COMPARING SOCIALIST APPROACHES

PITT LATIN AMERICAN SERIES

Catherine M. Conaghan, Editor

COMPARING SOCIALIST APPROACHES

Economics and Social Security in Cuba, China, and Vietnam

CARMELO MESA-LAGO

WITH COLLABORATION FROM BINGZI HE ON THE SECTIONS ABOUT CHINA'S SOCIAL SECURITY PROGRAM

University of Pittsburgh Press

Published by the University of Pittsburgh Press, Pittsburgh, Pa., 15260

Manufactured in the United States of America
Printed on acid-free paper
10 9 8 7 6 5 4 3 2 1

Cataloging-in-Publication data is available from the Library of Congress

ISBN 13: 978-0-8229-4847-6
ISBN 10: 0-8229-4847-8

Cover art: Images of flags via Adobe Stock

Cover design: Melissa Dias-Mandoly

To the millions of people all over the world who are not protected by social security, with my hope that in the not-too-distant future they achieve universal coverage, with equal treatment, adequate benefits, social solidarity, gender equity, efficient and participatory administration, and in a financially sustainable manner.

CONTENTS

PREFACE

Cuba, China, and Vietnam are all socialist countries with unique socioeconomic systems aimed at providing support and protection to their citizens. In Cuba, the social security system provides benefits to all citizens such as retirement pensions, disability insurance, and healthcare coverage. However, the benefits are relatively modest, and there have been serious challenges in terms of funding and sustainability. In contrast, China has made significant strides in expanding its social security programs and improving coverage for its citizens, including a wider range of benefits. Similarly, Vietnam's social security system has evolved over the years to provide more comprehensive social protection for its citizens. Each country has a unique social security system that reflects the respective political and socioeconomic contexts. Cuba's central plan and the so-called socialist-market model in China and Vietnam differ in fundamental ways in the delivery of social security outcomes to their citizens, the viability of their long-term financial sustainability, and their success in reaching goals such as universal coverage, equal treatment, social solidarity, gender equity, and efficient participatory administration.

In this groundbreaking study, Carmelo Mesa-Lago presents a comparative analysis of these socialist economic models, providing us with a unique opportunity to learn best practices across borders and share lessons to improve social protection for all. He argues that the socioeconomic model in China and Vietnam has consistently produced better economic and social performance than Cuba's. In addition, the social security system in China and Vietnam has developed gradually based on strong economies and therefore it is more sustainable and financially stable than Cuba's system. Finally, the overall economic-social performance of the Sino-Vietnamese model has been undoubtedly more successful than Cuba's central plan and the prospects for the island's future financial sustainability and provision of pensions, healthcare, and other services to its citizens are impaired by the country's aging population, which is projected to be among the oldest in the world by 2050. Accelerated aging has started to impact the social security system in China as well.

Mesa-Lago raises key questions about decision-making in socialist systems. Why has Cuba not adapted its socioeconomic system over time to implement selected reforms following the model in China and Vietnam? Although the author acknowledges the impossibility of providing a definite answer to this question, he takes us on a fascinating path to consider the likely reasons for Cuba's poor performance despite having started at a significantly higher level of economic-social development than the two Asian nations.

The study goes beyond a comparison of the two models and social security performance in the three countries. Mesa-Lago offers readers a compelling agenda of suggested social security policy reforms, based on a systematic evaluation of the problems faced in each of these nations. He delves into healthcare, pensions, and social assistance. The analysis helps us understand whether the existing model can adapt to new challenges or if there is a compelling need to implement structural changes. He makes a case for the importance of having an inclusive social dialogue with broad participation of all sectors as a condition of successful social security reform.

This book marks the culmination of an outstanding career. One of the world's most distinguished experts on social security, a leading scholar of Cuba, a beloved teacher and mentor, and an accomplished administrator who helped to position the University of Pittsburgh's Center for Latin American Studies among the best in the world, Carmelo Mesa-Lago is unrelenting in his quest to produce the highest quality of research with concrete impact on the policy world. Above all, his lifetime aspiration has been to study, document, and analyze the state of economic and social systems around the world to advocate for policies that improve the well-being of all people, seeking progress in ensuring that all individuals—regardless of their income level, employment status, gender, race, or ethnicity—have access to the support they need to live a dignified life.

Ariel C. Armony
Vice Chancellor for Global Affairs
Director, University Center for International Studies
Professor of International Affairs and Political Science
University of Pittsburgh

ACKNOWLEDGMENTS

I am solely liable for this study but gratefully acknowledge the support of many institutions, scholars, and people who generously helped. The Fulbright Commission granted me a Specialist Program grant to do research on China at the Max Planck Institut für Sozialrecht und Sozialpolitik at Munich in the spring of 2022 (Institute director Prof. Ulricht Becker and senior researcher Dr. Eva Maria Hohnerlein endorsed my application). A research grant to support my research on China was granted by the University of Pittsburgh Center for International Studies (my gratitude to its director and vice chancellor for global affairs Prof. Ariel C. Armony, who also wrote the preface), the Asian Studies Center, and the Center for Latin American Studies (CLAS). The latter also provided a part-time research assistant; a special thanks to CLAS associate director Manuel Roman-Lacayo who assisted in a myriad of ways. The book was improved by the magnificent editing done by Kelsey Trimm, with CLAS financial aid, and by Pippa Letsky. Finally, the Japan Institute for Developing Economies, Tokyo, granted me a visiting research award to study the Vietnamese experience (postponed because of the pandemic), and Dr. Kanako Yamaoka gave her support.

On China, very valuable help was provided by Bingzi He, associate researcher at the Social and Cultural Center, Institute of Latin American Studies, Chinese Academy of Social Sciences (CASS) in Beijing who answered many questions, made some calculations, carefully revised all social security sections on China, and provided legislation, comments, criticism, and additional sources (Bingzi is recognized as a collaborator in the book, but she is not responsible for what is said in it). Experts on China's social security formerly at the Max Planck Institute in Munich included Prof. Linxin He (now at the Sorbonne University) who answered questions; Yifei Wang, a doctoral candidate at the institute, who responded to a questionnaire, clarified many doubts, revised and commented on China's social security sections, and provided sources; and Prof. Barbara Darimont (now a professor of Chinese economics at the East Asia Institute of the University of Applied Sciences Ludwigshafen) who clarified doubts on Chinese health. Luis Frota, an International Labor Office (ILO) specialist on social security and manager of a project on China, and Zhou Jie, a national project coordinator at ILO Beijing, answered multiple queries, corrected some of my calculations, and supplied valuable statistics and information. Prof. Emerita of Political Science at University of California Irvine Dorothy J. Solinger revised China's social assistance sections and offered valuable materials and information on social assistance. Prof. Zheng Bingwen, director of the CASS Center for Social Security Studies, and Mao Xianglin, CASS Institute of Latin American Studies in Beijing, helped to make contacts with some Chinese scholars. Prof. Thomas Rawski of the economics department at the University of Pittsburgh read part of the manuscript on China, commented on it, and solved many doubts. Dr. Jerry La Forgia, former senior health economist at the World Bank and technical director of Acceso Global, in Washington, DC, answered several questions on hospital efficiency and healthcare in China. Prof. Martin Dimitrov, of the political science department at Tulane University, commented on a preliminary paper on China and on a presentation of this book at Tulane; he also supplied materials on Vietnam policies and statistics.

On Cuba, I am most grateful to Prof. of Economics Pavel Vidal at the Universidad Javeriana Cali for his useful comments and for sending some of his works. Prof. Henry Colina, formally in the department of economic development at the University of Havana and now with the UN Development Program (UNDP) in Havana, clarified points, contributed data on Cuba's social security, and suggested some recommendations for pension reforms. Prof. Juan Carlos Albizu-Campos, formerly at the University of Havana, gave advice on demographic issues and population projections. Dr. Vegard Bye, affiliate researcher at Chr. Michelsen Institute, Bergen, Oslo, read the sections on Cuba in the manuscript and offered useful comments. Dr. Jorge Pérez-López, prominent Cuban expert, helped on comparability issues. Dr. Sergio Díaz-Briquets, international demographer, aided in the calculation of Cuba's population growth rates. Prof. Ricardo Torres of the department of economics at American University provided arguments concerning the comparability of the three countries. Dr. Elaine Acosta, research associate of the Cuban Research Institute at Florida International University, helped on eldercare and data on procedures to receive social assistance in Cuba.

On Vietnam, I acknowledge help from Ca Tran Ngoc, associate professor and senior fellow at Vietnam Institute for Science, Technology and Innovation (Hanoi), who read the introduction and the first three chapters and commented on them. Dr. Hinhn T. Dinh, senior research fellow at the Policy Center for the New South (Rabat, Morocco), also read the introduction and the first three chapters and made suggestions. Huy Doung Quang, social worker who graduated from Vietnam Academy of Social Sciences and ILO consultant recommended by Dat Nguyen Hai (national program coordinator, Social Protection, ILO, in Vietnam), answered a long questionnaire (revised three times), checked some paragraphs, and solved many doubts. Yoilén Juan Rodríguez, informatic engineer in Hanoi coordinated a team of four social scientists who partially answered my questionnaires—Duong Xuan Minh, economist on economic issues; Hoàng Quynh, lawyer on social assistance; Nguyen Nam Thanh, economist on pensions; and Nguyen Thi Mai, lawyer on pensions (unfortunately, the project was not completed).

On general issues I wish to thank Yan Cai, doctoral candidate at the University of Pittsburgh and my research assistant, who provided crucial help in elaborating the standardized number-scale ranking among the three countries. Carla Moreno, doctoral candidate in economics at Emory University, made remarks on the methodology of ranking the three countries. My part-time assistant Akira Pinto Madeiro, doctoral candidate in political science at Pitt, helped with the figures, and two anonymous referees engaged by the University of Pittsburgh Press made many useful suggestions that enhanced the manuscript. Josh Shanholtzer, editor at UPP handled the manuscript professionally and fast, with my deep appreciation. A summary of two chapters of the book was published as "Evaluation of Economic-Social Performance of Two Socialist Models: Cuba (Central Plan) and China-Vietnam (Socialist Market)," *Latin American Research Review* 59, no. 2 (May/June 2024).

Last but not least, my deep gratitude to my wife, Elena, for her endurance, cheerfulness, patience, love, and support.

LIST OF ACRONYMS

ALOS—average length of hospital stays

ASEAN—Association of Southeast Asian Nations

CASS—Chinese Academy of Social Sciences, Beijing

CBIRC—China Banking and Insurance Regulatory Commission

CCP—Chinese Communist Party, Cuban Communist Party

CEE—State Statistical Committee, Cuba

CLAS—Center for Latin American Studies, University of Pittsburgh

CMEA—Council of Mutual Economic Assistance (also COMECON)

CPA—Agricultural Production Cooperatives, Cuba

CPI—Consumer Price Index

CPTPP—Comprehensive and Progressive Agreement for Trans-Pacific Partnership

CUC—convertible peso, currency of Cuba (ended in 2021)

CUP—national peso, only currency of Cuba since 2021
FDI—foreign direct investment
ECLAC—Economic Commission for Latin America and the Caribbean
GDP—gross domestic product
GDR—German Democratic Republic
GLF—Great Leap Forward (China)
GNI—gross national income
GOV—Government of China
GSO—General Statistical Office (Vietnam)
HDI—Human Development Index
ILO—International Labor Office
ILSSA—Institute of Labor, Science, and Social Affairs, Vietnam
IMF—International Monetary Fund
INASS—National Institute of Social Security, Cuba
MINSAP—Ministry of Public Health, Cuba
MLSS—Minimum Living Standard Scheme, China
MOH—Ministry of Health, Vietnam
MOHRSS—Ministry of Human Resources and Social Security, China
MOLISA—Ministry of Labor, War Invalids, and Social Affairs, Vietnam
MPI—Multidimensional Poverty Index
MTSS—Ministry of Labor and Social Security, Cuba
NBSC—National Bureau of Statistics, China
NCD—noncommunicable diseases
NCSSF—National Council for Social Security Fund, China
NDC—nondefined contribution
NHSA—National Healthcare Security Administration, China
NICE—National Institute for Health and Care Excellence, China
NRCMS—New Rural Cooperative Medical Scheme, China
NRPS—Voluntary New Rural Pension Scheme, China

OECD—Organization of Economic Cooperation and Development, Paris
ONAT—National Tax Administration Office of Cuba
ONEI—National Office of Statistics and Information, Cuba
OPHI—Oxford Poverty and Human Development Initiative
PAYG—pay-as-you-go
PPP—purchasing parity power (international dollars)
RCEP—Regional Comprehensive Economic Partnership
RMB—renminbi, currency of China (also yuan)
RR—replacement rate
SCI—Statistical Capacity Index
SHI—Social Health Insurance, China
SMEs—small and medium-sized enterprises
ISSA—International Social Security Association
TVET—Technical and Vocational Education and Training
UBPC—Basic Units of Cooperative Production, Cuba
UEBMI—Urban Employee Basic Medical Insurance, China
UNDESA—UN Department of Economic and Social Affairs
UNDP—UN Development Program
UNIDO—UN Industrial Development Organization
URRBMI—Urban and Rural Resident Basic Medical Insurance, China
US.SSA-ISSA—US Social Security Administration–International Social Security Association
USSR—Union of Soviet Socialist Republics (Soviet Union)
VCP—Vietnam Communist Party
VND—dong, currency of Vietnam
VSS—Vietnam Social Security
WHO—World Health Organization
WTO—World Trade Organization

AUTHOR'S NOTE

One billion herein is 1,000 million, and a trillion is one million million (twelve zeros).

Exchange rates are official, unless specified, and taken from the Internet.

n.a. = not available

COMPARING SOCIALIST APPROACHES

INTRODUCTION

For half a century, I have worked and published on comparative economic and social systems, developing diverse techniques to measure and rank their performance. My doctoral dissertation at Cornell University in 1968 dealt with employment, unemployment, and underemployment in socialist economies—the Soviet Union, the People's Republic of China (thereafter China), Yugoslavia, and Cuba (Mesa-Lago 1968). Later, I organized an international conference at the University of Pittsburgh on comparative socialist systems, analyzing economic and political issues, which was attended by prominent experts from all over the world; I edited a book with the best papers presented at the conference and contributed a chapter that elaborated a continuum model to compare the evolution of those economic systems (Mesa-Lago and Beck 1975). Some thirty books and more than one hundred articles or chapters in books of mine have compared social security systems (pensions, healthcare, unemployment insurance, and social assistance) and their reforms among all countries in Latin America and others in the Caribbean, Western and Eastern Europe, Asia, and Africa (the latest book is Mesa-Lago 2021b). In my historical comparison of three Latin American economic-social models (market in Chile, socialist in Cuba, and mixed in Costa Rica), I examined their policies, measured their results with dozens of indicators, and ranked their performance (Mesa-Lago 2000). Overall, I have conducted field research in and published on some thirty-six countries in the world. In the last three years, I have expanded my comparative research on the economies and social security systems and reforms of China and Vietnam (Mesa-Lago 2014, 2018a, 2024a). This latest work sparked my interest in deepening that line of research and motivated this book.

Based on my previous work and methodological contributions, herein I compare two main socialist economic-social models. One is Cuba's central plan with dominant, state-owned large enterprises over the market and private property along with mild structural reforms oriented toward the market that have been unable to generate economic growth, resulting instead in the opposite. The other model is the Sino-Vietnamese "socialist-market" model, in which small, median, and some large private enterprises and the market predominate under a decentralized plan that is more a guideline than a straitjacket, with the state regulating the economy and controlling the largest enterprises.[1] It should be noted that Vietnam has a wider preponderance of small enterprises (also household nonfarm enterprises) than China. The share of the state sector in gross domestic product (GDP) has declined significantly in the two socialist-market economies (shares in 2019 were 27 percent in Vietnam and 31 percent in China) but is the vast majority in Cuba (96.2 percent in 2008 and 90.8 percent in 2018—in the latter year, the state accounted for 67 percent of employment).[2]

To the best of my knowledge there are not all-embracing systematic comparisons of the economic-social models and social security systems of Cuba and China-Vietnam. There are academic articles that compare specific policies of the three countries: for instance, Malesky and London (2014) on the politics of development, Mesa-Lago (2018a) on social security reforms, Monreal (2018c) on economic reforms, and P. Vidal (2014) on monetary and exchange-rate unification. Some edited handbooks have chapters on each of the three countries treating different features: for instance, Aspalter (2023) encyclopedia on social welfare with chapters on Cuba (Mesa-Lago and Aspalter 2023), on China (C. Lee 2023), and on Vietnam (Diep and Hang 2023). These exercises are useful and informative but are not systematic comparisons of overall social welfare among the three countries.

ORGANIZATION OF THIS BOOK

The book is structured in three parts. The first part is comprised of the introduction and chapters 1, 2, and 3. In the introduction I provide the background, organization, and hypotheses of the book and analyze the key issue of the availability and reliability of statistics in the three countries. I start chapter 1 with the question of whether the three countries are truly comparable. In examining a series of indicators (the human development index, area and population size, demographics, and so forth), I find that most indicators are similar but a few are different; I discuss counterarguments to conclude that the divergent indicators are not an obstacle, hence the countries-models are comparable. In chapter 2 I contrast the two models focusing on five major economic policies: ownership of the means of production (the market vis-à-vis the plan); agrarian reform; industrialization process; employment, open unemployment, and self-employment; and currency and exchange-rate unification. I do not break new ground in this chapter but provide a synthesis of these policies in a comparative manner, which serves as a useful base for the rest of the book. In chapter 3 I contrast the economic-social performance of the two models and the three countries using twenty-seven indicators, of which fifteen are economic and twelve are social. Based on a selection of the most relevant and comparable twenty indicators (ten economic and ten social), I elaborate a composite average to rank the three countries' economic-social performance.

In the second part of the book (chapters 4 and 5), which is the most important and innovative, I focus on social security/social protection and its three major components: contributory pensions, healthcare, and noncontributory social assistance.[3] Each component is compared based on the following fundamental ILO principles of social security (for the history and analysis of these principles see Mesa-Lago 2007; Olivier 2022): unity and equal treatment; universal coverage (labor force on pensions, total population on healthcare, and elderly population on social assistance); benefit sufficiency; social solidarity and gender equity; administrative efficiency, reasonable costs, and tripartite representation; and financial and actuarial sustainability. Standardized tables and selected figures are elaborated along each of these principles to compare the three countries. The treatment of them in the text, whenever suitable, is done in the same order: China, Cuba and Vietnam.

There are two chapters (6 and 7) in the third part. Chapter 6 contains the conclusions, made up of four sections. In the first section I summarize the key social security indicators in the three countries and rank the countries for their performance in such indicators (social security principles), as well as their financial-actuarial sustainability. In the second section I discuss some methodological problems in the comparisons. The third section is a confirmation of the three hypotheses of this book. And in the fourth section I search for an answer to the intriguing question as to why Cuba has not followed the economically and socially successful model of Sino-Vietnamese socialist market.

Chapter 7 consists of policy suggestions to improve social security in the three countries; the suggestions are based on the book's diagnosis combined with my forty years of consulting experience in thirteen countries, working with international-regional organizations as well as governments and international foundations. In a brief subsection I explore the sustainability of the current model in each country and the potential alternatives or adjustments needed to increase sustainability. The rich and varied comparative experience of the three countries and the policy recommendations should be valuable for both developing and developed countries.

Several sources were used in the book. The first are statistical yearbooks from the three countries; an effort was undertaken to compile the data for both a specific time period (to identify trends) and the most recent year available. Although 2020 data was obtainable from the three countries, that year was affected by the pandemic and generated some distortions. In several cases, 2020 data is provided when such distortion does not occur or to show the impact of Covid-19 (in a few instances, statistics on 2021 and 2022 are supplied). A second source was a compilation of legislation in the three countries. A third source was consulting experts both in China and Vietnam. I had originally planned to conduct field research in both countries, but the pandemic impeded my trips.[4] Instead, I sent questionnaires to scholars, officials, and experts on the economic models and the three major components of social security in both countries, and these were answered and then tabulated by me. A fourth source was academic literature on economics and social security from the three countries. In addition to the materials obtained in the United States, I worked on the China collection at the Max-Planck Institute for Social Law and Policy in Munich and consulted with its experts. A planned stay at the Institute of Developing Economies in Tokyo to work on its excellent collection and to consult experts on Vietnam also had to be postponed due to Covid-19. A fifth source was books, academic articles, technical reports, and press articles on the three countries—more than five hundred bibliographical entries support this book.

HYPOTHESES

In the book I present three major hypotheses. The first is that the Sino-Vietnamese socialist-market model has had a better economic and social performance than the Cuban model of predominant central plan and modest ineffective reforms, even though the two Asian countries started with a much lower level of economic-social development than

Cuba, which demanded a greater effort to match and exceed Cuba's accomplishments. The second hypothesis is that Cuba developed social security much earlier, faster, and more expansively than it could financially support, making it unsustainable in the long run especially with the country's poor economic performance. Conversely, in China and Vietnam, social security developed gradually and is supported by a successful economic performance, thus it is more financially sustainable, although China is beginning to encounter several problems. The third hypothesis is that accelerated aging has had a strong adverse effect on the financial sustainability of the Cuban social security system and is beginning to have an impact in China but not yet in Vietnam. The first hypothesis will be tested in chapter 3, whereas the second and third hypotheses will be examined in chapter 6.

A brief summary related to the three hypotheses follows. At the eve of its revolution, Cuba was one of the most socially developed countries in Latin America, albeit with significant differences in living standards between the capital city of Havana and other large cities and the countryside, something that was also true concerning social security. Building on that base, and with generous aid from the Soviet Union, the revolutionary government virtually closed the urban-rural gap, making education and healthcare universal and free, whereas pensions became almost universal (social assistance and housing were considerably less developed). By 1989, at the eve of the collapse of the socialist camp, Cuba probably had the most advanced system of social security in Latin America, even better than that in many socialist countries in Central and Eastern Europe (Mesa-Lago 2000).[5] The cost of social services grew steadily and peaked in 2007 at 55 percent of the state budget and 37 percent of GDP, probably the highest proportions within Latin America, constituting a heavy burden for the state. In 2007 the president Raúl Castro announced that social services and other "gratuities" (such as subsidized consumer goods through rationing, free burials, social insurance, social assistance, and so forth) could no longer be supported at the same level and had to be reduced according to the economic capacity of the nation.[6] As a result, the cost of social services steadily decreased to 41 percent of the state budget and 25 percent of GDP in 2019. Said cuts reduced access to and quality of healthcare, the purchasing value of pensions, the number of social assistance beneficiaries, and the benefit amount (Mesa-Lago and Díaz-Briquets 2021). It is remarkable that such a significant amount of public resources are allocated to social expenditure despite the severe economic crisis. In 2021, however, 37.6 percent of total investment went into enterprise services, real estate, hotels, and restaurants (despite their significant decrease) whereas only 1.7 percent was assigned to healthcare and social assistance; the former showed an increasing trend while the latter a decreasing trend (ONEI 2022a).

Cuba has the oldest population in Latin America, and it is projected that by 2050 it will be among the most aged nations in the world. As part of this aging process, the population's old cohort is expanding fast, while the youngest cohort and the productive-age cohort are contracting, resulting in fewer active workers contributing to support the pay-as-you-go (PAYG) pension system, meaning a continuing decline of the ratio of active workers to one pensioner. Furthermore, as life expectancy rises, pensioners will be collecting their benefits for a longer period, increasing costs parallel to the revenue decline and hence boosting the pension deficit. Aging also increases healthcare costs because the elderly cohort suffers terminal and more complex and costly illnesses than those typical of the young and productive-age cohorts. The needed reforms to reduce said services (such as further age increases in pensions) face resistance from beneficiaries who fear losing or diminishing their entitlements.

The current economic crisis has made it more difficult to finance pensions and healthcare in Cuba. In 2016–2020, economic growth decreased at an annual rate of –1.3 percent, aggravating an already strained situation (see chapter 3). Cuban demographer Albizu-Campos properly characterizes the situation: "The real demographic storm is that the Cuban population has completed the process of 'reproductive revolution' [accelerated aging] but the current economic model has failed to materialize the needed 'productive revolution'" (2022c).[7]

Conversely, at the time of their revolutions, China and Vietnam had very poor social services/social security and their costs were quite low. In contrast to the Cuban case, there were no vast beneficiaries to resist the market-oriented reforms.[8] As the two Asian countries developed economically, because of high rates of GDP growth, wages rose, poverty and unemployment decreased, and coverage and benefits of social security were gradually expanded according to their respective economic capacity.[9] In his study of China's development of its health system, X. Huang (2020) proves that economic growth provided the resources needed for the distribution and expansion of social insurance, allocating to it a growing percentage of GDP and fiscal revenue. With more than one billion workers in the labor force covered by pensions and 1.35 billion of the population with access to healthcare in 2021, China has the largest social security system in the world ("Rising Pension Levels," 2021) but also the second-biggest economy.[10] Furthermore, both China and Vietnam have a mixed social security system where state services are combined with private facilities in healthcare (copayments are paid by users), and together with public social insurance, China has fully funded individual pension accounts. Vietnam has moderate but expanding aging, whereas now China is beginning to confront labor force decreases due to the one-child policy that have placed pressure on pensions.

It has been properly argued that Vietnam was better prepared than Cuba to confront the disappearance of the Soviet Union and the socialist camp in the early 1990s (P. Vidal 2016). Vietnam's reforms began before the collapse of socialism in Central and Eastern Europe, and the rise in economic growth cushioned the fall in trade and aid from the Union of Soviet Socialist Republics (USSR). In the same vein, China started its reform in 1978 and had more than a decade of growth before the Soviet collapse. In addition, China did not have the same dependence on trade and aid as Vietnam and Cuba did, and China had an ideological confrontation with the USSR to lead the communist movement globally. Cuba had the highest dependence of the three countries on the Soviet Union and the Council of Mutual Economic Assistance (CMEA) in trade, aid, and subsidies. Furthermore, in 1986–1990, Cuba turned radically to the left and away from the market ("Rectification Process"), which damaged economic growth and, therefore, was the most affected by the socialist-camp collapse: its GDP decreased 35 percent in 1989–1993 (Mesa-Lago 2000).

With its decades-long policy of one child per family, China is confronting accelerated aging that is a threat to the financial-actuarial sustainability of its pension program. The previous policy was changed, increasing the number of children allowed per family first to two and then to three, but such policy change cannot reverse the adverse demographic effects—though it will take longer for China to reach Cuba's critical situation. Opposite to these two countries, Vietnam has a much younger population and does not need to confront this threat in the short and middle term.

Now for a word about asymmetries in my knowledge and experience in researching the three countries. I have devoted sixty years of my life to the study of the Cuban economy and social policy, publishing about 45 books or monographs and more than 150 academic articles or chapters in books on those subjects. Conversely, my previous work on China was mostly comparative and limited to the cited doctoral dissertation and comparison on socialist-economic models, the pension model most applicable to China, and my recent piece on social security reform. My work on Vietnam has been on the comparison of its reform with Cuba's both on the economy and social security. In the last three years, I have tried to fill that vacuum with intensive study of the literature of the two Asian countries and the invaluable collaboration from many colleagues who are experts on their economy and social security policy. As this book indicates, I have substantially reduced the noted information gap with China and to a less extent with Vietnam, and I hope to continue in this pursuit in the future.

AN IMPORTANT NOTE ON THE AVAILABILITY AND RELIABILITY OF STATISTICS

This section is fundamental in comparing the quality of data in the three countries, in detecting missing statistics, and in regarding discrepancies in the comparisons and poor reliability of some data. The Statistical Capacity Index (SCI) measures 144 countries from 2004 to 2020 based on twenty-five criteria that are compressed into three scores (methodology, source data, and periodicity) and, in turn, into a composite scale—from 0 (best) to 100 (worst)—that is used to rank the countries (World Bank 2022b). Each country is also compared with its geographical region according to its three scores. In 2020, China's overall score was 80.0 and it was ranked thirty-first, meaning it has better statistical systems than about 80 percent of all countries and ranked eleventh among 34 Asian countries. Vietnam scored 74.4 overall and was ranked forty-fourth among 144 countries, or eighteenth among 34 Asian countries. Cuba is excluded from the SCI; it is the only excluded country in Latin America (SCI includes the least developed Latin American countries such as Haiti, Nicaragua, and Honduras). One potential explanation for such exclusion is that Cuba is not a World Bank member; nevertheless, the Bank provides several Cuban indicators, such as GDP, fiscal balance, population, and so forth.

In terms of availability, it is quite helpful that the major statistical yearbooks of the three countries, with the latest edition available at the time of finishing this book being 2021 (NBSC 2022a; ONEI 2022a; GSO 2022b), are easily accessible online, as well as other statistical materials, particularly those in China (the country with the largest number of online available statistical publications). Nevertheless, in recent years, the National Bureau of Statistics, China (NBSC), has discontinued hundreds of series of data that were used by experts to double-check the veracity of broader government statistics such as economic growth, making it progressively harder to access this data (Bradsher 2022b). In 2023, because of adverse data, the NBSC discontinued the series on consumer confidence, published for thirty-three years, as well as the series on youth unemployment (Bradsher 2023d; Fu 2023b). In 2007, Premier Li Keqiang privately acknowledged to the US ambassador to China that official economic statistics were "manmade" and unreliable (Buckley and Bradsher 2023). There are reports in the international press of censorship to criticism of some official statistics (Yuan 2023a). Concerning promptness in publishing the data, Cuba takes the most time, especially during economic crises. The production of statistics is highly centralized in the three countries (although data is also gathered locally), which generates some problems. The three countries prohibit private or independent collection of data, and it is quite difficult or impossible (depending on the subject) to conduct free surveys.

China requests official acceptance or approval of foreign researchers who want to conduct fieldwork and surveys; anthropology researchers can reside in rural communities only with the permission and cooperation of local authorities (Rawski 2022a), but in some cases, people taking surveys without permission are picked up by the local police. On the other hand, Brandt (2022) reports her experience on surveys as generally being positive (save for one case): her Chinese colleagues have been given permission from the authorities, although she cautions that said colleagues tried not to publicize differences with official data and that she knows of cases where scholars were declared persona non grata after they did so. Solinger (2022a) reports that in the 1990s and early 2000s, she worked through scholars in China to gain entry to communities where she held interviews but that it is not possible now to do any fieldwork in China. In Cuba and Vietnam, the government requires a special visa submitted with a research project approved by a ministry, an academic institution, or another official agency that guarantees the project. In Cuba, when the researcher arrives, a meeting ought to be held at the host institution, which thereafter arranges the necessary appointments (my own experience in Cuba; Pérez Villanueva 2022b). Therefore, there is no alternative independent data with which to check the national official figures, and this opens the door for potential manipulation by the government. Another common hindrance in Cuba is the lack of transparency regarding the methods used for data collection and/or calculation and the lack of information on how to analyze and interpret the official data. Finally, in the three countries, those generating or managing the data may have a personal interest that benefits them or the government; for instance, positive indicators on economic growth, output production, and social indicators could result in promotion and negative ones could result in demotion (Wei et al. 2019b; Mondorf 2020).

Reliable statistics on China are complex to obtain given the large territory, the second highest population in the world, and the significant diversity among regions. In 2006–2015, there were an increasing number of annual publications on China's statistical reliability (Plekhanov 2017). Most questionable data is on GDP in constant prices (overvaluation), inflation particularly on healthcare (undervaluation), industrial growth, investment, and unemployment (undervaluation) (Rawski 2001,

2002, 2022; Holz 2003; Orlik 2011; Wei et al. 2019a, 2019b; Yingyao and Jiaxiong Yao 2021; Wallace 2022; Yuan 2023a). Specific reliability problems have been more elaborated by Mondorf (2020): The National Bureau of Statistics, China, reports directly to the State Council, the highest administrative institution in China, which supervises the administration of the NBSC and provides its management staff and financial resources, corroborating that it is not an independent institution. In addition to collecting its own data, the NBSC also receives information from other agencies such as the Ministry of Human Resources and Social Security (MOHRSS), but this data cannot be checked by the NBSC for completeness and accuracy. Statistical inconsistencies in the same publication year have been found; for instance, adding up data from provinces comes to a total that is higher than the national GDP figure. In addition to the NBSC staff, there are 40 million civil servants at national, provincial, and local levels, making individual records hard to trace back to any one specific person, and there are incentives for local officials to manipulate data as it can have a positive impact on their careers. Public expenditure on healthcare and education in 2011 was reported as 8,000,000 million yuan, tantamount to 17 percent of GDP in that year, a percentage that did not match official statistics. The local statistical staff report directly to the respective government in the provinces but not to the NBSC, hence data may be "touched up" at the local level despite the fact that this is illegal. Nevertheless, since the economic reforms of 1978, there is no hard evidence that data is manipulated at the central level of government, but it might be at the local level, resulting in deviations when data is merged. There should not be any interest in inaccurate data at the national level because distorted data would lead to incorrect decisions. Finally, as part of President Xi Jinping's anticorruption campaign, investigation teams have been sent to several provinces to address some of the cited problems and try to improve the situation (Mondorf 2020).

In the case of Cuba, for more than fifty years I have assessed the availability and reliability of statistics (Mesa-Lago 1969, 2001, 2022) concluding that the weakest are macroeconomic indicators such as the calculation of GDP, economic growth rates, gross capital formation, inflation, unemployment, and so forth. Conversely, data on foreign trade is fairly reliable as it can be contrasted with the World Trade Organization (WTO) and other international trade data, but hyperinflation and devaluation of the Cuban peso has led to severe distortions in its conversion to US dollars (Mesa-Lago 2024). Tourism statistics on the number of visitors are reliable as they can be checked with those of the UN WTO, but data given in gross revenue does not subtract imports for the tourist industry. The availability of data has varied through time. For instance, during the severe crisis of the 1990s, the statistical yearbook was halted and was not resumed for a decade, creating a huge vacuum (Mesa-Lago 2000). Until 1989, social statistics were fairly reliable, but because of the crisis and subsequent economic-social deterioration, its reliability decreased (particularly for unemployment and infant mortality). It is common that a series is published when results are good and then suspended when they are bad, for instance on production of medicines (ONEI 2021). In 2021, out of twenty-four statistical tables relevant to Cuba in the annual statistical publication of the UN's Economic Commission for Latin America and the Caribbean (ECLAC), data on Cuba is only included in two: the GDP (absolute and per capita) and the consumer price index (CPI), both questionable indicators. The other nineteen countries in Latin America are included in those tables, even the least developed country, Haiti (ECLAC 2021; Mesa-Lago 2022). In an ILO study on informal workers, Cuba is the only country in Latin America that does not appear (ILO/WIEGO 2018). Key indicators available in most countries in the world—such as poverty incidence, the Gini coefficient, and coverage of the labor force on pensions and of the population on health—have not been officially published under the revolution.

A search for academic literature examining the reliability of Vietnam statistics was less successful than in China and Cuba. Trinh (2019) studied how agents at lower levels distort data; using nighttime luminosity data he measured the inflated GDP numbers estimated by provincial governments. Economist Ca Tran Ngoc (2022) noted that data on Vietnam economy by the General Statistical Office (GSO) could diverge with other sources such as World Bank, the International Monetary Fund (IMF), Asian Development Bank, and other international banking and financial organizations; but this is also true of many other countries of the world. I have detected statistical contradictions between official sources on the balance of pension revenue and expenses. There are three different series with a significant divergence among them (GSO 2021b; K. T. Nguyen 2017; ILSSA/ILO 2022). The first gives a much lower balance than the other two. In response to my questionnaire, an economist in Hanoi stated that GSO statistics "are the most reliable" and that "statistical information outside state statistics is less reliable because . . . these figures have no value as a substitute for state statistical information" (Hoàng 2022). Vu Hoàng (2014) quoted some Vietnamese officials, but without providing the sources, so their veracity could not be checked. Vũ Quang Viêt (2020), a lecturer on statistics in Vietnam, reported frequent inconsistencies in data collection by sampling on family income and spending. Le Dang Doanh, former director of the Central

Institute for Economic Management, stated that there are many experts, including himself, who have doubts on the accuracy of statistics; for instance, GDP growth reported from provinces is often double the reported national GDP growth (Huy 2022).

PART I

COMPARABILITY AND ECONOMIC-SOCIAL PERFORMANCE

CHAPTER 1

ARE THE THREE COUNTRIES COMPARABLE?

In this chapter first I analyze features that are similar in the three countries. Second, I examine those that are different, and concerning these, I present counterarguments that those differences do not impede the comparison. Finally, I examine a compensatory factor: prerevolutionary Cuba had higher socioeconomic development than China and Vietnam, which forced these two countries to make a greater effort to match and surpass Cuba.

SIMILARITIES AMONG THE THREE COUNTRIES

First, the three countries have communist regimes that were the result of popular uprisings (a significant difference with Central and Eastern European socialist countries where communism was imposed by the USSR). All are unitary states (the three have provinces), and all of them have a one-party political system where the communist party is in full control of the regime.[1]

The second similarity is that the three countries also have socialist economies, albeit of two different types. After sixty-five years and despite some ineffective reforms, Cuba still retains a predominantly centrally planned economy with overwhelming state ownership of the means of production over the market and non-state and private property. Cuban officials refer to the reforms as an "updated model," meaning that they did not transform the existing planned model but just mended or actualized it. Conversely, the other two countries have mixed economies that blend state and predominantly private ownership of the means of production with a key role of the market, although under decentralized planning.

The third similarity is that the three countries have similar postures in their antagonism toward the United States (much less in Vietnam, after the war was over, than in the other two) and the North Atlantic Treaty Organization (NATO, OTAN) in particular, as well as fair relations with Russia (except in China during the period of confrontation with the USSR for world hegemony). The three countries have supported liberation movements in colonial countries in several continents. They also endured a large emigration after the communist takeover, which harmed their human capital endowment (such exodus continued in Cuba by 2024). Both Vietnam and Cuba have suffered an embargo (called a "blockade" in Cuba) imposed by the United States; in Vietnam it was terminated in 1994, whereas in Cuba it still exists and was substantially strengthened under the first Trump presidency.

The three countries currently have relatively similar rankings and scores in the UN Development Program (UNDP) Human Development Index for 2021 (see table 1.1). The higher the score the better. The three are classified in the second group as "high human development." Their scores are relatively close: 0.004 points higher (better) in China (0.768) than in Cuba (0.764), which is 0.001 points lower in Vietnam (0.763); these scores compare with a maximum difference of 0.580 points between Switzerland (highest human development) and South Sudan (lowest human development).

Among 191 ranked countries, China is 79th, Cuba is 83rd, and Vietnam is 115th. Cuba and China are separated by only four places (2 percent of the total number of countries). The difference is wider concerning Vietnam: thirty-two places (16 percent of the total number of countries). Between 2007 and 2021, Cuba's Human Development Index (HDI) rank fell from 51st to 83rd place (a decline of thirty-two places), whereas China's rank rose from 92nd to 79th place (an improvement of thirteen places) and Vietnam's rank also increased from 116th to 115th place (an improvement of one place). As a result, the gap in HDI ranking between Cuba and China shrank from forty-one to four places in fifteen years (UNDP 2009, 2022; Albizu-Campos and Díaz-Briquets 2023).

In table 1.1, the demographic indicators in the three countries seem

Table 1.1: Human Development Index, Area, and Demographic Indicators in China, Cuba, and Vietnam, circa 2019

Indicators	China	Cuba	Vietnam
Human Development Index			
Ranking (among 191 countries) 2021	79	83	115
Scores (1.0 best)	0.768	0.764	0.763
HDI change in places 1990–2021	+13	–32	+1
Area (1,000 sq. Km)	9,596.9	110.9	331.2
Demography			
Total population (millions)	1,386.4	11.3	96.5
Urban (% of total)	63.9	77.1	36.8
Rural (% of total)	36.1	22.9	63.2
Population growth rate (x 1,000 inhabitants)	0.3	–1.4	1.2
Labor force (millions)	811.0	4.6	55.7
Population age 65 and over (%)[a]	13.7	15.7	8.0
Dependency ratio (%)[b]	39.5	45.8	43.3
Total fertility rate[c]	1.7	1.6	2.1
Life expectancy at birth (years), 2021			
Men	74.7	76.7	70.8
Women	80.5	80.6	76.1
Total	77.4	78.8	73.4

Source: My own elaboration based on UNDP (2020, 2022): China from NBSC (2021b, 2021c), B. He (2022); Cuba from ONEI (2020a), MINSAP (2021), ONEI/CEPDE (2021); Vietnam from GSO (2019, 2022a); others from OECD (2018), World Bank (2021a, 2021b, 2021c).

Notes: [a] Over total population.

[b] Aged 14 and under, plus aged 65 and older, divided by aged 15–64.

[c] Number of children born alive to women in their child-bearing years.

fairly similar. Life expectancy at birth is 78.8 years in Cuba, 77.4 in China, and 73.4 in Vietnam, a difference of 1.4 years between Cuba and China and 5.4 years between Cuba and Vietnam.[2] Dependency ratios are 45.8 in Cuba, 43.3 in Vietnam, and 39.5 in China, a variance of 6.3 points between Cuba and China and 3.8 points between Cuba and Vietnam. Total fertility rates are close in China and Cuba (1.7 and 1.6 respectively) but higher in Vietnam (2.1).[3] Percentages of the population aged 65 years and above, over the total population, are 15.7 percent in Cuba, 13.7 percent in China, and 8.0 percent in Vietnam, so the difference between Cuba and China is 2 percentage points and between Cuba and Vietnam 7.7 percentage points. In 2019, Cuba's population decreased by 1.4 per thousand inhabitants while China's population grew by 0.3 and Vietnam's by 1.2. All these indicators show that Cuba is the oldest country of the three, closely followed by China, where aging is accelerating because of the one-child policy that was in place for thirty-six years. Vietnam has moderate but expanding aging.[4] According to the ILO, Vietnam will move at a "very high pace of ageing" by 2035 (2018a, 3), a span of 18 years, a much shorter period than for other nations such as France (115 years) and the United States (69 years). The "window of opportunity" or demographic bonus has closed in Cuba and China but will not do so in Vietnam until 2042 (World Bank 2021b).[5]

DIFFERENCES AMONG THE COUNTRIES AND COUNTERARGUMENTS OVER ALLEGED IMPEDIMENTS FOR COMPARISON

There are five differences among the three countries that could play a positive or negative role on their respective performances and hence become significant barriers for comparison. First, China's territorial area is eighty-six times that of Cuba and twenty-nine times that of Vietnam, while Vietnam is only three times larger than Cuba. In addition, China's population is 123 times that of Cuba and 14 times that of Vietnam, whereas Vietnam is 8.5 times that of Cuba (see table 1.1). Second, the US embargo has lasted much longer and stronger in Cuba than in Vietnam, which could result in more adverse effects for Cuba. Third, the distribution of the population by urban (77.1 percent) and rural (22.9 percent) areas in Cuba is much wider than in China (63.9 percent urban and 36.1 percent rural) and virtually the reverse of Vietnam (36.8 percent urban and 63.2 percent rural). In Vietnam, agriculture had a higher share of GDP than in Cuba—these factors could have made structural reforms easier in China and Vietnam than in Cuba. Fourth, Vietnam had the smallest state sector and the largest proportional number of small enterprises, hence the transition from central planning to the socialist market was not as complex as in Cuba, which has very large state enterprises. Fifth, the three countries are oil producers; Vietnam is a net oil exporter hence it has an advantage over the other two countries. These differences—as potential advantageous factors for China and/or Vietnam vis-à-vis Cuba—are analyzed below.

The first difference concerns size. The larger area size and population of China (and to a less extent Vietnam) does not appear as an insurmountable obstruction in comparison with Cuba—for two reasons. The large populations living in the two Asian countries, particularly in China, suffered famines, and millions of people died of hunger; it was not until the socialist-market model was adopted that agricultural production significantly rose and eliminated starvation. Small countries, both in area and population, such as Switzerland, Netherlands, Denmark, and Estonia, have been quite successful in reaching very high levels of human development despite having a territorial area less than half that of Cuba (0.5 percent that of China and 46 percent that of Vietnam) as well as smaller populations than Cuba (even more so than China and Vietnam). Still, China's large domestic market may have a competitive edge in attracting foreign investment and technology transfer. The size issue is addressed whenever appropriate in comparisons moving forward.

The second difference concerns embargos imposed by the US government on Cuba for a longer period (sixty-two years) than in Vietnam (thirty years) and China (twenty-three years), another of the obstacles usually raised for comparison.[6] The strongest harmful effects of the embargo on Cuba were in its early stages (1960s) when the country was isolated in the Western Hemisphere save for Canada and Mexico. Without disregarding its posterior adverse effects on Cuba and its people, the embargo continued under the rapprochement in the Obama presidency, but it was much less damaging. Trump strengthened the embargo in 2017–2020, and yet Cuba had trade with some one hundred countries (including the United States as the eighth-largest importer, sharing 16 percent of food imports in 2019) as well as investment from several nations. The embargo's adverse effect was estimated by Cuba as US$130,000 million in 2021 (Reuters Staff 2021), but without providing hard data on how that estimate was achieved, and was largely compensated for by substantial economic aid, including nonrepayable grants and price subsidies to the tune of US$65,000 million in 1960–1990, at those years' prices, from the Soviet Union and US$100,000 million only in 2005–2017 from Venezuela (Mesa-Lago 2000; Mesa-Lago and Vidal 2019). Compare that last sum with the US$20,000 million granted to all Latin America in the two decades of the Alliance of Progress.[7] Using diverse methods (including counterfactual ones), Jales, Kang, Stein, and Garcia Ribeiro (2018) conclude that the impact of the Cuban revolution on GDP per capita was negative, taking into account both the adverse effects of the US embargo and the positive effects of the economic relationship with the USSR.

In addition, Cuba's foreign debt with most external creditors was forgiven in the amount of US$42,470 million: 100 percent of US$10,000 million from China, 90 percent of US$25,000 million from Russia, 80 percent of US$11,000 million from the Paris Club, 80 percent of 1,400 million from Japan suppliers' creditors, and 70 percent of US$500 million from Mexico (Frank 2013, 2015, 2021; Rapoza 2019; Spadoni 2022).[8] Canada has steadily been Cuba's fourth principal trade partner, major investor, and first sender of tourists to the island. Improved economic relations with and credits from the European Union have been another compensatory factor (Bye 2020). Raúl Castro himself, in several speeches in 2011, said that the embargo could not be blamed for all the economic problems of Cuba (Mesa-Lago 2015b, 4). In the closing of the communist party congress in 2011, Raúl stated: "We are convinced that the principal enemy that we confront and will confront will be our own deficiencies" (R. Castro 2011).

On the other hand, Vietnam suffered twenty-nine years of war against France (1946–1954) and the United States (1955–1975), which devastated its economy and made it one of the poorest countries in the world. Neither Cuba nor China was engaged in such prolonged and catastrophic wars. Agricultural reform in Vietnam (1986) began when that country was not a member of international financial organizations (Vietnam became a member of the IMF and the World Bank in 1994), and yet the positive fruits of the reform were tangible (agriculture contributed 1 percent to GDP growth in 1987–1993). Le asserts that the decline of Soviet aid and the continued US embargo on Vietnam during the 1980s, combined with the lack of aid from international financial institutions, were tough external constraints for economic development, hence the only suitable solution was a change in the country's economic model: "the new elected leadership after the party congress in 1986 was willing and determined to implement the market-oriented reform" (Le 1994, 9). Furthermore, "thanks to the reforms, Vietnam could not only survive the collapse of the USSR and the East European socialist countries but also expand and diversify international economic relations. The reforms contributed relevantly to the lifting of the U.S. embargo [and to normalize] relations with international financial organizations" (Le 1994, 41). Despite similar conditions as faced by Cuba, Vietnam was able to implement the successful socialist-market model that turned around the country's economic situation and contributed to the lifting of the US embargo.

Concerning the third difference, some scholars (P. Vidal 2016) argue that the structural reforms were easier in China and Vietnam because they were mostly agricultural economies and their populations mainly lived in rural areas, whereas Cuba was less agricultural and predominantly urban. Two counterarguments are as follows. First, the initial agricultural reform in Cuba, in the first year of the revolution (1959), distributed landownership (small and medium-sized parcels) to 200,000 peasants who already lived on and worked the land. Instead of expanding that successful policy, however, in 1961–1963 the government imposed restrictions on the private farmers, and only 97,341 were left in 2019 (ONEI 2020a). The government seized the medium-sized private farms, transformed cooperatives into state farms, took away common plots in state farms, then shifted back to co-ops, which became quite ineffective and contributed to the awful agricultural performance—the Achilles heel of the revolution and the perennial cause of food scarcity, particularly in the 1990s and currently. The second counterargument is that Cuba's second agricultural reform (under Raúl Castro, in 2008 and 2012) transferred idle state land in usufruct (see chapter 2) to small farmers, again with many restrictions and disincentives—such that, when that experiment failed, successive laws amended the ill-conceived initial law but without improving agricultural output. It is revealing that, in Cuba, 17 percent of the employed labor force in agriculture generates only 2.6 percent of GDP, the result of extremely low labor productivity in agriculture, and opposite to what happened in China and Vietnam (ONEI 2021).[9] If, instead, the government had followed the three golden rules of the successful Sino-Vietnamese agricultural reforms (allowing all agricultural producers to decide freely what to sow, whom they sell to, and the price to set by supply and demand), the reforms would have been powerful incentives for food-deprived workers in urban areas to move to work in agriculture; in a short period, Cuba would have substantially raised output, achieved food self-sufficiency, and generated a surplus for export.[10]

In a similar vein, Sachs (1996) argued that socialist economies with large state enterprises, such as the Soviet Union and Eastern Europe, confronted an economic structural obstacle to taking the Sino-Vietnamese path because it was difficult to advance in market-oriented reforms without restructuring state enterprises concentrated on heavy industry. Conversely, China and Vietnam were agricultural economies with underdeveloped industrial sectors. Torres (2023) has applied Sachs's argument to Cuba, adding that in China and Vietnam the economy greatly benefited by the expansion of the private sector without dismantling the relatively few large state enterprises. Nevertheless, compared with the USSR–Eastern Europe, the size of Cuban state enterprises was significantly smaller; so was the degree of prerevolutionary industrialization (it was also smaller than China's), and after 1989 Cuba endured a process of deindustrialization (Mesa-Lago 2000).

Concerning the fourth difference, the argument is that the predominance of small enterprises in Vietnam was a facilitator of the reforms (P. Vidal 2014, 2016). From the beginning of the Cuban revolution, the government confiscated thousands of small businesses, including even homes that were rented. It was probably the fastest collectivization process in the three countries, and it started the concentration in large state enterprises.[11] In 1968, fifty-six thousand tiny family enterprises (many of them street stands) were seized, virtually completing full collectivization, possibly in a higher degree than in China and Vietnam. Due to the failures of these policies, from 2007 to 2018 Raúl Castro's reforms tried to curtail the gargantuan state sector by allowing the expansion of the non-state sector, but the reforms still imposed many restrictions, taxes, inspections, and policy reversals that impeded the expansion's proper development. For instance, university graduates cannot practice self-employed in their own careers although they can do so in low-skilled jobs, which is a waste of the substantial state investment in their academic training. Furthermore, if microbusiness had been more developed prior to monetary unification, some of its adverse effects would have been avoided (Mesa-Lago 2000; Mesa-Lago et al. 2018; P. Vidal 2021). This analysis indicates that government policy, rather than unfavorable structural factors, was at the heart of the Cuban flop.

Concerning the fifth difference, finally, oil production in Vietnam is eleven times that of Cuba, whereas China's is six times that of Cuba. In per capita terms, however, Vietnam has the highest output (0.23 tons per capita), followed by Cuba (0.19 tons), and last China (0.01 tons); Vietnam is a net oil exporter whereas China and Cuba are net oil importers (China is the biggest oil importer in the world). Therefore, Vietnam has an advantage over the other two countries. Without disregarding this as an important Vietnamese advantage over Cuba, it should be pointed out that oil deposits were not discovered in Vietnam until the mid-1980s, and production did not begin until the 1990s. Even more important is that, in 1960–1990, the Soviet Union provided all the oil that Cuba needed, at subsidized prices and on credit (the resulting debt was never paid back). After a significant problem in the 1990s due to insufficient Cuban oil production and imports, since the early 2000s Venezuela began to supply oil to Cuba in exchange for professional services (which involve a substantial hidden subsidy). Venezuela also built an oil refinery in Cienfuegos, Cuba, and supplied it with crude oil; part of its output was sent back to Venezuela, but a surplus was kept by Cuba and exported to the world market. The crisis in Venezuela has reduced its oil supply to Cuba but has not completely stopped it. Last but not least, if Cuba had been able to generate enough non-oil exports to finance its oil imports (as was the case in many non-oil-producing countries in Europe, Asia, and Israel), then insufficient oil output would not have been a major obstacle.

PREREVOLUTIONARY CUBA'S ADVANTAGE IN ECONOMIC-SOCIAL DEVELOPMENT

There are no systematic comparisons of Cuba, China, and Vietnam, either at the time of their revolutions (1959, 1949, and 1945 respectively) or when each started their economic reforms. Nevertheless, statistics from those times and other statistics analyzed later herein strongly indicate that the two Asian countries were at a much lower overall level of development than Cuba. For instance, prior to the revolution of 1959 and based on eighty comparable economic and social indicators, Cuba's development level was the second- or third-best among the twenty Latin American countries, meaning that it was fairly developed by regional standards (Mesa-Lago 2009). According to Devereux, before the revolution, Cuban income per capita was on a par with those in Ireland and Finland and above that of Spain. It was a "fairly prosperous middle-income society . . . along with Puerto Rico and the Southern Cone, Cuba had the highest income of any Spanish-speaking society" (2021, 5, 9).[12] Furthermore, in 1978 when China began its reform, its GDP per capita was one-twelfth that of Cuba and, in 1986 when the transformation started in Vietnam, its GDP per capita was one-sixth that of Cuba (Monreal 2018c).[13] Therefore, the two Asian countries had to undertake a greater effort to raise their levels of economic-social development and living standards to close the gap and surpass Cuba within these metrics. The last point is supported by each country's change in HDI placement in the period 1990–2021: China increased thirteen places, and Vietnam increased one place, while Cuba decreased thirty-two places (see table 1.1). This demonstrates that the first two are rapidly closing the gap with the third (UNDP 2022).[14]

Sachs's argument (1996) that the USSR and Eastern Europe had an "over-extended social welfare state," while China and Vietnam lacked even a basic social safety net, might support my conclusion above concerning Cuba. And yet his point that social entitlements became a hindrance later while they helped the two Asian countries in supporting their financial sustainability is valid regarding Cuba.

In summary, there are twice as many similarities as differences (ten versus five) among the three countries, whereas divergences have been contested with counterarguments to discard or at least reduce their potential for being a barrier to comparison. In any case, the cited factors will be taken into consideration when they are relevant in the analysis of economic-social performance (chapter 3) and in the evaluation of the impact of the models on social security (chapter 5). Finally, Cuba's advantages vis-à-vis China and Vietnam in terms of the higher level of both economic-social and social security developments should be considered a compensatory factor against the other adverse factors examined.

CHAPTER 2

COMPARISON OF THE TWO ECONOMIC MODELS AND THEIR KEY POLICIES

Communist revolutions took over in 1945 in Vietnam, 1949 in China, and 1959 in Cuba—where socialism was not officially proclaimed until 1961. The two Asian countries preceded Cuba in their revolutions by fourteen and ten years, respectively. As in all other socialist nations, all three countries first copied the traditional Soviet model of central planning and virtual total state ownership of the means of production.[1] After the failure of such a model, market-oriented structural economic reforms began (in China, first was Mao Zedong's disastrous Great Leap Forward [GLF] away from the market), but they took a longer time relative to the start of the revolution: twenty-two years in China, forty-one years in Vietnam, and forty-nine years in Cuba. China and Vietnam did not follow the big bang approach that was typical in Central and Eastern Europe but instead used a gradualist approach. Nevertheless, the path and rhythm of such a process have been much faster and deeper than in Cuba.

EVOLUTION OF THE TWO MODELS IN THE THREE COUNTRIES

After the dire economic performance during the Mao era (particularly the GLF and the Cultural Revolution), China under Deng Xiaoping,

Zhao Ziyang, Jiang Zemin, and Zhu Rongji developed a "socialist-market" model, where the private sector, markets, and foreign investment, combined with an indicative plan and decentralization of decision-making, spurred the highest economic growth rates in the world (Wu 2005; Yasheng Huang 2008). Reforms were conducted in two stages. In 1978–1984 (six years, in comparison to the ten years of Raúl Castro's reforms), Chinese leaders mandated the division of agricultural communes into private plots, opening to foreign investment, allowing entrepreneurs to start businesses that rapidly increased their share in industrial output, and establishing several economic development zones, thereby authorizing and expanding private property. Following this, in the period between 1984 and 2005, leaders implemented state decentralization and increased the transfer of power to local governments, townships, and villages that legally owned enterprises but that in fact were private, along with the privatization and contracting out of much state-owned industry, although state monopolies in oil and banking continued (Brandt and Rawsky 2008). A communist party meeting in 2013 agreed to push forward new reforms, thwarting the party bureaucracy and its resistance to deeper economic changes. Between the government and the market, the latter was to play a decisive role in financing and the allocation of resources; competition was strengthened and restrictions on landownership were overhauled (Buckley 2013). However, the current president and first secretary of the communist party, Xi Jinping, has stepped back from the market opening, global cooperation, and private initiative and has instead supported state enterprises, top-down decision-making, and party involvement in business management and firms, significantly strengthening his political control and expanding his legal terms in power. (For the shifting policies under China's President Xi and its effects, see appendix 1).

Cuba's centrally planned model (Soviet style) was introduced with the first medium-term plan in 1962–1965, but it failed, and a debate on alternative models followed in 1964–1966 between pro-Soviet and Guevarist (Che) factions. Under Fidel Castro rule, in 1966–1970, the long-central plan was substituted by a short-run sectorial plan, and that also failed. This forced a reintroduction of the central plan in 1971–1985. However, in 1986–1990 Fidel launched the "Rectification Process" and a move further away from the market. The collapse of the USSR and Easter European socialism provoked a severe crisis in Cuba in the 1990s and a chaotic period (Mesa-Lago 2000). Fidel's illness in 2006 led to his replacement by his more pragmatist brother, Raúl Castro, who since 2007 endorsed (ineffective) market-oriented "structural reforms" (his own term), which were afflicted by a slow pace, contradictions, and lack of incentives, and these ground to a virtual halt in 2016. A party congress in 2011 stated the goal of "updating the economic model," not changing it. New president Miguel Díaz-Canel proclaimed continuity and began implementing the monetary and exchange rate unification in 2021 that contributed to another severe economic crisis, which was still unfolding in 2024. During all these years (save for the 1990s, because of the crisis), five-year central plans have been enacted but have failed; currently there is a long-term plan 2020–2030 (Mesa-Lago and Pérez-López 2013; Mesa-Lago 2024b). Today, Cuba and North Korea are the only two socialist economies in the world with the largest role of the plan and state property and the lowest role of the market and private property.[2] In 2023, Cuba and Russia signed several economic agreements, and the island, prompted by the severe economic crisis, seems to be moving to adopt the inefficient Russian model of oligarchic capitalism (see chapter 7).

Vietnam reforms ("Doi Moi," meaning "innovate" or "renovate") began in 1986 and also moved the country rapidly toward a socialist-oriented market economy.[3] The reforms encouraged private business (more than thirty thousand businesses were created in six years), foreign investment, and foreign-owned enterprises; agricultural cooperatives were abolished, as well as state control over agricultural production in the predominant private sector, which was allowed to sell in the market and to fix prices. In 2000, the Vietnam Communist Party (VCP) approved a ten-year plan to enhance the role of the private sector, and in 2003 private enterprises controlled more than one-quarter of industrial output. The 2000 bilateral trade agreement with the United States facilitated the transformation of a predominantly agricultural economy into a manufacturing-based economy. Furthermore, Vietnam has become an active member of many international economic and financial institutions' free-trade agreements.

COMPARISON OF FIVE KEY ASPECTS OF ECONOMIC POLICIES

There are five main aspects of the economic models: ownership of the means of production; agrarian reform; the industrialization process; employment, unemployment, and self-employment; and monetary and exchange rate unification.

Ownership of the Means of Production and the Role of the Market vis-à-vis the Plan

China's ownership rights are expansive and liberal. By 2005, because of the rapid process of privatization, 50 percent of China's GDP was generated by the private sector, reaching over 60 percent in 2018 (Brandt and

Rawski 2008; NBSC 2019). The property law of 2007 allowed national and foreign investors to own constructions on state-owned land and, once completed, granted them the right to sell, lease, and mortgage such rights (for seventy years, for residential use, and forty years, for commercial use), which are automatically renewable for residences or renewable every forty or fifty years for industrial and commercial businesses (M. Zhang 2008). The real estate sector became a pillar of the ascendant economy, accounting for about 30 percent of GDP, and Chinese households allocated most of their savings to housing. This resulted in a housing bubble, which led to government regulations (Wakabayashi 2022).

The expansion of the private sector has been remarkable. In 2019, out of the total number of enterprises (21 million): 0.4 percent were state owned, 0.6 percent were collectively owned or cooperatives, 1.2 percent had foreign investment or capital from Hong Kong or Macao, 7.9 percent were corporations either shareholdings or of limited liability, and 89.7 percent were private. However, state ownership was concentrated in large enterprises that generated 47.2 percent of the total output (although declining),[4] medium-sized enterprises that generated 22.5 percent of the total (rapidly expanding), and small enterprises that generated 30.3 percent of the total (stagnant).[5]

In 2018–2019, in the crucial industrial sector in China, 37.6 percent of the total were private assets, whereas 80 percent of total national employment was private (NBSC 2019, 2021b). The market approach was best articulated in the 2013 official document "China 2030," which envisioned a retreat of the state and state-owned enterprises and the domination of market forces. In practice, there was an absence of major reforms after China's entry into the WTO and the global financial crisis of 2008. Nevertheless, an anonymous referee argues that official statistics underestimate the shares of state enterprises because a very large share of the enterprises listed under other categories are in fact state enterprises. Furthermore, state enterprises sell shares to the public, but the public has no say at all in picking management, which is actually done by the organization department of the communist party. The fact that state enterprises have gained control, however, has happened under President Xi's reinforcement of state enterprises and reversal of socialist-market policies (Lardy 2019; see also appendix 1). This issue has to be researched more, but there is no doubt that, even if this argument is correct, still the size and power of the state sector and ownership in China and Vietnam is much lower than in Cuba.

Since 1990, when virtually all Cuban means of production were state owned, the market-oriented reforms (particularly under Raúl Castro) did not significantly change the predominant state and cooperative ownership, or central planning and hesitance about the role of the market.[6] In agriculture, only small farmers own the land, but their numbers dwindled by one-half in 1959–2020, and they are submitted to many controls.[7] State farms that used to be the majority in the 1960s have declined as they were converted into agricultural production cooperatives: Basic Units of Cooperative Production (UBPC by its Cuban acronym) and Agricultural Production Cooperatives (CPA). The state keeps landownership and tight control over said co-ops, granting indefinite leasing contracts to their members; a 2011 decree has been unable thus far to improve their independence.

The Cuban state also retains property of the land in usufruct. Non-agricultural-production and services co-ops started in 2013; their members are leasers, and such co-ops seem to have more autonomy than agricultural production co-ops, but their numbers have stagnated. Most self-employed are owners of their small or medium-sized enterprise (SME) but also leasers when receiving a small state enterprise. In 96 percent of enterprises with foreign capital, the state owns 51 percent of the shares. Foreign investment in real estate is forbidden; a foreign entity cannot have landownership but is only allowed to rent the land (Mesa-Lago et al. 2018; Mesa-Lago et al. 2020).

Out of Cuba's total entities in 2008, 44.3 percent were state owned and operated (combining enterprises and service agencies), 53.5 percent were cooperatives, and 2.2 percent were enterprises with foreign capital; in 2019, the respective percentages were 42.1 percent, 55.4 percent, and 2.4 percent, such that the combined state and co-ops share decreased only 0.3 percentage points in that period (ONEI 2009, 2020a). Small private farms and self-employed businesses, the only two groups with private ownership, were excluded from that percentage distribution—the former were in decline and the latter were rising. In terms of employment, however, in 2019 the state had 67.1 percent of the employed labor force, the cooperative sector had 10.4 percent, and the private sector had 22.5 percent. By 2021 the distribution had worsened to 67.6 percent, 21.9 percent, and 10.5 percent, respectively (ONEI 2021). No official data is available on the value of GDP generated by the private sector, but two scholars have calculated it: 7.7 percent in 2002, which decreased to 3.8 percent in 2008 and peaked at 9.2 percent in 2018 (Vidal and Alonso 2022).[8] According to Vidal and Alonso, Cuba's proportion in 2018 was 15.3 percent that of China and 14.7 percent that of Vietnam (see table 2.1).

In Vietnam, after the end of the war and the reunification in 1975, the congress of the party (1976) implemented the centrally planned-economy model as in Cuba in the 1960s, which included nationalization of the means of production, state ownership of enterprises (which received state subsidies to cover losses), planned output targets, monopoly of foreign trade, collectivization of agriculture and handicrafts, state-fixed prices for all relevant goods and services, and agricultural cooperatives with compulsory procurement quotas. Under the 1976–1980 five-year plan, many investment projects were not completed, planned targets were unfulfilled by a large margin, the economy deteriorated and reached a critical situation by 1980. Soviet aid financed budget and foreign-trade growing deficits (Le 1994). Between 1957 and 1975, the collectivization process in the North reduced the non-state sector (including cooperatives) from 72 percent to 8 percent, whereas the state sector grew from 28 percent to 92 percent. In the South in 1976–1985, the non-state sector declined from 72 percent to 60 percent and the state sector grew from 28 percent to 40 percent (Le 1992, 2018).

The party congress of 1986 strongly criticized the previous failures and approved market-oriented reform. Under Doi Moi, Vietnam returned land-use rights to private households and recognized them as autonomous economic units. The state retreated to a regulatory role, with the market determining the prices of goods and services. The collapse of the Soviet Union pushed the reforms further, and there were four successive enterprise laws that greatly invigorated the private sector. The 1990 law legalized and guaranteed private firms, whereas the 1992 constitution officially recognized the role of the private sector.[9] The law of 1999 in Vietnam provided the same legal framework for all types of enterprises, regulated enterprises with foreign direct investment (FDI), cancelled all licenses and permits required from ministries and provinces, prohibited the nationalization or expropriation of assets and investment capital of enterprises, and allowed foreign organizations and others to contribute capital to all enterprises. The enterprise law of 2005 abolished any remaining discrimination between state and private enterprises and recognized the lawful profitability of private businesses. The law of 2015 was accompanied by a new law of investment that replaced that of 2005; it pushed for an acceleration of the reform of state enterprises and substituted a previous list that allowed specific national and foreign investment with a "negative" list that denoted those activities where such investment is not allowed—this significantly expanded private and foreign investment. Corporate and income tax deductions were implemented to spur domestic and foreign investment.

After each of the four enterprise laws in Vietnam, there was an expansion of the private sector (Brundenius and Le 2014; Monreal 2018a). The number of private enterprises rose further, and by 1996 there were 190 joint stock companies and 8,900 limited liability companies. By

2010 their respective numbers had risen to 55,058 and 163,980, while the share of state enterprises in the total decreased to 1.1 percent.[10] In 1995–2011, the combined share of GDP of private and household enterprises jumped from 43.5 percent to 87.5 percent. Foreign direct investment (FDI) in Vietnam averaged 5.7 percent of GDP in 1990–2019 vis-à-vis 3.4 percent in China (Việt Vũ Quang 2020); Cuba's "materialized" FDI (meaning not promised but contracted and operational) averaged about US$500 million annually (virtually zero percent of GDP in 2020) compared to an official goal of US$2,500 million (Mesa-Lago and Svejnar 2020).[11]

In 2002, the Vietnam stock market opened. Economic growth expanded significantly, led by the private sector, which had annual rates of 9.9 percent in 1995–2005 and 11 percent in 2005–2011 (Brundenius and Le 2014). The number of households having nonfarm businesses was 32.2 percent in 2018, and 18.2 percent of households had two or three businesses; "communes" (local administrative units) with business enterprises increased from 57.2 percent in 2008 to 69.4 percent in 2018 (GSO 2019). In a lecture at the University of Havana in 2018, Secretary General of the Communist Party Nguyen Phu Trong (2018) defined the role of the market in the development of socialism in Vietnam based on three key points: the market has a central role in the economic model; the market is necessary to build socialism; and instead of being antagonistic with socialism, the market favors it. However, in 2019, the secretariat of the communist party of Vietnam central committee issued an instruction on the need to have party cells in all private Vietnamese economic entities so as to make such entities a driving force in that country's socialist-market economy; the cells were to coordinate with the management boards to ensure that workers' rights, obligations, and interest were protected ("More Party Cells Needed," 2019). At first sight this could resemble Xi's creation of party cells in private enterprises, but such cells in China now control most decision-making; I was not able to find further information on this instruction in Vietnam.[12]

In 2019, the distribution of GDP by ownership in Vietnam was 27.1 percent state, 42.7 percent non-state (out of which household ownership was 29.4 percent, private was 9.7 percent, and collective was 3.6 percent), and 20.4 percent foreign owned—hence, combining domestic and foreign owned, the contribution of non-state was 72.9 percent. Investment shares were 31 percent state, 46 percent non-state, and 23 percent foreign. The number of active enterprises was 668,500: only 0.5 percent were fully state owned, 96.7 percent were non-state, and 2.8 percent were foreign owned. In addition, there were 5.2 million nonfarm individual enterprises (e.g., owned by one person, group, or family), at an average of 7.9 per 1,000 inhabitants, that employed more than one-half the number of total employees in active enterprises (GSO 2019). Furthermore, professional activities (in law, architecture, engineering, travel, health, education, and research) accounted for 7 percent of total employment (whereas professionals cannot practice their own profession in Cuba) and generated 1.2 percent of GDP. In the tourist sector, only 12 percent of the number of visitors is handled by the state, while 77 percent is privately owned and operated and 11 percent is foreign owned (GSO 2021b). The private sector is clearly predominant in Vietnam and China, whereas the state sector is dominant in Cuba. One of the key drivers of Vietnam's development is the special Resolution No.10/2017 of the Party on the development of the private sector: Once ignored and discriminated against for a long period of time, now the private sector economy is well recognized and supported officially by policies and incentive mechanisms.

Agrarian Reforms

In China under Mao, virtually all land was organized as communes, with disastrous effects on agricultural production that led to periodical famines and the death by hunger of millions of people. Under the market-oriented reforms, although ownership is legally kept by the state (as it is in Cuba and Vietnam), virtually all agriculture has become managed privately by individuals, families, autonomous co-ops, and villages, who sign contracts for between thirty and fifty or seventy years depending on the type of land, or for an indefinite amount of time. There is freedom to hire workers; investment is not limited; and farmers decide freely what to sow, whom they sell to, and the price to set based on supply and demand. At the start, the price of a few key products such as rice was set by the state but soon liberated.[13] The Chinese restoration of household farming, along with partial decontrol of rural marketing and individual entrepreneurship, propelled significant increases in agricultural output and productivity as well as rural incomes (Brandt and Rawski 2022; see chapter 2).

There have been several agrarian reforms in Cuba, with an increasing trend toward state collectivization until about 2008. At the start of the revolution in 1959, all large private domestic and foreign plantations were seized by the government; two hundred thousand farmers who were working the seized land received titles for small parcels (instead of "private" farmers they were and still are officially called "small" farmers). In 1961 the remaining land was quickly organized as state-controlled cooperatives, but in 1962 all co-ops were converted into state farms and co-op members became state-salaried employees, although they also received small collective parcels for their own cultivation and consumption. In 1963, private farms were reduced in size by the state, which began to buy such farms when private farmers died or retired, thus leading to a reduction of them by one-half. In 1967, the small collective parcels in state farms were taken by the state. Experiments with China-style communes were tried in some state farms, and once briefly allowed, farmers' markets were eliminated in 1986. By 1988, 97 percent of all Cuban land was collectivized, either as state farms or as state-controlled cooperatives, and the remaining 3 percent comprised of private farmers was submitted to tight government regulations. All Cuban farmers (private, co-op members, usufruct farmers) must follow planning guidelines on what to sow; they have to sell most of the crop to the state (mandatory procurement quota or *acopio*) and at a price set by the government below the market price (Mesa-Lago 2000; Álvarez 2004).

Raúl Castro's major agrarian reform, which started in 2008, was the expansion of usufruct; it began in 1995, amid the severe crisis of the 1990s, but later stagnated. Usufruct consists of the transfer of idle state land to farmers who lack ownership but who can work the parcel and appropriate the fruits of their labor. The land is transferred under contracts signed with the state for ten years, renewable to another ten—the contract period was extended to twenty years in 2012. If the state denies the renewal, all investment done by the usufruct farmer is assessed by the government, which decides a sum that is reimbursed to the owner. Tight restrictions are imposed on usufruct: the farmer must sell to the state as much as 70 percent of the crop at state-set prices (below the market price); investment is limited to a tiny percentage of the parcel land; the farmer must be "tied" to a cooperative; hiring workers requires state authorization; building a house or a stable was banned but then was later permitted when submitted to state approval, which involves considerable red tape. The contract could be terminated by the state if the usufruct farmer violates any of the above obligations or if the land is not "used in a rational manner," a clause left to government interpretation (Mesa-Lago et al. 2018). Under these conditions, it is not surprising that agricultural production has sharply decreased in Cuba.

For more than one decade, Cuban academic economists have unsuccessfully recommended that the government allow freedom to all agricultural producers to plow what they want, sell their produce to whomever they desire, and set prices according to supply and demand (see Nova 2013).[14] Sugar and cattle are two examples to illustrate failures in agricultural planning. Sugar production reached 8 million tons in the 1980s. In 2002, a restructuring of the sugar sector took place, substantially reducing sugarcane plantation area and the number of mills, supposedly to increase productivity and profits. This policy was followed by a steady decline in sugar output, down to 474,000 tons in 2021, the lowest harvest in Cuban history and a decrease of 94 percent relative to the 1980s level (Álvarez 2004; Mesa-Lago and Pérez-López 2013; ONEI 2022a; Rodríguez 2022). Restrictive bovine cattle policies included top prices set by the state for thirty-eight categories of cattle (well below the market price); a 5 percent tax for commercialization; and a discount of 3–5 percent for each cattle unit delivered to slaughter. In addition, in 2022, sixteen fines and penalties (up to 20,000 Cuban pesos per animal, eight times the average annual state salary at the time) were imposed for "violations," such as undeclared cattle and failure to regularly count the herds and properly identify each animal. As a result, the number of head of cattle decreased 26 percent in 1989–2021 (down 36 percent in 1958–2021), and cattle for slaughter fell 59 percent in the same period (González-Corzo 2022). Cuba's agricultural contribution to GDP declined from 5.7 percent to 2.6 percent in 2007–2020, and the nation must annually import about US$2,000 million in food (22 percent of total import value) that could be produced domestically (ONEI 2008a, 2021).[15]

North Vietnam collectivized all land and centrally fixed prices, which were lower than the cost of production, hence provoking huge inflation and a sharp decline in agricultural output and economic growth that forced the importation of food. Soviet assistance (US$2,000 million) was tantamount to 80 percent of GDP in 1975 (Le 2015). On April 5, 1988, Vietnam General Secretary of the Party Nguyen Van Linh promulgated Resolution No. 10-NQ/TW (known as Khoan 10) on the change of agricultural economic management. The resolution recognized households as autonomous economic units and gave farmers parcels, land-use rights, and long-term contracts. In addition, the policy of trade liberalization allowed farmers to do business freely in the market; this transformed the cooperative (the agency responsible for the whole production management organization) to focus on providing services to the farmers. In 1989 the abolishment of compulsory procurement quotas in agriculture, along with price liberalization and approval of crop trading for the private sector, led to an immediate increase in rice production and exports (Le 1992, 2018). Khoan 10 was the base for regulation of long-term and stable land allocation to farmers. It was further ratified by the 1993 land law, a significant incentive for increasing agricultural output and productivity as well as development of rural areas in the late twentieth century and early twenty-first century that ended the chronic food shortages of the past. While, in 1976, Vietnam was a large importer of rice (up to 450,000 tons of rice), since 1989 it has satisfied domestic rice demand and quite soon exported 1.2 million tons of rice, becoming the second-largest exporter in the world (the harvest peaked at 45 million metric tons in 2015) and exported 6.5 million tons in 2021–2022.[16] Vietnam annually exports to Cuba 250,000 tons of rice, which could be produced domestically if Cuba followed Vietnam agricultural policies (Mesa-Lago and Svejnar 2020).[17] China and Vietnam agrarian reforms ended the historical food deficit that had generated famines and tens of millions of deaths (particularly in China), achieving food self-sufficiency and a surplus for export (particularly in Vietnam).

The Industrialization Process

There are fundamental differences among the three countries in the industrialization strategies. Influenced by ECLAC inward strategy of import substitution industrialization (combined with the Soviet-Stalinist model), in 1959 Cuba embraced rapid industrialization, but the program failed in four years, forcing a return to sugar and the outward model, which also was unsuccessful. Conversely, China and Vietnam also tried the Soviet model of industrialization first and later shifted to the export model, which was successful. However, such model is virtually exhausted in China and is moving to the inward approach supported by a huge population and the needed industrial structure.

Brandt et al. (2017) argue that China's industrialization was a 150-year process through which enterprises developed manufacturing abilities based on two steady features: openness to the international economy, which allowed for access to new technology, FDI, importing intermediate and capital goods and new ideas; and domestic market liberalization, a source of new opportunity and competition to upgrade products and reduce costs.[18] In China, modern industry started with labor-intensive products that demanded modest skills and gradually became more skilled-labor and capital-intensive products. Brandt, Ma, and Rawski identify other key factors that contributed to the success of industrialization: (a) since the 1950s, China received technical support from the USSR and CMEA in the largest technological transfer in human history, a solid base for the post 1978 reforms; (b) the Chinese diaspora was a substantial source of financial and human capital (except in the planned-economy era);[19] (c) FDI jumped six times from US$3,500 million in 1990 to US$21,822 million in 2019, mainly from Hong Kong and Taiwan; (d) the spread of mass education (ministries and state-owned enterprises established a network of universities and technical schools) provided factory-level skills; (e) since the mid-1950s, a rural development industry was developed that employed 20 million workers by 1978; (f) special economic development zones, mostly in coastal areas, facilitated an opening to the global economy; (g) favorable coastal region conditions (better education, skills, and experience) were expanded to central and western regions; (h) security concerns and the goal to narrow the gap with the West promoted investment and expansion of producer-goods sectors such as steel, machine tools, chemicals, and so forth; (i) the reforms allowed market forces to exert growing influence over the industrial product mix while government agencies continued to promote the replacement of imports with domestic production of computers, chemicals, machine tools, etc.; (j) by 1991, market forces had surpassed "state directives" in determining prices; (k) the reforms' introduction of profit retention by enterprises and bonuses for workers were powerful incentives for increasing productivity; and (l) entry in the WTO in 2007 gave another push to China's exports and its transition to an export-oriented economy.[20]

China's industrial structure and technological level has progressively advanced. As a percentage of total export value, the proportion of low-value-added products (such as textiles and processed materials) has kept falling since the late 1990s, while the proportion of products in the higher end of the value chain (like electronics and heavy manufactures) has steadily accelerated since the early 2000s (Meng 2019) and even more so since the 2020s. The combination of all the cited factors prompted high annual industrial growth rates: 12.3 percent in 1952–1965, 10.2 percent in 1965–1978, 11.6 percent in 1978–1995, and 13.8 percent in 1995–2008 (Brandt et al. 2017). Other industrialization policies have focused on the development of larger state enterprises as well as the concentration in sectors deemed to be too fragmented, the encouragement of technological advances and use of specific local techniques, and the heavy reliance on direct administrative intervention and shift of top resources to preferred sectors (World Bank 2013). The Index of Industrial Output rose 153 percent in 2010–2020, and today China is the dominant manufacturer in the world of everything from cement to solar panels as well as the main trade partner of and principal lender to most of the developing world (NBSC 2021b; Bradsher 2022a).

Prior to the revolution in Cuba, there was a very high dependency on sugar production—the agricultural-industrial branches of sugar generated about 29 percent of GDP, and sugar exports were 81 percent of total exports. Cuba lacked the prerevolutionary industrial base of China, but there were indicators that sugar dependency was decreasing, thus non-sugar industrial output grew 47 percent in 1947–1958 (Pérez-López 1974). In 1959–1963, the new revolutionary government launched an ambitious plan of import-substitution industrialization to eradicate sugar dependency, with machinery and equipment provided by the USSR and the socialist camp. By 1964 this plan had failed, and Cuba returned to an export strategy mostly relying on sugar production (a return to the prerevolutionary strategy of sugar as the major engine of growth), but with increasing production (a 1970 target of 10 million tons) and an expansion of nickel, fishing, and cattle. The 1970 sugar output target was not met, and the decline in GDP that year led to an increase in the modernization and mechanization of the harvest in 1971–1985 (resulting in steady crops of about 8 million tons in the 1980s), combined with a push in nickel, citrus, tourism, selected industry, and biotechnology. Soviet and CMEA aid amounted to US$65,000 million in 1960–1990, but the government was incapable of properly utilizing those resources to promote productive industrialization (part of the aid was invested in a further expansion of free social services).

Furthermore, between 1986 and 1990, there was an ideological radical shift to the left with a predominance of moral stimulation instead of economic incentives (an attempt to forge a "new man") that provoked a decline in GDP, weakening Cuba economically to confront the collapse of the socialist camp (opposite to the beneficial effects brought by opening to the market in Vietnam). In 1991, a new strategy prioritized foreign investment, external remittances, and hard-currency exports, but the collapse of the USSR provoked a GDP decline of 35 percent in 1990–1993 (Mesa-Lago 2000). Many Soviet and GDR industrial plants, such as nuclear energy plants and oil refineries, were left uncompleted. Starting in 2002, the "restructuring" of the sugar industry—aimed at reducing sugarcane plantations and factories with the hope of producing less sugar with higher productivity—also failed as sugar output fell about 80 percent relative to the 1980s. The sharp decrease in GDP and gross capital formation, poor foreign investment, and the restructuring of the sugar sector led to a significant "deindustrialization."

Since the beginning of the 2000s, substantial Venezuelan aid allowed a few advances, such as the completion of the oil refining plant in Cienfuegos, which led to a brief partial recovery. And yet, the failure of the reforms to transform the resilient planned model, Trump's strengthening of the US embargo, combined with the severe economic crisis in Venezuela, the pandemic, and the subsequent crisis of 2017–2024 doomed those efforts. Some of Raúl Castro's reforms, such as a new foreign investment law and the creation of one Special Economic Development Zoom, had very poor results (unlike China's and Vietnam's) because of many restrictions and bureaucracy. Cuba has a very well-educated labor force, but it has not increased productivity, largely because of the government ban on university-educated professionals working in the private sector. Despite some brief trials, state enterprise profit retention and bonuses for workers have not been effectively implemented. Even after the reforms and the current economic crisis, centrally fixed prices continue to predominate over market-set prices. Finally, the Cuban diaspora has not been legally and effectively allowed to invest in the island and generally has a hostile attitude toward the Cuban regime. The official Index of Industrial Output of 1989 clearly reflects the industrialization fiasco: by 1993, the worst year of the severe crisis, output had fallen by 61 percent; there was a recovery until 2017, but still output was 32 percent lower than in 1989; by 2021 industrial production decreased again to about one-half that of the 1989 level (ONEI 2022a). All eleven key manufactured products in 2020 were either below the 1989 level (six) or below a peak achieved in 2007–2018 (five); output decreases vis-à-vis 1989 oscillated from 10 percent to 33 percent in six products and from 73 percent to 99 percent in the other five (Mesa-Lago 2021c).

The situation of Vietnam at the end of the war in 1975 was a mirror of Cuba's current situation: "inappropriate emphasis on state-owned economy ['unsuccessful collectivization'], restrictions on the private sector, lacking incentives for farmers, and inefficient public investment were the main causes for negative growth," whereas state investment into state-owned enterprises, aiming at building an autarkic economic structure and emphasizing heavy industry, was highly inefficient and costly in terms of both time and money (Le 2018).[21] In order to start a new private enterprise, a lot of red tape was required (more than three hundred licenses and permits were needed in 1999), which blocked the private sector (Le 2015). The Doi Moi reforms of 1986 were a turning point for Vietnam, moving it from a centrally planned to a socialist-market economy and integrating it into international markets, a move that has continued via subsequent reforms including the four enterprise laws already analyzed (Dinh, Zafar, et al. 2013). The market-oriented reforms accounted for two-thirds of the remarkable increase in Vietnam GDP (World Bank 2021b).

Many of the main features in Vietnam's industrialization process are similar to China's, such as domestic and trade liberalization, deregulation, reliance on skilled low-cost labor, expansion of the private sector in manufacturing and its exports (mobile phones are the major export [in Cuba, even after recent reforms, the private sector cannot export-import directly but rather through state agencies]), establishment of eighteen coastal economic zones (vis-à-vis only one in Cuba in 2022),[22] incentives to attract FDI, massive education and training of the labor force (with emphasis on quality),[23] and prices set by the market. But there were autochthonous features too. According to Dinh, Mishra, et al. (2013) and Dinh, Zafar, et al. (2013), industries such as wood products, garments, and shoes boomed in Vietnam because of three main factors: the country's ability to attract FDI that caters to its comparative advantage of semi-skilled and cheap labor; its capability to secure a strong supply chain of imported raw goods and overall reliability in infrastructure; and financing costs that are relatively low through bank loans with advantageous interest rates as well as government subsidies and low tariffs.

Other factors were industrial competitiveness and the ease of doing business, as well as the elimination of tariffs and restrictions to trade that allowed integration into the global economy by signing sixteen free trade agreements, including one with United States in 2001, and joining regional trade associations such as the Association of Southeast Asian Nations (ASEAN), the Comprehensive and Progressive Agreement for Trans-Pacific Partnership (CPTPP), the Regional Comprehensive Economic Partnership (RCEP) of fifteen countries in Asia and the Pacific, and the EU-Vietnam Free Trade Agreement. Entry in WTO in 2007 pushed such integration further (Eckardt et al. 2018; Le 2018; Minh 2022). These agreements allowed Vietnam to diversify its external economic relations, to be not too dependent on any particular market, and to turn a trade deficit into a trade surplus at the beginning of the 2011–2020 period. In 2020 the export value reached US$282,600 million, up 2.9 times relative to 2011, while import value was US$262.7 million, up 2.5 times relative to 2011 (ILSSA/ILO 2022).

In addition, the reforms made Vietnam's economy an integral part of the international framework and one of the most open economies in the world (Tran Ngoc 2022). From 2006 to 2016, Vietnam climbed twenty-seven positions (from sixty-ninth to forty-second place) in the UN Industrial Development Organization (UNIDO) Index of Competitive Industrial Performance. In 2018, Vietnam had also rapidly escalated in the World Bank ranking on ease of doing business. Resolution Khoan 10 of 2018 set the goal of bringing Vietnam into the top three competitive countries in the ASEAN by 2030 (J. Nguyen 2020).[24] The share of industry in GDP rose from 23.2 percent in 1990 to 38.6 percent in 2013 and is projected to reach over 40 percent by 2030, whereas the industrial share in employment increased from 11 percent to 22.7 percent and is projected to reach 37.2 percent (Politburo 2018; Le 2018).[25] These progressions have led to an average GDP annual growth of 6.8 percent in 1988–2017, a constant increase in income, and a decrease in the incidence of poverty (Dinh, Zafar, et al. 2013; Le 2015, 2018). The Index of Industrial Output rose 57 percent in 2010–2020 (GSO 2021b).

Employment, Open Unemployment, and Self-Employment

Under Mao Zedong employment was virtually guaranteed to all workers, but with market reforms and the closing of many state-owned enterprises and communes, open unemployment significantly increased (Ringen and Ngok 2013). The reforms have advanced substantially in expanding employment in the private sector going beyond self-employment and cooperatives (as in Cuba) to engage wage workers, and professionals can work on their own or in the private sector. About 75 percent of the employed labor force is in private enterprises and self-employment (22 percent of the total labor force in 2019), which contribute from 50 percent to 60 percent to GDP and half of total taxes; cooperatives are autonomous and usually own their business (Mao 2013; ILO 2021d). In 1998, a round of reforms was aimed at reducing the number of redundant workers in state-owned enterprises, which were overly burdened with unneeded workers who were paid salaries, resulting in poor performance in production, productivity, and profitability (again, as in Cuba). To avoid massive open unemployment, the government set up a basic livelihood guarantee scheme targeted at supporting workers who had been laid off from state-owned enterprises (Gongcheng and Scholz 2019).[26] There were differences in the process of reducing superfluous labor: the most developed regions rapidly achieved it, but in the northeastern region, the private and foreign sectors were too small to absorb all redundant labor (X. Huang 2020). Although there is still some surplus labor in China, the processes of privatization and competition, combined with social assistance, have largely eliminated it; the average open unemployment rate in 2019 was 3.6 percent (NBSC 2021b).[27] Prior to 2018, unemployment data was based on urban administrative registration at the local level and was widely criticized as underestimated. However, since that year, household surveys have been used according to ILO standards and have been judged as more independent of local governments and more reliable (Mondorf 2020). Despite a significant effort, it was not possible to get data on underemployment, which is reportedly unavailable (L. He 2022; Y. Wang 2022). Notwithstanding unavailable data, lower levels of education and skills and a lack of opportunities in rural areas result in persistent underemployment, while university graduates find it increasingly difficult to get jobs and may be underemployed. On the other hand, wages and opportunities for lower-skill migrants are increasing, and there is a labor shortage as the economy rebounds from Covid-19. Finally, there is a new government effort to revitalize and develop rural areas (Huy 2022).

Cuba virtually eradicated open unemployment by allowing "hidden" unemployment. For instance, a factory required one hundred workers but hired two hundred, striving for full employment at the cost of halving labor productivity and wages. Devereux (2021) estimates that "labor productivity has hardly increased in over six decades [1957–2017]" (13–

14). In my doctoral dissertation in 1968 I analyzed employment, unemployment, and underemployment in socialist economies and proved the existence of the labor surplus in Cuba, which I estimated as 27 percent of the labor force in 2010 (Mesa-Lago 2018b). In 2008 the "open" unemployment rate was 1.6 percent of the labor force, one of the lowest in the world, but two years later about 1.8 million workers (36 percent of the labor force) were officially estimated unnecessary, higher than my previous estimate.[28] In 2011 a dismissal of the surplus was decreed, aiming for employment in an expanding non-state sector in self-employment, usufruct farming, and service cooperatives.

Self-employment occupations are generally quite specific and unskilled (such as water suppliers to street workers, clowns, bathroom attendants, street vendors), though there are very few skilled (such as translators, real-estate agents, insurance agents, bookkeepers). University graduates are banned from working as self-employed in their professions; an engineer cannot work as such but may be a taxi driver, hence wasting Cuba's huge investment in human capital. Inspectors frequently close microbusinesses or impose fines on them. Taxes are many and heavy: the tax on the labor force has a rate rising in tandem with the number of hired employees, arguably to prevent wealth concentration but in fact punishing self-employment, which creates more private jobs, and obstructing the dismissal of superfluous state employees. Microcredit and inputs are grossly insufficient, and a couple of wholesale markets were opened and later shut down. Ups and downs in the history of self-employment engender uncertainty, as did state actions in 2014–2016: closure of stands in Havana porches, bans on the sale of imported products, shutting down 3D cinemas, and the confiscation of tons of lobster destined for small restaurants. One-fifth of the self-employed failed and returned their licenses. Bureaucracy has been a strong barrier, largely due to conflict of interest: the manager of a state restaurant that offers bad food and worse service is threatened by a small nearby private restaurant that is cheaper and serves excellent cuisine. To be approved, nonagricultural and service co-ops went through four reviews and the final decision was made by the State Council. Additionally, a license from the Cuban Central Bank was required for co-ops to open bank accounts in pesos, only one bank accepted these accounts, commissions were charged for banking services, and no interest is paid for deposits (BCC 2014). The pandemic and the economic crisis have forced many co-ops to shut down.

In August 2021, a law authorized private SMEs (mipymes) and co-ops to operate in more than two thousand activities but still does not permit professionals to practice their own trade in those activities (Pérez

Villanueva 2021). In 2022, the government approved a regulation that self-employed workers with more than three employees could become mipymes; by the end of 2022, there were 4,665 of them, but only 25 percent were middle-sized—the rest were micro or small (ONEI 2023; Pérez Villanueva 2022a). In January 2024, a new income tax regulation imposed several heavy taxes on mipymes: a 20 percent tax on monthly earnings above 30,000 CUP (US$109), an increase over the previous tax of 15 percent on earnings above 9,510 CUP; in addition they have to pay 10 percent on sales and services, 5 percent tax on payroll plus 14 percent on social security, 20 percent on dividends, and 35 percent on profits; finally, mipymes cannot have more than one hundred employees (Gámez 2024a). A new law enacted in August 2024 imposed new obligations, permits, and restrictions on mipymes: Cubans that acquire shares in a mipyme will lost their status as shareholders (*socios*) if they cease to be "effective residents" in the nation (such condition still has not been defined by the law); the condition of socio may be lost also if a third party exercises the socio's functions or by the reiterated absence of the socio in the general board meetings (Decreto-Ley 88, 2024).

State employment declined from 82 percent to 74 percent of the labor force between 2006 and 2013, whereas non-state employment grew (ONEI 2014). At the end of 2014, 418,000 state employees had been dismissed, which was about one-fourth of the official target for 2015 because non-state job creation was insufficient to provide jobs to those earmarked for dismissal. The number of workers in the non-state sector ascended to 767,000 in 2014; such a number had to increase more than twofold in 2015 to meet the target of 1.8 million total dismissed state workers. There were about 200,000 private farmers in 1959, which decreased by half to 97,341 in 2019 due to deaths, retirement, and the state buying of farms. The number of usufruct farmers fell 12 percent in 2013–2019, from a peak of 312,572 to 275,762. The number of new co-ops in operation rose from 198 to 439 in 2013–2017, about half of those approved, and then stagnated at 431 in 2019; there were 16,700 new co-op members in 2019 vis-à-vis 459,000 agricultural-production co-op members. On the other hand, the number of self-employed increased to 617,000 in 2019 (four times the 2010 number), but then it decreased to 602,400 in 2021 because of the economic crisis, and this is an insufficient number to provide employment to surplus labor in the state sector. Open unemployment was 1.2 percent in 2019, but underemployment was 29.2 percent (ONEI 2014, 2021; Mesa-Lago et al. 2020).

Finally, the labor force has been declining as well as the rate of active economic participation. In 2011 the labor force was 5,174,500 and by 2019 had decreased by 10.3 percent to 4,642,300. In turn, the rate of economic participation shrank from 76.1 percent to 65.2 percent in the same period (ONEI 2012, 2020a). There are various explanations of these trends: the declining fertility and reproduction rate since 1978 (ONEI 2008b, 2010a, 2010b; MINSAP 2021); significant emigration (of which 80 percent is people aged 15–59 and 15 percent is people with a university degree); and feminization of the emigration, as there are 117 women for every 100 men (Albizu-Campos 2020). Another problem is that a high percentage of workers either are not interested in working or reject state job offers because of very low state wages; instead, these workers seek employment in the non-state sector, particularly self-employment, because it is much more remunerative. In 2008, 300,000 workers were disconnected from work (*desvinculados al trabajo*), tantamount to 6 percent of the labor force in comparison to the official 1.6 percent of open unemployment ("Editorial," 2008; ONEI 2009).

The expansion of the private sector in Vietnam spurred employment creation (as in China): from 1.6 to 2 million new jobs, equivalent to 90 percent of newly created employment, and this is an important factor in reducing unemployment and poverty (Brundenius and Le 2014). The open unemployment rate was 5.6 percent of the labor force in 1990, peaked at 6.7 percent in 1994, and decreased to 6.1 percent in 1995 and to 5.1 percent in 1996. However, this situation did not last long, for the rate increased in 1997–1998 from 6 percent to 7.4 percent, largely because of the economic-financial crisis in the Asian region but also because of an increase in the labor force, not enough creation of jobs, and displacements provoked by the application of advanced science, engineering, and technology. Conversely, the unemployment rate of the labor force by age groups in the region and by urban and rural areas from 2010 to 2019 had a general tendency to decrease, falling from 2.9 percent in 2010 to 2.2 percent in 2019, but increasing to 2.5 percent in 2020 because of the pandemic (GSO 2009, 2017–2021b). School-aged youth do not continue to attend school in large numbers, leading to an increase in underemployment in rural areas from 1 percent in 1996 to 2.2 percent in 1997, still overall low rates. Opposite to the case of Cuba, underemployment in Vietnam has declined nationally: from 1.9 percent of the working age population in 2016 to 1.5 percent in 2019, to 2.5 percent in 2020 due to the pandemic. Self-employed persons in Vietnam account for 35.7 percent of the labor force (more than twice the Cuban rate), and members of agricultural cooperatives are 0.1 percent of the labor force compared with 10.4 percent in Cuba (GSO 2021b). Self-employment, calculated as percentage of the population aged 15 years and over, was 66.7 percent in 2008 and decreased to 54.3 percent in 2018; proportions of self-employment were much higher in rural than in urban areas, but all showed decreasing trends (GSO 2020). Self-employment accounts for 48 percent of informal employment (Ramírez and Arza 2021).

MONETARY AND EXCHANGE RATE UNIFICATION

"The experience of Vietnam and even China, suggests that there is no special monetary policy strategy for socialist-market economies: Both have tended toward an international approach, albeit with more controls on the exchange rate and the financial system" (P. Vidal 2014, 75). Cuba, still a centrally planned economy with partial reforms, has more government controls than the two Asian economies; for instance, Cuba has a state monopoly of foreign trade and an incipient private sector and has not implemented a socialist-market system parallel with or before monetary unification. The three countries refer to their monetary unification process as "gradualist," but actually Vietnam's approach was fast (close to the "big bang" approach), and all applied divergent policies.

In China

In precommunist China, several currencies circulated—mostly denominated as yuan but also with other names. In 1948, even before the communist takeover, the People's Bank of China started to issue a unified currency for the controlled territories (usually denominated yuan but also with different names) until 1949 when they were unified as the renminbi (RMB). In 1978, a dual-track currency treatment was established: with the RMB used domestically and foreign exchange certificates for foreigners. In 1993 this dual-track system was abolished, and the RMB was made more convertible and had more realistic exchange rates through subsequent devaluations. Between 2010–2013, there were successive steps taken to make the RMB internationally convertible with several currencies; currently, the RMB is the eighth most internationally traded currency.

The effects of unification on inflation and the fiscal deficit were rapidly controlled by the government, whereas exports increased substantially. In 1979 China's fiscal deficit was US$11,362 million dollars; the government made payments that were not covered with deposits and hence went into debt (US$7,352 million) to banks. The following year, the respective figures declined to US$8,299 million and US$6,534 million. In 1979–1980, banks issued an additional US$8,689 million, equivalent to 60 percent of the previous twenty-nine years. As a result of such financial overdraft, the retail price index rose by 6 percent in 1980 and urban prices by 8.1 percent. The policy at that time was to reduce fiscal expenditures, balance finances and overdrafts to banks; not overdrawing banks was a very important policy that continued into the 1990s. The leadership decided in 1978 to make the central bank independent, because it could not be the "money box" for financing, hence printing money required permission from the central bank. In 1981 the government tightened finances and prohibited bank overdrafts.

As a result of these policies, the inflation rate dropped to 2.4 percent, but thereafter China has experienced three inflation peaks: in 1987–1989 it was 18.8 percent; and in 1993–1996 (when the major advance in unification was introduced) the economy overheated. Inflation rose to 24 percent in 1994; this is the strongest inflation after the market reform, and there has never been a double-digit rate again. After 1997 the inflation rate dropped and the country entered a stage of low inflation, but in 2008 inflation reached 8.2 percent. The next decade was a period of low inflation (2.4 percent in 2020) and even deflation. The fiscal deficit as a percentage of GDP in 1994, after a major step in unification, was 1.2 percent; it oscillated from 1 percent to 2 percent in 1995–2014; rose to 3–4 percent in 2015–2019; increased to 4.9 percent in 2019; peaked at 6.2 percent in 2020; and decreased to 3.8 percent in 2021 (all the above is based on NBSC 2008, 2021b; China Government Network 2022; B. He 2022).

In Cuba

From the start of the revolution until 1994, Cuba had one single currency, the peso. From 1995 to 2000, two currencies, as well as the US dollar, circulated: the national peso (CUP) and the "convertible peso" (CUC), which was not traded in the world market. The value of the CUC was slightly higher than the dollar. The exchange rate set by state agencies to the population was 24 CUP = 1 CUC, but in the state enterprise sector 1CUP = 1CUC = 1US dollar, hence the exchange rate was, and still is, greatly overvalued. This monetary duality created severe distortions: (a) market segmentation, with a large income gap between those dependent on wages, pensions, assistance, and subsidies vis-à-vis those who have access to foreign remittances, hard-currency/CUC earnings, and private income sources (also workers are paid their salary in CUP but some of their expenses are in CUC); (b) adverse effects on the efficiency of economic decisions and resource allocation; (c) hiding subsidies that keep some enterprises fallaciously profitable and others deceitfully unprofitable; (d) making it impossible to assert profitability of exports and competitiveness with imports; and (e) lack of proper assessment of domestic investment feasibility and the creation of disincentives to foreign investment. It also generated the illusion that monetary unification would increase income and reduce inequality, when such problems are actually the outcome of state enterprises' low efficiency and productivity (P. Vidal 2014).

The monetary and exchange-rate unification was postponed for at least one decade, despite urgent need and its promise to bring long-run benefits if properly implemented, such as increases in exports, labor productivity, and enterprise profitability that would help promote economic growth and new jobs. In 2014 a timetable and regulations for monetary unification in the enterprise sector were enacted. Several times, the leadership announced the unification, but it did not happen until January 1, 2021 (after twenty-five years of monetary duality), when the country suffered the worst economic crisis since the 1990s: "The majority of Cuban experts recommended [and they were right] that it was better to fully implement the structural reforms before unification in order to have an economy [able to expand production of goods and services and meet the increase in demand brought up by salary increases]; this should have included market liberalization, especially the expansion of private enterprises. After the unification there has not been an increase in the supply of agricultural and industrial goods to reduce their prices" (Pérez Villanueva 2021).[29]

At the start of 2001, Cuba eliminated the CUC and, by mid-year, fully replaced it with the CUP, which is now the only national currency, albeit the US dollar, the euro, and other hard currencies are used to buy goods in state shops. The CUP that was once exchanged one to one with the dollar in the state-enterprise sector was devalued to 24 (the gap in the exchange rates was 1 ÷ 24 x 100 = 2,300 percent). This means that exporting enterprises should see the value of exports multiplied by twenty-four, while imports should cost twenty-four times more. In addition, monetary unification unveiled the cost of postponing the needed structural reforms. Unprofitable enterprises—suffering decapitalization and technological obsolescence—should no longer get state subsidies to cover losses, thus they would be shut down and their workers dismissed (five hundred of these enterprises, one-third of the total, were identified by the government in 2021). Conversely, profitable enterprises should be able to expand and hire more workers. Yet the leadership decided to postpone those effects for one "transitional" year in order to avoid shutdowns and a sharp increase in open unemployment.[30] For that purpose, US$750 million were assigned to subsidize 31 percent of state enterprises in the red, which signed "commitments" promising to eliminate losses in one year without guarantees that said "commitments" would be fulfilled (Mesa-Lago 2021c).

The subsidies continued in 2022, when 24 percent of state enterprises ended the year with losses and the government declared that it will not allow them to shut down ("La ineficiencia," 2022). Cuba's official exchange rate in July 2022 was still frozen at twenty-four CUP to one dollar, which was grossly overvalued, as the exchange rate in the informal market was three times higher. In August 2022, the Cuban government resumed buying dollars from the public at a rate of 110 CUP to compete with the informal exchange, but the rate in the black market rapidly doubled to 200 CUP to the dollar in 2022 and to 322 to the dollar in 2024 (Frank 2022; "Tasa representativa del mercado," 2022, 2024).

Wages, pensions, and social assistance benefits were raised to compensate their devaluation due to inflation, which actually exceeded those increases. The official inflation rate based on the CPI in 2021 was 77 percent, whereas the consumption deflator was 1,062 percent (ONEI 2023); other experts estimate inflation oscillated from 500 percent to 700 percent (Albizu-Campos 2022a). The deflator is fourteen times the CPI, a difference explained by the 2,300 percent devaluation of the peso in 2021 (Luis 2023). If the government were able to transfer the labor surplus at the inefficient state enterprises toward an expanding private sector and maintain fiscal equilibrium, then inflation would decrease, but this has not happened. Just the opposite: the fiscal deficit was 18 percent of GDP in 2020 and estimated at 12 percent in 2021, but it was probably much higher due to the distortions caused by inflation. Exports declined by 17.4 percent in 2020 and 67.7 percent relative to 2013 (ONEI 2021). There is neither a plan for macroeconomic stabilization nor a plan to control devaluation of the CUP (P. Vidal 2022; ONEI 2022a).[31]

Starting in the second half of 2021, the economy began to operate with the unified currency, but most unification objectives will take time because of the problems. Meanwhile, the short-term adverse effects of the process prompted street protests throughout the country in July 2021 (Mesa-Lago 2021a; P. Vidal 2021; Pérez Villanueva 2021). Pavel Vidal concludes that "there are only two possible paths: seriously advance toward structural reforms and [liberal] opening, or the economy will provoke a hyperinflationary spiral with difficult austerity measures of high socio-political costs" (2021, 5). In 2023 such structural reforms had not been introduced, and to control hyperinflation, the government enacted a tough austerity program to begin in 2024, which includes cuts in rationing quotas and food subsidies as well as sharp increases in the prices of gasoline (528 percent), transportation (180 percent), electricity, and cooking gas, combined with restrictions on SMEs (Gámez 2024b).[32]

In Vietnam

In the mid-1980s, Vietnam had two official exchange rates that were excessively overvalued, both far below the real market exchange rate. In August 1985 there was an attempt to restore the command economy to stop creeping inflation, but it failed. The government tried to set prices, wages, and the new currency at one-tenth of previous levels.[33] This required the exchange of old currency to new currency at a ten-to-one rate at banks, thus restricting personal money withdrawals, keeping the remaining funds at the banks, and thereby restricting consumption. Against the goal that such policies would set proper command prices for transactions, there was a widespread refusal to sell products to the state, forcing authorities to raise prices and print more money, which destroyed public trust in cash; instead, people invested their money in gold and other physical goods. Inflation quickly jumped from 50 percent to 90 percent before 1986, peaking at 454 percent in 1986, whereas GDP fell sharply.

At the end of 1988, three crucial economic decisions were made. Prices were market-determined, save for electricity and gasoline; interest rates on deposits were set higher than the inflation rate in order to attract money back to the banks; and interest rates on loans were kept at low rates to avoid bankruptcy of state-owned enterprises, thus slowing down growth of the money supply to reduce inflation (Viêt Vũ Quang 2020). The government deflationary policy brought inflation under control in 1989, and it was only 2.8 percent in 2019 (GSO 2021b). In 1989, there was a single exchange rate of 4,500 dong per one US dollar; the gap between the official rate and the market exchange rate was reduced from 770 percent in 1985 to 10 percent in 1989 (Le 1994).

The devaluation of the exchange rate occurred along with important structural reforms such as the elimination of the state monopoly of trade and exporter access to imported capital goods and intermediate exports, something that by October 2024 still had not happened in Cuba. Even during the Doi Moi, the Vietnamese fiscal deficit peak was 7.5 percent of GDP in 1989, and it dwindled to 3.3 percent in 2019; whereas in Cuba, it exceeded 30 percent of GDP in 1992–1993 and, after a decline, increased again to 18 percent in 2020 (ONEI 2021). Vietnam's realistic exchange rate had very positive effects in the promotion of exports, which grew at a 25 percent annual rate in 1989–1993. GDP growth rates were brought from 4 percent in the 1980s to an annual rate of 6.8 percent in the period 1990–2018; in 2018, per capita GDP reached US$1,964 at current prices, and Vietnam joined the club of lower middle-income countries (Viêt Vũ Quang 2020). Labor productivity in 2011–2020, calculated at 2017 prices and in international dollars, increased at an annual average of 4.9 percent, higher than the average growth rate of ASEAN countries. Tourism grew at an annual rate of 30 percent per annum, reaching 18 million arrivals in 2019, an increase of more than 10 million relative to 2015 (ILSSA/ILO 2022).

Vietnam renounced direct (administrative) instruments of monetary policy such as central price fixing and relied instead on indirect tools such

Table 2.1: Economic Policies and Their Results in the Three Countries, Different Time Periods

Policies	China	Cuba	Vietnam
Ownership of Means of Production			
Non-state owned (% of total enterprises)	89.7	21.9	96.7
Contribution to GDP (%)	60.0	9.2[a]	62.7
Agrarian Reform			
Privately managed agriculture	Large majority	Minority	Large majority
Agricultural output	Increasing	Decreasing	Increasing
Food self-sufficiency	Yes	No	Yes
Industrialization			
Degree of progress	Very advanced	Deindustrial-ization	Advanced
Index of industrial output[b]	157	−46	57
Index of global innovation (rank)	11	Excluded	48
Employment			
Elimination of redundant labor in state sector	Most[c]	No	Yes
Remaining underemployment (% labor force)	Small	29.0	1.5
Monetary and Exchange-Rate Unification			
Single currency and rate, process completed	Yes (1 year)	No	Yes (3 years)
Structural economic reforms	Yes	No	Yes
Inflation	Decreasing	Increasing	Decreasing
Fiscal deficit/GDP (%)	Decreasing	Increasing	Decreasing
Currency traded in international market	Yes	No	Yes
Exports	Increasing	Decreasing	Increasing

Source: My own elaboration based on analysis in the text.

Notes: [a] There is no official data. The figure is estimated by Vidal and Alonso, 2022.

[b] China and Vietnam 2010–2020, Cuba 1989–2020.

[c] But labor productivity, TFP, and quality control, and so on remain far from global frontiers.

as open market operations, legal reserve requirements, discount rates, and incentives. So far Cuba has not followed these policies—conversely, Cuba has set centralized prices for many goods and services (Pérez Villanueva 2021). In 1975, Vietnam took the seat of South Vietnam in both the IMF and the World Bank (World Bank 2011) but did not receive loans to support the unification process; said unification was initiated before the collapse of the USSR, and Vietnam had received Soviet aid. Cuba is not a member of these international financial organizations; its major trade partner and subsidizer, Venezuela, is in a deep financial crisis, and this has harmed Cuba, which has very scarce domestic resources to help in the crisis (P. Vidal 2014).

SUMMARY ON COMPARATIVE KEY POLICIES AND THEIR RESULTS

Because Cuba continues to be a centrally planned economy and has not implemented market-oriented reforms as in China and Vietnam, it is lagging those two countries in the five key policies analyzed above. For a summary of the major features of such policies and their results in the three countries, see table 2.1. Out of fifteen indicators in the table, Cuba ranks third in all, whereas China and Vietnam are virtually tied in first place. Further research is needed to gather comparable numbers in most indicators.

Concerning ownership of the means of production, in Vietnam, 96.7 percent of the total number of enterprises are non-state owned, plus 2.8 percent foreign owned, hence only 0.5 percent are state owned. In China, 89.7 percent of the enterprises are private, and only 1.3 percent are state owned. Cuba does not provide data on the ownership distribution of the total number of enterprises, but 67.6 percent of total employment is in the state sector, with only 21.9 percent in the private sector, and the remaining 10.5 percent is in agricultural cooperatives, which are strictly controlled by the state. In China, 60 percent of GDP is generated by the private sector, compared to 62.7 percent in Vietnam; there is no Cuban official data on the non-state sector contribution to GDP; Vidal and Alonso (2022) estimate that it is 9.2 percent. Finally, on the role of the plan and the market, Cuba continues with what is essentially a planned model (with minor ineffective reforms), China appears to be moving somewhat toward the plan and away from the market, and Vietnam steadily continues in the market path.

Because of reforms in China and Vietnam, virtually all agriculture is privately managed under fifty-year contracts or for indefinite time: agricultural producers can plant whatever they want, sell to whomever they desire, and sell their produce at free market prices. Agricultural output has steadily risen, chronic periodical famines are a thing of the past, and both countries are food self-sufficient, though China has to import wheat and soybeans. Vietnam is the second major world exporter of rice. The key feature of Cuba's agricultural reforms in 2008 and 2012 was usufruct, where the state maintains landownership and usufruct farmers till the land under a twenty-year contract and keep the fruits of their labor, but they submit to selling a big part of the crop to the state at prices set by the government below the market price. The rest of the agriculture sector is operated by the state and cooperatives, save for a tiny private sector that shrank by half in 1959–2020 but still produces much of the food. Agricultural contribution to GDP decreased from 5.7 percent to 2.6 percent in 2007–2020, and Cuba has to import food (22 percent of total import value) that could be produced domestically.

Under the socialist-market model, China and Vietnam industrialized rapidly through fairly similar strategies: expansion of the private sector in manufacturing and its exports, deregulation, domestic and trade liberalization, reliance on low-skilled labor cost, development of economic zones, incentives to attract FDI (including from the diaspora), government subsidies and incentives to innovations and key industrial lines, rural development industry, and so forth. China achieved increasingly higher industrial annual growth rates ranging from 10.2 percent to 13.8 percent, whereas Vietnam steadily rose in the UNIDO Index of Competitive Industry and in its industrial share of GDP. In the Global Innovation Index for 138 countries in 2022, China ranked eleventh, Vietnam forty-eighth, and Cuba was excluded from the Index (WIPO 2022). Cuba pursued the import substitution industrialization strategy under the Soviet-style centrally planned model in 1959–1963, but it failed in 1964 and returned to its historical dependency on sugar production and exports, and later on foreign remittances, export of professional medical services, and tourism—all three in sharp decline because of the economic crisis of 2019–2024. There has been a severe deindustrialization process after 1989. The Index of Industrial Output rose 157 percent in China and 57 percent in Vietnam, both from 2010 to 2020, whereas it declined by 46 percent in Cuba from 1989 to 2020.

China's labor reform of 1998 aimed to reduce redundant workers in the state sector. In order to avoid massive open unemployment in state enterprises, a basic livelihood scheme to support laid-off workers was implemented, which helped to reduce open unemployment to 3.6 percent in 2019 (but there is substantial open unemployment among young urban workers and unneeded white-collar workers in state-controlled coal mines) and sharply reduced the surplus, hence increasing labor productivity and wages. Conversely, Cuba sharply reduced open unemployment by expanding underemployment at the cost of decreased productivity and wages; in 2010–2015, the government estimated redundant labor in the state sector at 1.8 million workers or 36 percent of the labor force and planned to eliminate such a surplus by expanding the non-state sector, mainly self-employment, without a social scheme to support laid-off employees. In reality, only 418,000 were dismissed, because self-employment, instead of jumping 100 percent (as was needed to absorb the state labor surplus), rose only 18 percent. As a result, in 2019 there was 1.2 percent open unemployment but 29 percent underemployment. Vietnam reduced open unemployment to 5.6 percent and underemployment to 1.5 percent of the labor force in 2019 (one-fifth of Cuba's); self-employment increased to 36 percent of the labor force (almost three times Cuba's 13 percent).

Vietnam's monetary and exchange-rate unification was accomplished much faster than in China, though both countries were implementing the structural economic reforms when the unification process began. China started unification shortly after 1949 and in 2010–2013 made the yuan internationally convertible; currently, the yuan is the eighth most internationally traded currency. Inflation peaked at 24 percent in 1994, then decreased to 8 percent in 2008 and to 2.5 percent in 2019–2020; the fiscal deficit at a key time of unification was 1.2 percent of GDP, whereas exports increased significantly after monetary unification. China became a member of the IMF and the World Bank in 1980. In Vietnam, unification occurred between 1986 and 1989, and by 1989 the country had achieved a single exchange rate. Initially, inflation rose and peaked at 350 percent, but it was controlled and fell to 2.8 percent by 2019, whereas the deficit relative to GDP peaked at 7.5 percent; on the other hand, exports rose at 25 percent annually in 1989–1993. Vietnam took the South Vietnam seat at the IMF and the World Bank in 1975 but did not receive loans for unification, although the country did receive some aid from the USSR. After announcing unification, Cuba took one decade to start unification in 2021, amid a severe economic crisis; a single currency was created but it is not traded in the international market, whereas structural economic reforms have not been implemented. A one-year transition period was decreed so that state enterprises with losses (one-third of the total) might keep receiving government subsidies in order to avoid shutting down and increasing open unemployment. The official fixed exchange rate from unification until July 2022 was 24 CUP for one US dollar, but in the informal market, CUP was traded three times higher; in August, the official rate was increased to 110 per one US dollar but the informal rate rapidly increased to 200 and in October 2024 rose to 322. The official inflation rate was 400 percent in 2021, and foreign estimates are even higher; the fiscal deficit was 18 percent of GDP, and exports declined 17 percent in 2020 and were 68 percent below the 2013 level. Cuba belongs neither to the World Bank nor to the IMF. Monetary reform is far from completed, and so far, the results have been adverse.

The unification process in China was very fast, but in Vietnam it took three years. It could be argued that Cuba has had little more than two years since unification began, hence the results cannot be properly compared. There are several counterarguments. First, China had multiple and Vietnam had two currencies respectively at the time of their revolution, whereas Cuba had only one and later introduced two currencies plus the use of the US dollar; the dual (triple) monetary system provoked significant economic and social distortions that did not exist beforehand. After withdrawing the US dollar and unifying the domestic currency, Cuba reintroduced the US dollar and other hard currencies. Second, China began to take steps to unify its currencies even before the national takeover. Vietnam began unification parallel with that model's inception. Conversely Cuba waited twenty-six years to begin the unification process, despite a fair consensus among domestic economists and foreign experts urging to do it (as well as several unfulfilled announcements by the government). Third, China and Vietnam started their structural economic reforms at the same time as the unification process; Cuba has not done them, hence creating a severe obstacle to unification success. Fourth, the two Asian countries devalued their currency rapidly and steadily, whereas Cuba, after the initial devaluation, has set a fixed exchange rate that significantly overvalues the unified currency. Finally, Cuba has actually postponed the potential positive effects of unification by establishing at least one year of transition to avoid the shutdown of unprofitable enterprises and a surge of open unemployment.

CHAPTER 3

ECONOMIC AND SOCIAL PERFORMANCE OF THE THREE COUNTRIES

In this chapter, first I evaluate the economic and social performance of the two models in the three countries. Second, I select the twenty most relevant and comparable indicators (ten economic and ten social) and rank the countries accordingly. Third, I address some methodological problems in the comparison. Fourth, I confirm hypothesis 1.

EVALUATION OF ECONOMIC AND SOCIAL PERFORMANCE

The performance of the two models and three countries is assessed based on twenty-seven indicators, fifteen economic and twelve social (see table 3.1).

Economic Indicators

GDP per capita in US dollars in 2019 was calculated by converting the national currency into dollars based on the official exchange rate: 10,410 in China, 3,500 in Vietnam, and 384 in Cuba (the latter was 3.7 percent that of China and 14 percent that of Vietnam).[1] However, UNDP estimate of Cuba's gross national income (GNI) per capita at international

TABLE 3.1: Economic and Social Performance of the Three Countries, 2019–2020, unless Specified

Indicators	China	Cuba	Vietnam
Economic			
GDP (million US$, 2019)	14,195,716	4,297	340,800
GDP per capita (US$, 2019)	10,140	384	2,741
GNI per capita (US$ PPP, 2017)	16,057	8,621	7,433
GDP average growth rate (%, 2009–2020)	7.4	0.9	5.9
GDP composition 2019 (percentage distribution)			
Primary	7.1	4.0	14.0
Secondary	39.0	22.5	34.5
Tertiary	53.9	73.5	51.5
Gross capital formation 2019 (% of GDP)	43.1	11.5	26.8
Fiscal deficit 2019 (% of GDP)	4.9	6.2	3.3
Inflation 2020 (% over the previous year)	2.5	18.7	3.2
Index of industrial output[a]	152.6	–46.2	57.0
Agricultural-cattle-fish output[b]	398.0	–58.8	235.7
Oil production (metric tons per capita)	0.01	0.19	0.23
Economic (trade) openness 2019 (% of GDP)	38.4	22.9	211.5
Balance of trade goods 2000–2019 (% of GDP 2019)	0.3	–123	6.3[c]
Number of foreign tourists (% rise 2016–2019)	13.0	6.6	55.3
Exchange rate (to 1 US$ mid 2019)[d]	6.91	24.00	23,060
HDI average annual growth (1990–2021, %)	1.50	0.38	1.22
Social			
Poverty incidence (% of population)	0.6	25–30	4.8
Misery index (highest is worst)	4.3	1,227.6	11.3
Open unemployment 2019 (% of labor force)	3.6	1.2	2.0
Underemployment (% of labor force)	n.a.	29.2	1.5
Inequality in income (Gini coefficient)	0.385	0.407[e]	0.357
Change in real average wage/income (%)[f]	217	–53	289
Real average or mean monthly pension in US$[g]	486	18	193
Literacy rate (percent of population aged 15+)	96.8	100.0	95.8

Indicators	China	Cuba	Vietnam
Mean years of schooling	7.9	11.8	9.0
Infant mortality rate (x 1,000 born alive)	5.6	5.0	13.9
Maternal mortality rate (x 100,000)	17.8	176.6[h]	46.0
Gender inequality index (scores)	0.168	0.304	0.296

Source: My own elaboration from NBSC (2021a, 2021b, 2021c, 2022a), MOHRSS (2020d), K. Li (2021) for China; from ONEI (2018, 2020a, 2021), "Cuba registra" (2022), Espina (2022a) for Cuba; from GSO (2021b), IMF (2021), Dinh (2021b) for Vietnam; other data from UNDP (2020, 2022), World Bank (2020, 2021a), Hanke (2022).

Notes: [a] China 2010–2020, Cuba 1989–2020, Vietnam 2010–2020.

[b] China 2000–2019, Cuba 2014–2021, Vietnam 2016–2020.

[c] 2010–2020 surplus as percentage of 2020 GDP.

[d] China yuan, Cuba CUP, Vietnam dong.

[e] Estimate for 2016 by Espina (2020).

[f] China 2009–2019, Cuba 1989–2019, and Vietnam 2008–2018.

[g] China urban employee scheme in 2020; Cuba mean pension in 2020; Vietnam in the mandatory system in 2022.

[h] 2021.

US dollars (purchasing parity power [PPP]) in 2017 was only 54 percent of China's and 115 percent of Vietnam's. The reason for this significant divergence is that the UNDP substantially overestimates Cuba's GNI (see Mesa-Lago 2020b, 2022; Devereux 2021); because of that flaw, the UNDP estimate was disregarded.[2] Even more, average annual economic growth rates in China and Vietnam are the two highest in the world whereas in Cuba the rate is substantially lower. In 2009–2020, China's annual GDP at constant prices grew 7.4 percent, Vietnam's grew 5.9 percent, and Cuba's grew 0.9 percent (see figure 3.1). Covid-19 affected economic growth in all three countries, but in 2020 Vietnam still grew 2.9 percent and China grew 2.3 percent whereas Cuba decreased 10.9 percent, the second-worst performance in Latin America (Mesa-Lago 2021a; ECLAC 2021).[3]

In 1978–2019 Chinese GDP climbed 3,929 percent, averaging around 10 percent yearly in 2003–2012, although it slowed down to 6.7 percent in 2015–2019 (NBSC 2008, 2021b). Vietnam's average GDP annual growth was 5.6 percent in 1987–1993, 7 percent in 1994–2000, 5.9 percent in 2011–2015, and 6.7 percent in 2016–2019 (GSO 2021b). In 1985–2018, Vietnam's income per capita jumped eightfold, pushing

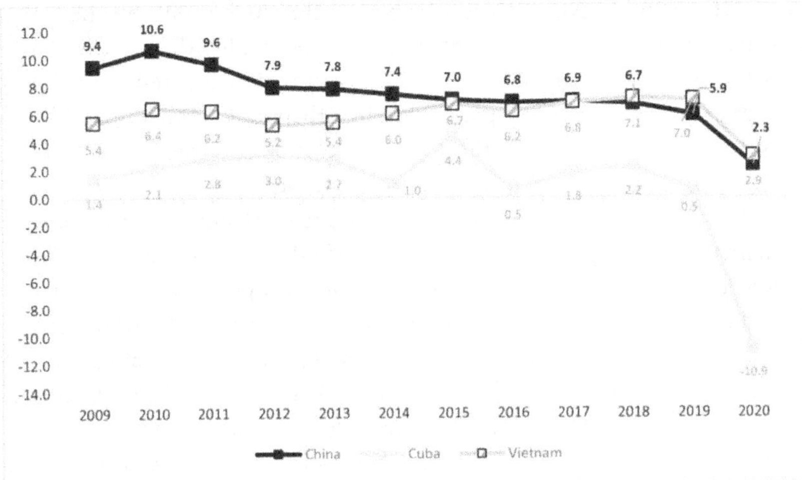

FIG. 3.1. GDP Annual Growth Rates in the Three Countries, 2009–2020 (at constant prices). *Source*: My own elaboration based on World Bank (2022a) for China and Vietnam; ONEI (2013, 2018, 2021) for Cuba; and GSO (2009, 2021b) for Vietnam.

the country from the low-income to the middle-income group, and it is projected to join the high-income group by 2045 (World Bank 2021b). Cuban GDP annual average growth shrank from 7.8 percent in 2006–2008 to −0.8 percent in 2016–2021 (ONEI 2009, 2013, 2022a). Devereux estimates that between 1957 and 2017, Cuban "GDP per capita increased at an annual growth rate of 0.6 percent—among the lowest anywhere. . . . GDP per capita was below 1957 levels for 33 of the 59 years of revolutionary rule" (2021, 5, 14). In 2022, China's GDP growth was 3 percent, Cuba's was 1.8 percent, and Vietnam's was 8 percent; in 2023 China and Vietnam grew 5 percent while Cuba declined from 1.9 per cent (ONEI, 2024).

Gross capital formation as a percentage of GDP shows an increasing trend in China and a declining trend in Cuba: in 2019 it was 43.1 percent in China, 26.8 percent in Vietnam, and 11.5 percent in Cuba (down from 25 percent in 1989, at the eve of the severe crisis of the 1990s).[4] The fiscal deficit as a percentage of GDP in 2019 was 3.3 percent in Vietnam, 4.9 percent in China, and 6.2 percent in Cuba—the latter rose to 18 percent in 2020 (ONEI 2021). Inflation in 2020 was 2.5 percent in China, 3.2 percent in Vietnam, and 18.7 percent in Cuba; due to monetary unification, inflation in Cuba in 2021 (measured as deflator of GDP) was officially reported as 1,062 percent (ONEI 2023; 740 percent estimated by EIU 2022), whereas in Vietnam it declined to 1.8 percent (GSO 2022b).

GDP composition in 2019 diverged in the three countries: the primary sector in Vietnam (14 percent) is 3.5 times higher than in Cuba (4 percent) and twice that in China (7.1 percent), which is reflected also in the distribution of the population by urban and rural sectors. The two Asian countries at the time of the revolution and the reforms were largely agricultural societies, which arguably facilitated agrarian reform and its success (see chapter 2), whereas in Cuba, urbanization was much higher and the agricultural component of GDP was lower. Nevertheless, the urbanization process has been quite fast, particularly in China, and so is the percentage of industry and construction in GDP in both Asian countries: it is 16 percentage points higher in China and 12 percentage points higher in Vietnam than in Cuba, a remarkable success considering the low point of departure in the two Asian countries. There has also been a deindustrialization process in Cuba since 1989. Finally, the tertiary sector is considerably higher in Cuba than in the other two countries. However, the respective components of such a sector in GDP are different: in China and Vietnam, the majority of the tertiary sector is made up of finances, banking and insurance, real estate, lodging and gastronomy, transportation, and professional services, while in Cuba it consists of social services such as education and health, as well as state administration and defense—at 28.3 percent vis-à-vis 6.6 percent in Vietnam (GSO 2021b; ONEI 2020a).

GDP composition largely explains why the index of industrial output in Cuba declined by 46.2 percentage points in 1989–2020; the participation of manufacturing in GDP decreased at an annual rate of 12 percent in 2019–2021 (ONEI 2021, 2022b). Conversely, China's industrial index rose 157 points in 2010–2020, and Vietnam's index rose 57 points in 2010–2019.[5] Agriculture, cattle, and fishing output in China increased 398 percent in 2000–2019 and increased in Vietnam by 235.7 percent in 2016–2020, whereas in Cuba it decreased by 58.8 percent in 2014–2021. In 1989–2019, Cuba's production of sugar (the main export prior to the revolution) fell by 87 percent, citrus fruit by 91 percent, head of cattle by 22 percent, milk by 44 percent, rice by 42 percent, and fish caught by 76 percent (CEE 1991; ONEI 2020a).[6] The comparison of rice output between Vietnam and Cuba is revealing: in the former, it rose by 8.7 percent in 2010–2019, while in the latter, it decreased by 13.8 percent; in 2019 yields were 65.7 and 3.4 tons per hectare, respectively (nineteen times more for Vietnam). As has been said, Vietnam is the second-largest rice exporter in the world (after India) and sells to Cuba about 250,000 tons annually that could be produced on the island (ONEI 2020a; GSO 2021b). Vietnam has the highest oil output per capita (0.23 tons), followed by Cuba (0.19 tons), and China (0.01 tons); Vietnam is a net oil exporter whereas Cuba and China are net oil importers (China is the greatest oil importer in the world).

Economic openness (foreign trade/GDP) in 2019 was 211.5 percent in Vietnam, 38.4 percent in China, and 22.9 percent in Cuba (decreasing from 44 percent in 2013). There is no data on Cuba's balance of payments, so I have to rely on the balance of foreign trade (goods) as a percentage of GDP.[7] In 2000–2019, China had a steady annual surplus accumulated at US$44,210 million, equivalent to 0.3 percent of the GDP of 2019, whereas Cuba had a steady annual deficit accumulated at US$127,070 million, equivalent to 123 percent of the GDP in the same year.[8] Vietnam's trade balance of goods in 2012–2020 accumulated a surplus of US$17,000 million dong or 6.3 percent of GDP of 2019.[9] While the governments of China and Vietnam have extensive links with their communities abroad, which have been a significant source of direct foreign investment (particularly Hong Kong and Macau for China), Cuba has none. Tourism is the third source of hard currency in Cuba, and in 2016–2019 the number of tourists increased by 6.6 percent, whereas in China it rose by 13 percent and in Vietnam by 55.3 percent (ONEI 2021; NBSC 2021b; GSO 2021b). Vietnamese foreign tourism in 2019 reached 18 million visitors, 3.6 times Cuba's 5 million in the same year (ILSSA/ILO 2022; ONEI 2020a). Cuba does not publish any data on international reserves and releases only partial data on the external debt, hence these variables could not be compared.[10]

The HDI annual average growth in 1990–2021 was 1.50 in China, 1.22 in Vietnam, and 0.38 in Cuba (UNDP 2022). If the HDI inflated GNI per capita in international dollars (accounting for one-third of the HDI, whereas two-thirds are health and education variables) had been more realistic, Cuba's annual average would have been even lower. Therefore, China and Vietnam were ahead of Cuba in all economic indicators.

Social Indicators

The poverty incidence in China was 0.6 percent of the population in 2019 (declining from 97.5 percent in 1978), whereas it was 4.8 percent of households in Vietnam in 2020, decreasing from 60 percent in 1990 (State Council Information Office 2021; World Bank/State Council of the PRC 2022; GSO 2021b).[11] Under the revolution, Cuba has not published statistics on poverty; neither are there figures for 1958 at the eve of the revolution.[12] There is a wide consensus, however, that revolutionary policies reduced poverty significantly until the end of the 1980s; the severe crisis of the 1990s reversed the previous trend (Añé 2007). After measuring living standards in Cuba during sixty years under the revolution, Devereux concludes that "the revolution impoverished Cuba relative to any plausible counterfactual" (2021, 5). Cuban sociologist Espina (2008) estimated poverty incidence in Havana at 20 percent in 2000 and from roughly 25 percent to 30 percent in 2016 (Espina 2022a).[13] This is between forty-one and fifty times higher than in China (0.6 percent) and between five and six times higher than in Vietnam (4.8 percent). Poverty must have increased under the current economic crisis. Based on official data on consumption decline in 2022, Cuban economist Monreal (2023) estimates that prices of consumer goods rose 4.5 times the median salary, and seven times if sales in the black market are included in the calculation. More than one million workers (one-fifth of the labor force of 2022) earned less than the median wage (drastically reduced because of inflation), whereas pensions do not meet basic food needs, hence "inflation has had a negative impact on poverty."

A similar vacuum for Cuban data exists concerning income inequality. According to UNDP (2020), income inequality in 2010–2018 was lower in Vietnam (18.1) than in China (27.4), and the respective Gini coefficient figures were 0.385 and 0.357; UNDP does not publish any of those two figures for Cuba. In 1989, Cuba was probably the most egalitarian society in Latin America and among many Eastern European socialist economies, but structural reforms since 2007 overturned the situation. Estimates of Cuban Gini coefficient showed an increase from 0.250 in 1989 to 0.407 in 2016, but they exclude transactions in CUC and external remittances, hence the real coefficient should have been higher (Espina 2008, 2020; Monreal 2018c).[14] The structural economic reforms introduced by Fidel Castro in the 1990s resulted in a sharp increase in income inequality (Romanò and Barrera 2021), and the more advanced structural reforms implemented by Raúl in 2007–2018 must have expanded such inequality. In 2015, the income from most lucrative microbusinesses was from 229 to 236 times the state mean salary (Mesa-Lago 2015a; see also Bye 2020), hence Cuban current inequality should exceed that in China and Vietnam (see also Monreal 2023).[15] Table 3.1 shows the Gini coefficient for China and Vietnam based on the HDI as well as Espina's estimate for Cuba for 2016, which underestimates it for the reasons already explained. Espina (2020) identified the obstacles that impeded research on income inequality in Cuba, among them the absence of statistics, restrictions on financial resources, and obstructions to public academic institutions trying to work on that theme.

The misery index (a mix of social and economic variables) ranks 156 countries based on four indicators: unemployment, plus inflation, plus bank lending rate, minus real economic growth rate. In 2021, Cuba's score was 1,227.6 percent (ranked worst in the 156th position), whereas Vietnam's was 11.3 (ranked 99th) and China's was 4.3 (ranked 143rd, above Switzerland), hence Cuba was 285 times worse than China and 108 times worse than Vietnam (Hanke 2022). Out of the three countries, the gender inequality index among 191 countries is lowest in China (ranked in 48th place), while Vietnam and Cuba are much higher and almost similar (71st and 73rd, respectively).[16]

Open unemployment in 2019 was 1.2 percent in Cuba, 2 percent in Vietnam, and 3.6 percent in China (2.5 percent in 2020 but 4.9 percent in 2022).[17] The Cuban rate was the smallest not only among the three countries but one of the lowest in the world, but underemployment in Cuba was estimated at 29.2 percent and increasing (Mesa-Lago 2021a), whereas in Vietnam it was 1.5 percent (no rate available for China, but see chapter 2). The mean salary in the state sector, annually adjusted for inflation, decreased 53 percent in Cuba by 2019 (based on 1989), but the average rose 217 percent in China (based on 2009) and 289 percent in Vietnam (based on 2008), which largely explains Cuba's deterioration in living standards since the 1990s crisis vis-à-vis the substantial improvement in such standards in the two Asian countries.[18] The average/mean monthly pension in 2020–2022 was US$486 in China, US$193 in Vietnam, and US$18 in Cuba (for calculations, see chapter 5), the latter did not cover basic food needs.

Mean years of schooling are 11.8 in Cuba, 9.0 in Vietnam, and 7.9 in China; Cuba's literacy rate is universal while China and Vietnam are about 3 percentage points lower than Cuba but rapidly reaching 100 percent. Infant mortality rates per 1,000 children born alive are similar in Cuba (5.0 in 2019, decreasing from 10.7 in 1990, but rising to 7.6 in 2021 [ONEI 2022a]) and China (5.6, declining from 50.2 percent in 1991), but higher in Vietnam (13.9, shrinking from 32.6 in 1990). The maternal mortality rate was lowest in China (17.8 per 100,000 child births, declining from 80 in 1991) whereas Vietnam's was 46 in 2019, declining from 233 in 1990. Cuba's was 176.6 in 2021, rising from 32.6 in 1991.[19]

While in China and Vietnam health indicators have increased steadily since the early 1990s, the quality of and access to public facilities and personnel have severely deteriorated in Cuba. Access has declined because of the exportation of physicians and nurses to foreign countries (for instance, one-half of primary care doctors), which generates the first source of hard currency for Cuba, whereas the government pays a tiny fraction of that revenue to Cuban health personnel abroad. Services worsened during the crisis of the 1990s, and despite a partial upturn, some indicators have not recovered to the precrisis levels. The current crisis combined with Covid-19 has contributed to the virtual collapse of the health system (Mesa-Lago and Díaz-Briquets 2021).

RANKING OF THE THREE COUNTRIES BASED ON SELECTED INDICATORS

I selected the most relevant and comparable ten economic indicators and ten social indicators from table 3.1 in order to elaborate in table 3.2 the ranking of such indicators. In eleven indicators, the higher the number the better the situation: GDP per capita in US dollars, GDP average growth rate, gross capital formation, index of industrial output, agriculture-cattle-fish output growth, economic openness, foreign trade balance of goods as percentage of GDP (a surplus is positive while a deficit, marked by a minus sign, is negative), real wage growth, real average monthly pension, years of schooling, and annual average growth of the HDI. Conversely in nine indicators, the lower the number the better the situation: inflation, fiscal deficit, poverty incidence, income inequality, gender inequality index, open unemployment, misery index, infant mortality rate, and maternal mortality rate.

Total scores are 29 in China, 37 in Vietnam, and 54 in Cuba, and the average rankings of the twenty indicators are 1.45, 1.85, and 2.70, respectively. Hence, China is first, followed by Vietnam, and Cuba lags behind. The maximum difference in the ranking is 2.00 points; the distance between Cuba and China is 1.25 points and from Vietnam 0.85 points, while there are only 0.40 points between China and Vietnam. Cuba ranked third in all economic indicators, whereas out of the ten social indicators, it ranked third in seven and first in three. These last three indicators were open unemployment (but with a very high underemployment rate), infant mortality (but showing an increasing trend, the opposite of China and Vietnam), and years of schooling (fairly similar in the three countries). In the average of social indicators, Cuba performed a little better than in the average of economic indicators with a shorter gap vis-à-vis the other two countries. China ranked first in twelve indicators, second in seven, and third in one; Vietnam ranked second in thirteen indicators, first in five, and third in two. The two Asian countries performed much better in economic than in social indicators but were still well ahead of Cuba.

ANALYSIS OF SOME METHODOLOGICAL PROBLEMS

The comparisons face some methodological problems. First is the lack of Cuban official statistics on poverty incidence and Gini coefficient; these indicators were analyzed in the text and scholars' estimates were provided for the ranking. Another missing indicator was underemployment in China and only one-year estimate from a scholar on Cuba, thus prompting its elimination from the comparison. The indicator agricultural-

Table 3.2: Ranking of the Three Countries based on Twenty Economic-Social Indicators, circa 2019

Indicators	China	Cuba	Vietnam
Economic			
GDP per capita (US$)	1	3	2
GDP average growth rate in 2009–2020 (%)	1	3	2
Gross capital formation	1	3	2
Inflation	1	3	2
Fiscal deficit	2	3	1
Index of industrial ouput	1	3	2
Agriculture-cattle-fish output	1	3	2
Economic openness	2	3	1
Foreign trade balance of goods (% of GDP)	2	3	1
Annual average growth in HDI 1990–2019	1	3	2
Social			
Poverty incidence	1	3[b]	2
Misery index	1	3	2
Open unemployment	3	1	2
Income inequality	2	3[b]	1
Real wage/income growth	2	3	1
Real average/mean monthly pension (US$)	1	3	2
Mean years of schooling	2	1	3
Infant mortality rate	2	1	3
Maternal mortality rate	1	3	2
Gender inequality index	1	3	2
Total scores	29	54	37
Ranking average[a]	1.45	2.70	1.85

Source: My own elaboration based on table 3.1, figure 3.1, and data in the text.

Notes: [a] The lower the number the better the situation; total scores in the twenty indicators were divided by twenty to obtain the average.

[b] There is no official figure on this indicator, it is based on a Cuba expert's estimate and the analysis in the text.

cattle-fish output growth lacks a numerical figure, and the countries were ranked based on the comparative analysis in the text on the output in a given period of the most important products in the three countries.

The second methodological problem is the need for better standardization in the periods for most comparisons. Out of the twenty indicators, fourteen relate to the performance in the most recent available year, whereas only six refer to performance in a given time period (annual average GDP growth, annual average growth in HDI, industrial output growth, agricultural-cattle-fish output growth, foreign trade balance of goods, and real wage growth). It would have been ideal to compare all twenty indicators' performance within a specific time period, from the year the model began to the most recent year, but this was not possible because of the different starting years of the two models in the three countries and the lack of comparable data at the starting point (further discussion in chapter 6).

The comparisons, nevertheless, show consistent orders in the three countries across the twenty key economic-social indicators, therefore allowing for a fair average ranking among them (see table 3.2). China is first in twelve indicators, second in seven, and third in one; Vietnam is second in thirteen indicators, first in five, and third in two; Cuba is third in seventeen indicators, second in none, and first in three. Overall, Cuba is worst in economic indicators but slightly better in social ones, but still below China and Vietnam in 70 percent of them. Based on the average rankings of all twenty indicators (the lower score the better), China is first with a score of 29 (average ranking of 1.45), followed by Vietnam with a score of 37 (ranking of 1.85), and Cuba is third with a score of 54 (ranking of 2.70). Cuba's gap with China is 1.25 points and 0.85 points with Vietnam, whereas the gap between China and Vietnam is only 0.40 points (out of a total of 3 points).

The third problem is that, because there are only three countries, the ranking range is quite narrow: from 1 to 3 (from best to worst). The ideal would have been to include more countries, but that was not feasible because, after the collapse of the USSR and the Eastern European countries, there are very few socialist economies left in the world. Laos follows the socialist market, and North Korea adheres to the centrally planned model, making both excellent candidates, but there is very little data available on the former and virtually none on the latter, hence they had to be excluded.

Fourth, the ranking does not properly show the relative range among the three countries, but in the overwhelming majority of indicators, there is significant distance among the three countries. In a couple of cases, however, the three countries have relatively close scores; for instance, in infant mortality, the distance between China and Cuba is only 0.6 percentage points. To alleviate that problem, scores are given in all the ranking tables, which better detect the distance among the countries. Another snag is that each indicator has the same weight for the calculation of the ranking. Ideally, a weight should be assigned, but this would require a significant level of subjectivity to determine which indicator is more important and by how many points.

To cope with the fourth problem, a more sophisticated ranking was elaborated based on standardized number scales that measure the space between each indicator, comparing unusualness or oddness in a batch.[20] The batch in table 3.2 has twenty indicators or numbers but not all were comparable and that left only sixteen; six indicators were converted; the indicators that were eliminated were poverty incidence, misery index, and gender inequality; in addition, it was decided to delete the indicator GDP growth (despite supporting the key hypothesis) because it could potentially overlap with GDP per capita and gross capital formation/GDP.[21] To standardize a batch, the mean is subtracted for every indicator number in the batch and the result is divided by the standard deviation of the batch. The resulting batch has standard scores or z scores. For each number in the original batch, the z score indicates how many standard deviations it falls above the mean (for a positive z score) or below the mean (for a negative z score). See appendix 3 for the total score and average ranking of all indicators for each country (the higher score the better): China is first (0.38), followed by Vietnam (0.28), a difference of 0.10 points, and Cuba is third (–0.65), 1.03 points behind China and 0.93 points behind Vietnam. So, the ranking is the same, but distance between Vietnam and Cuba is a little bit expanded whereas distance between Cuba and China is a little bit reduced. The elimination of four indicators might be responsible for this difference.

CONFIRMATION OF THE FIRST HYPOTHESIS

The above analysis supports my first hypothesis in this book. The socialist-market model of China and Vietnam has had a better economic and social performance than the Cuban model of a predominant central plan and modest structural economic reforms, even though the two Asian countries began reform with a much lower level of development than Cuba and hence required a greater effort to match and exceed Cuba's accomplishments. (For an analysis of the potential argument that, in addition to the models, there might be external factors that influence the performance, see chapter 6.)

PART II

COMPARISON OF SOCIAL SECURITY PROGRAMS AND THEIR PERFORMANCE

CHAPTER 4

GENERAL OVERVIEW OF SOCIAL SECURITY INSTITUTIONS AND PROGRAMS

My aim in this chapter is, first, to identify all social security programs in the three countries and, second, to explain briefly in a comparative manner the three main programs under review. (For the existence or absence of social security programs in China, Cuba, and Vietnam see table 4.1.) Although all programs are listed, the focus is on the three major ones: contributory pensions (protecting against old-age, disability, and death risks); sickness, maternity, or health (both cash and medical benefits); and social assistance (noncontributory programs).[1] Work injury and unemployment insurance are briefly mentioned in some sections of this chapter but are not examined in detail.

PENSIONS

The purpose of a contributory pension is to "smooth" individuals' consumption across the life cycle and in the face of shocks. Usually, contributions from employers and employees plus the investment of an accumulated pension fund are expected to be sufficient when the insured person retires; in some countries, the state finances the system through taxes. Pension systems can be of two types: either "public," which is

TABLE 4.1: Social Security Programs in the Three Countries, 2022

Programs	China	Cuba	Vietnam
Contributory			
Pensions (O-A, D, S)[a]	X	X	X
Sickness-Maternity			
Cash benefits	X	X	X
Medical benefits	X	X[b]	X
Work injury	X	X	X
Unemployment	X		X
Noncontributory			
All means-tested	X	X	X

Source: My own elaboration based on legislation and questionnaires answered by Chinese and Vietnamese experts.

Notes: O-A, D, S = Old-age, disability, and survivor pensions.

[a] All pensions are earnings-related.

[b] No social insurance but a public health system.

characterized by defined benefit, pay-as-you go financing (PAYG) or collective partial capitalization and is administered by social insurance or the state, or "private," which is characterized by defined contribution and full capitalization ("fully-funded") with individual accounts and is administered by private profit-seeking corporations (in some countries, it may be managed by public entities or by a mix of private and public). In public systems there are transfers among generations, as the younger generation helps finance pensions of the older generation. This does not happen in private systems because individual accounts are owned by the insured and cannot be shared—at least theoretically (Mesa-Lago 2021b). China has a mixed pension system that combines a basic social insurance with individual accounts, whereas Cuba and Vietnam both have public systems.

In China

After the market reform, China's social security system emerged piecemeal through a series of regulations and provisions in the Labor Law of 1994 and the Labor Contract Law of 2007 (GOV 2007). It was not until 2010, however, that these separate parts were codified into a comprehensive national framework in the Social Insurance Law (2010), which was implemented in 2011 and revised in 2018. Social security has three key programs: (a) social insurance pensions (old-age and disability),[2] (b) social insurance sickness-maternity (health program), and (c) social assistance. Employment-injury and unemployment insurance will not be examined. Under Mao Zedong, pension and health systems were tied to large urban state enterprise units (which are now largely decentralized) as well as rural communes (now disbanded). The government provided the needed resources to those work units to secure their social security obligations (Meng 2019; Y. Wang 2021).[3] In order to adjust social security to the new socialist-market economy, it was essential to make it independent of state-owned enterprises, farms, and government agencies, thereby expanding its coverage and improving its benefits and bolstering acceptance of the reform by a large stratum of society (Gongcheng and Schulz 2019). Until the 1990s, pensions were financed entirely by the state; there were no contributions from employers or workers (Chen and Turner 2021).

Other key laws include those of 2010 and 2011 (social insurance), 2014 (unified scheme for urban and rural residents), and 2015, a reform that integrated civil servants and public sector employees into the urban-employee program (US.SSA-ISSA 2019).[4] China's pension reforms were influenced by the World Bank (1994) multi-pillar system and structural reforms in Latin America, specifically the mixed model. The Chinese system was highly fragmented and exacerbated inequalities among groups and generated regressive effects; it rewarded the privileged rather than the disadvantaged (Leung and Xu 2015). These problems have been reduced by several social insurance reforms and unification processes, but some still persist. Currently, there are three major pension schemes.

The first major pension scheme is a mandatory pension for urban employees in the "market" sector; it has two pillars or tiers.[5] The first pillar is the basic social insurance (PAYG), and the second pillar is the fully funded individual ("personal") accounts, which are publicly managed. However, in China, a combination of the two is considered to be the first pillar, which creates confusion. The whole scheme is financed by contributions on payroll paid by employers and employees (16 percent and 8 percent, respectively); employers' contributions go to the basic social insurance, and employees' contributions go to individual accounts. Since the 2015 social insurance reform, all civil servants and other public employees have been integrated into this scheme, hence there is now only one mandatory program with the same features (GOV 2015).[6] "Flexible" employees and migrant workers can join the urban-employee scheme if they have a labor relationship with the employer or if they pay by themselves at a rate that is less than the total percentage paid by the employer and the employee (otherwise, they could join the voluntary urban-and-rural-resident scheme explained below).[7]

Some small and middle-sized enterprises provide only pensions and health insurance because of their financial incapacity to finance the rest. Conversely, large corporations with strong profits as well as government employees have voluntary occupational pension plans; this is the third pillar, and it is of two types. In the enterprise sector (93,422 enterprises) since 2004, the employer pays up to 8 percent and the employee up to 12 percent, and in the government and public sector, since 2015, the respective percentages are 8 percent and 4 percent. These occupational pensions are paid in addition to the other two pillars (GOV 2015; KPMG 2020).

A fourth pillar, voluntary commercial supplementary pension, was created in China in 2018 and features fully funded and defined contributions for families and individuals. In 2020, the government further elaborated on the new fourth pillar, which is an addition to the basic pension, individual accounts, and occupational plans for urban employees and urban and rural residents (CBIRC 2020a).[8] This plan is a corporate, occupational annuity with voluntary tax-deferred contributions not to exceed 12 percent of the payroll, and participants can select the amount and frequency of their contributions, which are managed and invested by both profit-seeking private companies (note the difference with the public administration of the second pillar individual accounts) as well as state-owned profit-seeking corporations. These insurance companies must develop a simple affiliation, flexible payments, and stable investment yields. In addition, the companies must submit quarterly reports on their progress in fulfilling the objectives and regulations. By 2020–2021, only big companies that can guarantee a high return had set up the scheme: at the end of 2020 only 3.5 percent of the total employed labor force was enrolled, virtually leaving out urban and rural residents (FIAP 2021; "China's Social Security System," 2021). Other obstacles to this fourth pillar are the slow progress in pilot advancement, cumbersome tax deferral procedures, and low tax incentives—a maximum contribution of 6 percent of wages is tax deductible, which makes it difficult to stimulate enthusiasm for people to participate (Lou Yuekai Securities, cited by A. Lee 2021). According to Chen and Turner, "the resulting situation is of a dominant first tier with weaker second and third tiers" (2021, 52).

In April 2022 the State Council issued guidelines for the fourth pillar (GOV 2022c): (a) all those in the first pillar are eligible; (b) participants can contribute up to 12,000 yuans (US$1,739) annually, the employers don't contribute; (c) there is a fiscal deduction up to the maximum contribution and a reduction in the taxes applicable to the pension; (d) instruments must meet certain legal standards and focus on long-term yields; (e) withdrawal from the account is accessible at the retirement age or upon disability and can be received in a flat sum or in monthly amounts; (f) if the insured dies before the retirement age, then the amount saved is inherited. At the start of 2023, over 24 million commercial pensions accounts had been opened, equal to 3.2 percent of the employed labor force—slightly less than the estimate in 2020 (FIAP 2023; GOV 2023). It is projected that the new pillar could grow up to 15,000 to 20,000 billion by 2030 (KPMG and ASIFMA 2023).

The second major pension scheme, the voluntary pension, is for urban (nonsalaried) and rural residents aged 16 years and over who are not covered by the mandatory urban-employee scheme—such as informal employees, and those in small enterprises, migrants, the self-employed, farmers who had their land expropriated by the government, rural workers in nonagricultural activities, the unemployed, nongovernment agencies, and housewives (it excludes students in schools). This scheme resulted from the 2014–2015 integration of the Voluntary New Rural Pension Scheme (NRPS), originally established in 2009, and the urban resident scheme set up in 2011. It also has two pillars: a basic social insurance pension and individual accounts. The central and local governments finance in full the basic social insurance pension.[9] Individual accounts are financed mainly by insured flat contributions at twelve different levels that diverge significantly in various areas (the level is chosen by the insured and is paid for fifteen years), as well as subsidies from local governments and village collectives.[10] This scheme could be called contributory-subsidized, with the caveat that its financing is mostly public, hence its similarities with a social assistance program. Flexible employees (including the self-employed), informal workers, and the unemployed can participate either in the resident scheme (at the place of household registration *hukou*) or in the urban-employee scheme, but only if they have a local hukou.[11]

In 2014, however, the central government proposed to unify urban and rural hukou, and the distinction between agricultural hukou and nonagricultural hukou was cancelled; they are now uniformly registered as resident hukou (China State Council 2014). Beijing and several cities on the coast have done the unification, but the process is slow, and specific local policies vary (Y. Wang 2022). The resident scheme is more inclusive and accommodating, less discriminatory than the urban-employee scheme, another reason for its increased capacity to expand coverage (Zhao and He 2021). In 2019, of the total insured in the basic insurance pension in both schemes (967 million), 55 percent were in the resident scheme and 45 percent in the urban-employee scheme, similar to the previous distribution (Chen and Turner 2021; "China's Social Security System," 2021). At the end of 2021, out of the total number of insured in the basic urban-and-rural-resident pension scheme, 95 percent were rural residents, such that the share of urban residents should have been only 5 percent (Conglong et al. 2022).

The third major pension scheme is the military's own social insurance. The Military Personnel Insurance Law of 2012, Veterans Protection Law of 2020 (GOV 2020), Military Status and Right Protection Law of 2021 grant the military better benefits relative to their contributions (including unemployed accompanying spouses) as well as social assistance when people are having difficulties with pensions and medical care. Military personnel who complete military service and conditions for retirement receive the benefits of that regime. Military personnel who have completed their service but have not fulfilled conditions for retirement must transfer their contributions and subsidies for pension and medical benefits to the urban-employee or the urban-and-rural-resident schemes. Policemen are affiliated to the urban-employee scheme, as are other public servants (save for military police, who belong to the special military scheme).[12] In all schemes, dependents of the insured are not covered, except for the military scheme, which covers them when they are unemployed.

As indicated in the above discussion, the fragmentation of the pension system in China continues with diverse sectors and groups covered by different basic social insurance, individual accounts, occupational plans in large enterprises, and individual commercial insurance—all with divergent contributions and benefits. At least until 2019, "China still has no nationally unified scheme for its pension program" (Meng 2019, 6), and pension management remains the domain of local authorities, which concentrate 86 percent of pension expenditures, whereas the central government controls only 14 percent.

In Cuba

Cuba was among the pioneer countries in the introduction of social insurance pensions in Latin America: its first dozen schemes were established in 1913–1929, together with Uruguay (1919), Chile (1924), and Brazil (1930). Other countries followed in the 1940s and 1950s, with the most recent in the 1960s. Some of the Cuban schemes were created between 1930 and 1955 (CERP 1964; Mesa-Lago 2007). In total, Cuba had fifty-four pension schemes prior to the revolution; they were all PAYG, some were privately administered, and others were publicly managed, but all were independent. The schemes were fragmented along occupational lines for the most organized groups in the economy and society (e.g., civil servants, armed forces, policemen, legislators, judicial power); the main export sectors, such as sugar and tobacco; university professionals such as teachers, lawyers, physicians, architects, engineers, accountants; and strong trade-unionized workers in sectors such as transportation, communications, electricity, gas, and water. Therefore, Cuba preceded by many years China's first pension scheme, which was created in the early 1950s, as well as Vietnam's, which was created in 1945 for civil servants and extended to other groups in 1961.

Under the revolution, between 1959 and 1963, all Cuban contributory pension schemes (old-age, disability, and survivors) were gradually unified into a mandatory public pension system. The funds were seized by the state and consolidated into a single PAYG state fund, which was soon after absorbed by the general state budget, lacking a reserve (even a contingency one). There are neither individual accounts nor company pension plans. A 2008 law implemented a parametric reform (to be explained later). In addition to the general system, the military, the interior ministry employees, and party executives have a separate scheme (Mesa-Lago 2003).

In Vietnam

In Vietnam, the first pension law was enacted in 1945 for civil servants, and it was extended in 1961 to public-sector salaried employees, the military, the police, and members of the communist party, The 1992 constitution stipulated that the state provide social insurance pensions for state employees and wage earners (under the 1986 market-oriented reform, it was added that the state encourages other forms of social insurance). A 1995 law created the Vietnam Social Security (VSS) institute, expanded coverage to private sector workers (including enterprises with more than ten employees), and incorporated new army and police forces and members of the party into the mandatory pension system.[13] The groups insured prior to 1995 received state transfers to finance their pensions.

The social insurance law enacted in 2006 and effective in 2007 established two schemes: one was compulsory for public-sector employees (including the armed forces, internal security, and the party), salaried private employees with labor contracts of one month or more, and some co-op workers; and one was voluntary for nonsalaried (e.g., workers with contracts of under twelve months, the self-employed, and workers without wages). This law also introduced noncontributory pensions (National Assembly 2006). The 2006 law was revised in 2014 (it is currently in force with amendments).[14] Changes included altering the reference salary from the last five years to lifetime, as well as making more types of salary/income subject to contributions; allowing participants in the mandatory and voluntary programs to combine their pension rights; permitting those in the mandatory program who have not yet completed twenty years of contributions to participate in the voluntary program and keep contributing until completing the vesting period; and regulating pension fund investment (Law No. 58 2014).

Those insured who reach the retirement age and have exceeded the years of contribution to obtain the maximum replacement rate (RR) of 75 percent receive both a regular retirement pension and a lump sum benefit for the years contributed in excess. Such a lump sum is equal to half the monthly salary base per year of contribution exceeding those required to get the maximum RR. In addition, a termination lump sum is offered to insured workers who have reached the retirement age without being eligible for a pension and are either demobilized military, settled abroad, or have a fatal disease; such lump sum is equal to between 1.5 and 2 times the monthly salary base for each year of insurance. Most termination lump sums are taken by workers in the private sector and are particularly appealing at young ages and among women; in 2019, about 69 percent of termination lump sums received by women were taken before age 35 and are insufficient to cover years after retirement particularly because of female longer life expectancy (Ramírez and Arza 2021).

In addition to the social insurance compulsory pension program in Vietnam, there are voluntary supplementary pension plans offered by big companies in large cities. These plans began to be implemented after Circular No. 115 (2013). Other regulations are Decree No. 88 (2016) and Circular No. 86 (2017).

There are two models of supplementary pension schemes. The first is organized under a trust fund and managed by a life insurance company under the supervision of the Ministry of Finance. The second is organized according to a contract model and managed by the pension fund enterprise; the contract is signed between the fund management enterprise and individuals, employees and employers; the enterprises entrust this pension fund to an independent fund management company. Participating employees are entitled to receive payments from their retirement accounts during the time the employee is a part of the workforce. Currently, there are sixteen life insurance companies, and six of them offer supplementary pension schemes.

Party Resolution No. 28 (Socialist Republic of Vietnam 2018) studied reforms to improve all aspects of the social security system. Among the objectives of the resolution are to expand coverage (particularly to the informal sector and women) so as to achieve the target of social insurance for all; to develop a diversified, multipillar, modern, and integrated social insurance system based on the ILO principles; and to enhance the capacity, effectiveness, and efficiency of state management. These goals will be analyzed and evaluated in the rest of the book.

HEALTHCARE

In China

China has a fragmented healthcare system and multiple laws regulate it: 1953, 1988, 1994, 1998 (basic insurance scheme for urban employees), 2003 (pilot for urban workers medical insurance), 2012 (pilot plan for urban and rural residents), 2016 (integrated program for urban nonsalaried and rural residents), and so forth. X. Huang (2020) contends, along the lines of the second hypothesis of this book, that the expansion of the healthcare system was carried out in a gradual and incremental manner—it was tied to economic development and available resources, hence avoiding a commitment to an excessively generous welfare state.[15] The current system resembles the pension program and currently comprises three schemes.

The first scheme, the mandatory Urban-Employee Basic Medical Insurance (UEBMI) for urban and rural employees, was established in 1998 and has two tiers: basic social insurance and individual accounts. In 2015 the separate mandatory scheme for civil servants and public employees was merged with the UEBMI, but certain civil servants retained free medical services. As in the case of pensions, flexible employees (including self-employed) may participate in this scheme, as well as migrant workers, if they have a labor relationship with the employer. If not, they may join the voluntary scheme explained below. The UEBMI is financed by contributions on the payroll (6 percent by employers and 2 percent by employees).

The second scheme is the voluntary Urban-and-Rural-Resident Basic Medical Insurance (URRBMI) for urban and rural residents such as informal workers, self-employed, unemployed, housewives, children, the disabled, and the elderly who are not covered by the mandatory UEBMI.[16] This scheme only has basic social insurance, since in 2019, individual accounts were eliminated; the basic scheme is financed by a flat contribution from the insured and another flat contribution from the government. Flexible employees, including the self-employed as well as members of urban cooperatives and domestic workers, may affiliate to the URRBMI, but if they have labor relations with an employer and the needed resources, they can join the UEBMI. The URRBMI resulted from the integration in 2016 of two previous programs: one was the voluntary New Rural Cooperative Medical Scheme, which was launched in 2003 for members of rural cooperatives, rural self-employed, and other workers or residents who choose to enroll; the other was the urban-resident basic insurance scheme, which was established in 2007 exclusively for urban residents (GOV 2016).[17] Most places closed the cooperative scheme, but some retained it; in 2019 the government ordered its closure before the end of 2020 (GOV 2019) and it was done.

The two basic medical insurance schemes only cover partial medical expenses below a given amount. The rest of the expenses are partly covered by supplementary catastrophic illnesses insurance that was implemented in 2015 and that covers patients with critical illnesses whose out-of-pocket expenses are more than the average disposable income per capita in the local area, providing extra reimbursement (Fang et al. 2019).[18] For urban and rural residents, there is a nationwide unified scheme, whereas for urban employees, coverage is provided on a local basis. Those entitled to social assistance also receive aid for critical illnesses (Y. Wang 2022).

Third, the military has its own scheme (Interim Provisions, 2021) as well as separate health facilities and medical staff. At the grassroots level, there are usually sanitation teams that are open to the public and responsible for minor illnesses of military personnel. At the higher (mostly provincial) level, there are also army hospitals, normally of high quality with good medical resources, and generally open to the public. However, military personnel could have priority access, special inpatient wards, and better treatment (Y. Wang 2022). Policemen are in the UEBMI scheme and use the same facilities as other urban employees.

Despite China's positive unification process, in practice, there are disparities. Various population groups can opt to affiliate with the UEBMI or the URRBMI according to their labor relations with an employer, and some civil servants are entitled to free medical care, whereas the military has better benefits and its own facilities and medical staff. In addition, other factors influence access, benefits, and quality of care, such as the local economy, medical culture, and the availability of staff, all generating disparities (Leung and Xu 2015; Huang 2020; B. He 2022).

Since 2017, China's sickness and maternity cash benefits have been included as part of basic medical insurance, a change made after the one-child policy was abolished (GOV 2017). The maternity cash allowance is calculated based on the average monthly salary of all the employees in an enterprise in the previous year, but the process of setting said allowance can differ according to local regulations, for instance, basing it on the city average salary. Unemployed spouses of employees with the right to maternity benefits are entitled to maternity medical expenses (Presidential Decree 2010, latest version 2018). Sickness leave is financed by the employer; it is set as a percentage of wages and lasts between three months and two years, both of which are based on the employee's length of employment.

In Cuba

Cuba significantly departed from the two Asian countries and most of Latin America in its lack of a social insurance program for healthcare services. Instead, there is a unified universal free public health system, save for separate hospitals for the armed forces and internal security personnel, as well as special paid services for foreigners.[19] In addition, there are neither private facilities nor copayments, and doctors and other health personnel cannot work privately. A 1963 law established mandatory sickness and maternity paid leave and regulated cash benefits; other related laws were enacted in 2008, 2013 (labor code), 2016, and 2021 (Decreto-Ley 56, 2021). Both types of leave are paid by the employer in the case of salaried workers or by the state budget in the case of self-employed; the 60 percent pay leave is based on the average salary or income in the year before the leave (Colina 2022a). In 1986, the government created a national family doctor program in charge of primary care.

In Vietnam

The Vietnamese health system is somewhere between those of China and Cuba. The 1992 constitution established the right for healthcare for all citizens including the poor. The same year, the National Vietnam Health Insurance Program was introduced to facilitate financial access to healthcare for all. A law of 2003 created the Healthcare Fund for the Poor financed by public resources. Another law in 2008 stipulated compulsory coverage for children under six, the elderly, the poor and near poor, and ethnic minorities, providing full subsidies for these groups and partial subsidies for students (ILO 2018a). A goal of universal coverage by 2014 was set by a law in 2009, and although it was not met, coverage was at 89 percent by 2020 (Huong et al. 2013; GSO 2022b). The system is public and relatively unified with a growing emphasis on primary care. The state finances most expenses, but there are copayments that increase with the complexity of treatment. In addition, there is a network of private hospitals and other facilities that care for high-middle-income and high-income groups that can pay the insurance or cash in exchange for services. The best hospitals are those owned and operated by foreign nations.

The government's future strategy for healthcare comprises three principal plans. The Twelfth Communist Party Central Commission (Resolutions 20 and 21 of 2017) provided orientations for 2018–2025 and a vision for 2030, such as strengthening primary healthcare through a family medicine model and setting priorities for the population's most vulnerable groups. The Ministry of Health National Action Program established the bases for healthcare for the elderly in 2017–2025. The prime minister launched the Health Program for 2018–2030, developing a network of family doctors that will provide services to manage chronic diseases and long-term care for older persons. These three programs must be evaluated to trace results.

SOCIAL ASSISTANCE

Social assistance consists of many programs: cash transfers for the poor and near poor, relief for the needy, means-tested pensions for the elderly poor, universal pensions for the old-old, eldercare in-home or at institutions, aid for children and pregnant women in need, minimum living standards, assistance to the disabled and mentally ill, emergency aid, temporary assistance because of unpredictable hazards, unemployment aid, and healthcare assistance for those in need (exemptions of fees, health certificates, coverage of the poor through universal free healthcare, etc.). Covid-19 led to new and substantial health and monetary assistance. Because of the large number and diversity of programs, as well as changes over time, it is quite complex to compare social assistance among the three countries and even more difficult to quantify the number of beneficiaries, but an effort is made to have rough estimates (see chapter 5). An overall picture of the main social assistance programs in the three countries follows.

In China

China has the longest history of social assistance (for monetary and health benefits), which is fragmented and multilayered with intertwined programs geared toward the poor, families with income below local standards, the unemployed, and families who confront a sudden burden of medical expenses.[20] Schemes of poverty reduction ran parallel to social assistance schemes; the two have separate budgets and administrations (Y. Wang 2022). The oldest program (*danwei*) dates from premodern China but was modified in the more recent republican and socialist periods with influences from the Soviet Union and other socialist countries (Bray 2005); danwei gave protection to full-time workers in state enterprises (including medical care). Next was the *sanwu*, implemented in the early 1950s, which means "three without" (livelihood source, ability to work, and legal support), but its benefits were meager. In rural areas, the "five guarantee" program to reduce poverty also went back to the 1950s and apparently still exists.

After 1978, four other social assistance programs were established. The first and longest-running is the Minimum Living Standard Scheme (MLSS) or Minimum Livelihood Guarantee (*dibao*) introduced in 1993 in Shanghai (the most developed city in China) as an anti-poverty safety net to improve assistance related to urban unemployment and poverty (resulting from the transition to the socialist market and shut down of state enterprises). By 1999, dibao had been implemented nationwide in urban areas, and by 2007, it was nationwide in rural areas as well (Jiandong and Barrientos 2006; Gao 2017; L. Yang 2018; Solinger 2022b). Dibao recipients are families whose members' joint per capita annual income is lower than the locally set minimum living standard and whose assets do not exceed the local standards; they receive a supplement to meet the subsistence standard. Such recipients must pass an annual means test and are expected to search for work.

Dibao is centrally regulated and locally implemented. Financing should mostly come from local governments but has been heavily subsidized by the central government. The program's positive effects have been that the number of beneficiaries increased from 3.7 million in 1999 (in urban areas, zero in rural areas) to a total peak of 75.9 million in 2011 (22.8 million in urban areas but decreasing; 53 million in rural areas, declining after 2013 [Solinger 2022b]);[21] rising expenditures in both areas by 718 times in 1999–2016; increasing poverty line benefit levels by 232 percent in urban areas and by 330 percent in rural areas (L. Yang 2018); and improving social stability (or placating protests). On the other hand, two divergent estimates of dibao coverage of the total population show 5.6 percent at its peak in 2010 decreasing to 3.3 percent in 2018 (based on L. Yang 2018), and 2.2 percent in 2004 rising to 3.9 percent in 2018 (Solinger 2022b).

Despite increases in expenditures and the poverty line benefit levels, dibao still did not meet subsistence levels.[22] The program's anti-poverty effectiveness has been modest at best, due to low allowances and targeting problems (see chapter 5). It has been more effective at reducing the depth and severity of poverty than the poverty rate; it maintains a gap between urban and rural areas (based on the hukou), despite some reduction. And still in 2016, the dibao standard in rural areas was 63 percent that of the urban area (L. Yang 2018). Dibao also maintains gaps between regions, has scarcely reduced income differences, does not promote enough work among its members, and has not been systematically evaluated (Gao 2017).

The second social assistance program is the "subsistence allowance" (cash), introduced in 2002–2004, granted by the state to those who lack income or receive very low income in urban and rural areas, such as the extremely poor, the marginal family members of the subsistence allowance recipients, and the rural poor who are prone to return to poverty, as well as severely ill patients who do not meet the above requirements but suffer serious difficulties in basic family life because of high medical expenses—taking into consideration the family's economic status, health expenses and medical insurance premium, the region, province, or municipality determines the conditions for identifying patients with severe illness in the last group (B. He 2022).

The third program is "targeted poverty reduction" introduced in 2014 to improve the effectiveness of previous programs and geared toward the extreme poor and other vulnerable groups such as the elderly, the disabled, or children without work capacity, income, or family support.[23] Recipients have access to "special social assistance benefits," which include sickness aid.[24] In recent years, this program has been increasingly integrated into social assistance (also merging urban and rural programs) in order to further improve effectiveness in fighting rural poverty.

The fourth program is the "temporary benefit" established in 2014, which is more accessible and flexible than dibao; it is based on family emergencies that increase expenditures, such as sudden serious illnesses (including to dibao families) among other causes; this scheme is regulated by local governments.[25]

During Xi's leadership, since 2012, several changes have been introduced in dibao: those able to work must do so to receive dibao, regardless of their skills and education; targeted are the "especially difficult" poor, such as the disabled, elderly, and minors unable to work (under the "targeted poverty reduction" scheme); a fight against corruption, correcting improper use of social assistance funds, and accounting for all recipients' assets to exclude those who exceed the minimum; and the improvement of benefits for residents in agricultural projects so that the poverty line in the countryside eventually reaches the same level as in urban areas. These measures eliminated almost one-half of dibao recipients, from 74.9 million in 2012 to 41.5 million in 2021 (estimates based on L. Yang 2018; Solinger 2022a). A social assistance law was drafted in 2020 and submitted for public discussion; its goal is to broaden social assistance and generalize benefits in order to tackle poverty in a more effective manner. Social assistance is to be extended to low-income families who are not recognized as dibao families based on low-income standards that are also set locally. In addition, temporary benefits are to be granted to low-income families and individuals in sudden urgent or temporary difficulties who are not covered by other social assistance benefits (Ministries of Civil Affairs and Finance 2020).

In 2021 the State Council released the "Human Rights Action Plan on China for 2021–2025," which seeks to help all those in need with a wide social safety net. For instance, urban and rural residents who face difficulties would receive state help to cover part of their premiums in the basic social insurance system, whereas a mechanism would be established to adjust basic pension rates for urban employees; in addition, subsidies would be granted for family dependents of the deceased. If this goal is achieved, there would be a larger role of social assistance, and it should be more integrated with social insurance. Whether this ambitious plan is implemented will have to be tested ("China to Accelerate," 2021).

China lacks a centralized social assistance pension that targets the poor. The central government has encouraged the poor to join the subsidized urban-and-rural-resident scheme, but few have done so (some local governments help them to pay for such pension). The elderly poor without coverage get social assistance subsidies under the MLSS (B. He 2022).

In Cuba

In Cuba, social assistance is nationally unified. Social assistance pensions are provided to the elderly in need (for men aged 65 and over and for women aged 60 and over) who lack a contributory pension. Assistance is also granted to certain vulnerable groups such as the disabled, mothers with children suffering from severe disabilities, and people confined to their homes and living alone. Assistance includes monetary benefits, medicine, food, and personal services (ONEI 2021). Law 105 of social security and the new Cuban Family Code determine that rightful family members are ascendants, descendants, siblings, and spouses. The Party Guidelines of 2011 stipulate that social assistance is submitted to a strict means test, which includes the lack of any family able to economically help the beneficiaries.[26]

The process to request aid by the family includes a declaration that identifies all members, the report on a socioeconomic investigation, and supporting documents. The person in charge of the socioeconomic investigation (who also submits the request for aid based on the cited documentation) is a municipal social worker from the Office of Social Prevention, Assistance, and Work at the Ministry of Labor and Social Security (MTSS). In addition, the information is verified by the community where the candidate lives. Official guidelines for social workers define the vulnerable situations of individuals, families, homes, groups, and communities and establish the procedure to follow (Consejo de Ministros 2021). Rita Machín, under-director of social prevention in the MTSS, stated in 2022 that there were six thousand social workers, but only half of those who perform "the important means test [have] special formation for such task" ("Prevención y asistencia social," 2022). The public healthcare system is universal and free; hence, it legally covers the poor.

In Vietnam

In Vietnam, social insurance and social assistance have been independently designed and implemented. The 1992 constitution stipulated the exemption or reduction of hospital fees for the poor (by 2012, 15 million poor received free health insurance cards). In 1998, the National Target Program for poverty reduction was approved (Nguyen et al. 2012). In 2010–2016, social assistance was expanded significantly, particularly among the elderly and to a greater extent in rural rather than in urban areas. Benefits more than doubled, especially for the elderly; about half of the old-old received a noncontributory pension both in urban and rural areas.

A means-tested noncontributory pension is granted to those aged 60–79 who are under the poverty line, whereas a universal noncontributory pension is awarded to those aged 80 and above who are poor, live alone, and do not receive a contributory pension. As a result, poverty has sharply declined (World Bank 2021b).[27] However, among those aged 65 and above, the contributory pension reduces poverty by 32 percent (from 23.7 percent to 16.1 percent), whereas the noncontributory pension reduces it by only 3 percent (ILO, n.d.). In 2018, 25.3 percent of households benefited from poverty reduction policies, out of which 22 percent were aided in buying health insurance and 2.3 percent benefited from fee remission for medical examination and treatment. The most supported regions were the most vulnerable (Northern Midlands and Mountain Areas, North Central and Central Coastal Area, and Central Highlands). Households benefited from public assistance to get health insurance cards or health exemptions to the poor, which rose from 22.2 to 24.4 percent in 2009–2018 (GSO 2020).

The Master Plan on Social Assistance Reform and Development for the period 2018–2025 and a vision to 2030 has the following objectives. The overall goal is to aid all those facing unexpected difficulties, particularly through the expansion of social allowances to the elderly facing difficult circumstances and lacking pension, also through state subsidies to those living in mountainous and island areas as well as to ethnic minorities. This goal is gradually expanded upon in various stages. In

2017–2020 the aim is to provide social services to 50 percent and at least 10 percent with comprehensive social assistance, in 2021–2025 to 70 percent and at least 30 percent with comprehensive social assistance, and in 2030 to 90 percent and 50 percent respectively. In 2021–2025 the aim is to increase the monthly social allowance, with support for children under 36 months of age, pregnant women from poor or near poor households, as well as for households in difficult circumstances, those living in mountains or islands, and for ethnic minorities. In 2030 the aim is to expand the previous services and adjust social allowances according to budgetary capabilities and international trends (Decision No. 488 2017).

By mid-2022, there was not an evaluation of these goals; however, it has been reported that beneficiaries, policies, resources, and mechanisms for policy implementation have been identified (Hoàng 2022). In addition, assistance is granted to other groups in need, mostly those living in poor households and lacking the capacity to work, such as the disabled, the mentally ill, those infected by HIV/AIDS, single mothers, children of low-income families or children with no supporting adults, and those who adopt orphans or abandoned children.[28] As in China, Vietnam has attained a sizable reduction in poverty, contrary to Cuba's increasing trend.

CHAPTER 5

COMPARISON OF FEATURES AND PERFORMANCE BASED ON SOCIAL SECURITY PRINCIPLES

Now it is time for an evaluation of the countries' performance in the three targeted programs. The evaluation is based on six key ILO social security principles: (1) unity and equal treatment; (2) universal coverage and access; (3) benefit sufficiency; (4) social solidarity and gender equity; (5) administrative efficiency, reasonable costs, and tripartite participation; and (6) financial and actuarial sustainability.

UNITY AND EQUAL TREATMENT

This principle pursues unity among diverse groups of insured to avoid unequal treatment based on power (armed forces, civil servants), significant geographical differences (including country regions and urban-rural locations), uneven development, and/or ethnic and gender discrimination. The opposite of unity is fragmentation and stratification within which occupational groups or regions have preferential entitlement conditions and benefits that are financed not by their own contributions but largely through fiscal subsidies. Fragmentation increases administrative costs, and small groups of the insured face serious difficulties in maintaining financially stable systems. Conversely, unity facilitates plans to extend coverage and protect the uninsured and the poor, allows centralized collection of contributions, reduces administrative costs, permits redistribution mechanisms from the wealthiest to the poorest (social solidarity), such as a wide pool of resources that also strengthens financial sustainability. My aim is to summarize the state of unity and equal treatment in each of the three countries and develop qualitative indicators to assess unity; unfortunately, this cannot be done to measure equal treatment.

China's pension, health, and social assistance systems are the most fragmented of the three countries, with inequalities among social groups and geographical units, although measures of unification, standardization, and a regional adjustment fund have somewhat reduced said fragmentation. To start, there is a combination of social insurance and individual accounts. In pensions there are two schemes that cover two diverse groups: urban employees (since 2015, including civil servants that used to have the most generous entitlement conditions and benefits) and urban and rural residents not covered by the first scheme.[1] These two schemes have both basic insurance and individual accounts with diverse entitlement conditions, benefits, and financing, and there are substantial differences between urban and rural residents. Not only is there low unity but also unequal treatment. In the urban-employee scheme, both the employer and the employee pay a percentage contribution based on salary; employees do not contribute to social insurance but do so to their individual accounts, and employers contribute over the payroll, which goes toward the basic social insurance. Urban and rural residents pay annual flat contributions at twelve diverse levels and receive local and central subsidies. Civil servants and workers in large corporations with good profits have occupational pension plans, and wealthy persons can buy additional commercial insurance. The military has its own separate pension scheme with less strict entitlement conditions and more generous benefits and fiscal subsidies.

In the healthcare program there is also a dual system: urban employees in the public and private sectors, some social groups, and nonprofit organizations have basic medical coverage through social insurance plus individual saving accounts, whereas urban and rural residents only have basic social insurance.[2] The military has its own separate facilities. Flexible employees (including the self-employed) and migrant workers with a long-term relation with an employer (at least six months) who join the urban-employee scheme theoretically have lower contributions than salaried workers, but their contributions are subordinate to those of their employers. If the latter do not actually pay, then the whole contribution is due from the migrant or flexible worker.[3]

There are other examples of unequal treatment. In the basic pension social insurance, salaried workers pay 8 percent (plus 16 percent from the employer for a total of 24), whereas the migrant or flexible worker pays 20 percent (2.5 times what salaried workers pay). In the health basic social insurance for urban employees, migrants and flexible workers pay 6 percent vis-à-vis 2 percent paid by salaried workers (plus 6 percent from the employer for a total of 8 percent), which amounts to three times what the salaried worker pays. In line with the recent health program reform, if migrants and flexible workers do not have a relationship with an employer (or it is temporary) or are having financial difficulties, then such workers can join the the voluntary urban-and-rural-resident scheme, in which case they lack individual accounts and pay an annual flat sum that goes toward basic social insurance (B. He 2022). Services are provided at accredited ("designated") urban and rural hospitals, clinics, and pharmacies, both public and private. Uninsured people with resources may resort to private facilities and staff. For those who are insured, reimbursement for the use of private facilities depends on regulations and insurance conditions; usually, they must pay up front and then request reimbursement. The military has its own hospitals, facilities, and staff.

Dependents of the insured across all schemes are not covered; but unemployed dependents of certain military insured are covered. In 2016, the government called for an integration of the urban-and-rural-resident scheme with the new rural medical insurance scheme. In 2018, the National Healthcare Social Security Administration was established to accomplish that goal. Currently, the maternity scheme is integrated into basic medical insurance. Ideally, a national unified health insurance of the two major schemes, as well as the military, should be established. Despite the unification process, various groups in the population can enroll in the mandatory or voluntary scheme depending on whether they have a labor relationship with an employer or not. The military has better pension benefits, its own facilities, and medical staff, whereas some civil servants are entitled to free medical care. In China, there are four social assistance schemes with different norms by regions, localities, and so forth; these schemes are undergoing a gradual process of integration.

Cuba's pension system is as fragmented as China's, but the opposite is true of the healthcare and social assistance systems. The general pension system has fairly uniform entitlement conditions, but the armed forces and security personnel have separate schemes with better entitlement conditions and more generous benefits than the general system.[4] In addition, there are different pension regimes and associated contributions for agricultural-production cooperatives, non-agricultural-production-and-services cooperatives, the self-employed, and artists. The self-employed pay more than the sum of the percentage contributions paid by the employee and the employer (for details, see Colina 2016).

There is a national, public, unified healthcare system, but the armed forces, internal security, and high officials in the communist party have separate health facilities. In addition, hard-currency-paying foreigners have access to distinct and considerably better quality healthcare treatment than the overall population, who face a decrease in access and quality of healthcare. On the other hand, there are no private facilities. Health personnel are banned from private practice, but paying bribes to the personnel has become increasingly popular, hence those with better incomes have faster access and care than those with less income. Social assistance is nationally unified.

Vietnam's social security system is comprised of a collection of programs that lacks a well-defined strategy and fails to operate as an integrated and coherent system (World Bank 2019). However, the pension system is more unified (less fragmented) than in China and Cuba. The health system in Vietnam is as fragmented as China's but less fragmented than Cuba's, and the social assistance system is unified as in Cuba and much less fragmented than China's. The legal system deals with contributory and noncontributory programs as two separate frameworks with a diversity of legal instruments; social security schemes are scattered across several pieces of legislation with overlaps and inconsistencies (Olivier 2022). Of the three countries, Vietnam's pension system is the most unified: the private and public sectors are covered by the compulsory scheme, and there are no separate groups such as the urban employees or the urban and rural residents in China. The military and police personnel are part of the general system (instead of separate, as in China and Cuba), though contributions and benefits may differ; for instance, their ages of retirement are five years less than in the general system, and male officers with twenty-five years of service in the army and female officers with twenty years may retire regardless of their age.

There is a voluntary system for those not covered by the compulsory system (those who choose to be insured this way have to pay a double percentage contribution because they lack an employer). For instance, private sector employees' base salary used to calculate the pension is the entire contribution period, but for those who work in the public sector, the period could be from five to twenty years prior to retirement depending on when they began contributing. In 2025, this will change to the entire contribution period. The lower the base salary, the higher the pension.

The healthcare system in Vietnam is as fragmented as China's but with a trend toward unity. Initially, mandatory coverage was provided for four groups: civil servants, employees of state-owned enterprises, employees of private companies (with more than ten employees), and pensioners; the rest of the population could enroll in a separate voluntary scheme. Successive laws incorporated the poor, ethnic minorities, households living in disadvantaged municipalities, children under age 6, the near poor, students, farmers, workers in agriculture and fishing, the self-employed, and family dependents. In 2008, all these groups were integrated, and one single pool was established for Social Health Insurance and Healthcare for the Poor, but some fragmentation remained at the provincial level.

A revision of the 2014 law gradually extended mandatory enrollment to the entire population, but there are five groups (and thirty-five different subgroups) based on the payment source of their contributions: employer/employee, social insurance, state budget (partial subsidies), households, and employees (dependent on the military and internal security) (ILO 2018a). Inequalities in access exist across groups by income, ethnicity, location (mountain areas), and gender. Theoretically, public and private employees have access to private physicians and hospitals, but costs are much higher and usually prohibitive for them. A small copayment must be paid at the primary care level, but it increases at higher levels and also when the patient chooses a facility different from the one assigned. Some employed by private foreign companies have better health insurance that allows access to private hospitals and covers more treatments than in the general programs, but their insurance still requires a copayment.

The quality of public and private hospitals is often similar, but the former often have long queues, whereas the latter offer faster access. Foreign private hospitals (French, Japanese, and so forth) are the best and the most expensive, and users tend to be foreigners and those working for foreign companies. Poor households, children younger than age 6, the disabled, and students are entitled to free medical services at public hospitals but are subjected to the queue (near-poor households pay a reduced rate); the government grants subsidies to these groups. Dependents of insured persons pay a premium depending on the number of members in the household. To have access to social insurance, the self-employed must pay the sum of the percentage contributions paid by employees and employers; hence, they probably have lower access, poorer services, and pay more than employees. In social assistance, different legal definitions apply to key concepts (Olivier 2022), but Vietnam's system is still more unified than China's and similar to Cuba's.

Table 5.1: Degree of Unity of Social Security Programs in the Three Countries, 2020–2021

Diverse Groups/Schemes	China	Cuba	Vietnam
Pensions	7 (2)	7 (2)	2 (1)
Healthcare	6 (2)	3 (1)	6 (2)
Social assistance	4 (2)	1 (1)	1 (1)
Private facilities/personnel	Yes (2)	No (1)	Yes (2)
Total scores	8	5	6
Average ranking of four indicators[a]	2.00 (3)	1.25 (1)	1.50 (2)

Source: My own elaboration based on analysis in the text.

Notes: The first figure is the number of separate programs; the second figure is the ranking of each indicator among the three countries. Equal treatment could not be measured but is assessed in the text.

[a] Average of four indicators; the lower the number the better.

Summary concerning Unity and Equal Treatment

For a qualitative ranking of the degree of unity among the three countries, see table 5.1. Scores were assigned as follows. China in pensions: urban employees (basic insurance and individual accounts), urban-rural residents (basic insurance and individual accounts), military, occupational pension plans, commercial insurance (7); in healthcare: urban employees (basic insurance and individual accounts), urban-rural residents (basic insurance), military, some civil servants, flexible employees, and migrants (6); and in social assistance: dibao, subsistence allowance, targeted poverty reduction, and temporary benefit (4). Cuba in pensions: general system, military, internal security, self-employed, agricultural cooperatives, service cooperatives, and artists (7); in healthcare: general system, military-internal security-party officials, foreigners (3); and in social assistance: unified (1). Vietnam in pensions: mandatory and voluntary (2); healthcare: six groups with different financing and benefits (6); and in social assistance: unified (1). Concerning private facilities/personnel, they exist in China and Vietnam (2) but not in Cuba (1). Total scores (the lowest number signifies the most unified or least fragmented) result from adding the countries' scores in the various programs and estimating an average. The ranking is first Cuba (1.25), second Vietnam (1.50), and third China (2.00). I could not estimate numerically the different entitlement conditions, financing, and benefits among the diverse schemes and groups as described in the text, but poor levels of equal treatment are indicated in all three countries (see table 5.1).

UNIVERSAL COVERAGE AND ACCESS

A fundamental ILO principle is to reach universal coverage on social security for all citizens. In this section I first compare legal coverage by programs and population groups in the three countries. Second, I measure—mostly based on official statistics but also estimates by local experts and international organizations—the three countries' positions regarding the universal goal across three dimensions: coverage of the labor force on contributory pensions, access and coverage of the total population on healthcare (medical and cash benefits), and protection of the vulnerable population or the needy by social assistance. I also identify which groups are not covered. Third, countries are ranked based on their quantitative coverage.

Legal Coverage

Table 5.2 is a summary of coverage based on the law, by groups and programs, of the three major social security programs—distinguishing between mandatory (M) and voluntary (V). Cuba has the most extensive legally mandatory contributory pension coverage because it includes the self-employed, who have voluntary coverage in Vietnam and the option of either mandatory or voluntary coverage based on labor relations with an employer in China. Sickness-maternity legal coverage on cash benefits (sickness and maternity leave) is mandatory in the three countries for private and public employees, but not for the self-employed in China and Vietnam. Medical benefits are mandatory in all cases except for flexible employees (including self-employed) and migrant workers in China, who have the choice between voluntary and mandatory. The military has separate (S) mandatory coverage in pension and healthcare facilities in China and Cuba but not in Vietnam, which integrates them. Social assistance for the needy is granted to the poor or near poor in China, the poor in Vietnam, and the poor in Cuba, but not when they have a family who can help, which is quite difficult because of the dire economic situation.

Contributory Pension Coverage

According to the statistical yearbook (NBSC 2021b), pension coverage in China was 81.8 percent based on urban employees and urban and rural residents relative to the employed labor force, but was 42.5 percent relative to the total labor force.[5] The urban-employee-scheme labor force coverage is given as 68 percent but varies significantly among provinces, for example, it is 32 percent in Guangxi (Cousins 2021). Meng found that "a province tends to have a higher level of coverage if it has been more often governed by locally promoted insider leaders, enjoys a higher

Table 5.2: Legal Coverage by Programs and Groups in the Three Countries, 2019–2021

Legal Coverage	China	Cuba	Vietnam
Pensions (O-A, D, S)			
Public-private (market) employees	M	M	M
Civil servants	M	M	M
Cooperative members	V	M	M
Household (domestic) workers	V	M	V
Self-employed and/or flexible employees	M or V	M	V
Military	M-S	M-S	M
Sickness-maternity			
Cash benefits			
Public-private employees	M	M	M
Self-employed	No	No	No
Medical benefits			
Public-private employees	M	M	M
Self-employed	M or V	M	M
Social assistance			
Needy persons	Poor, low-income families, emergencies	Poor lacking family help	Poor

Source: My own elaboration based on national legislation: from ILO (2017) for China; from Colina (2021b) for Cuba; ILO (2021c), Ramírez and Arza (2021) for Vietnam; also US.SSA-ISSA (2019, 2020).

Note: In China rural cooperatives have been integrated into the urban-and-rural-resident scheme.

level of economic development [it's more urbanized], has deeper market-oriented reforms, and receives more subsidies from the central government" (2019, 186). In 2019 the combined number of migrant workers and flexible employees accounted for 42.9 percent of the labor force, the majority of which was not effectively covered by basic social insurance in pensions and health although their coverage by the urban-and-rural-resident scheme has expanded faster than that of the urban-employee scheme (Zhao and He 2021).[6] In 2021 the Ministry of Human Resources and Social Security, in its forty-fifth-year plan for the development of social security, acknowledged that the 95 percent target for coverage

TABLE 5.3: Degree of Coverage of the Total Labor Force on Pensions, Total Population on Health, and the Needy on Social Assistance in the Three Countries, 2019–2020

Coverage (percent)	China	Cuba	Vietnam
Labor force on pensions	42.5 (2)	68.5 (1)	32.5 (3)
Total population on healthcare	96.6 (1)	n.a.	88.8 (2)
Needy on social assistance			
All beneficiaries as % of total population[a]	4.5 (1)	1.6 (3)	3.2 (2)
Pensioners as % of population 60+	70.7 (1)	3.9 (3)	14.7 (2)
Total scores	5	7	9
Average ranking of four indicators	1.25 (1)	2.33 (3)	2.25 (2)

Source: My own elaboration: figures for China from NBSC (2021b); figures for Cuba from ONEI (2019b); figures for Vietnam from GSO (2021b), ILSSA/ILO (2022); other sources ILO (2017) and text.

Note: [a] Excludes medical assistance and long-term eldercare.

of the labor force by the basic pension insurance had not been met and postponed it until 2035 (MOHRSS 2021). See table 5.3.

Legally speaking, Cuba's contributory pension coverage should be virtually universal (given the lowest informal labor sector among the three countries and mandatory coverage of the self-employed); the Cuban government claims it has achieved universal coverage on pensions, placing the country ahead of China and Vietnam. Unfortunately, pension coverage statistics have never been published (neither by the Cuban government nor by international organizations). Nevertheless, Cuba's national survey on aging reports that 68.5 percent of the population aged 60 and above received either a contributory or a noncontributory pension in 2017 (ONEI 2019b). That coverage, however, is not of the total labor force but of the population aged 60 and above, and therefore it is not comparable with the figures from China and Vietnam.

Cuba has not conducted a yearly household labor survey as seventeen other Latin American countries do; that survey asks those of legal retirement age (65 and above) if they receive a pension (contributive or noncontributive), which is a similar approach to estimate the figure of 68.5 percent given by the 2017 aging survey in Cuba. Still, the latter is based on ages 60 and over, hence it overestimates coverage. The Latin American surveys taken in 2016–2018 show that Bolivia, Chile, Brazil, Uruguay, Argentina, and Panama (in that order) cover from 96.8 percent to 80.8 percent of the old-population cohort; Bolivia, a less developed country than Cuba, has the highest coverage at 96.8 percent (IADB-SIMS 2019). Another alternative manner to estimate coverage by old-age pensions is to compare Cuba's eligible population (all of whom are of legal retirement age) with the number of old-age-pension beneficiaries: in 2020 there were 3,041,796 persons in the eligible population (adding men aged 65 and above and women aged 60 and above, which are the legal retirement ages) and 1,666,954 beneficiaries of old-age, disability, and survivor pensions (ONEI 2021), which results in coverage of 54.8 percent of the eligible population; coverage by old-age pensions alone must be smaller. Despite legally mandatory pension coverage of the self-employed in Cuba, there are barriers to effective coverage, such as the payment of contributions that combines the percentages of the employee and the employer (that they lack); evasion and underdeclaration of income are frequent.

In Vietnam, contributory pension coverage rose from 27 percent to 32.5 percent of the total labor force in 2017–2020; much less than Cuba's and China's but increasing. Out of the total, 31.2 percent was covered by the mandatory scheme and only 1.3 percent by the voluntary scheme; coverage of the former alone rose to 36.8 percent, so total coverage should be close to 39 percent (GSO 2022b; Olivier 2022).[7] Vietnam is the only one of the three countries that provides coverage by gender. In 2019, 31.1 percent of women and 21.1 percent of men were covered (GSO 2021b); despite higher female coverage, in 2019 only 16 percent of women aged 65 and above received a pension vis-à-vis 27.3 percent of men, which is the result of a high proportion of women leaving the labor force after age 26 (Ramírez and Arza 2021).[8] Those covered by Vietnam's mandatory program are in the formal sector and in the top 40 percent of income (World Bank 2021b). The voluntary program was mainly geared to the self-employed, independent farmers, and other informal workers; these groups had to pay the combined percentage contribution of employers and employees (22 percent), as well as meet twenty years of contributions. The informal sector is 61 percent of total employment and mainly represents the self-employed, concentrated in agriculture and afflicted by poverty (ILO/WIEGO 2018; ILO 2021a).[9] Self-employment accounts for 35.7 percent of the labor force, and I estimate that only 1.5 percent of them were covered around 2017, largely explaining the low overall coverage of the labor force.

In 2018, the state began to pay contributions for participants in the voluntary program as a proportion of the monthly payment according to the rural poverty line (the aid declining from 30 percent to 10 percent of the payment), subject to a maximum support of ten years (Socialist Republic of Vietnam 2018). As a result of this measure, the number of participants in the voluntary scheme rose from 100,000 in 2011 to 1.1 million in 2020, and the percentage distribution of coverage between the mandatory program and the voluntary program changed from 99 and 1 percent in 2011 to 93.3 and 6.7 percent in 2020, respectively.[10] Another goal—that informal workers and farmers insured in the voluntary program would reach 1 percent of the labor force by 2021—was exceeded as 2.2 percent were insured in 2020. Furthermore, self-employment decreased from 51 percent to 47 percent of total employment in 2009–2020, whereas the informal sector declined from 61 percent to 55 percent, and the target for 2025 is to further reduce it to 35 percent (ILSSA/ILO 2022). Small and medium-sized enterprises (SMEs) have coverage of 33.5 percent but exclude household enterprises, which are the majority of SMEs, and very few enterprises with five employees or fewer are enrolled. There are many reasons for this: high contributions that increase labor costs, the long period of twenty years of contribution, a lack of trust in the system, complex procedures for registration, and employees being complicit with nonenrollment (Castel and Pick 2018).[11] In addition, unpaid family workers (mostly women), another group in the informal sector, rose from 64 percent to 68 percent of total employment in 2009–2020; their coverage probably is very low but no data is available (GSO 2022a). Finally, domestic workers (mainly women) can only join the voluntary program, hence it is not legally enforceable for employers to register these workers; in addition, they are not entitled to sickness, disability, or maternity cash benefits (ILO 2018b; Ramírez and Arza 2021).

Coverage pension targets set in 2012 by Vietnam's central committee of the communist party (Socialist Republic of Vietnam 2012; Huong et al. 2013) compared with actual achievements show nonfulfillment: the target was 29 million insured (26 million in compulsory insurance and 800,000 in voluntary insurance) for 50 percent coverage of the labor force, and actual data in 2020 shows that 16.2 million are insured (56 percent of the target) and there is 28.3 percent (22 percentage points less than the target) coverage of the labor force (ILO 2021d; World Bank 2021b; Ramírez and Arza 2021). A new pension coverage target for the labor force set in 2018 compared with actual data is positive: the target of 31 percent by 2021 was exceeded by actual coverage of 39 percent in that year. Current targets are 45 percent by 2025 and 60 percent by 2030 (Socialist Republic of Vietnam 2018).

Coverage and Access in Healthcare

According to Leung and Xu, China "has attained almost full coverage of the national population" (2015, 84), but there have been huge differences among all schemes in terms of access, covered treatments, quality of services, and financing. Between the two major health schemes, the distribution of total coverage at the end of 2020 was 75 percent of the urban and rural residents and 25 percent of the urban employees—out of which 6 percent were retired. Although rural coverage is impressive, benefits are very limited ("China's Social Security System," 2021). According to the ILO (2017), medical coverage increased tenfold in 2003–2013 and was 96.9 percent of the population by 2017. The Ministry of Human Resources and Social Security (MOHRSS 2021), based on the number of social security cards, reported healthcare coverage of the total population as 95.4 percent in 2020. B. He (2022) estimated that the combined coverage of the total population by urban-employee and urban-and-rural-resident schemes as 96.7 percent in 2019. The statistical yearbook (NBSC 2021b) refers to both "participants" and "workers" with payment records; for 2019, coverage of the total population with basic medical insurance, based on participants, was estimated as 96.6 percent. Gongcheng (2022) estimated that basic healthcare covers 1,367 million people, about 96.8 percent of the total population in 2020. Therefore, most estimates for 2020 are virtually alike.

Those without pension and health coverage in China are mainly rural-to-urban migrant workers, flexible employees, including the self-employed and informal workers.[12] Expanding coverage on pensions is difficult because about 43 percent of workers in the labor force are either migrants or flexible workers, most informal works are concentrated in rural areas, and one-third of the labor force in six urban areas is informal (ILO/WIEGO 2018; Giles et al. 2021; ILO 2021d; "China's Social Security System," 2021).[13] It should be noted that not all persons covered by basic pension and health insurance pay their contributions because they, particularly in rural areas, allegedly do not know about said insurance; local authorities have tried to inform them, but still, many do not pay. According to B. He (2022), the MOHRSS target for 2035 is that all those covered by basic social insurance must pay (save those that receive state subsidies) in order to reach 95 percent of the "population," which probably refers to the total labor force because health coverage of the total population already exceeds 96 percent.

Coverage through Cuba's public healthcare system is universal and free for all the population (including the poor), but statistics have never been published by the Cuban government nor estimated by scholars. Effective access to healthcare has dwindled because of the exportation of medical personnel for the government to earn hard currency (the number of primary-care family doctors has halved), as well as deterioration of services and severe scarcity of medicine and other inputs. Since the government proclaims universal coverage and the subject is not discussed by domestic scholars, there are no plans to achieve full coverage or to cope with the decrease in access.

Healthcare coverage of the total population in Vietnam was 88.8 percent in 2019 (GSO 2022b).[14] The official target of 90 percent by 2020 was achieved (Olivier 2022). Furthermore, people treated in the previous year using health insurance or free healthcare certificates increased from 61 percent in 2008 to 95 percent in 2020 (GSO 2021a, 2021b). There are several key factors in this achievement: making coverage mandatory, assigning the needed tax resources, integrating the system under a single government agency (the Ministry of Health), and an incremental approach with achievable and monitored targets (Olivier 2022). A healthcare coverage target set in 2012 by Vietnam's central committee of the communist party was 77 million insured for 70 percent coverage of the population vis-à-vis actual 2020 data of 88 million and 89 percent (19 percentage points more than the original goal) (ILO 2021d; World Bank 2021b; Ramírez and Arza 2021). Nevertheless, coverage remains inequitable, with low enrollment of the near poor, irregular contributions, and low awareness of the benefits of the system, which all contribute to coverage gaps (ILO 2021d). There is less access and poorer quality of health services in rural areas (Olivier 2022).

Coverage by Social Assistance

Most difficult to calculate in China is social assistance coverage relative to the total population, because of the multiple programs, their changes through time, and uncertainty as to whether programs have been terminated or partly continue. Estimates were made in 2020: the minimum living standard scheme was 8 million in urban areas and 36.2 million in rural areas, relief and support for the elderly poor was 4.7 million in both areas, temporary assistance was 13.8 million, and medical assistance was 99.8 million (GOV 2021c; NHSA 2021). The total was 162.5 million, or 10.2 percent of the total population. Total social assistance coverage also excludes long-term care, part of which is state provided, and the total covered 10.3 percent of the population (the specific portion of social assistance is not available).

Cuba's coverage of the elderly population (aged 60 and above) was 3.9 percent in 2020, much lower than China's (70.7 percent) and Vietnam's (14.7 percent). Furthermore, coverage is being sharply cut despite an expanding vulnerable population: in 1989–2020, as a percentage of GDP, social assistance expenditure decreased from 2.2 percent to 0.3 percent, whereas, in terms of beneficiaries per 1,000 inhabitants, it fell from 5.3 to 1.7 (ONEI 2011–2021).[15] Conversely, coverage is expanding in the two Asian countries whose poverty incidence is declining.

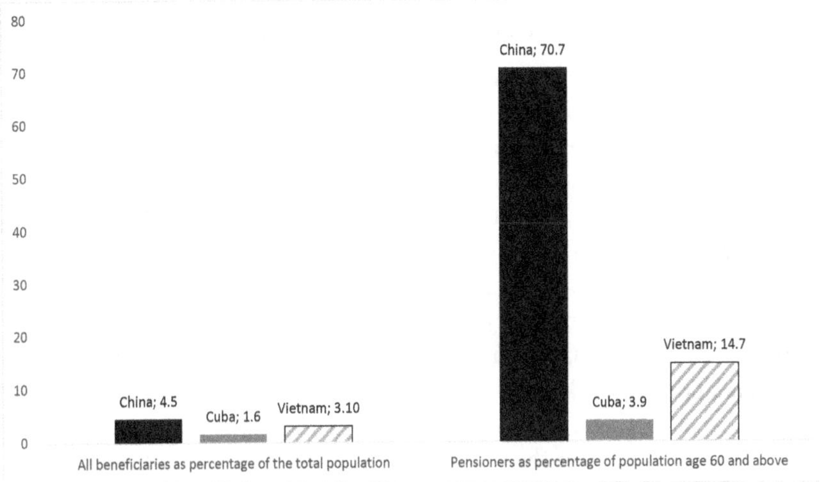

Fig. 5.1. Indicators of Social Assistance Coverage in the Three Countries, 2019–2020. *Source*: My own elaboration based on table 5.3. *Note*: All beneficiaries exclude healthcare assistance.

In Vietnam, coverage of the population aged 60 and above by pensions (contributory and noncontributory) was estimated at 14.7 percent in 2020. ILSSA/ILO (2022) calculates 57 percent coverage of elderly people who are poor and living alone and people aged 80 and above without contributory pensions (Quang 2022). In 2012, Kidd et al. (2016) calculated that 10.2 percent of all households received social assistance transfers. Olivier (2022) estimated 10 percent of all the vulnerable population in 2020; I have estimated 24 percent based on other sources. The target for coverage was 3 million beneficiaries and 3 percent of the population and in 2020 both were met and increased 81 percent over coverage in 2012.

The Social Assistance Explorer was utilized to check the above results on social assistance coverage. The Explorer consists of a harmonized panel dataset of social assistance indicators spanning the period 2000–2015 that compares social assistance (in cash and in kind) financed by the state in low- and middle-income countries. The indicator used was the absolute number of individuals ("participants") that received social assistance in 2015, the latest year available (Barrientos 2018).[16] The number of individuals under social assistance was divided by the total population of each country to obtain the following ratios, similar to the ranking done above: China 4.5 percent, Vietnam 3.1 percent, and Cuba 1.6 percent. For a visual comparison on social assistance coverage, see figure 5.1.

Summary concerning Coverage and Access

Comparisons on pension coverage among the three countries are obstructed due to lack of proper data in Cuba and of diverse calculations in the other two countries. China appears to have the higher coverage on pensions based on the employed labor force (81.8 percent) but seems to come second behind Cuba based on the total labor force (42.5 percent vis-à-vis 68.5 percent). It must be recalled, however, that Cuba's figure is not comparable, because it is based on the population aged 60 and over covered by contributory and noncontributory pensions. Cuba has the advantage over China and Vietnam of a higher proportion of the urban labor force, a lower proportion of informal workers, and a much older pension system that predated the revolution of 1959. Vietnam has the lowest coverage of the total labor force (32.5 percent) although it is rapidly rising. Comparison on healthcare coverage is even more challenging due to the lack of Cuban data. Legally, healthcare coverage is universal whereas China's 96.6 percent is close to universal, followed by Vietnam with 88.8 percent, but Cuban access has declined. Concerning social assistance, coverage by healthcare could not be included because it is available only for China (10.2 percent) and not for the other two countries. For the rest of programs focused on the needy, it was 4.5 percent of the total population in China, 3.1 percent in Vietnam, and 1.6 percent in Cuba. Coverage of the population aged 60 and over by assistance pensions was 70.7 percent in China, 14.7 percent in Vietnam, and 3.9 percent in Cuba. The overall ranking (see table 5.3) is China first (average 1.25), Vietnam second (2.25), and Cuba third (2.33), the latter excluding total population coverage on healthcare due to lack of data, and replacing contributory pension coverage of the total labor force by coverage of the population aged 60 and over.

BENEFIT SUFFICIENCY

This principle seeks adequate social security benefits: pensions should maintain the minimum income of pensioners; healthcare benefits should have the necessary quality; and social assistance benefits should eradicate or reduce poverty and, ideally, be set above the poverty line. In this section I first summarize, in a comparative manner, entitlement conditions of contributory pensions in the three countries (retirement ages, years of contribution, and the adequacy of both) and then evaluate sufficiency of said pensions (replacement rates, average contributory pension, minimum pension, indexing of benefits). Second, I assess healthcare based on different aspects, such as packages of benefits, inputs (facilities, hospital beds, medical personnel) and outputs (infant and maternal mortality

TABLE 5.4: Entitlement Conditions and Other Pension Features in the Three Countries, 2017–2020

Indicators	China	Cuba	Vietnam
Contributory statutory pension age			
Men	60[a]	65	60
Women	50/55[a]	60	55
Minimum years of contribution for pensions	15[a]	30	20
Legal replacement rate (%)	40–60	60	45
Effective gross replacement rate (%)[b]	48.5	36.9	63/40
Base/reference salary (average number of years)	15	5	15
Noncontributory statutory pension age			
Men	60	65	80/60–79[c]
Women	60	60	80/60–79[c]
Average contributory pension (US$)[d]	486	18	193
Average social assistance pension/benefit (US$)[e]	25	7	12.50
Indexing of contributory pensions	Yes, to wages/CPI	No, gov't discretion	Yes, to wage growth

Source: My own elaboration from MOHRSS (2019), NBSC (2021b), ILO (2017), OECD (2018, 2019b), B. He (2022) for China; from ONEI (2021b), Colina (2021a) for Cuba; from GSO (2021b), Ramírez and Arza (2021) for Vietnam; also from Allianz and Hermes (2020), US.SSA-ISSA (2019, 2020).

Notes:

[a] Ages are to be gradually increased between 2023 and 2040: men from 60 to 63 and women from 50/55 to 55/58; years of contributions will increase from fifteen to twenty (V. Wang 2024).

[b] In China and Cuba only government and state enterprises (private sector excluded); in China urban-employee scheme; in Vietnam men/women; there is no disaggregation by gender in China and Cuba.

[c] Two programs: one universal for all citizens age 80 and over and another means-tested based on poverty at ages 60–79.

[d] China is the basic social insurance pension for urban employees in 2020 to which the pension from the individual account should be added; Cuba is the mean pension in 2020; Vietnam is the compulsory system for a worker with the lowest skill.

[e] China is the resident pension (really a noncontributory pension) in 2018; Cuba is the mean social assistance benefit in 2020; Vietnam is the average social assistance pension in 2019.

rates, morbidity rates), the impact of Covid-19, and eldercare. Third, on social assistance, I analyze the average noncontributory pension, its requirements, its amount, and whether it covers essential needs.

Contributory Pensions

Table 5.4 is a comparison of entitlement conditions of social security pensions (contributory and noncontributory) and other features across the three countries.

Retirement Ages and Years of Contribution

China has the lowest retirement ages for contributory pensions and the shortest minimum years of contribution: in the urban-employee scheme, the retirement age is 60 for men and 50/55 for women (blue- and white-collar workers, respectively), plus fifteen years of contributions.[17] In the urban-and-rural-resident scheme, the age is 60 for both genders (that is, from five to ten years more for women than in the urban-employee scheme); among civil servants it is age 50 for women. Ages were set in the 1950s and have become unrealistic due to aging: life expectancy in 2019 was 77.4 years (80.5 women and 74.7 men) and about 12 percent of the population is over 65 years old (World Bank 2020; WHO 2021).[18] In practice, the insured continue working under the "deferred retirement plan" and in the public sector usually retire at age 65 (men) and at age 60 (women) (Zheng 2019).

Cuba's retirement ages are 65 (men) and 60 (women), plus thirty years of contributions. Cuba has the highest retirement ages and the longest years of contribution due to its status as the oldest of the three countries. Retirement ages used to be like those in China and Vietnam but were increased by five years for both genders in the parametric reform of 2008. Accelerated aging is putting pressure on Cuba to increase the age again.

Vietnam's retirement ages are 60 for men and 55 for women (gradually rising annually to reach 62 for men by 2028 and 60 for women by 2030), plus twenty years of contributions. It is possible to retire five years before the statutory age for physical work in certain industries (China), for dangerous work (Vietnam and Cuba), and for demobilized military and reduced working capacity (Vietnam). In the latter case, the pension is reduced by 2 percentage points of the insured's average monthly earnings for each year the pension is taken before the statutory age (OECD 2018). Ages of retirement in China and Vietnam are five years lower in each gender than in Cuba and require fifteen and ten less years of contributions, respectively.

Ages of retirement in China and Vietnam are notably below those of the countries ranked by the Human Development Index (HDI) as

TABLE 5.5: Eighteen Countries Ranked by HDI and by Ages of Retirement, circa 2020

Countries	HDI Groups	HDI Rank	Age of Retirement	Countries	HDI Groups	HDI Rank	Age of Retirement[a]
Barbados	Very	58	66	Cuba		70	65-60
Bahamas	High	58	65	Brazil	High	84	65-60
Costa Rica	Level	62	65	Libya	Level	105	65-60
Mexico		74	65	Vietnam		117	60-55
Peru		79	65	China		85	60-55/50
Saint Lucia	High	86	65	Guatemala		127	65
Botswana	Level	100	65	Bangladesh	Medium	133	65-62
Philippines		107	65	Honduras	Level	133	65-60
Belize		110	65	Micronesia		136	65-60

Source: My own elaboration based on ages from ILO (2021a); ranking by HDI from UNDP (2020).

Note: [a] Men-women.

"very high level of development" (age 65). Within the same rank of "high level" as China and Vietnam, however, there are six countries with a retirement age of 65 and three with ages 65 (men) and 60 (women); five of those countries are HDI ranked as less developed than China. Surprisingly, four countries ranked below China and Vietnam at the "medium level" have retirement ages of 65 (men) or 60 (women). Finally, ten countries out of the eighteen have an equal age for men and women (see table 5.5). Retirement ages for women in China and Vietnam are among the lowest ten countries of the seventy compared in 2020 (Allianz and Hermes 2020).

Replacement Rates Both Legal and Effective

The replacement rate (RR) is the percentage applied to an average salary period of the insured ("base" or "reference" salary) to calculate the amount of the pension. A distinction is made herein between the legal RR, as set in the law, and the effective RR, which results from calculations based on actual pensions (the effective RR could, in turn, be net or gross depending on whether the tax on salary is deducted or not). The legal minimum RR rate in China, combining the basic social insurance pension and the individual account pension, oscillates between 40 percent and 60 percent of the average monthly local wage in the previous year.[19] In Cuba, the RR is 60 percent of the best-five-year wages from the last fifteen years of employment, and it increases 2 percent for each year of employment exceeding thirty, with a maximum of 90 percent. Vietnam's basic RR is 45 percent for the first fifteen years of contribution for women, and for men a gradually increasing period (during 2019–2022) from seventeen to twenty years of contribution; in addition, accrual rates of about 2 percent are assigned for each additional year of contribution up to a maximum of 75 percent.

The effective gross RR, in China's urban-employee basic pension insurance, is estimated as 68 percent for men and 45 percent for women (Allianz and Hermes 2020).[20] The men's RR is well above the ILO recommended minimum RR of 45 percent, whereas the women's RR is equal to the minimum. In 2016, OECD (2018) estimated the RR at average earnings for men as 52.9 percent and for women as 52.3 percent. For the year 2056, OECD projects a hypothetical gross RR of 76 percent for men at average earnings, only surpassed by Pakistan, Italy, and India.[21] The most reliable RR estimate combines basic insurance pension and individual accounts in the urban-employee scheme—limited to government, state-owned enterprises, urban collective units, joint ventures, and other not private entities. The estimate is based on China's statistics (dividing the average pension in the year by the average salary in the previous year) and results in an RR of 48.5 percent for 2019 (MOHRSS 2020c; NBSC 2020a), above the ILO minimum. However, an ILO official and expert on China estimates an RR of 30 percent (without the pension from the individual account) for urban employees whose average monthly wage for thirty years equals the average monthly local wage.[22]

In reality, due to a skewed income distribution, the median is well below the average wage, and therefore many urban employees enjoy a higher than average RR. Other outliers serve as redistributive mechanisms in this formula, as average wages also reflect steep salaries in high-tech industries and high wages in the public sector. Furthermore, individual accounts do have some minimum floor: according to government guidelines, the bookkeeping interest rate should not be lower than the bank fixed-term deposit interest rate. Before 2016, the bookkeeping interest rate was in line with the bank interest rate, between 2 percent and 3 percent annual rates. In 2017, another government instruction stipulated that the rate of interest on individual accounts should henceforth be linked to increases in the average social wage, but the exact formula is not known and is therefore difficult to project (Frota 2021).

Cuba's gross RR decreased from a peak of 57 percent in 2008 to 36.9 percent in 2020 (Colina 2020, 2021a). The latter is well below the ILO minimum rate of 45 percent. It shows a declining trend that will probably continue.

Vietnam's RRs are estimated as 63 percent for men and 44 percent for women (Allianz and Hermes 2020), but local experts said that these are not effective RR (Quang 2022). For the year 2056, the OECD (2018) projects a hypothetical gross RR of 75 percent for men with average earnings, which is surpassed only by China and the three other countries cited above. In Vietnam, there is a significant difference in the RR calculation for workers in the private and public sectors. In the former, the average reference salary is the entire contributory period, but in the latter, the contributory period is the average of the final few years; hence, the public sector RR is twice that of the private sector and one of the highest in the world. On the other hand, 75 percent of private sector workers leave the scheme before meeting the twenty years of contribution and only receive a lump sum equivalent to one and a half months of their average monthly earnings in the last five years (for years of contributions before 2014), plus 2 percent of their average monthly earnings in the last five years for contributions since 2014 (OECD 2018; World Bank 2021b).

Average Contributory Pensions

China provides a statistical series on the average monthly basic insurance pension in the urban-employee scheme (without the individual account pension) for the period 2004–2018.[23] The average pension rose 388 percent from 646 yuan (US$78) to 3,153 yuan (US$476) (MOHRSS 2019). Estimates for 2019 and 2020 (based on MOHRSS 2020d; NBSC 2020a, 2021b) show 3,332 yuan (US$482) and 3,350 yuan (US$486), respectively, and all these averages are above the urban poverty line (B. He 2022).[24] Although the two periods of estimates may not be comparable, the increase in 2004–2020 would be more than five times. On the other hand, the urban-and-rural-resident scheme average monthly pension was 58 yuan (US$9.16) in 2010 and 174 yuan (US$25) in 2020, for an increment of 200 percent (NBSC 2010–2021b; MOHRSS 2019, 2020d). Hence in 2020, the urban-employee scheme average basic pension was nineteen times the average resident pension, which was below the urban and rural poverty lines.

Cuba estimates a mean rather than an average contributory pension. In 2020 the mean monthly pension was 441 CUP, equivalent to US$18.38 at the official exchange rate of 24 CUP per one US dollar; this is grossly insufficient to cover all basic needs (ONEI 2021). The 2021 monthly mean contributory pension was 1,607 CUP, an increase of 264 percent over the 2020 level, but with inflation at 400 percent, said pension in real terms decreased significantly (ONEI 2022a). There is virtually no supply of hard currency on the formal market (recipients of foreign remittances receive them in national currency at the official exchange rate), and most food and other goods are available only at hard-currency state shops; most people must buy at the informal market at very high prices. The mean monthly pension in 2021 for a family of two only covered the cost of electricity and water (600 CUP), thirty eggs (600 CUP), three pounds of rice (210 CUP), one pound of sugar (100 CUP), and one liter of vegetable cooking oil (100 CUP) (Pumar 2022), without any fish, chicken, beef, or vegetables, and neither transportation nor medicine. Data is not available on the 2022 mean pension, but consumer-goods market prices increased several times in that year; for instance, a carton of fifteen eggs jumped five times in price from 300 CUP to 1,600 CUP (Vicent 2022).

Vietnam's average monthly contributory pension in 2022 was set equal to the monthly minimum regional wage, and there were four regions where such average was highest in region 1 and lowest in region 4. In addition, there were three categories of workers—those with minimum skills, those with training skills, and those working under dangerous or hazardous conditions. The first category was equal to the regional wage, and the other two were the regional wage plus an increase of 7 percent. Based on region 1 and the minimum-skill category, the average monthly pension was calculated at 4,420,000 dong (US$193); if based on the trained category, it was 4,735,714 dong (US$207); and if based on region 4 and the trained category, it was 3,294,440 (US$144).[25] These averages are above the poverty line (Ramírez and Arza 2021).

Minimum Pension

The three countries grant a minimum pension that should provide a basic level of economic protection for pensioners—particularly important for workers with low earnings and for those with a short contributory history. China grants the minimum pension in the urban-employee program and requires fifteen years of contribution; such pension is above the poverty line (B. He 2022). Cuba's minimum pension does not cover basic food needs. In 2021 the minimum pension was raised to 1,528 CUP, which was equivalent to US$64 at the official exchange rate, but the informal rate jumped to 70 CUP per one US dollar, hence the pension actually decreased to US$13.83. Vietnam's minimum pension in the mandatory system is equal to the basic salary in the public sector, around 1.7 times the urban poverty line and two times the rural poverty line (Ramírez and Arza 2021).

Pension Indexing

In China, pensions in the urban-employee scheme (both the basic and individual accounts) have been annually indexed to wages and the CPI

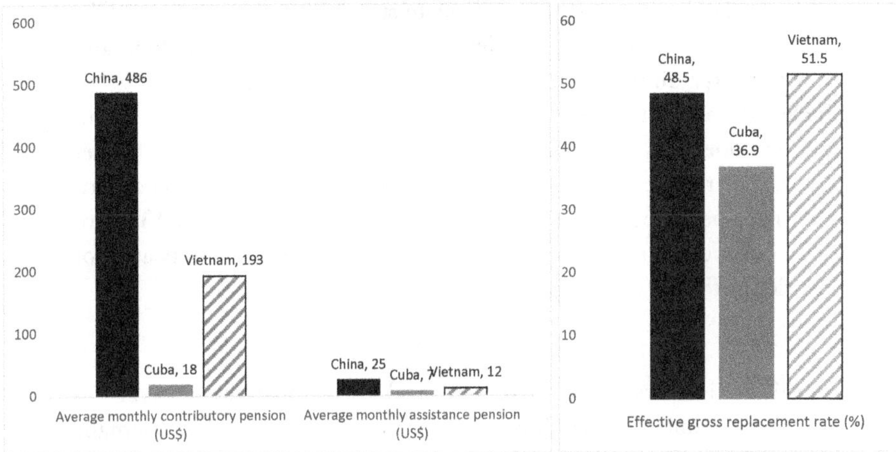

Fig. 5.2. Selected Indicators of Pension Sufficiency in the Three Countries, circa 2020. *Source*: My own elaboration based on table 5.4.

since 2005 (MOHRSS and Ministry of Finance 2005); this regulation became an article in the 2011 law. In 2021, for the seventeenth consecutive time, the pension in seventeen provincial-level regions was increased and other provinces followed suit ("China: Raising Pension," 2021), and in 2022 the eighteenth increase in pensions took place (Gongcheng 2022). There was not a national norm to adjust urban-and-rural-resident pensions, as local governments had autonomy and discretion to do it. In 2018 the MOHRSS (2018) set the adjustment by national policy and made the central government responsible for annual adjustment.

In Cuba, contributory pensions and social assistance benefits are not annually adjusted to inflation. The state has ample discretion to adjust both types of benefits based on available fiscal resources such that, between 1989–2019, the value of the mean pension adjusted to inflation decreased 36 percent (Mesa-Lago et al. 2022).

According to the law, Vietnam adjusts its pensions based on the "increase in the consumer price index and economic growth to suit the state budget capacity and social insurance fund." But in practice, indexation has followed wage growth; the government is considering a shift toward adjustment based on the increase in the consumer price index (Ramírez and Arza 2021). It was not possible to get a statistical series on the real pension from 2000 to 2020; however, from 2008–2020 the annual average CPI growth was 7.21 and the rate of pension indexation averaged 12.35 annually, hence a gain of 5 percentage points in the period (my calculation based on raw data from Quang 2022).

A ranking of seventy countries in 2020 based on the "adequacy" of pensions (ability to provide an adequate standard of living) placed China twenty-sixth, just beneath Germany and the United Kingdom, and Vietnam fifty-ninth, just beneath Argentina and Mexico. Cuba was not included among the seventy countries, but considering that its mean pension does not cover basic needs in addition to the ranking of other Latin American countries such as Argentina, Chile, Mexico, and Peru that have better pensions, Cuba should be ranked well below Vietnam (Allianz and Hermes 2020). For a comparison of selected indicators of pension sufficiency, see figure 5.2.

Healthcare

In this section, first I aim to compare packages of healthcare benefits in the three countries, including reimbursement (in China and Vietnam, as well as the role of individual accounts in China), primary vis-à-vis curative care (including hospital centralism), quality of services, availability of medicine, family doctors, and policies to confront health problems. Then I comparatively analyze and assess health inputs and outputs and the impact of Covid-19. Finally, I describe and evaluate long-term eldercare.

Packages of Benefits and Reimbursement/Financing

China has different packages of benefits largely based on local rules, resulting in substantial divergence in such packages. Most vaccines are provided free by the public health system (for instance, for influenza), whereas others require payment. The basic medical insurance schemes are not preventive but, rather, curative and do not provide vaccines (L. He 2022). The medical social insurance fund guarantees hospitalization and treatment for serious diseases, whereas individual accounts guarantee outpatient care for minor illnesses. Since the absorption of the maternity program by the social insurance, the latter also covers birth control, prenatal checkups, delivery and antenatal care, as well as maternity leave allowances.

Historically, there has been a strong hospital bias ("centralism") in China (Xu et al. 2019). In 2010, 53 percent of total health expenditures were allocated to hospitals; more recent data is not available. Patients usually go directly to hospitals even for outpatient care and vaccination because there are relatively few public primary care facilities (most are private) (World Bank 2013), and people do not trust lower facilities. Because of this vacuum, hospitals are overcrowded with long lines waiting for services (X. Li 2020; Hu 2021; L. He 2022). Notwithstanding, a 2019 law on basic medical hygiene and health promotion stipulated that primary medical services should be provided by health institutions organized by the government, whereas those organized by "social forces" are encouraged to provide basic medical services. The law added that the state should guide nonemergency patients to go first to primary health-care institutions but went on to state that primary services will be "gradually established at the grassroots level" (Law of the Public Republic of China on Basic Medical . . . , 2019, art. 30).

If the basic medical insurance does not cover a treatment in China, the insured can withdraw funds from their individual accounts, and the same is true for care of dependent family. Similarly, treatments outside of designated hospitals must be paid out of individual accounts or the insured's own pocket. In 2020, the average amount in individual accounts was 2,919 yuan (US$422), which was probably insufficient to pay for costly medical treatments that were not covered ("China's Social Security System," 2021). The Social Insurance Law of 2010 stipulated that medical insurance funds should cover insured medical costs by directly paying service providers (hospitals and clinics, public and private), but in most cases the insured must pay upfront and request reimbursement later. Furthermore, to be eligible for social insurance funds, hospitals must be on a preapproved government list; the insured can choose among those hospitals for treatment (some hospitals are automatically "chosen" for the insured), but if the insured change their place of work or residence, they need to apply for a change of designated hospitals (Y. Wang 2022). Diverse rules apply for reimbursement in provinces, regions, and localities. For instance, in Beijing (the biggest and highest-income city), in the UEBMI scheme the maximum reimbursement for outpatient care is 20,000 yuan and 500,000 for inpatient care for a total of 520,000 yuan; in the URRBMI, the maximums are 4,500, 250,000, and 254,000 yuan, respectively, such that the latter maximums are 22.5 percent, 50 percent, and 49 percent of the former (B. He 2022).[26] Reimbursement for inpatient services and medicine is even more limited.[27] People need to buy additional private medical insurance, pay out of pocket, or forgo treatment.[28]

There is a positive trend toward supplying the same package of benefits and reimbursements for all. Based on a regulation in 2016, most prosperous cities adopted a "universalist" approach providing the same health package of benefits to all social groups (e.g., urban-rural), and two pioneers were Dongguan City in Guangdong Province and Shenmu County in Shaanx Province (China State Council 2016; X. Huang 2020). In 2021, eleven more provinces had completed the integration of the basic medical insurance for urban residents with the rural cooperative medical system and established a unified basic medical insurance for urban and rural residents (B. He 2022). The limitations explained above mean that some localities have established general outpatient clinics and strengthened the guarantee for social insurance and outpatient care: increasing and adjusting the social insurance fund, for instance, and allowing individual accounts to pay for out-of-pocket expenses in designated medical institutions (including any medical expenses incurred by the spouses, parents, and children of the insured) and pharmacies (GOV 2021a). The government also encourages people to buy supplementary private health insurance, but people with low incomes cannot afford the associated premiums ("China's Social Security System," 2021).

Finally, China's law stipulates that the state will promote the implementation of family doctor contract services in primary healthcare institutions, and that they will sign agreements to provide medical and health services according to the health status and medical needs of residents. Under this law, a general practitioner signs a contract that sets a long-term therapeutic relationship with community members to manage their health needs.[29] The family doctor contract system began in 2009, and by 2017–2019, 500 million residents had signed contracts with 365,082 practitioners. Despite some success, "contracts were not implemented effectively"—only some of the doctors were able to perform the contracted services, and the number and frequency of contracted services per capita was "suboptimal" (a low compliance rate of 37.2 percent) because many doctors signed without an agreement, which is essential for good performance (Wang et al. 2021).[30]

An evaluation in 2020 of the performance of said program in Dongguan City in Guangdong Province (one of the first cities to implement the program) found a contract rate of 82 percent and a compliance rate of 75 percent, higher than the national averages, hence it was presented as a successful example to follow (Wang et al. 2021). Yet the survey was limited to 100 family doctors, making its extrapolation value questionable given the 1,400 million inhabitants of the nation. In March 2022, the National Health Commission announced a goal to expand family doctor services to cover at least 75 percent of the population by 2035: they are expected to serve about 85 percent of priority patients including the elderly, pregnant women, children, people with disabilities, as well as those with chronic and mental illnesses; the percentage of those registered with family doctors would rise by 1–3 percentage points annually from 2022; fees would be covered by the basic medical insurance scheme, the government, and copayments from users ("Seventy Per Cent," 2022).

The small territorial size of Cuba and the centralization of the health administration together have facilitated a fairly unified package of benefits, though there are some differences among provinces and municipalities, mostly based on divergent incomes and central budget allocations. The Cuban benefits package has three levels: primary, secondary, and tertiary. The primary level includes prevention based on a wide program of vaccination against communicable diseases, supported by a network of primary healthcare offices staffed by family doctors.[31] There is also a network of hospitals at the three levels (local, regional, and national), as well as a network of clinics and urban and rural health posts. Legally, the system is free, so there is no reimbursement (no individual accounts and private facilities either), and the government finances all services out of the general budget. Cubans endure long lines waiting for services, particularly for specialists and surgery, largely because of the exportation of physicians and the lack of inputs. Medicines used to be provided free at hospitals, but now they have to be paid for by patients; there is a severe scarcity of medicine, even paid for in hard currency (a result of the economic crisis, a reduction in domestic production, and a cut in imports). In addition, patients have to provide food, bedsheets, surgical inputs, and so forth. The physical healthcare infrastructure continues to suffer as resources are unavailable to support routine maintenance and most basic repairs (Mesa-Lago and Díaz-Briquets 2021).

As in China, there is a strong emphasis on hospitals and doctors, which tends to increase costs; tertiary-level hospitals are overcrowded because of the underutilization of lower-level services. Cuba was the first of the three countries to start the family doctor program in the mid-1980s. It became a pillar of the health system, but the exportation of half of the family doctors and the lack of medicines and other inputs in family-doctor offices have caused the program to wane substantially. The healthcare system peaked at the end of the 1980s but was severely damaged by the crisis of the 1990s and had not fully recovered by 2024, aggravated by the current economic crisis. The national survey on aging found that the population's self-perception on health was mostly mediocre ("regular") or bad and very bad; such negative self-perception increased with age—in the age group of 75 and over, 60 percent of men and 80 percent of women declared themselves to be in mediocre, bad, or very bad health (ONEI 2019b).

Vietnam's social insurance health system has developed a broad package of benefits to all members, which covers preventive services including immunization and control of communicable diseases, curative and rehabilitation services, and reimbursement for the costs of select medications. Efforts focus on primary care, basic health service packages for local facilities (including 80 technical services for medical care and 241 drugs provided by health stations), and inclusion of the poor and near poor. However, access to the package is hindered by limited health facilities and equipment and the low quality of services at the primary level. Moreover, the set of benefits covered also lacks prioritization, and about half of the reimbursement expenditures on select medicines is judged to be inappropriate based on specific guidelines (ILO 2018a).

There is an extensive network of government and private curative care facilities in all provinces, districts, and communes; in 2018, 99.7 percent communes had medical stations (GSO 2020). Public facilities are set at different levels: commune and ward stations, towns, family doctors, civilian army medical stations, and clinics. In addition, there are 32,000 private specialized clinics and 240 private hospitals, which are rapidly expanding and tend to be more concentrated than public facilities in urban areas because of their higher purchasing power (premiums in the private sector are higher than in the public sector).[32] The private sector requires better state regulation (World Bank 2021b).

There has been a relatively recent move to strengthen primary care, the prevention of noncommunicable diseases (NCD), early detections, chronic disease management, and health education. Provincial centers for disease control are responsible for preventive health programs and often have clinics that provide services to the people; district health centers and commune health stations implement preventive programs at the local level. A family medicine model responsible for primary care, immunization, health education, and family planning is reaching into the most remote areas; family medicine facilities are the first place to receive primary care, prevention, emergency, and curative care. And yet, the current organization still relies on expensive hospital-centric acute care, and the overcrowding of central and provincial hospitals (as in China and Cuba) continues to be widespread. Health service utilization relies on hospitals for outpatient care rather than primary care clinics despite the fact that hospitals are more expensive for providing those services (World Bank 2021b). In Vietnam, almost all districts (communes) have primary healthcare posts, but only about half of them meet national standards, many posts are deteriorating, and there is a shortage of or poorly qualified medical personnel (De Miranda and Yamaoka 2014). Recent data indicates that the population receiving health treatment in the previous year is expanding, but still there are differences by areas, regions, quintiles, and ethnic groups.

Health Inputs and Outputs

In this section first I compare inputs in the health system of the three countries, such as available health facilities and personnel, both in 2019 and in the period 2008–2019 to test if there is an increasing or decreasing trend (see table 5.6). Second, I evaluate output indicators such as

TABLE 5.6: Health Facilities, Personnel, and Other Indicators in the Three Countries, 2019–2020

Indicators	China	Cuba	Vietnam
Physicians per 10,000 inhabitants	2.0	8.6	8.8
Hospital beds per 1,000 inhabitants	5.5	3.0	2.8
Changes in period 2008 to 2019 (%)[a]			
Number of hospitals	79	–32	11
Number of local facilities[b]	11	–9	2
Number of physicians	79	39	89
Number of nurses	164	–21	97
Number of technicians	98	–80	n.a.
Ratio hospital beds (1,000 inhabitants) p.p.[c]	2.7	–1.0	1.1

Source: My own elaboration: from NBSC (2021b) for China; from ONEI (2009, 2014, 2020b) for Cuba; from GSO (2009, 2021b) for Vietnam.

Notes: [a] In Vietnam the end year may be 2017–2018.

[b] In China, these are local units; in Cuba, they are clinics (all rural and urban posts were shut down in 2011); in Vietnam, they are communes.

[c] Change in percentage points.

infant and maternal mortality rates, the stage of the epidemiological transition (causes of deaths), and morbidity rates.

In 2019, Vietnam had the highest ratio of physicians for 10,000 inhabitants at 8.8, closely followed by Cuba at 8.6, and China lagging at 2; whereas China had the highest ratio of hospital beds per 1,000 inhabitants at 5.5, Cuba had 3.0, and was very closely followed by Vietnam at 2.8. It has been hypothesized that, at the time of their revolutions, the two Asian countries were well behind Cuba in development level and social indicators, hence they had to exert significant effort to match and exceed Cuba in these areas. To support that hypothesis, a decade trend (from approximately 2008 to 2019) in six health indicators is compared in table 5.6. China and Vietnam show greater progress than Cuba in all the indicators, and Cuba exhibits a declining trend in five of them.

The number of hospitals rose by 79 percent in China and by 11 percent in Vietnam but decreased by 32 percent in Cuba.[33] In local facilities, the figures were 11 percent, 2 percent, and –9 percent, respectively. The number of physicians is the only indicator where Cuba exhibits an increase in the period (39 percent), but it is surpassed by Vietnam (89 percent) and China (79 percent). Furthermore, about 40,000 Cuban

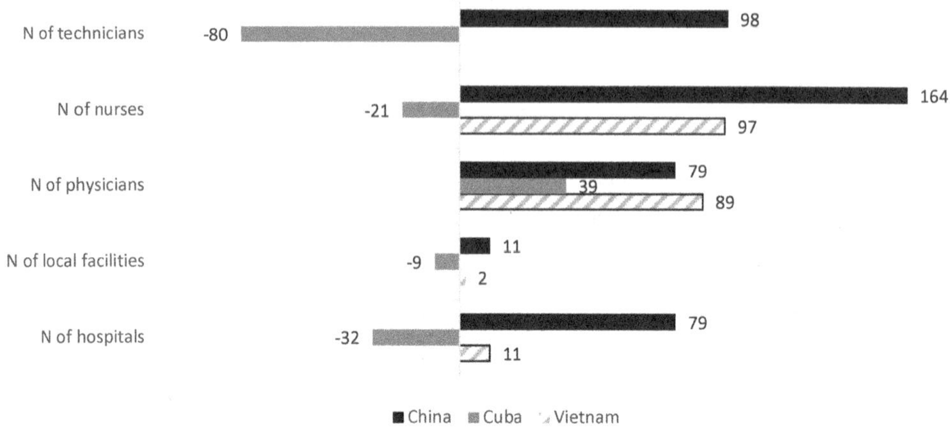

Fig. 5.3. Input Indicators of Health Sufficiency: Changes (%) in Facilities and Personnel in the Three Countries, 2008–2019. *Source*: My own elaboration based on table 5.6.

medical personnel, mostly physicians, are working abroad and generate the first source of hard currency for the nation, but this also results in fewer physicians being available domestically, such that the actual ratio of physicians per 10,000 inhabitants is lower than 8.6 (indicated in table 5.6). For instance, the number of family doctors abroad is about half of the total, thus reducing access to primary care in Cuba by the same proportion (ONEI 2009, 2021). In addition, not all doctors who are in Cuba work in their profession because of very low wages and the ban on private practices; therefore, many doctors work as taxi drivers, owners of small restaurants, and other more lucrative private jobs that are permitted by the government.

The number of nurses rose 164 percent in China and 97 percent in Vietnam but shrank 21 percent in Cuba, whereas technical personnel increased 98 percent in China and declined 80 percent in Cuba. Finally, the ratio of hospital beds per 1,000 inhabitants augmented 2.7 percentage points in China and 1.1 points in Vietnam but fell 1 percentage point in Cuba. Other indicators related to hospital efficiency, such as hospital average length of stay and hospital bed occupancy rates, will be analyzed below. (For the evolution of key output indicators of health sufficiency in the period 2008–2019 see figure 5.3.)

For health outputs, infant mortality, and maternal mortality rates, see table 3.2, which shows that Cuba has the lowest infant mortality (5 per 1,000), very closely followed by China (5.6), and then Vietnam

TABLE 5.7: Rates of Communicable Diseases in the Three Countries, 2019 (per 100,000 inhabitants)

Diseases	China	Cuba	Vietnam[a]
Acute diarrhea	N.R.	1,465.0	272.7
Acute respiratory	N.R.	39,093.2	N.R.
AIDS	5.1	131.7	1.16
Brucellosis	3.2	0.2	N.R.
Cholera	0.0	N.R.	0.0
Dengue	1.6	N.R.	149.8
Dysentery	5.8	N.R.	N.R.
Gonorrhea	8.4	26.4	0.3[b]
Leptospirosis	0.0	N.R.	0.0
Malaria	0.2	0.3	7.0
Measles	0.2	N.R.	5.1
Pertussis	2.1	N.R.	0.4
Poliomyelitis	0.0	N.R	0.0
Rabies	0.0	0.0	0.7
Scarlet fever	5.8	18.0	N.R.
Syphilis	38.4	38.1	2.1
Tetanus	0.0	0.0	0.2
Viral hepatitis	92.1	5.2	12.9
Covid-19 excess mortality means[c]	2.0	163.0	53.0

Source: My own elaboration: information on China from NBSC (2021b); information on Cuba from ONEI (2020a); information on Vietnam from Ministry of Health in 2018, Quang (2022); Covid-19 excess mortality means from WHO (2022a).

Notes: N.R. = Not reported, this could be because it is eradicated; nevertheless, in Cuba, epidemics acknowledged by the Pan American Health Organization such as cholera and dengue (as well as others reported by the news media such as leptospirosis) are not regularly reported.

[a] Year 2018.

[b] Underreported; it is estimated that there are 10,000 new cases annually.

[c] See explanations in the text.

(13.9); conversely, China has the lowest maternal mortality rate (17.8 per 100,000), followed by Vietnam (46), and Cuba lagging well behind (177).[34] It's intriguing that trends in those two rates are opposite in Cuba—infant mortality declining and maternal mortality climbing. Three peer-review academic articles have contested the statistical reliability of Cuba's infant mortality rate, indicating that it is underestimated (see sources in Mesa-Lago and Díaz-Briquets 2021). In 2019, mortality rates per 1,000 in children below age 5 was lower in Cuba (6.6) than in China (7.8); however, China has achieved greater reduction, from 18.1 to 7.8 in 2008–2019 (NBSC 2008, 2021b) vis-à-vis an increase from 5.7 to 6.6 in Cuba in 2016–2019 (ONEI 2017, 2020a). Cuba does not publish data on child malnutrition rates and instead publishes data on underweight children below age 5: the rate increased from 5.1 in 2008 to 5.6 in 2020 (ONEI 2021). Vietnam publishes data on malnutrition among children below age 5: it decreased from 14.1 percent in 2015 to 12.2 percent in 2019 (GSO 2021b).

The three countries are in a similar stage in the epidemiological transition. The percentage distribution by type of disease in 2019 in China was 89 percent noncommunicable diseases, 4 percent communicable diseases and maternal and nutrition condition, and 7 percent others, whereas Cuba was 83 percent, 9 percent, and 8 percent, and Vietnam was 81 percent, 9 percent, and 10 percent, respectively (World Bank n.d.). Therefore, the ranking of disease transmission is China first, Cuba second, and Vietnam third, with the last two very close together. A 2019 comparison of ratios of eighteen communicable diseases per 100,000 inhabitants between the three countries is obstructed by several nonreported diseases: seven in Cuba, four in Vietnam, and two in China. This is particularly worrisome in Cuba because the country suffers from epidemics in some of the nonreported diseases, such as cholera, dengue, leptospirosis, and so forth (Mesa-Lago and Díaz-Briquets 2021; "Con dengue," 2022). In Vietnam, some communicable diseases such as tuberculosis have rates that are among the twenty highest in the world: the morbidity rate of tuberculosis in 2012 was 215 in Vietnam and 6.7 in Cuba (Huong et al. 2013; De Miranda and Yamaoka 2014; ONEI 2014). Comparable rates in table 5.7 show that China has either the lowest rate of the three (or lower than at least one other country) in nine diseases, Vietnam in eight diseases, and Cuba in four diseases. China has eradicated five diseases, Vietnam has eradicated three diseases, and Cuba two. There is data available in the three countries for only seven diseases out of the total of eighteen, and the averages were very close. More data is needed to fill gaps and confirm eradicated diseases.

Impact of Covid-19

The divergent effects of Covid-19 in the three countries have been recently assessed by the WHO by measuring "excess mortality," which is the difference between the total number of deaths that have occurred and the number of deaths that would have been expected in the absence

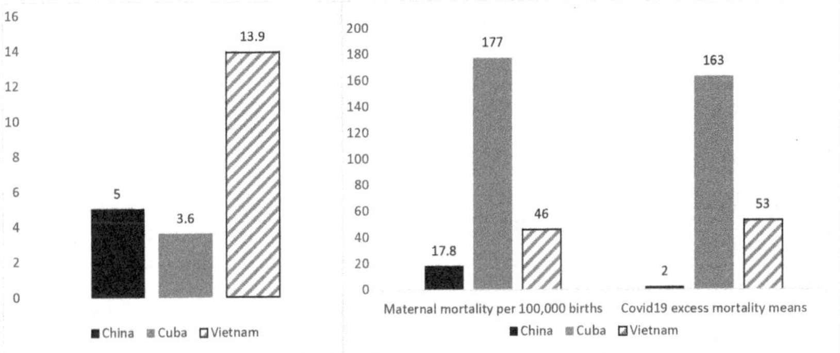

FIG. 5.4. Selected Output Indicators of Health Sufficiency, circa 2020. *Source*: My own elaboration based on table 3.1 and text.

of the pandemic. Excess mortality includes a variety of instances: deaths attributable directly to Covid-19 that were counted and reported by countries to WHO; deaths attributable directly to Covid-19 that were not accounted and reported by countries; deaths indirectly associated with Covid-19 due to other causes and diseases, resulting from the wider impact of the pandemic on health systems and society. Excess mortality also calculates deaths that would have occurred under normal circumstances but that were averted due to pandemic-related changes in social conditions and personal behaviors (e.g., less traffic deaths or influenza deaths due to less travel and local lockdowns). This tool provides us with "a more comprehensive understanding of the impact of Covid-19 beyond the number of Covid-19 deaths reported by countries," and the global excess mortality was 9.49 million more deaths than those globally reported as being directly attributable to Covid-19 (WHO 2022b). WHO calculates, for all countries, the mean excess mortality per 100,000 inhabitants in the years 2020, 2021, and 2020–2021. However, the year 2020 is distorted due to the diverse start of the pandemic across countries, whereas in the year 2021, the time is the same for all countries (one full year) because the pandemic had already occurred in all of them at that point. For this reason, the year 2021 is selected for the comparison in the three countries (see table 5.7): China had the lowest mean of 2, Vietnam had 53, and Cuba had the highest mean with 163, hence excess mortality in Cuba was eighty-two times that of China and three times that of Vietnam (WHO 2022a).[35] Published after the WHO estimates, Cuba's demographic statistical yearbook of 2021 shows that the total number of deaths in 2021 were 167,645 instead of the 117,908 reported by WHO (the latter did a projection based on the Cuban figure for March), for a total of 49,737 more. Based on the new total deaths and the

Table 5.8: Ratio of Elder Persons per Elderly Bed in the Three Countries, 2020

Indicators	China	Cuba	Vietnam
Percent of elderly/total population			
Age 60 and above	18.7	21.3	12.3
Age 65 and above	13.7	15.7	8.0
Thousands in population			
Age 60 and above	264,020	2,386	11,997
Age 65 and above	190,640	1,759	7,789
Thousands of beds for elderly	8,220	12	10
Ratio elderly person per bed			
Age 60 and above	32.2	198.8	1,199
Age 65 and above	23.2	146.5	778

Source: My own elaboration based on GOV (2021c) for China; ONEI (2021) for Cuba; MOHRSS (2020c), Quang (2022) and https://www.vietnamplus.vn/phat-trien-mang-luoi-tro-giup-xa-hoi-de-dap-ung-yeu-cau-nguoi-cao-tuoi/666890.vnp/ for Vietnam.

total population of 11,147,405, "excess mortality" increased from 163 to 446 (ONEI 2022b).[36] For selected output indicators of health sufficiency, see figure 5.4.

Eldercare

Aging demands eldercare and Cuba is the most aged country of the three. Table 5.8 shows the degree of aging and a comparable indicator of eldercare—the ratio of the number of elderly persons (at alternatives aged 60 and above and 65 and above) per elderly bed in 2020 (the lower the number the better). China has the lowest (best) ratios of 32 and 23 per bed, respectively; Cuba (the oldest country) has the second-lowest ratios of 199 and 146, respectively (in other terms, six times China's ratio); Vietnam has the highest ratio (worst) of 1,199 and 778, respectively.[37]

In China, there are three types of eldercare institutions with varying quality and cost. First are "registered beds" (or residential, 60 percent of the total), which are managed by profit-driven commercial or market enterprises as well as by state-owned enterprises and private corporations for their retired employees. These "registered beds" usually have the best services—the market charges high fees while state-enterprises provide eldercare as part of their package of benefits.[38] Second are "communities" that care for local residents and don't charge fees, but their services are usually of lesser quality (though there are exceptions). Third is the "third sector" (public) geared toward disadvantaged groups such as poor elders without family; these normally don't charge fees, but their quality is lower. The last two groups ("communities" and "third sector") account for 40 percent of the beds (B. He 2022).[39]

Public facilities often have long waiting lists, and private facilities are very expensive. In addition, there is the problem of facilities becoming properly licensed to offer nursing care, a process complicated by bureaucratic requirements. The government either should provide more long-term-care facilities itself or make it easier for private companies to do so (Wang and Dong 2023). Chinese private companies, including foreign companies, are actively entering the nursing home market that targets seniors with mid to high incomes; a resolution allowed companies from the United States, Japan, and France to form partnerships with Chinese firms (World Bank 2021b; Glinskaya et al. 2022).

China's Fourteenth Five-Year Plan for National Aging Development and Eldercare (2021–2025) stipulated the establishment of an integrated institutional framework to improve eldercare services in urban and rural areas. It included the improvement of the basic medical care; new professional nursing services for the aged still living at home; supplying fuel, food, clothing, transportation, and rehabilitation services; constructing geriatric facilities; and increasing the basic old-age pension for urban-rural residents. The plan also set six goals for 2025: 9 million beds for eldercare (only 778,000 more than in 2020 despite accelerating aging, though 90 percent of the elderly prefer home-based care by relatives); 100 percent visitation of elder persons with special difficulties; 100 percent construction of pension service facilities in all new cities; 55 percent of nursing beds in aged-care institutions; more than 60 percent of geriatric departments in second-level and higher hospitals; and more than one social worker per 1,000 elderly persons (GOV 2022b). In 2022, two pilot projects for national long-term care as part of the urban-employee and the urban-and-rural-resident schemes covered 49 cities, included 5,000 established new service providers with 300,000 staff positions, insured 145 million people (10.3 percent of total population), and had 1.65 million beneficiaries. The composition of service delivery was 75.7 percent home-care services, 11 percent nursing homes, and 6.5 percent healthcare providers (community care services at only 0.01 percent), thus the option of home care comprised the wide majority.

The fund expenditure of the program was 50,300 million yuan (US$7,896 million), and the composition of financing sources varied between the urban-employee and the urban-and-rural-resident scheme with 70 percent and 64 percent from health insurance, 16 percent and

22 percent from the insured, 3 percent and 13 percent from public finance, and 11 percent and 0 percent from employers (residents don't have employers), respectively. Thus, the insured had a heavier financial burden in the resident scheme that was not compensated by public finance and health insurance. The annual average benefit per capita was 16,000 yuan (US$2,512), and the annual per capita contribution was 180 yuan (US$28) at 1.1 percent of the average benefit. But the contribution varied 18 times between Shanghai and Anqing Province (US$112 and US$6) because of diverse living costs, and there was also a difference of 3.6 times in the average annual financing per capita in the urban-employee and the urban-and-rural-resident schemes. No information was available on the per capita benefit in both schemes, but the previous data indicates that it was much higher in the urban-employee scheme (Fan 2022).

The shortage of well-trained long-term-care workers and allied health professionals is a major barrier for quality improvement and for the effective integration of medical and long-term-care services (Glinskaya et al. 2022). The government encourages nursing homes to build medical facilities and hospitals to offer nursing services, but the separation of the state departments that oversee medical care and nursing care complicates the needed integration (Wang and Dong 2023). WHO projects that 400 million elderly people will need eldercare by 2040, which is one-third of the total population (cited in "China Is Going to Have to Figure," 2023).

In 2023, the communist party issued a new guidance to all provinces to build a basic eldercare system by 2025 based on factors such as economic-social development and financial situation. The long-term-care security system should integrate insurance, welfare, and assistance; services will include material assistance, nursing, and caregiving, particularly for elderly people living alone and families with financial difficulties. China's National Health Commission projects that, by 2025, there will be a need for 40 million beds in community facilities and nursing homes up from 8 million now ("China Issues Guidance," 2023).

In Cuba, eldercare is mainly provided by families either because state institutions are insufficient or because the cost of market services is unaffordable. As the state has been unable to satisfy the demand for eldercare, it has allowed marketization to mitigate the severe scarcity of public services (this is the only social service in Cuba where that is allowed). There are virtually no statistics on the number, tariffs, and other key data on eldercare services. Important providers are self-employed workers in the private sector who get a state license as "caregivers of sick, disabled or elderly people." Those workers are strictly regulated, with a maximum number of people in their care, and their services are fully paid by the families, sometimes in foreign currency and with a steady increasing cost (there is no state regulation of the prices for these services).[40] Furthermore, the family must pay for food, other essential consumer goods, and beds for the self-employed caregivers, hence they are financially out of reach for most of the population.

Service cooperatives have been authorized to perform such services; there is no data on the number of these co-ops, but it should be very small (Ación and Colina 2022). The state had 157 "elder homes" (nursing homes) in the nation in 2020 (the same number as in 2008), which were financed by the state with fees paid by the elder person or their family. In addition, there are also 292 "grandparents' houses," where the elderly spend part of the day, which are also partly financed out of pocket. Elder homes and grandparent houses may be certified (approved by the state when meeting minimum requirements) or uncertified; the former is of better quality than the latter but also seven times more expensive, and prices have escalated because of the hyperinflation generated by monetary unification (ONEI 2009, 2021; Acosta 2019; Ación and Colina 2022). In 2020, the monthly fee for the certified elder home was 217 CUP monthly (48 percent of the mean monthly contributory pension of 441 CUP and 18 percent of the mean monthly state salary of 1,194 CUP). After monetary unification at the start of 2021, the fee increased to 1,260 CUP (78 percent of the mean contributory pension of 1,607 CUP and 33 percent of the mean salary of 3,830 CUP). Fees for grandparent homes jumped fourteen times in 2020–2021 (my calculations based on Resolución 351/2000; Carmona et al. 2021; ONEI 2021, 2022a). If the elderly person pays the fee, their monthly pension is reduced to 347 CUP (US$3.47) for all other expenses. As social assistance pensions are denied when the beneficiary has relatives who can provide help, most of the fees for those at elder homes are paid by a relative who must use a hefty portion of their meager salary. The Catholic Church has several nursing homes for the elderly that provide the best services and usually don't charge fees, but these are in high demand and are grossly insufficient relative to the demand; they also depend on international donations (Mesa-Lago 2020a).

According to the previous analysis, service care for the elderly, the disabled, and the sick is unequal, and the low-income population has little access to it, hence the only viable alternative is family care (provided mainly by women), which impedes the ability of those taking care of relatives to perform remunerated work. A comparison of adult care in the three most-aged Latin American countries (Cuba, Uruguay, and Chile, in that order) based on multiple indicators ranked Cuba behind the other two because of the scarce provision of adult-care services, the decline in the value of pensions, the rise in neglected groups (women, people living alone, people not receiving external remittances, and residents in rural areas), and the decrease in healthcare facilities and personnel.[41]

These problems have led to a deepening of the adult-care crisis, aggravated by the incapacity of social policy to anticipate and plan for problems related to aging, as well as the concomitant economic deterioration and a virtual lack of adult organizations to influence public policy (Acosta et al. 2018; Acosta and Ángel 2020). Overall, 40 percent of Cuban households include an elderly person (ONEI 2019b). A Cuban demographer reports that each incapacitated adult demands the care of an average of 1.6 people. Providing adult care is a great challenge: homes for the elderly are insufficient to meet demand, and the burden of eldercare falls mostly on unpaid women (García Quiñones 2019). Despite accelerated population aging, in 2012–2020, the number of homes and beds for the elderly was stagnant—156 and 155 homes in 2012 and 2020, and 12,046 and 12,561 beds respectively (ONEI 2013, 2021).[42]

There is not a long-term plan for eldercare in Cuba, as there is in China and Vietnam, but the law of the new Cuban Family Code stipulates the rights of elderly persons, regulates the work of care providers, and so forth. It also establishes (chapters I and II) the obligation of sons and daughters—as well as siblings, aunts, uncles, nieces, and nephews—to provide food, housing, clothing, and personal care to their elderly relatives (parents and grandparents), either by supplying the necessary monetary resources or by providing a home and care for the adults. Such obligation ceases when the person obliged to provide food lacks the resources to meet their own needs. The law, however, does not make any reference to the state obligation set in the party orientations of 2011 to provide a social assistance pension to the elderly whose relatives cannot help them because of their own lack of resources, which creates a hefty vacuum (Ley 156, 2022). It has been shown that Cuba ranks below China on the ratio of elderly population to beds but is well above Vietnam, which is the least aged country of the three; Cuba also virtually lacks geriatric hospitals despite being the oldest country of the three.

In Vietnam, the 1992 constitution stipulates that poor vulnerable older persons without family shall be supported by the state and society. But, according to Glinskaya, Feng, and Suarez (2022), there is neither a comprehensive long-term care model nor any national integration of long-term-care service provision. Most assistance is focused on institutional care rather than on providing people with support to remain in their homes and communities (Kidd et al. 2016). In 2020, there were 411 social assistance facilities (43.8 percent public and 56.2 percent private), but only 33 of them provided care for the elderly; another source reported 425 nursing homes in the same year (Quang 2022). The number of beneficiaries receiving care and service at social assistance facilities increased at an annual growth of 2.2 percent between 2017 and 2020, but still there is a significant gap (ILSSA/ILO 2022).

The law encourages the development of the private sector for eldercare, and "social" enterprises are entitled to receive preferential treatment in land allocation, taxes, and loans. There are public and nonpublic residential homes for the elderly poor; public nursing homes are fully funded by the state, whereas nonpublic ones are financed by the state, charitable organizations, and fees paid by residents. Private providers are mainly located in Hanoi and the surrounding provinces. Nursing homes are mostly located in urban areas and can be afforded mainly by the wealthy (Glinskaya et al. 2022). Part of elder care is done by informal caregivers, mainly family, such as spouses and adult children (80 percent of wives care for their husbands, and 30 percent of husbands care for their wives). However, family help is rapidly declining due to urban migration by the young, decreasing fertility, and other factors (World Bank 2021b). A survey confirmed that only 22 percent of the working-age population expect to be dependent on their family for retirement, whereas 62 percent expect to depend on the state (ILO/Japan 2019).[43] Vietnam's National Action Plan for the Elderly for the Period 2012–2025 seeks to improve the quality of care for the elderly, including delivery of healthcare for those unable to take care of themselves, as well as raising private provision with government stewardship and expanding the network of facilities in geriatric medicine; no data was available on the implementation of this plan, its finances and benefits. In 2016, at the central and provincial levels there were one hundred hospitals with a geriatric department (World Bank 2021b).

Social Assistance

Noncontributory Pensions

China does not have a typical social assistance pension; instead, the basic social insurance old-age pension provided by the urban-and-rural-resident scheme (US$25 monthly) is actually a noncontributory pension fully financed by the state (see table 5.4).[44] The age for this pension is 60 for both genders, hence from five to ten years more for women than in the contributory pension. Since 2018, such pension is annually adjusted by the central government. The Fourteenth Five-Year Plan for National Aging Development and Eldercare (2021–2025) stipulates an increase in the resident old-age pension by US$15.70 (GOV 2022b), hence increasing the monthly amount to US$40.

In Cuba, there is no disaggregated data for the social assistance pension, but the average monthly social assistance benefit (including such pension) was US$6.75 in 2020. Ages for the old-age noncontributory pension are from 60 to 65 (for women and men), the same as for contributory pensions. Cuba's average social assistance benefit is about one-third of the mean contributory pension and therefore grossly insufficient to cover basic food needs. Social assistance benefits are not indexed to inflation. The average monthly social assistance benefit decreased by one-half in 2017–2021 from 153 CUP (US$6.38) to 79 CUP (US$3.29), while inflation was 1,062 percent in 2021 alone (my calculation based on ONEI 2022a).[45] The 2017 Cuban aging survey found that 20 percent of retired men and 10 percent of retired women worked because of "economic reasons," including that "money is not enough"; the most affected were Afro-Cubans—"blacks and mestizos" (at 41 percent and 43 percent, respectively). In addition, 40 percent of women aged 60 and over and 10 percent of men of that age had no income of any kind (no pensions, wages, or savings) and depended on transferred monetary support either from family members or from external remittances.[46] Finally, 70 percent of people aged 60 and over who were retired said they had deprivations because the income they received was insufficient (ONEI 2019b).[47] Cuban pensioners and social assistance beneficiaries are among the poorest groups in the population and survive because of foreign remittances, because they are working, or because of help from relatives (Espina 2008, 2020).

Vietnam has two social assistance pensions—one universal for everyone aged 80 and above who does not get a contributory pension and another means-tested pension for those poor aged from 60 to 79. These ages are higher than the 55/60 ages for contributory pensions. Because of the gradual increase in the age for contributory retirement (60 for women and 62 for men), the age for the noncontributory pension should be 67 by 2030 (ILO, n.d.). The average monthly social assistance pension in Vietnam was US$12.50 in 2019 (see table 5.4). Other social assistance benefits are based on a "norm" that is periodically (but not annually) adjusted according to socioeconomic development (thus it is discretionary). It was adjusted in 2007, 2010, 2013–2021, and 2022, and in the last year the monthly benefit was set at 360,000 dong, which is equal to US$15.60 and represented 64.7 percent of GDP per capita (ILSSA/ILO 2022). The World Bank (2021b) estimates that the ratio of Vietnam's contributory pension to the noncontributory pension is 18:1 (but based on the figures in table 5.4, it is 15:1).[48]

Poverty in Vietnamese households has decreased steadily among the elderly as they have benefited from contributory and noncontributory pensions as well as from other social assistance programs (World Bank 2021b). Around 33.5 percent of people aged 65 and above received a pension in 2016 (based on the household survey), out of which 18 percent received a contributory pension and 16 percent received a noncontributory pension.[49] In contrast, all those aged 80 and above received a noncontributory pension, therefore there should not be a coverage gap in this age group, but "this does not appear to be the case in practice," because the level of the noncontributory pension is very low (Kidd et al. 2019, ix–x).[50] Neither the latest household survey taken in 2020 nor the statistical yearbook of 2021 provides poverty rates by age group, which would have helped to clarify this controversy (GSO 2021a, 2022b).

Summary concerning Benefit Sufficiency

Pensions

Ages of retirement in China and Vietnam are five years lower in each gender than in Cuba and require fifteen and ten less years of contributions, respectively. Ages in the two Asian countries are low compared with other countries at the same development level, and even compared with some countries at a lower level of development; Cuba's ages are also low because of accelerated aging. Cuba's legal RR is the highest among the three countries, but its gross effective RR is the lowest of the three, below the 45 percent minimum set by the ILO, and it is shrinking. Comparisons of China's and Vietnam's RR are difficult because the former is an aggregate while the latter disaggregates by gender. Additionally, RR are diverse according to schemes, they discriminate against Vietnam's private sector, and there are divergent estimates and sources; but both Asian countries' RR appear to be high by international standards. In 2020, Cuba's mean monthly pension was 3.8 percent the Chinese average urban employee's pension and 9.5 percent the Vietnamese pension.

Average pensions in both China and Vietnam are above the poverty line; Cuba's is well below that line. Cuban pensioners and social assistance beneficiaries are among the poorest groups in the population; poverty increased during the crisis of the 1990s, later during the structural economic reforms (2007–2018), and finally, in 2019–2024 as a result of the economic crisis. The three countries have minimum pensions; in China and Vietnam, they are above the poverty line, whereas in Cuba they don't cover basic food needs. China and Vietnam annually adjust contributory pensions, the former based on wages and CPI and the latter in practice based on wage growth. Conversely, Cuba lacks a legally mandated annual adjustment mechanism and the government does it discretionally. Adjusted pensions in the two Asian countries have in-

TABLE 5.9: Degree of Benefit Sufficiency in the Three Countries, 2020–2021

Indicators	China	Cuba	Vietnam
Contributory pensions			
Effective gross replacement rate (%)	48.5 (1)	36.9 (3)	63/64 (1)
Average monthly contributory pension (US$)	486 (1)	18 (3)	193 (2)
Indexing of pensions	Yes (1)	No (3)	Yes (1)
Pensions above poverty line	Yes (1)	No (3)	Yes (1)
Healthcare			
Physicians (per 10,000 inhabitants)	2.0 (3)	8.6 (2)	8.8 (1)
Hospital beds (per 10,000 inhabitants)	5.5 (1)	3.0 (2)	2.8 (3)
Infant mortality rate (per 1,000 born alive)	5.6 (2)	5.0 (1)	13.9 (3)
Maternal mortality rate (per 100,000 births)	17.8 (1)	176.6 (3)	46.0 (2)
Causes of death (NCD % of total)	89 (1)	83 (2)	81 (3)
Covid-19 excess mortality	17.8 (1)	163 (3)	46.0 (2)
Changes in 6 indicators in 2008–2019[a]	5 (1)	6 (3)	4 (2)
Eldercare (population 65+ per bed)	23.2 (1)	146.5 (2)	778 (3)
Social assistance			
Average/mean assistance pension (US$)	25 (1)	7 (3)	12.50 (2)
Total score[b]	16	33	26
Average ranking in 13 indicators[b]	1.23 (1)	2.54 (3)	2.00 (2)

Source: My own elaboration based on analysis in the text.

Notes: [a] China ranked first in five and second in one; Cuba ranked third in six; Vietnam ranked second in four, first in one, and n.a. in one.

[b] The lower the number the better.

creased significantly, whereas Cuba's average real pensions have declined dramatically. For comparable data on four contributory pensions indicators see table 5.9.

Healthcare

Many features of the health system cannot be quantified to allow a comparison; even qualitative appraisals are difficult because of differences among the three countries. China has the most diverse package of benefits, while Cuba's and Vietnam's are more uniform; there is a movement toward universalism in China. Curative medicine tends to predominate over preventive medicine and primary care, but there are efforts in the two Asian countries to reverse the situation. Hospital centralism is a common characteristic of the three countries, as well as overcrowding. In China and Vietnam, there are reimbursements for services (individual accounts in China), as well as public and private facilities, but none in Cuba, where all is financed by the state budget (though still insufficient). The three countries have family doctor programs; Cuba was the pioneer and the one with the most expansion, but the program is in disarray because one-half of the family doctors are exported and there is a lack of medicine and other inputs at the family-doctor offices. Cuba conducted the only survey on self-perception, which shows that most users ranked health services as mediocre, bad, or very bad, with the negative evaluation increasing with users' age. Comparable data is compiled on eight input and output healthcare indicators in table 5.9.

Social Assistance

China's urban resident pension (similar to the social assistance pension) was 3.5 times Cuba's average social assistance benefit, whereas Vietnam's noncontributory pension was 1.8 times Cuba's benefit. Due to a substantially higher coverage of the elderly by the social assistance pension (see table 5.3) and a higher benefit amount, China and Vietnam have notably reduced poverty, contrary to Cuba. However, the ages for Cuba's social assistance pension are the same as those required for the contributory pension, whereas in China, the required age for women is from five to ten years more and in Vietnam ages in the two types of social assistance pensions are substantially higher. Cuba's social assistance average benefit decreased by half in 2017–2021 amid hyperinflation in the last two years, and it is grossly insufficient to cover essential food needs. In 2021, Vietnam's average social assistance pension was equal to 64 percent of GDP per capita, whereas Cuba's average social assistance benefit was 1.9 percent of GDP per capita.

The ranking of the three countries by thirteen indicators related to benefit sufficiency is laid out in table 5.9. In seven indicators, the higher the number the better the situation; the opposite is true in four indicators: physicians, hospital beds, causes of death (NCD), and eldercare beds. In two indicators (indexing of pensions and pensions above the poverty line), "yes" is assigned rank 1 in China and Vietnam and "no" is ranked 3 in Cuba. The average scores of the thirteen indicators are China the lowest with sixteen (best), followed by Vietnam with twenty-six, and Cuba lagging behind with thirty-three (twice the China score). Average ranking is the same: China first and best (1.23), Vietnam second (2.00), and Cuba third and worst (2.54).

SOCIAL SOLIDARITY AND GENDER EQUITY

The principle of social solidarity implies solidarity among generations (for instance, contributory pensions require that the younger generation contributes to finance the older generation), as well as among income groups (transfers from the higher to the lower). Factors favorable to solidarity are state subsidies to the lowest income groups, to the disadvantaged (e.g., poor ethnic groups or regions), and to finance social assistance. Conversely, factors against solidarity include low coverage of the labor force and of the total population; inequalities in benefits or financing based on income, regions, or ethnic groups; and separate schemes with better entitlement conditions than the general system. Gender equity posits that women receive equal treatment as men; gender inequalities are generated by the labor market (lower participation of women, lower salary for the same task, unremunerated care to raise children or to care for the sick or the elderly) and also by the system itself—for instance, in private pension systems with individual accounts, mortality tables differentiated by sex result in lower pensions for women.

Social Solidarity

In China, solidarity is negatively affected in the pension system because of several things: various schemes based on labor relations with an employer, location, or income (diverse benefits and financing); the urban-employee scheme has individual accounts on health but not the urban-and-rural-resident scheme since 2020; the military has separate pension and healthcare schemes with better entitlement conditions and benefits than the urban-employee scheme, and even more so than the resident scheme; large and highly profitable enterprises provide additional occupational pension plans.[51] In addition, significant disparities exist between the urban-employee and the urban-and-rural-resident pension programs—as well as within the latter between the urban and the rural insured on contributions, entitlements, and benefits. There are also financial inequalities between rural and urban areas and among regions, provinces, and municipalities, as some of them generate surpluses and others suffer deficits. Insured individual accounts both in pension and in health prevent transfers between generations, income groups, and genders (although they are attenuated by basic social insurance).

The health system is fragmented across several schemes (flexible employees and migrant workers are assigned to the UEBMI or the URRBMI based on a relationship or not with an employer) and also by the role of the market (e.g., private facilities and services, copayments, etc.). Several health programs also have diverse benefits and financing, and additional differences exist by regions, provinces, and wealth. Zhao and He (2021) have shown significant inequalities in coverage according to income, education, employment, and migrant status in the urban-employee scheme but considerably less in the urban-and-rural-resident scheme, which explains the faster expansion of coverage through the latter vis-à-vis the former. Cousins (2021) has also noted disparities in the urban-employee pension scheme among provinces concerning coverage, contributions, average pensions, and indexing. Based on a national representative sample in 2018, Giles et al. (2021) documented sharp variations between the urban-employee program and the urban-and-rural-resident program and, within the latter, between the urban and the rural insured with consideration to contributions, retirement ages, early retirement, work after retirement, benefits, RR, wealth, and major source of support among the retired. X. Huang's (2020) theory of "stratified expansion" of healthcare analyzes healthcare inequalities by regions, social groups, employment sectors, levels of development, industrialization, and urbanization, which all lead to stratification along three divides: urban-rural, labor market insiders and outsiders, and public versus private sectors.

Here are some concrete examples of inequalities in China. The large majority of rural residents contribute to the minimum flat sum and receive the lowest state subsidy; hence their pensions are very low. Urban residents aged 50 and above have a retirement rate more than twice the rate of rural residents (63.4 and 31.1 percent, respectively). The average basic pension in the urban-employee scheme in 2020 was about twenty times the average basic pension in the resident scheme. RR in the urban-employee scheme are from 45.5 to 48.9 percent, whereas in the urban-and-rural-resident program, they are from 10.7 to 15.3 percent (rural residents are at the lower end of the range); RR in the urban-employee scheme are at the same level as some OECD countries and cover living expenses, while RR for rural residents do not even cover essential needs. Of urban residents, 82.8 percent rely on pensions and only 12.4 percent need child support, whereas 20.8 percent of rural residents rely on pensions and 67.6 percent need child support. After retirement, most urban employees get consultant or self-employed jobs, but rural residents continue working until they are forced to retire because of illness (Giles et al. 2021).

Moreover, health expenditure per capita in the urban-employee scheme in 2020 was almost five times the per capita rate in the resident scheme; the urban-employee scheme per capita health expenses in Beijing, which has the most expensive facilities, was 2.5 times that in Guangdong (where there is a higher working-age population); and the number of hospital beds per 1,000 inhabitants in cities is twice as high as in rural areas ("China's Social Security System," 2021; X. Huang 2020). Thresholds, caps, and reimbursement rates are much better in the urban-employee scheme than in the resident scheme. In the former scheme, retirees who have paid in for ten to thirty years according to local regulations do not have to pay any more (Y. Wang 2022), whereas in the resident scheme, they have to keep paying. Finally, out-of-pocket expenses in the resident scheme are higher than in the urban-employee scheme, partly because of copayments or shallower benefit packages that, in turn, result in higher rates of catastrophic spending (Fang et al. 2019). Therefore, the overall pension and healthcare systems contribute to disparities, which go contrary to the current government priority of more balanced growth and equity among different regions, urban and rural areas, and households (Lu et al. 2019).

Improvements in the last decade have alleviated some of the inequalities (B. He 2022) but not eradicated all of them. There are several improvements: the very high population coverage of the health system (who then have reduced out-of-pocket expenses); the integration of the civil servant and public employee scheme into the urban-employee scheme (also the relative standardization of their norms); state and local government subsidies granted to the urban-and-rural-resident scheme; targeted social assistance that has substantially reduced poverty; the establishment of the "central adjustment fund" in 2017 paid by provincial basic pension funds and used to adjust the pension insurance funds of various provinces (there are transfers from the wealthiest to the poorest provinces);[52] "provincial and city adjustment funds" for basic medical insurance schemes also operate similar transfers that improve social solidarity; and transfers from the economically developed coastal areas in the east to less developed areas in the middle and western areas, but still the overall level of services in those deprived areas is not comparable with those in the developed regions.[53] Qi Tao (2022), an official from the MOHRSS, reported in 2022 that the pooling of pension funds among regions in 2020 (transfers of surplus to regions with deficit) had not been enough to assure that retirees in the less developed regions will get their pensions sufficiently and in a timely manner ("China Starts Nationwide Pooling," 2022).

Cai and Yue (2020) conclude that social security transfers have a positive effect on reducing inequality in China, but of all components of such transfers the formal-sector pensions (urban-employee scheme) have the most inequality impact, whereas dibao and rural pensions have equalizing effects on income distribution.[54] Y. Wang (2022) adds that individual accounts harm solidarity. In 2021, President Xi announced a program to reduce the wealth gap, pressing the wealthiest to share with the lowest-income citizens; the goal is to improve income distribution, make healthcare less costly and more evenly available outside of big cities, and cover all workers by basic pension insurance. If this is achieved, a bigger middle class would develop and its purchasing power would launch a new stage of economic growth. This plan requires careful balance so as to avoid both alienating and harming the wealthy and causing a decline in economic growth, hence the call on the wealthiest to share their wealth with the less fortunate; there are appeals for a property tax and a more progressive income tax (Buckley et al. 2021).

In Cuba, no social security scheme has been privatized or "marketized" (there are no individual accounts), except partially in eldercare. Social security is public and mostly state-financed such that it supports social solidarity by facilitating transfers among generations, genders, and income groups (except for the armed forces and internal security personnel). Differences between urban and rural areas as well as among provinces are not as wide as in China because of a much smaller territory, a more unified and centralized social security system, and early revolutionary policy geared toward the reduction of inequality. Still, there are disparities in health indicators among the fifteen provinces (particularly between the wealthiest and most urbanized and the poorest and most rural); for instance, in 2020 the range in those provinces between the lowest and the highest maternal mortality rate was 15.6 and 78.1 per 100,000 (a 62.5 percentage point gap), and said disparities have been increasing in the last decade (ONEI 2021). In the same vein, the practice of giving informal "gifts" to healthcare personnel so as to get faster and more personalized treatment has become significantly more common in the last ten years, hence providing an advantage to those who have higher incomes (Acosta 2019). Finally, poverty has risen while the social assistance net has contracted, particularly affecting the elderly and Afro-Cubans.

Vietnam allows for social solidarity among income groups, generations, and genders in the pension system because it is all public and there are no individual accounts. Least benefited are the old-old, especially in rural areas, the elderly without education, and the elderly without children, as well as those in the least developed regions, ethnic minorities, and microenterprises. The last group coverage among the top 1 percent in pretax profits was 50 percent in 2016 compared with an overall average of 95 percent (ILO 2021a). As in China, during the planning era (1975–1986), household registration was introduced—the *ho khau*.[55] According to the Law on Residence 2020, as of July 1, 2022, all information related to residence will be updated in the Residence Database, which is connected and shared with the Citizen Database. Therefore, when removing the ho khau, citizens only need to present their citizen's card, and a competent authority will be able to look up the associated residence and identity information. Under the 2020 law, when a citizen carries out the procedure for permanent residence registration, the registration authority will revoke the issued family registry or temporary residence registry, update information in the residence database in compliance with regulations of the Residence Law, and not issue a new family registry or temporary residence registry or reissue the old family registry or temporary residence registry to the citizen (Quang 2022). In 2017, the government announced that ho khau would be phased out in a few years (World Bank 2021b).

Inequalities in pension coverage among the elderly has been detected by geographic regions (extremes of 20 and 44 percent), urban and rural areas (46 and 27 percent), and income (20 percent for the poorest 5 percent versus 69 percent for the wealthiest 5 percent) (Kidd et al. 2019). In the health system, coverage remains inequitable. Enrollment rates are highest in low- and high-income groups but persistently low in the middle-income group. Even when they are enrolled, irregular collection of contributions from self-employed and informal workers generates gaps in coverage; and 40 percent of the elderly population, many of whom are poor and live in rural areas, are not covered.

The population receiving health treatment in the previous year is expanding, but still there are differences by areas, regions, quintiles, and ethnic groups. Overall access grew from 34.2 percent to 38.9 percent in 2008–2018, but in urban areas in 2018, coverage was 41.3 percent vi-à-vis 37.7 percent in rural areas. In less developed regions (Northern Midlands and Mountains Areas), coverage was 29.6 percent, and in the wealthiest region (Mekon River Delta), it was 49 percent. By income quintiles, coverage was 36.9 percent in the first (the poorest) and 41.8 percent in the fifth (the wealthiest)—a gap of five percentage points. By ethnic groups, coverage was 48.7 percent among Kho me and 17.6 percent among H'Mong.

Concerning social assistance, there are four groups that receive state health subsidies as of 2018: members of near-poor family households; multidimensional-poverty households that have a shortage of health insurance as defined in the law; members of family households doing business in agriculture, forestry, and aquaculture; and workers in the salt industry who earn an average income below standards set by the law (Decree No. 146, 2018). The wealthy use mostly central and provincial hospitals, while the poor and near poor primarily use community health centers and district hospitals, which can be partly attributed to the perception of low-quality care at the local level. In addition, the fifth quintile (the wealthiest) are more likely to frequently use certain health services than the poor; for instance, there is a significant gap in skilled attendance rates. The SHI is fragmented with sixty-three provincial funds, and only marginal equalization is done through central reserves; therefore, redistribution effects are often regressive, from poorer to richer regions and groups (ILO 2018a). Infant mortality rates vary among regions. They are higher in the less developed Central Highlands and Northern Midlands and Mountains (24 and 22 per 1,000 respectively) and lower in the Red River Delta and the southeast regions (12 and 8.5 respectively) (World Bank 2021b).[56]

Gender Equity

The gender inequality index ranks China as the lowest with a score of 0.163 (thirty-ninth place among 189 countries), whereas Vietnam and Cuba almost double that score and are very close together at 0.296 and 0.304, respectively (sixty-fifth and sixty-seventh) (UNDP 2020). As in other countries of the world, women suffer discrimination derived from the labor market in the three countries. First, data for 2020 is available for the three countries, and women have a lower share in the labor force. Cuba's shares were 39.4 percent women and 60.6 percent men, and the distribution of employment was virtually the same (ONEI 2021).[57] China's shares of employment were 43.5 percent women and 56.5 percent men, and there was no data available on the labor force (GOV 2021b).[58] Vietnam's labor force was 47.4 percent women and 52.6 percent men (GSO 2022a). Therefore, the lowest female share was that of Cuba (39.4 percent), followed by China (43.5 percent), and the highest was in Vietnam (47.4 percent); gender gaps were 21.2, 13.1, and 5.2 percentage points, respectively. In Vietnam, women are more represented in formal jobs than men and contribute more to their pensions, which is explained by their relatively higher education at the primary and secondary levels (World Bank 2021b; GSO 2022a). In China, pension coverage of the labor force for women was 27.3 percent, whereas for men it was 59.3 percent for a gap of 32 percentage points in favor of men; conversely, in Vietnam, figures in the mandatory program were 56.1 percent (women) and 43.9 percent (men), a 12 percentage point gap in favor of women (NBSC 2021c; ILSSA/ILO 2022).[59] No data was available for Cuba. Furthermore, most women are not insured directly but, rather, are insured as dependents of husbands, fathers, sons, and brothers.

Second, women are paid a salary lower than men for the same task even when the law demands equal pay. In Vietnam, the average female wage relative to men was 86 percent in 2019 (ILSSA/ILO 2022); no data was available for the other two countries. Third, women retire earlier than men: five years earlier in all three countries and ten years earlier for blue-collar women in China. On average, Vietnamese women's contributory histories are four years shorter than those of men (Ramírez and Arza 2021).

Fourth, in all three countries, women who leave the labor force to raise their children or to take care of the sick and the elderly are not remunerated for that work and do not contribute when out of the labor force. In Cuba, 21.6 percent of women left their jobs before they completed the requirements for an old-age pension, making them ineligible for said pension (Acosta and Ángel 2020). In Vietnam, most women between age 20 and 49 do not work, citing their housework responsibilities as a cause; unpaid home care is a critical impediment, particularly among ethnic minorities (World Bank 2021b). Women dedicate a much larger share of their time to unpaid care than men: 14.5 percent and 5.5 percent, respectively (ILO 2021b).

Fifth, in addition to the market, women endure discrimination by the pension system itself. In the private pension system, mortality tables differentiated by sex are applied and—due to a higher female life expectancy—stretch the pension for a longer period than men hence reducing the amount of their pensions (the latter happens in China's individual accounts).

As a result of these five factors, women's contribution density in pensions as well as their RR and their pension level are all lower than men's. In China, a survey from the Resident Income Distribution Project found that the average monthly pension of urban workers in 2018 was 3,157 yuan for women and 3,965 yuan for men, hence women got 20.4 percent less than men. The gap was worse in the enterprise sector (–22) than in the government sector (–8) (Yake and Huizhen 2021). In Vietnam, the female average pension was 20 percent lower than the average male pension in 2016 and about the same percentage in 2019 (ILO/Japan 2019; ILO 2021b). There was a gap of 10 percentage points against women compared with men in 2019 regarding the number of new pensioners (Ramírez and Arza 2021). In addition, women take early lump sums, which are 12.8 times what they receive from pensions (only 5.8 times men); survivor pensions for women require that their husbands have contributed fifteen years and female benefits are relatively low (Ramírez and Arza 2021). No data on this indicator could be found for Cuba. Public pensions often allow gender transfers from men to women but this could not be tested in the three countries. However, individual accounts for pensions in China should result in a lower fund accumulation for women, due to the five factors explained (Mesa-Lago 2021b).

China provides data, which is not available from Cuba and made only partially available by Vietnam, on female participation in all social insurance schemes in the period 2010–2018 (all are women's percentages in total coverage in 2018, men's percentages are the difference based on a total of 100 percent): 44.6 percent in urban-employee basic pension (increasing trend); 46.4 percent in urban-and-rural-resident basic pension scheme (higher in urban than in rural); 47.2 percent in urban-employee basic medical insurance; 43.8 percent in urban-and-rural-resident basic medical insurance; 43.7 percent in maternity insurance (stagnant); 42.5 percent in unemployment insurance; 39.0 percent in work injury; 44.8 percent in urban residents receiving minimum subsistence allowance; and 42.0 percent in rural residents receiving minimum subsistence allowance. In all these figures, women have a smaller participation than men, oscillating from 5.6 to 22 percentage points, although an increasing trend has occurred during this period (save maternity insurance, which stagnated). In addition, the proportion of enterprises that have implemented the special provision of labor protection for female employees rose from 54.9 percent in 2010 to a peak of 72.6 percent in 2014 and decreased to 68.4 percent in 2018 (NBSC 2020b).

In Vietnam, the proportion of women in productive ages (from 15 to 49 years) amply surpasses that of men (Ramírez and Arza 2021). The ILO (2021b) estimates coverage on sickness insurance relative to the labor force in 2019 as 31.3 percent of women and 22.1 percent of men; these figures refer to cash benefits and not to medical/hospital coverage that was almost 89 percent of the total population in 2020 (see table 5.3). Concerning healthcare insurance and free healthcare certificates, male patients are 95 percent and female patients are 94.7 percent—virtually the same (GSO 2020). In addition, women have higher healthcare treatment (42.3 percent) than men (34.7 percent). Although indicators are not the same and there is more data in China than in Vietnam, it appears that women have a higher participation in Vietnam. Because of the lack of Cuban figures and the difference in indicators, this variable could not be used to compare the three countries.

China pays maternity leave at 100 percent of the average salary in the previous year, and Vietnam does the same with the average salary in the previous six months (a period of previous employment and/or contributions is required in the three countries), whereas Cuba pays 60 percent based on the average salary in the previous year. Granted periods for leave are different: China pays urban employees for from fourteen to twenty-three weeks depending on the province; Cuba for eighteen weeks; and Vietnam for twenty-four weeks (the longest) and also pays a birth grant (US.SSA-ISSA 2019). The self-employed are excluded in

TABLE 5.10: Degree of Social Solidarity and Gender Equity among the Three Countries, 2020–2021

Indicators	China	Cuba	Vietnam
Social Solidarity			
Number of separate social security schemes	17 (3)	11 (2)	9 (1)
Coverage of the labor force on pensions (%)	45 (2)	68 (1)	28 (3)
Existence of individual accounts	Yes (3)	No (1)	No (1)
Central adjustment fund among regions/ provinces	Yes (1)	No (2)	No[a] (2)
Subtotal score	9	6	7
Average ranking of four indicators	2.25	1.50	1.79
Gender Equity			
Gender inequality index (coefficient)	0.168 (1)	0.304 (3)	0.296 (2)
Proportion of the labor force that is female (%)	43.5 (2)	39.4 (3)	47.4 (1)
Weeks paid for maternity leave	14–23[b] (2)	18 (2)	24 (1)
% of previous year[c] average salary paid	100 (1)	60 (3)	100 (1)
Female advantages over men in calculating RR	No (2)	No (2)	Yes (1)
Subtotal score	8	13	6
Average ranking of five indicators	1.60	2.68	1.20
Total score[d]	17	19	13
Average ranking of nine indicators[d]	1.89	2.11	1.44

Source: My own elaboration based on analysis in the text.

Notes: [a] Marginal adjustments that do not significantly correct inequalities; however, London (2023) argues that there is substantial redistribution of wealth across provinces.

[b] Depending on regions.

[c] Six months in Vietnam.

[d] The lower the number the better.

Cuba and Vietnam, whereas those who are not affiliated with the two main basic schemes or who are not poor are also excluded in China.

Vietnam grants women several advantages over men: the period of contribution to set the basic RR is five years less for women; the maximum RR of 75 percent also requires five years less; and in the first fifteen years of contribution, women have an accrual rate of 0.75 percent more than men. As a result, women can get a higher replacement rate than men (Ramírez and Arza 2021)—these advantages are not granted in China or Cuba. None of the three countries compensates women for the time they are out of the labor force raising children, as is the case in some Latin American countries such as Chile and Uruguay. In Vietnam, however, the maternity system pays a lump sum benefit equal to two times the basic salary of the insured mother for childbirth or adoption of a child less than 6 months old.

Summary concerning Solidarity and Gender Equity

The above information on the three countries is not steadily comparative in most indicators, making it difficult to elaborate a table with the most meaningful variables. For a preliminary attempt at such a comparison see table 5.10, but it requires further research on key indicators such as, for instance (concerning social solidarity), on disparity among regions/provinces for average pensions, and (related to gender equality), on women's participation in the labor force, average wages, and pensions levels by gender.

The indicators are positive with regards to improved social solidarity and gender equity as follows: a lower number of separate schemes; a higher labor force coverage; the nonexistence of individual accounts, because they impede transfers among generations, income groups, and genders; the existence of a central adjustment mechanism, because it transfers surplus from wealthy regions and provinces to those with a deficit; a lower gender inequality index (maximum inequality = 1.00); a higher participation of women in the labor force; a larger number of weeks paid for maternity leave and a higher percentage on salary. The ranking in social solidarity places Cuba first (1.50), Vietnam second (1.79), and China third (2.25), whereas the ranking on gender equity places Vietnam first (1.20), China second (1.60), and Cuba third (2.68). The overall average ranking is best in Vietnam (1.44), followed by China (1.89), and last Cuba (2.11).

ADMINISTRATIVE EFFICIENCY, REASONABLE COSTS, AND TRIPARTITE PARTICIPATION

An efficient administration saves resources that could be assigned to improve benefits or finances, and the ILO recommends tripartite administration (by workers, employers, and the government) in social security administration in order to improve participation by stakeholders. In this section I analyzes (a) decentralization in the administration; (b) managerial costs; (c) centralized collection of contributions; (d) digital information system and unified ID; (e) government mechanism to buy medicines and other inputs; (f) law compliance/enforcement; (g) fraud, corruption, and bribery; (h) targeting errors in social assistance; (i) length of hospital stay; (j) bed occupancy rate; (k) other indicators of hospital efficiency; (l) tripartite administration; and (m) plans to further modernize the administration. It has been difficult to find concrete comparative statistics to measure administrative efficiency and, in particular, costs, hence the evaluation herein is largely qualitative. I identify key missing data for future research and make a preliminary effort at the end of the section to evaluate administrative performance and rank the three countries accordingly. There have been some problems in getting hard indicators. In three programs, efficiency is defined and measured differently. There is a lack of or poor international comparative statistics on administrative efficiency, and there are discrepancies on the interpretation of some indicators, such as average length of hospital stay and hospital bed occupancy rate.

Decentralization

The more decentralized the social security system the better, as those at the lower levels can play a role and participate in decisions. Centralized systems usually concentrate power and decisions and vertically impose them on the bottom.

The Chinese administration is the most decentralized. At the national level, the Ministry of Human Resources and Social Security (MOHRSS) Department of Pensions and Rural Social Insurance exercises general supervision over the pension programs, including management of the individual accounts. The National Health Commission (which integrated functions of the MOHRSS, the National Health and Family Planning Commission, and the Ministry of Civil Affairs) supervises medical providers. The National Healthcare Security Administration exercises general guidance to local governments on medical insurance and sickness-maternity insurance. The Ministry of Civil Affairs is in charge of social assistance at the central level. The Ministry of Finance supervises and balances all budgets. At the subnational level, provincial governments collect the investable pension funds in each province into a provincial social security account, managed (but not the investment itself) by the National Council of Social Security Fund authorized by the State Council and under the supervision of the MOHRSS and the Ministry of Finance (Tang 2022). Local social insurance agencies manage their respective urban employee health pools (there was an announcement that the pools would be gradually integrated into a national pool but significant differences among the provinces have impeded its implementation).[60] Provincial municipal agencies also manage the pension schemes for urban-rural residents, as well as the medical insurance programs for urban employees and urban-rural residents (and the cash benefit programs)—they also contract with credited hospitals and clinics to provide medical services and pay monetary benefits.[61]

The investment of pension funds is entrusted to professional agencies (public, private, and Sino-foreign joint ventures) approved by the government, and such agencies are divided into trustee, custodian, and investment and are supervised by the People's Bank of China, the Banking and Regulatory Commission, and the Futures Commission (Tang 2022). Until 2019, and depending on the provinces, either the tax administration local agencies or the social security authorities collected contributions for all programs (the collection was unified in 2019 under the state taxation bureau); most provincial and local agencies determine the contributions. In general, the central government sets policy, which is interpreted and implemented by provincial and municipal governments, and also supervises the system; the national ministries have limited control over implementation at the local level.[62] Decentralization and the lack of an integrated approach have contributed to low compliance (Cousins 2021). It should be recalled that the second-pillar individual accounts are publicly managed, whereas the fourth-pillar commercial insurance accounts are privately administered.

Cuba's administration is the most centralized of the three countries via three national agencies. The Ministry of Labor and Social Security, through the National Institute of Social Security (INASS), manages the pension program, sickness-maternity, and work injury cash benefits, and its municipal offices handle social assistance. The Ministry of Health, through the National Health System, administers medical provision. And the National Tax Office collects contributions for pensions that are paid by the People's Bank.

Vietnam's administration of the system is the second most decentralized of the three countries. At the national level, the Ministry of Labor, War Invalids and Social Affairs (MOLISA) controls social insurance agencies, social assistance, and gender equality. It also exercises general supervision of the whole system including sickness-maternity cash benefits and unemployment insurance. Finally, it collects contributions, processes benefit payments, designs policy for the pension, health, and social assistance systems, and sets basic standards or norms.[63] At the subnational level, the provincial MOLISA departments are responsible for implementation of national policies—for instance, the identification of vulnerable households via the compilation of a list of poor and near-poor households. Provinces must ensure MOLISA minimum standards but may upgrade them when they have budget surpluses. The Vietnam Social Security (VSS) administers the pension program under the supervision of MOLISA and collects all contributions. The Ministry of Health (MOH) manages preventive, curative, rehabilitation, and reproductive health; regulates and supervises the social insurance health system; reports the system performance to the National Assembly of Vietnam; and sets prices of medical services. And the Ministry of Finance supervises the financial regime of all social insurances (US.SSA-ISSA 2019; Hoàng 2022).

There are few mechanisms for effective communication and collaboration between the MOLISA and the MOH, although some progress has been achieved (see below). The MOLISA has a network of public and private facilities with the aim of maximizing both geographical access and users' choice. Private facilities must be licensed and registered at said ministry; in 2018, out of a total 2,316 contracted facilities, 23 percent were private. A number of facilities included on the list of approved facilities have not yet met the license requisites (ILO 2018a).

Administrative Costs, Collection of Contributions, Buying Medicines, and Information System

Costs are not available in China and Cuba. Costs are impossible to estimate in Cuba as pension, healthcare, and social assistance are separate programs that are managed by diverse entities and have different financing. Furthermore, the Ministry of Public Health, responsible for healthcare, and INASS, which manages pensions, do not supply any data on administrative costs. In China's commercial insurance pillar, a mix of profit-seeking state-owned and private corporations manage the funds under state supervision (B. He 2022). Such private corporations in other countries typically charge high fees and have substantial administrative costs. In the few countries where there is the same mix as in China, competition from state-owned entities has often been able to reduce administrative costs (Mesa-Lago 2021b). So far, there is no information about this issue in China.

Vietnam is the only country that provides data on administrative costs. Operational costs as percentage of total expenditures (mandatory and voluntary insurances) decreased from 4.1 percent in 2017 to 3.1 percent in 2020 (VSS 2018, 2021). This is a key indicator that should be tabulated and published by international organizations, and they should also provide standards for reasonable costs.

Abundant evidence, particularly on pensions in Latin America, shows that state centralized collection of contribution and taxes significantly reduces costs and helps to control evasion and underdeclaration of employment and salaries (Mesa-Lago 2007). In China before 2019, and depending on the provinces, either the tax administration local agencies or the social security authorities collected contributions for all programs; since 2019, all social insurance contributions as well as all taxes have been unified and collected by the state taxation bureau, which allegedly has reduced administrative costs (GOV 2018). In Cuba, the National Tax Administration Office (ONAT) oversees collecting all contributions for social security pensions; there are no contributions to healthcare as the whole system is state provided and financed. In Vietnam, the VSS collects all contributions.

China, under the reform of the digital system, implemented a social security digital card to be used in pension, health, social assistance, and similar services; both central and local governments have positively evaluated such a card (GOV 2022a). Digital archives and databases have allowed the dissemination of identification cards according to national poverty alleviation standards (Y. Wang 2022). In August 2020, Cuba began a program for electronic payment of pension checks ("Cuba jubila," 2020). Preliminary steps have been taken to digitalize the process of granting pensions, but these steps exclude the small private sector. The digital identification card has been proposed but does not exist yet (Colina 2022a). In Vietnam, the MOLISA modernization plan until 2020 and orientations for 2030 include the application of information technology to improve social security policy and the development of a unified information system and database for issuing an integrated social security card ID that facilitates better integration of the social protection system (Decision No. 488, 2017). An evaluation in 2021 of the plan implementation reported that holders of health insurance cards had seen their benefits guaranteed and upgraded.

In China, since 2019, there has been a centralized government mechanism to buy medicines in order to negotiate and reduce prices. In Cuba, all production of medicines, vaccines, and other medical inputs are entrusted to state-owned enterprises, and the government is the only importer of medicines and other health materials, hence there is no need for bidding—but the current system is not transparent. Vietnam also has a central mechanism through national drug bidding; MOLISA and MOH negotiate for the state-public sector with firms and pharmaceutical companies, saving hundreds of billions dong.

Law Compliance and Enforcement

Enforcement of the law has been low in China, particularly with migrant workers and flexible employees because many corporations, in pursuit of increased profits, evade or underreport these employees and their salaries. If said contributions are not paid, the employees will not qualify for the social benefits (Z. Wang 2011; Y. Wang 2021). Enforcement of social insurance coverage is very relaxed in many areas, and in practice many workers are not covered (Cousins 2021). Compliance decreased from 20 percent to 16 percent from 1995 to 2019, and enterprises barely face penalties. Local governments, anxious to attract investment, turn a blind eye to nonpayment by employers. A reform was planned to increase the effectiveness of the collection of contributions, but it faced strong resistance from employers. The government reduced the employer's contribution to pensions from 20 percent to 16 percent, alleging that high contributions were an incentive to evade, but in practice, it was a political concession granted to employers, yet legally questionable. Since then, the state has virtually "withdrawn from its responsibility to collect contributions," and the courts are now in charge of civil liability of employers for compensation to cover the damage inflicted on the insured; but "the primary claims under public law are replaced by secondary claims under private law" (Y. Wang 2021, 123). In 2019 there were 290.8 million migrant workers and 41.5 million flexible employees (in the "gig" economy), with an increasing trend; combined, they accounted to 42.9 percent of the labor force (based on MOHRSS 2020d), and the majority are not effectively covered by basic social insurance in pensions and health. Many migrant workers have labored for fifteen years or more, but there is no record of their contributions; if they work with several employers, they are legally able to transfer their contributions and benefits (portability), but if they do not have enough accumulated, either they can reach an agreement with previous employers or make up the shortfall themselves depending on local regulations of the resident scheme. Most flexible employees lack labor contracts—they may pay contributions in multiple locations but still not meet the fifteen-year requirement in one specific district; furthermore, their employers may have treated them as service providers instead of employees and refused to pay due contributions.

During the 2007–2008 global financial crisis, the central government allowed struggling companies to postpone social insurance contributions for up to sixth months, and during the 2020–2021 pandemic, another six-month holiday was approved. Due to these various factors, it is said that only a fraction of contributions has been made in the last two decades, placing pressure on the social insurance funds' financial sustainability, which is also aggravated by accelerated aging ("China's Social Security System," 2021).[64] The government now acknowledges the need to reform social insurance but has been unable to force employers to comply with their legal obligations. Since January 1, 2019, all collections (taxes, social security contributions, etc.) are unified under the State Tax Organization (B. He 2022).

In Cuba, ONAT oversees enforcing of the law on mandatory coverage and compliance. In the predominant state sector, the contribution for pensions is withheld from the salary of the employee; in the minority non-state sector, annual ONAT reports pinpoint frequent violations of social insurance payments, and yet forcing the growing number of self-employed to pay is difficult because of the obstacles posed by verifying incomes, compounded by the economic crisis. An official report in 2014, based on a sample of 30,000 self-employed workers, revealed that 95 percent underdeclared their income; furthermore, ONAT lacks the resources to verify self-employed workers' income and their deductible expenses (Mesa-Lago et al. 2018).

In Vietnam, compliance was low given that many employers delay payments, especially in the private sector and from the micro and small enterprises (Huong et al. 2013; Jackson and Peter 2015; ILO 2021a).[65] According to Olivier (2022), compliance among private enterprises was 50 percent. However, late payments of contributions to pensions fell markedly in 2011–2019; the ratio of debt to revenue decreased from 7.2 percent to 3.9 percent (ILSSA/ILO 2022).[66] Inspections carried out in 2017 to verify payment of health and unemployment social insurance among 10,055 employers found a debt of US$122 million for evasion and late payments (N. Dao 2018). Decree No. 12 of 2022 introduced tougher sanctions to execute the social security law and to penalize its violators. The sanctions included charging employers several fines, such as from US$33 to US$2,507 for each violation of the law, from 12 to 15 percent of the amount of contributions due on the wages of the employees not registered, and due contributions inflated by two times the VSS fund return of the previous year; suspending the certification of occupational health in the enterprise from one to three months; forcing payment of the full contribution with interest for evasion, late payment, underestimation, or misappropriation of payments; and refunding to the employee the sum of the due benefit jeopardized by nonpayment of contributions.

Fraud, Corruption, and Bribery

In China, fraud and corruption in medical care have been reported (Leung and Xu 2015; Gao 2017; Gongcheng and Scholz 2019; Y. Wang 2021). Hospital physicians forge fictitious patients and provide unnecessary tests for them (crimes can be done also by a gang of malicious patients), which substantially increase premiums and cause fatalities. Losses caused by medical fraud and abuse account for about 10 percent of healthcare system expenditures; inspections of 197,000 medical institutions in 2018 detected that nearly one-third had healthcare violations

(Zhang et al. 2020). There is evidence of the existence of gangs committing crimes that require the assistance of hospital insiders to access subscribers' medical insurance cards and use them to forge tests and/or resell drugs; gangs also falsify medical records or collude with pharmacies to obtain prescription drugs. Insured people made informal payments ("red pockets") to hospitals and employees so as to receive prompt care and avoid long waits, and local governments in some western and northeast provinces tolerate or even encourage duplicate enrollment (in urban-employee and resident schemes) to help meet financial needs (X. Huang 2020). Under President Xi, there has been a fight against corruption to correct the improper use of social assistance funds. Legislation to combat medical fraud has not yet been enacted; the government primarily uses administrative measures to prevent or punish fraudulent behavior (Li et al. 2022).

On the other hand, there are policies to deal with fraud and corruption in healthcare. In 2020, the National Health Commission issued policy to deal with fraudulent activities, such as "red pockets" (NHC of the PRC 2020). Special campaigns against fraudulently obtaining medical security funds include inspections of 627,000 medical institutions by medical insurance departments, which detected 401,000 institutions that had violated laws and regulations; 26,100 people were sanctioned, and a total of 22,310 million yuan were recovered. The National Health Insurance Administration organized sixty-one unannounced inspection teams to carry out on-site inspections in various provinces in ninety-one designated medical institutions, fifty-six medical insurance agencies, and forty commercial insurance companies that undertake medical insurance and critical illness insurance for urban and rural residents. A total of 540 million yuan of funds were found related to violated laws and regulations (NHSA 2021). Still, the proportions of people sanctioned and funds recovered are tiny: 26,000 persons comprise virtually zero percent of 1,400 million people, and 22,850 million yuan are 0.1 percent of a GDP of US$14,195,716 million.

In Cuba, official data is not available on fraud and corruption (Espina 2022b) as in China and Vietnam. In practice, however, the theft of medicines and other medical supplies from hospitals, clinics, warehouses, and pharmacies for sale in the black market is widespread; many state employees run medical practices under the table, charging in hard currency while using public equipment and facilities (Molina 2005; Díaz-Briquets and Pérez-López 2006; Hirschfeld 2007a, 2007b). During the last two decades, there has been a virtual universalization of the practice of bribery (kickbacks or gifts) by patients to doctors and healthcare personnel in order to get faster access and more personalized care, medicines, and so forth (Acosta 2019; Hernández 2019).

In Vietnam, corruption is widespread. In 2016, an anti-corruption campaign began with dozens of health officials (including generals) arrested for crimes; it culminated in mid-2022 when the minister of health Nguyen Thanh Long, the mayor of Hanoi Chu Ngoc Anh, and the deputy science minister Pham Cong Tac were expelled from the communist party and submitted to criminal charges for overpricing the Covid-19 test kits supplied to hospitals (to the tune of US$172 million), bribing health officials, and causing big losses and much damage to the pandemic campaign ("Vietnam Minister," 2022). Earlier that year, the Hanoi former chairman was arrested for abusing his position and power in a fraud related to water pollution ("Hanoi Former Chairman," 2022). In addition, political connections facilitate access to superior services (London 2023).

Targeting Errors in Granting Social Assistance

In China, targeting errors have been detected, including families mistakenly excluded from or included in dibao, particularly in rural areas. The percentage of people who reported a "need" for hospital admission but did not receive inpatient care decreased from 29.6 percent in 2003 to 17.1 percent in 2013, whereas the average number of outpatient visits per capita rose from 1.7 in 2003 to 5.9 in 2017 (Fang et al. 2019). A new program, Creating Archives and Identification Cards, collects detailed information on families in rural areas, identifies those in need, finds out the causes of poverty, and delivers assistance on a case-by-case basis (Y. Wang 2022).

In Cuba, official data is not available on potential errors of exclusion or inclusion (Espina 2022b). But errors should be small, in theory, because of strict state control in awarding the aid—for instance, checking annually if the recipient has one of the defined situations of vulnerability and lack of family capable of help, an essential requisite to grant the benefits (Consejo de Ministros 2021). Nevertheless, there are reports of bureaucratic denial of assistance by social workers to persons suffering severe sickness or disabilities (CiberCuba 2021).

In Vietnam, targeting errors occur. For instance, half of the households identified in the poorest decile of the population in 2012 were excluded and 40 percent of people over 80 do not receive the benefit because of flaws in the "Poor List." These flaws include difficulty for the most vulnerable in obtaining documents, weak mechanisms of complaints and grievances, and inadequately trained staff (Kidd et al. 2016).

Concerning Hospitals

Average Length of Hospital Stays

In 2019, average length of hospital stays (ALOS, often regarded as an indicator of efficiency) was 9.5 days in China, 7.4 days in Cuba, and 6.6 days in Vietnam (NBSC 2021b; MINSAP 2021; Quang 2022). According to OECD: "[A] shorter stay reduces the cost per discharge and shifts care from inpatient care to less expensive outpatient care. Longer stays can be indicative of poor-value care: inefficient hospital processes may cause delays in providing treatment; errors and poor-quality care may mean patients need further treatment or recovery time; poor care coordination may leave people stuck in hospital waiting for ongoing care to be arranged. At the same time, some people may be discharged too early, when staying in hospital longer could have improved their outcomes or reduced chances of readmission" (OECD 2017, 176). The OECD (2022a) average for ALOS in 2020 was 6.6 days; China's has remained consistently above that average (according to OECD, China's average was 9.5 days in 2020), whereas in Cuba it is also above but less, and in Vietnam it is exactly the average. Nevertheless, the OECD average refers to acute stay hospitals only, and several developing countries mix data from long-term and acute facilities. Furthermore, China is among some outliers that drive up the OECD ALOS. China's systems tend to be hospital-centric and combine weak supply and poor quality of long-term-care facilities and primary care.

There are several reasons for this. First, senior citizens with chronic conditions tend to remain in hospitals longer than necessary, in part because of lack of long-term-care options (nursing homes, residential homes). Second, patients may remain in hospitals longer because there is inadequate follow-up care at primary or ambulatory facilities, there is little confidence in the quality of lower-level facilities, and there is poor integration or coordination between hospitals and primary care. Third, the fee-for-service payment system incentivizes high complexity care at hospitals; reimbursement rates are higher for services performed and drugs prescribed in central and provincial hospitals compared to similar services at local levels (World Bank/WHO 2019; La Forgia 2022).

Vietnam's ALOS is much lower than China's, partly related to patient flow and bed management. Overcrowding compromises quality of care, physicians spend relatively little time with patients during consultations, and staff is often rushed to provide care. Due to bed sharing, both providers and patients seek early discharge in Vietnam. Also, insurance coverage is shallow, and longer stays result in higher out-of-pocket spending, another incentive for shorter stays (La Forgia 2022). In Cuba, poor bed management is a driver of ALOS, including the lack or disrepair of diagnostic equipment as well as severe scarcity of medicines and long waits for surgery that prolong the hospital stay.

Hospital Bed Occupancy Rate

The rates in 2019 were 83.6 percent in China (91.2 percent in public hospitals and 61.4 percent in non-public hospitals), declining to 72.5 percent in 2020; 77.6 percent in Cuba in 2019, decreasing to 65.2 percent in 2020; and 129 percent in Vietnam in 2020—the rate may go up to 170 percent, among the highest in the world (NBSC 2021b; MINSAP 2021; Quang 2022; Statista 2020).[67] There is no agreement about the "optimal" occupancy rate: the National Institute for Health and Care Excellence (NICE 2018) suggests a maximum of 85 percent, WHO recommends 80 percent, and the OECD average was 76 percent in 2019. Based on these three indicators, Vietnam is well above, with 129 percent; China, at 72.5 percent in 2020, would be below the WHO figure and match the OECD average, but a public hospital rate of 90 percent would be above all recommendations; Cuba, with 65 percent, would be well below all the recommendations. High occupancy rates are driven by inappropriate admissions, unnecessarily long ALOS, poor patient flow, poor bed management, and distorted incentives. Hospitals are usually the first point of entry into the healthcare system for most care seekers in China and Vietnam (increasingly so in Cuba). Dysfunctional referral systems cause many patients to bypass lower-level facilities, resulting in the hospital being the first point of contact for an illness episode (La Forgia 2022).

Inappropriate demand is also an issue. For example, in a study of inappropriate hospital stays in Vietnam, 30 percent of inpatient days were for conditions that could technically and cost-effectively have been treated on an ambulatory basis (MOH 2007). The same also applies to China. It is important to note that hospital beds per 1,000 population are decreasing in nearly all high- and middle-income countries. China is an exception: in 2013, China had more beds per 1,000 population than Canada, Spain, the United Kingdom, and the United States (OECD 2022a). Cuba has the lowest occupancy rate, and it is declining; many hospital beds are not actually operational (hospitals are closed or under repair), thus the actual rate should be even lower, and the only plausible reason is a lack of effective access because of the deterioration of the healthcare system (Mesa-Lago and Díaz-Briquets 2021).

Other Indicators of Hospital Efficiency

In China, profit-driven hospitals deliver inappropriate and less-cost-effective services that waste scarce national resources. Although the government has tried many pilot programs to reform its public hospital system and to control its rising expenditure since 2012, most of these programs have not yielded significantly positive results because they are piecemeal remedies. A model of systemic reform of public hospitals in China (Sanming) shows evidence of substantially reduced medical costs without sacrificed medical quantity and quality of services (Hongqiao et al. 2017).

Cuban hospitals are all state-owned and operated based on central plan norms, so they are not driven by profit. Despite the lack of indicators (particularly costs), however, there is ample evidence of their inefficiency. In addition, there are significant wasted resources in their allocating priority to further reduce infant mortality (which is already quite low) and to training physicians for export despite the decrease of professional medical services purchased abroad (Mesa-Lago and Díaz-Briquets 2021).

In Vietnam, the cost of treatment increases at higher levels of the health service delivery system. Factors causing such increased cost are numerous: provider payment mechanisms that do not incentivize efficient use of resources;[68] an overreliance on hospital-centered service delivery at the central and provincial levels (the health service delivery system is hospital-centric, which is both expensive and not well-suited to the management of chronic conditions and noncommunicable diseases); inefficiencies in hospital investment decisions, policies, and practices that result in excessive spending on pharmaceuticals in addition to weaknesses in monitoring and accountability mechanisms (Quang 2022). In 2016, almost one-half of all outpatient visits in Vietnam took place in a hospital, and this share has been rising steadily over time even as overuse of hospital care has long been recognized as a health system problem, given that primary care clinics are less expensive. In 2018, outpatient visits were concentrated in state hospitals (50.9 percent and increasing since 2008), followed by private health facilities (27.9 percent and declining) and commune health centers (15.9 percent and decreasing); the remaining 5.3 percent were in regional policlinics, traditional medical practitioners, and others (GSO 2020). A large share of the total health spending in Vietnam (73 percent) occurs at hospitals.[69]

Tripartite Representation in the Administration

The ILO recommends tripartite administration of social security. In China and Vietnam's decentralized systems, the central government delineates broad guiding principles for reform (indicative rather than mandatory), and local governments are encouraged to experiment with diverse solutions according to their unique circumstances, taking responsibility in management and decision-making. In China, the social insurance law mandates "social insurance regulatory committees, consisting of representatives of the employers . . . the insured, . . . trade unions, experts, etc.," to analyze income and expenditures; management and investment operations of social insurance funds; advice and suggestions offered on social insurance; and supervision to be implemented. In addition, social insurance agencies must periodically report their income and expenditures, their management, and their investment operations of funds to the social insurance regulatory committees; the latter may employ accounting firms to conduct an annual audit and special audits (open to the public). Finally, when said committees find problems in social insurance operations and financing, they shall offer suggestions to the relevant departments on the illegal acts of social insurance agencies and their staff members (Presidential Decree, 2010, art. 80). Although there is no direct participation in the administration, it is obvious that workers, insured persons, and employers have powers of supervision and oversight of social insurance funds. Since 2012, participation in social organizations has increased; village committees play a significant role in selecting dibao beneficiaries.[70]

Cuba lacks effective worker participation in the management, monitoring, and evaluation of social security. Furthermore, most enterprises are owned and operated by the state, and until mid-2001, the private enterprises and cooperatives lacked legal recognition; hence there is also no representation of employers in the administration. Provincial organizations of "peoples' power" (largely controlled by the central government) oversee health administration at that level, but the ministry is the director ("rector") and is methodologically in charge. In turn, local organizations play a role in vaccination and the verification of social assistance beneficiaries' income for means-testing (ONEI 2021). The state monopoly bans private, cooperative, and individual medicine practice.

In Vietnam, the General Confederation of Labor, the Chamber of Commerce and Industry (employers), and cooperatives have representation in the Social Insurance Board. The confederation, together with the MOLISA, presides over a program that annually supervises the implementation of social insurance legislation and policies and also makes recommendations to enact and modify social insurance laws and policies (Hoàng 2022). Trade unions' and employers' representatives can investigate firm enrollment in social insurance; twice a year employers must report to their employees the amount of contribution paid, while local social insurance agencies must also report once a year (Castel and Pick 2018). Complaints about social insurance and grievances on social security issues can be presented by employees and employers to agencies or organizations that review previous decisions or actions when there are grounds to believe that such decisions violate the law on social insurance and infringe their lawful rights and interests (National Assembly of Vietnam. 2006. Social Insurance Law No. 71, art. 118).[71] Nevertheless, healthcare plans and legislation are generally designed from a top-down perspective without adequate consultation with diverse representation from regions and groups of the population; and mechanisms for addressing grievances are inadequate (World Bank 2021b).

Administrative Modernization Plans and Their Evaluation

Concerning the elderly, China's Fourteenth Five-Year Plan for National Aging and Development and Eldercare (2021–2025) and Vision for 2035 has goals to improve administrative efficiency in healthcare, including aging-appropriate levels of medical institutions and processes for elder doctor care, both aiming to provide nearer medical facilities for the elderly (GOV 2022b). Similar plans are not implemented in other programs.

Cuba does not yet have a plan for modernization or for improvement of the social security administration. In 2018, the government elaborated a National Plan of Economic and Social Development to 2030. A decree enacted in 2021 stipulated the organization of a group including the minister of labor and social security to implement that plan, but there is no mention of social security (Decreto Presidencial 2021). However, the decree section on human development, equity, and social justice briefly mentions two goals: "improvement of healthcare services" and "coverage and sustainability of social security." There is a program of decent work and, within it, a project on coverage and sustainability of social security, which apparently includes administrative issues, but such a program is not available (Colina 2022a). In the 2022 Inter-American Conference on Social Security (Mexico), the director of Cuba's INASS presented a paper on that program, but it is also not available.

Vietnam has the most comprehensive vision for modernization of the social security administration that has been fully evaluated, and it includes the MOLISA modernization plan until 2020 and orientations for 2030 that seek to digitalize the system and introduce ID cards; simplify administrative procedures, including registration and payments to beneficiaries; increase the effectiveness and efficiency of state management; and promote online public services on social security (Decision No. 488, 2017; Decision No. 708, 2017; ILO 2018a). Highlights of the evaluation

TABLE 5.11: Degree of Administrative Performance in the Three Countries, 2019–2021

Indicators	China	Cuba	Vietnam
Decentralization	Most (1)	Least (3)	Middle (2)
Managerial cost (% of total expenses)	No data (2)	No data (2)	3.1 (1)
Centralized collection of contributions/ taxes	Yes (1)	Yes (1)	Yes (1)
Digital information system and unified ID card	Yes (1)	No (3)	Partly (2)
Central state mechanism to buy medicines	Yes (1)	Not needed (1)	Yes (1)
Law compliance/enforcement[a]	Poor (2)	Poor (2)	Poor (2)
Fraud, corruption, bribery[a]	Yes (2)	Yes (2)	Yes (2)
Targeting errors (inclusion/exclusion)[a]	Yes (2)	Yes (2)	Yes (2)
Length of hospital stay (days)[b]	9.5 (3)	7.4 (2)	6.6 (1)
Bed occupancy rate[b]	83.6[c] (1)	65.2 (2)	129 (3)
Tripartite administration	Yes (1)	No (3)	Yes (1)
Comprehensive administrative modernization plan	Middle (2)	No (3)	Best (1)
Total score	19	26	19
Average ranking of 12 indicators[d]	1.58 (1)	2.17 (3)	1.58 (1)

Source: My own elaboration based on analysis in the text.

Notes: [a] More quantitative data is needed for a proper ranking.

[b] Different interpretations about this indicator make ranking tentative; international standards and a more unified consensus on how to read the indicator are needed.

[c] In the private sector, it is 91 percent, and in the public sector, it is 62 percent; the former is too high and the latter is too low.

[d] Total score divided by 12.

of the fulfillment of such a plan in 2021 were that, after six years of implementing the revised SHI Law, health coverage rose from 71.3 percent to 91 percent in 2016–2021, with 100 percent coverage of the poor, elderly, and other vulnerable groups. The quality of medical services has significantly improved, particularly at the grassroots level, which has helped to reduce overcrowding at higher levels of care. The health insurance policy enhances equity in healthcare among social groups, and the health insurance fund, although overspent in 2016 and 2017, had a surplus by the end of 2018, which is an important point for calculating the adjustment of health insurance premiums and the price of medical services toward more adequate calculation. The evaluation identified several challenges: participation in health insurance was not universal, as 10 percent of the population was not covered; pending issues in law compliance remained; the quality of medical treatment was still low, especially at the grassroots level and in mountainous, remote, and isolated areas because of the conditions of the facilities, the equipment, and limited staff capacity; and there was overcapacity of the healthcare system at the central level.

Summary concerning Administrative Efficiency, Costs, and Participation

The evaluation of administration efficiency, costs, and tripartite participation does not provide enough quantitative information to elaborate a precise ranking; nevertheless, a qualitative order can be achieved based on the key issues analyzed. There is a summary of a dozen features related to the administration of social security in table 5.11, elaborating a preliminary ranking of the three countries, but most of the indicators lack figures and when figures are present they are not always certain or they have different interpretations that obstruct a proper ranking. More research is needed to develop proper indicators.

Some indicators are straightforward: decentralization, the centralized collection of contributions, the existence of a digital database and unified digital ID, a central state mechanism to buy medicines (in Cuba there is none, but it is not necessarily due to state production and direct importing), tripartite administration with the participation of stakeholders, and the most comprehensive administrative modernization plan. Other indicators are much more complex. Problems of law enforcement and compliance are found in all three countries (most detailed in China) but without concrete data. Poor compliance is concentrated in the private sector (95 percent of the self-employed underdeclare income in Cuba, and 50 percent of microenterprises do not comply in Vietnam). The trend appears to be increasing in China and Cuba but decreasing in Vietnam, mainly because of recent legislation that imposes tough sanctions on violators, an example for the other two countries to follow. Because of these problems, the same rank (2) was given to the three countries on compliance.

Hospital length of stay has been measured in the table based on the OECD average of 6.6 in 2020 (a shorter average usually reduces the cost of stay, whereas a larger average increases such cost). China has been consistently above that average and had 9.5 in 2020 (and increasing), while Cuba was above the OECD average but still lower than China, and Vietnam was on par with the average. Causes that drive up the average in China (preference for hospital facilities instead of primary care, which has lower standards and a lack of adequate long-term care) and push down the average in Vietnam (bed sharing moves providers and patients to seek early discharge) do not dispute the average itself, and the same is true about Cuba's relatively high average (broken equipment, lack of medication, long wait for surgery). As a result, the following rankings were assigned: Vietnam 1, Cuba 2, and China 3. The ranking of the bed occupancy rate, based on the suggestions of NICE and WHO and the average of the OECD, indicate that China is below the first two and matches the third, but public hospitals are well above all; Vietnam's 129 percent is obviously too high (because of bed sharing), and Cuba's 65 percent is too low and declining. As in the case for ALOS, explanations about the occupancy rates do not contest the figures, hence the ranking was China first, Cuba second, and Vietnam third.

Targeting errors of inclusion and exclusion are officially reported in China (a declining trend) and Vietnam, but not in Cuba, although they should be small because of very strict government regulations and checks on social assistance beneficiaries. Yet there is evidence of bureaucratic denial of assistance by social workers to persons suffering severe sickness or disabilities; hence, the same rank (2) was given to the three countries (as in law enforcement). There are reports of fraud and corruption in the three countries, as well as the practice of "red pockets" in China and "bribes" in Cuba (growing in use); only China had data on the magnitude of the problem (medical fraud causes 10 percent loss in health expenditures while inspections detected that one-third of institutions had health violations). No legislation has been enacted to fight these problems in the three countries, although a tough campaign against corruption is going on in Vietnam and policies and actions are being taken in China. So, the fact that there is detailed information in China that is not available in the other two countries should not penalize China. As in the cases of law enforcement and fraud, it was decided to rank the countries alike (2). This analysis makes evident the urgent need for more quantitative comparative data on the last two indicators, and a more consensual interpretation, along with international standards, to properly judge hospital length of stay and bed occupancy rates. It was impossible to rank other indicators of hospital inefficiency.

The average ranking of the twelve indicators is that China and Vietnam tied in first place (1.58), and Cuba came third (2.17), with 0.59 more points than the other two countries. Because of the problems explained, a small variation in the scores assigned to the indicators could have changed these results, stressing further the importance of developing more quantifiable and meaningful indicators.

FINANCIAL AND ACTUARIAL SUSTAINABILITY

The principle of financial sustainability is fundamental to social security because, without it, all other principles cannot be preserved. This principle is at the core of the second and third hypotheses in this book. The second hypothesis is that Cuba developed social security much earlier, faster, and more expansively than it could financially support, hence making social security unsustainable in the long run, especially with the country's poor economic performance. Conversely, China and Vietnam developed social security gradually, and it is supported by much more successful economic performance and is therefore more financially sustainable.

The third hypothesis is that accelerated aging has had a strong adverse effect on the financial sustainability of the Cuban social security system and is beginning to have an impact in China but not yet in Vietnam. Cuba's social security system was established much earlier than in China and Vietnam, was developed faster and in a more expansive manner, but lacked strong economic performance in contrast to China and Vietnam. The aim here is to test the financial sustainability of the social security system and the impact of aging in the three countries.

China and Vietnam have higher percentages of wage contributions on payroll and much lower social security costs relative to GDP than Cuba, hence their systems generate a surplus and are more financially sustainable in the long run.[72] Economic growth has been high in the two Asian countries: in 2020, even under the worst effects of Covid, Vietnam's economy grew by 2.9 percent and China's economy grew by 2.3 percent, whereas Cuba's economy decreased by 10.9 percent. Each country's economic model played a key role in these outcomes (see chapter 3); whereas Covid-19 resulted in more excess mortality in Cuba than in the other two countries, and Cuba was shut down for almost two years, which badly affected tourism, a major source of foreign hard currency. Furthermore, the US embargo on Cuba was strengthened and the economic crisis in Venezuela forced a cut in substantial aid to Cuba. All these circumstances generated Cuba's worst economic crisis since the 1990s.

Another influential factor for Cuba is aging—Cuba is the oldest country out of the three, and an older population generates higher pension and healthcare costs, which negatively affects financial sustainability. Aging is accelerating in China and presenting a threat to future

Table 5.12: Insured Person and Employer Social Security Contributory Rates (%) by Country and Program, 2019–2021

Programs	China	Cuba	Vietnam
Pensions			
Insured person	8.0[a]	5.0[b]	8.0[c]
Employer	16.0[a]	14.0[b]	14.0
Subtotal	24.0[a]	19.0[b]	22.0
Sickness-Maternity			
Cash benefits[d]			
Insured person	0.0		0.0
Employer	1.0		3.0
Subtotal	1.0		3.0
Medical benefits[e]	n.a.		
Insured person	2.0[a]		1.5
Employer	6.0[a]		3.0
Subtotal	8.0[a]		4.5
Work injury (average)			
Insured person	0.0		0.0
Employer	0.75		0.5
Subtotal	0.75		0.5
Unemployment		No	
Insured person	1.0[f]		1.0
Employer	2.0[f]		1.0
Subtotal	3.0[f]		2.0

Programs	China	Cuba	Vietnam
Total (all programs)			
Insured person	11.0	5.0	10.5
Employer	25.75	14.0	21.5
Subtotal	36.75	19.0	32.0

Source: My own elaboration based on legislation of the countries; also in Cuba, Colina (2021b).

Notes: [a] This is the urban-employee scheme only. The urban-and-rural-resident scheme and the self-employed scheme are described in the text.

[b] Salaried employees only. Contributions of other groups are described in the text.

[c] The self-employed contribution is described in the text.

[d] In Cuba, out of the 14 percent employer contribution for pensions, 12.5 percent goes to pensions and 1.5 percent to sickness-maternity cash benefits; work injury is the employer's responsibility.

[e] In Cuba, this is fully financed by the state.

[f] Since 2019, the central government has encouraged provinces to reduce the unemployment contribution; in 2022 the total contribution was about 2 percent (1.5 percent the employer and 0.5 percent the employee).

financial sustainability. Vietnam is the youngest of the three countries and, so far, the least affected by aging.

Finally, Cuba has the lowest wage contributions as percentage of the payroll but the highest cost relative to GDP, hence the pension system has suffered a steady deficit that is financed by the state. The public health system is entirely financed by the state out of general revenue, and its cost is substantially higher than in the other two countries. As a result, the social security system is financially unsustainable unless a radical parametric or structural reform is implemented.

In this section my first aim is to show contributions over the payroll in all social security programs. Second, I evaluate the cost and sustainability of pensions, healthcare, and social assistance, Third, I summarize information from the latest available actuarial valuation. Fourth, I condense the key indicators of financial and actuarial sustainability from the section, select the most important and comparable ones in order to rank the countries, and evaluate the financial-actuarial sustainability of the three countries. Finally I aim to test the second and third hypotheses of this book.

Cost and Sustainability of Pensions

For a summary of contributions to all social security programs (total and in each program) as percentages of salary/income in the three countries, see table 5.12. Cuba's total contributions to social security amounts to 19 percent compared to 32 percent in Vietnam and 36.8 percent in China.[73] The employer pays 14.0 percent in Cuba, 21.5 percent in Vietnam, and 25.75 percent in China, whereas the respective figures for the insured's contributions are 5.0 percent, 10.5 percent, and 11.0 percent. The Chinese central government sometimes sets guidelines for local governments to decide the contribution rates on pension, maternity, and health insurances, so the exact contribution rates could diverge in different provinces and cities, especially for basic medical insurance.

For each of the three countries, I will now summarize contributions to pensions (by the employee, the employer, and the government); accumulated balance, reserves, and assets (in individual accounts only in China); investment and capital returns; the annual financial balance (surplus or deficit) as percentage of expenses and the GDP (and pension cost/GDP); the impact of aging on sustainability and government plans to improve financial sustainability and/or cope with aging. At the end there is a comparison of pension costs and financial sustainability.

Pensions in China

Contributions

The urban-employee pension scheme is financed by a 24 percent contribution, with 8 percent paid by the insured and 16 percent paid by the employer. The scheme has two pillars: PAYG, financed by employers' contributions; and fully funded individual accounts, financed by employees' contributions (individual accounts do not exist in Cuba or Vietnam).[74] In addition, the government transferred so-called state-owned capital to the urban-employee scheme for the years of work before the creation of the scheme when such employees did not make contributions; such years of work were deemed years of contribution.

The urban-and-rural-resident scheme also has two pillars: a basic flat rate pension that is totally state financed (PAYG) and individual accounts (fully funded). The individual accounts are financed by affiliates that select among twelve flat contribution scales (from 100 to 2,000 yuan annually, or US$15 to US$300, respectively). Local governments subsidize the accounts. In turn, the central government provides subsidies to all regions but at a different level. Local subsidies are related to the flat contributions but are proportionally higher than the lowest contributions (e.g., the lowest contribution of 100 yuan receives a 30 yuan subsidy, whereas contributions of 500 yuan and above receive a subsidy of 60 yuan). Subsidies are also paid by village collectives and by social and charitable organizations (GOV 2014). Despite the fact that the resident scheme is voluntary, the state-financed basic pension has been a strong incentive for affiliation and expansion of this scheme (ILO 2017).[75]

Accumulated Balance, Reserves, and Funds

Initially, China's funding of the basic social insurance pension was separated from that of the individual accounts, but local administrations did not know what to do with the individual account money, so they used it for other purposes (Leung and Xu 2015). Since 2000, both funds have been separated, but in 2011 accounts were still 89 percent behind the target and fourteen provinces had deficits; this problem continued in 2022 (Darimont 2022; Y. Wang 2022). The basic pension insurance in the urban-employee scheme (PAYG) had an accumulated balance of 6,330,000 million yuan in 2019 (US$912,000 million), whereas the individual accounts had 2,500,000 million yuan (US$362,000 million).[76] The occupational pension plans had 700,000 million yuan (US$101,000 million); therefore, 66 percent of the pension fund was in the basic insurance scheme. The total accumulated (including all programs) of 9,500,000 million yuan (US$1,375,000 million) was equivalent to 9.6 percent of GDP (Zheng 2020).[77]

The size of the fund of the recently created additional pillar of commercial insurance is difficult to assess. A government source set it at 22,120 million yuan (US$3,203 million) but that is only 0.02 percent of GDP in 2019 (CBIRC 2020b). Lastly, a national pension company has been established in Beijing with a capital of US$1,730 million, which comprises seventeen financial institutions, including China's five biggest banks, as well as insurance corporations. Its objective is to create a third (or fourth) pillar of individual accounts (Insurance Industry Association of China 2021; FIAP 2021).[78] At the end of 2023, more than 50 million accounts had been opened, but only 20 percent had contributions, averaging 2,000 yuan (US$ 275) per account ("The World's Largest Pension Fund," 2024).

All the previous figures refer to the cumulative balance amount but not to the reserve, which should be put aside in order to meet future pension liabilities. The National Social Security Fund is a reserve (although this is not exactly the definition of a traditional reserve, it is the only reference found in the literature) used to supplement and adjust social security expenditures such as the endowed basic insurance pension during the peak period of population aging. This fund consists of contributions from employers and employees, budget allocations, transfers of state-owned capital, investment income, and other funds raised by the State Council investment (NCSSF 2020). The transfer of state-owned capital was the amount that the state had to transfer to the fund in order to fill the gap in the basic old-age insurance scheme that was generated by the deemed contribution years before that scheme was created, which totaled 1,680,000 million yuan (U.S.$258,846 million) in 2021 (NCSSF 2019b).

In 2020, the China Banking and Insurance Regulatory Commission (CBIRC), together with other twelve ministries and government agencies, referred to a government target of 6,000,000 million yuan in "pension insurance liability reserves for insurance persons by 2025" but did not report what the reserve was in 2020 (CBIRC 2020b). In turn, Zheng (2019, 17) estimated the "cumulative balance" of the basic insurance pension for urban employees in 2019 as 4,260,000 million yuan (US$616,000 million) and projects 6,990,000 million yuan (US$1,012,152 million at 2019 dollars) for its peak in 2027. The 2025 target reserve, though limited to pensions, is 2.9 percent of the officially reported total social security liabilities of 206,000,000 million yuan in 2019 (NCSSF 2020), whereas the cumulative balance of 2027 (at 2019 yuan) is 3.4 percent of said liabilities. Both figures are low.

Investment and Capital Returns

The National Social Security Fund reported investment in 2021 as 2,600,000 million yuan (US$406,200 million), with an annual average real capital return of 5.6 percent in 2016–2020 that jumped to 13.4 percent in 2020 (NCSSF 2017–2021).[79] Another source gives a real annual average of 3.89 percent for the same period, with a record of 8.45 percent in 2020 (Tang 2022). Investment in the basic social insurance and individual accounts fund is in the form of bank deposits, government bonds, other fixed-income instruments, securities, trust loans, stocks, national projects and construction, and other equity instruments—the proportion of equity instruments is capped at 30 percent (Tang 2022). China's capital market is in a developing stage and lacks sufficient alternative instruments to invest the fund (Meng 2019; B. He 2022). In 2020, 90.3 percent of the fund was invested in domestic asset holdings, and only 9.7 percent was in foreign instruments (NCSSF 2021). Fund administrators have long requested permission to invest in private assets, such as equities and credit, to increase returns (Zhou 2021).

Annual Financial Balance

In 1990–2019, China's basic social insurance program (pensions and health for both urban employees and urban and rural residents) generated a steady annual surplus equivalent in 2019 to 23.7 percent of total expenses and 9.2 percent of GDP (respectively, 28.7 percent and 9.8 percent, if the work injury and unemployment schemes are added), whereas the pension fund surplus alone was 20.1 percent of total expenses and 6.4 percent of GDP (NBSC 2021b; Zheng 2020). The pension scheme represented 69 percent of total expenses in 2019 (NBSC 2020a). Due to diverse development levels among regions in China as well as different degrees of aging, there are significant differences in pension insurance balance among provinces (State Council Information Office 2022). For instance, in 2019, Heilongjiant Province had a deficit of 56,000 million yuan (US$8,832 million), whereas Beijing Province had a surplus of 103,500 million yuan (US$16,325 million). Such a large gap makes the regional adjustment fund even more important and the need to convert it into a national adjustment mechanism. In order to combat their deteriorating financial status, more provinces are asking the National Council for Social Security Fund (NCSSF) to manage their investments, aiming for improved capital returns and better-managed risk. In 2019, nineteen provinces (from only two in 2015) and 966,000 million yuan (US$152,366 million) were managed by the NCSSF. The NCSSF is developing policies to face the future by seeking higher capital returns from its investment portfolio and by further diversifying it, including professional management, overseas investments, and financial advice on new technological tools. In addition, the government is encouraging workers to take more individual responsibility to supplement public social insurance with the additional fully funded pillars, which should be better regulated (KPMG 2020).

Impact of Aging

The major threat to Chinese financial equilibrium was revealed by the 2020 census: "China is facing a unique demographic challenge that is the most urgent and severe in the world. . . . It is a long-term time bomb" (Jianzhang Liang, demographer at Peking University, cited by Wee 2021, A-12; see also Leng et al. 2021). Because of the one-child policy imposed from 1980 to 2015, which prevented 400 million births, and cultural changes regarding the cost and benefit of having children, population annual growth in the last decade was 0.53 percent, the lowest since 1961, when a national famine killed millions.[80] Additionally, the total fertility rate (average number of children born per woman of reproductive age) in 2020 was 1.3, well below the replacement rate of 2.1 children born during a woman's years of fertility. The productive-age population (from 15 to 59) shrank by 6.8 percentage points in the last decade. Moreover, the population aged 60 and above was 18.7 percent of the total population and rose 5.4 percentage points (NBSC 2020b; Wee 2021).[81] In 2021, the ratio of births per 1,000 people was the lowest since Mao Zedong founded the communist party in 1945 ("China's Birth Rate," 2022). Most of these indicators are worse in Cuba. Recall that China's retirement ages are considerably low (although a gradual increase will begin in 2025): for blue-collar female workers, retirement age is 50, ten years less than in Cuba; the average retirement age for both genders is 54. Life expectancy at the age of retirement is 14.7 years for men and from 26 to 30 years for women.

Trying to cope with this problem, in 2015 China's government first allowed couples to have two children, and in 2021 the authorization was expanded to three children. In addition, the government significantly lengthened paid maternity leave, introduced paid parental leave in some provinces, granted bonuses to mothers for second and third babies born alive (but only in some regions). The government also provided clothing and toys, increased child allowances, reduced taxes, subsidized fertility treatments and pregnancy, and built daycare centers and kindergartens.[82]

Data on the impact of these policies on increased fertility is still not available, but Cuban policies since 2014 (admittedly much more modest than China's) had the opposite effect. Other Asian developed countries that face similar problems, such as Japan and South Korea, have implemented sophisticated and expensive incentive policies without any results (Rich 2024). An immigration policy has been suggested to ameliorate the adverse effects of aging on social security (Bruni 2018), but so far Beijing is reluctant to change its anti-immigration policy (at least China does not have a negative net emigration rate, as is true for Cuba). And yet, young Chinese couples do not seem to be responding to the government policies, as children are viewed as a financial burden. Very few can afford the cost of raising an urban child from birth to eighteen years, which is US$93,410, the second highest in the world (Hawkins 2024). In addition, children no longer take care of their elderly parents. Once the demographic change starts, it will spiral exponentially: with fewer births, fewer girls grow up to have babies. Furthermore, the sex ratio in China is 105 males per 100 females due to the traditional preference for male children, although this gender attitude is ebbing (NBSC 2020b; Cave et al. 2021).

Government Plans to Improve Sustainability

China's current five-year plan (2021–2025) stipulates an increase in coverage of the basic pension insurance system to raise revenue; the plan allows work after retirement and increases the retirement age, which is strongly opposed by the people. However, in 2021, China's then-premier

Li Keqiang, in his report to the National People's Assembly, stated that "the statutory retirement age will be raised in a phased manner" (2021, 13). Such a gradual increase of the statutory retirement age is being implemented. On February 21, 2022, the State Council issued the Fourteenth Five-Year Plan for National Aging Development and Eldercare Service in 2021–2025 and Vision for 2035 (GOV 2022b). The following day, the Jiangsu Province approved a gradual increase in the retirement age, but on a voluntary basis through agreements between workers and enterprises. Workers who accept such an agreement will work more years and their pension amounts will increase, and it is expected that other provinces will follow suit ("Retirement Age to Be Progressively Raised in China," 2022).[83] Finally, in September 2024, the government approved a national plan to increase retirement ages gradually, between January 2025 and 2040: from 60 to 63 years for men, from 55 to 58 for white-collar women workers, and from 50 to 55 for blue-collar women workers. The period of contributions is also increased gradually from fifteen to twenty years. Insured workers will have the option to retire three years earlier, if they have met the twenty-year contribution period (V. Wang 2024).

Pensions in Cuba

Contributions, Capital Returns, and Financial Balance

Of the three countries, Cuba's total contribution to pensions of 19 percent is the smallest, compared with 22 percent in Vietnam and 24 percent in China (urban-employee scheme).[84] But the ratio of pension costs relative to GDP is the highest at 9 percent, about twice that of Vietnam (4.4 percent) and China (5.3 percent). There are caps on the salary for contributions in Cuba as in Vietnam (but not in China). The only revenue that the pension system receives is from contributions, as Cuba lacks a pension reserve (even a contingency one) hence there is not an accumulated balance but actually a financial deficit as will be shown later. It also lacks individual accounts and supplementary pension programs, hence there is neither investment nor capital returns. The state collects pension contributions and pays the benefits, and in healthcare the state finances everything; enterprises are directly responsible for work injury, and a fraction of the pension contribution by employers is transferred to finance sickness-maternity cash benefits.

Impact of Aging

Cuba is the oldest country among the three countries and also in Latin America. The annual population growth rate was negative in the period

2017–2020, and it is projected that, in 2035, this rate will decrease 4 percent The total fertility rate has been declining since 1978; it was 1.57 in 2019, well below the 2.1 replacement rate and the lowest in Latin America.[85] Both the active population and the labor force decreased by 7.8 percent in 2010–2020. Conversely, the population aged 60 and above rose from 17.8 percent in 2010 to 21.3 percent in 2020 and is projected to reach 32.5 percent by 2035. For many years, there has been a high net emigration rate (e.g., –2.8 percent in 2017); in 2022 there were 369,393 emigrants (tantamount to 3.3 percent of the total population), including a substantial proportion of women of reproductive age. In the period from October 2021 to April 2024, Cuba had 1.9 million inhabitants (reducing the total population by 17 percent), and 77 percent were aged 15–59 (Albizu-Campos, 2024a, 2024b). Cuba's old-age population ratio (the population 65 and above per hundred persons in the working-age population ages 20–64) is the highest of the three countries: it was 24.9 in 2019 and is projected to grow to 37.0 in 2030.[86] The same figures in China are 17.7 and 27.4; in Vietnam, 12.1 and 20. Cuba's number of pensioners will overtake the number of state-sector workers by 2025. In 2011–2013, life expectancies at the retirement age for women were 23.6 years and for men 17.3 years, but in 2020 these decreased to 22.7 for women and 16.2 for men (ONEI 2015, 2020b, 2021; ONEI-CEPDE 2020; Albizu-Campos 2021; Albizu-Campos and Díaz-Briquets 2023).

Government Plans to Cope with Aging

The Cuban government has implemented policies to cope with aging; for instance, a mother returning to work following her maternity leave but before her child is one year old is allowed to retain her maternity allowance in addition to her regular salary for the rest of the year. In 2019, seventy-six additional measures were enacted to increase the birth rate, out of which sixty-two have been implemented and monitored on a quarterly basis. Pro-fertility measures include improving access to daycare centers for children of working women (demand vastly exceeds supply, as only 18 percent of potential users are served) and assigning 50 million CUP (US$2 million) to build housing for mothers with three or more children under age 12, given that lack of adequate housing is a major reason women avoid having children (Silva 2019).

Another program, established for couples who want children but are unable to conceive, is the Service Network for Non-fertile Couples, which is available in all municipalities with technology centers in four hospitals. Despite implementation of these measures, the number of births declined by 9.7 percent in 2018–2020 (from 116,333 to 105,038), mothers' total fertility rate decreased from 44.3 to 41.5, and the gross reproduction rate (daughters per woman) shrank from 1.68 to 1.52 (MINSAP 2021). Such negative outcomes are consistent with those achieved in comparable programs in other low-fertility countries. When achievements result, they usually entail high price tags.

Pensions in Vietnam

Contributions

The pension scheme is financed by a contribution of 22 percent, in which 14 percent is paid by employers and 8 percent paid by workers. Those in the voluntary program (mainly the self-employed) pay the total contribution of 22 percent (as they lack an employer). The state matches such a contribution, although its amount is small.

Accumulated Balance, Reserves, and Funds

Vietnam has company plans that offer a supplementary pension but only cover 0.8 percent of the labor force (Quang 2022). In 2019, total assets of the supplementary pension fund were 3,350,000 million dong (US$144 million). Premium collected from supplementary pension schemes grew strongly in the period 2015 to 2019, averaging about 30 percent annually. A "reserve fund" was established for the purpose of controlling the risks of the investment activities of the social insurance fund in general. Its main component is the social insurance pension fund that is used to pay old-age, disability, and survivor pensions. By the end of 2010, said fund had a cumulative balance of 113,685,000 million dong (US$5,828 million). The amount of the fund could not be obtained for 2020.

Investment and Capital Returns

In 2019, total retirement insurance capital returns reached 703,000 million dong (US$30 million). However, the pension fund is largely concentrated on government securities, which have poor yields (World Bank 2021b).[87] It was impossible to find out what the real capital returns have been as data is confidential.

Annual Financial Balance

In 2015–2020, the pension program generated a steady surplus; in 2019, said surplus declined slightly but immediately resumed growth; and by 2020, it was tantamount to 10 percent of pension expenses and 0.38 percent of GDP (GSO 2021b). To maintain equilibrium in the fund, a 1 percent increase in contribution is planned every two years. MOHRSS gave a report on the status of the Social Insurance Fund in the fourth quarter of 2021, stating that the short-term funds were large and basically guaranteed the solvency of those programs, but while the pension fund (old-age, disability, and survivors) still had a large surplus, careful calculations were required to ensure a long-term balance, especially with changing characteristics of its size and the population's aging rate. Vietnam's cost of pension relative to GDP is 4.4 percent, the lowest of the three countries.

Impact of Aging

Aging is currently not a problem in Vietnam, but the total fertility rate has declined from 6.3 to 2.1 between 1960–2019.[88] It is projected that the percentage of the population aged 65 and over, which is currently at 7 percent, will grow to 18 percent by 2040 (from 6.3 million to 18 million).[89] The old-age dependency ratio is predicted to increase from 12.1 to 20 in 2019–2030 (UNDESA 2020; World Bank 2021b). Aging is less problematic than in the other two countries, but some measures are already being taken to cope with it.

Government Plans to Cope with Aging and Improve Sustainability

For more than twenty years Vietnam's fertility rate was equal to the replacement fertility rate; hence it maintained its population size. Resolution 21-NQ/TW of 2017 on population attempted to keep that balance by compensating nineteen provinces and cities (accounting for 36.7 percent of the total population) with a fertility rate lower than the replacement family rate, with forty-four provinces and cities (accounting for 63.3 percent of the population) with a fertility rate higher than the replacement family rate. A recent analysis based on the 2021 population census indicates that the plan is not working. Vietnam will not be able to maintain said balance by 2030 and the following years; a review of the 2017 Resolution is expected to address that problem ("Vietnam Strives to Maintain," 2023). Financial sustainability is strengthened by the plan to increase the contribution by 1 percent every two years to keep the fund in equilibrium.

Comparison of Financial Sustainability of Pensions in the Three Countries

Total social security expenses (all programs) relative to GDP in 2020 vis-à-vis total contributions on salaries in the three countries were, respectively, 8 percent and 36.8 percent in China, 6.9 percent and 32 percent in Vietnam, but 21.9 percent and 19 percent in Cuba (see figure 5.5). In addition, China and Vietnam have reserves that are invested with capital returns while Cuba has neither. Cuba's social security costs were about three times those of China and and Vietnam, whereas Cuba's

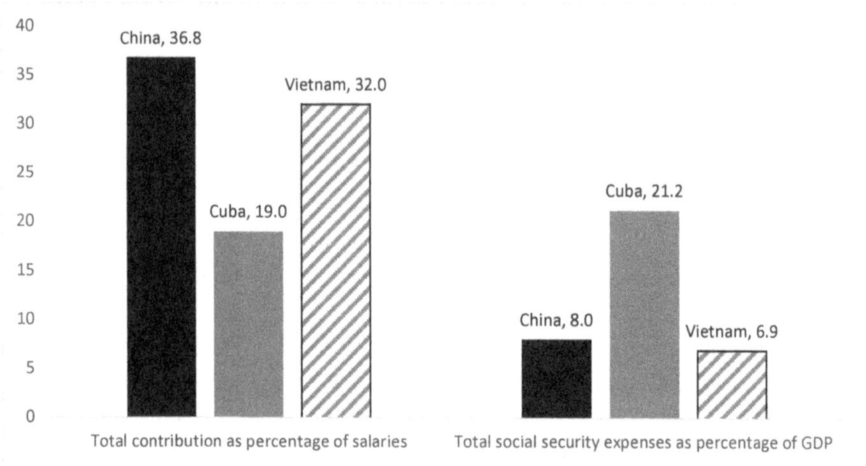

FIG. 5.5. Indicators of the Cost of Social Security in the Three Countries, circa 2019–2020. *Source*: My own elaboration based on tables 5.12 and 5.13.

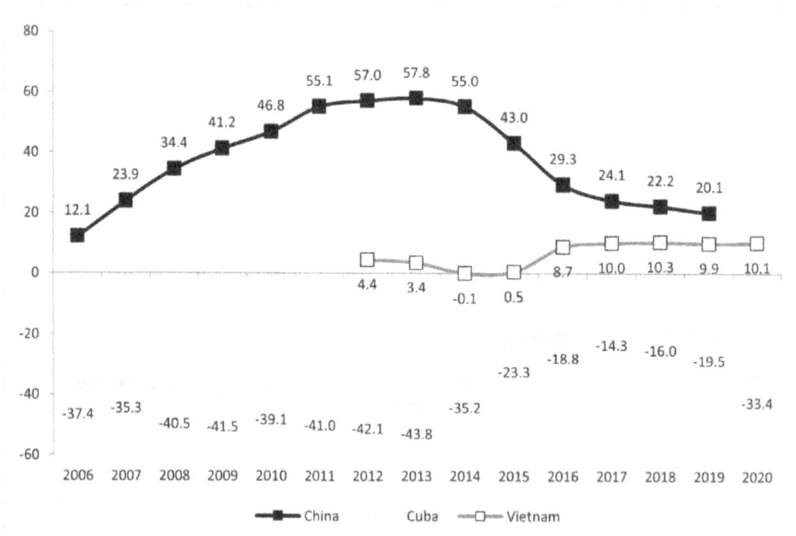

FIG. 5.6. Pension Financial Sustainability in the Three Countries, 2006–2020. *Sources*: My own elaboration based on NBSC (2021a) for China; ONEI (2007–2021) for Cuba; GSO (2017, 2018, 2019, 2021b) and VSS (2019a, 2021, 2022) for Vietnam. Another series places Vietnam's balance above China's (see text). *Note*: Balance [(revenue – expenditures) ÷ expenditures] x 100 – 1; in China, urban-employee scheme plus urban-and-rural-resident scheme.

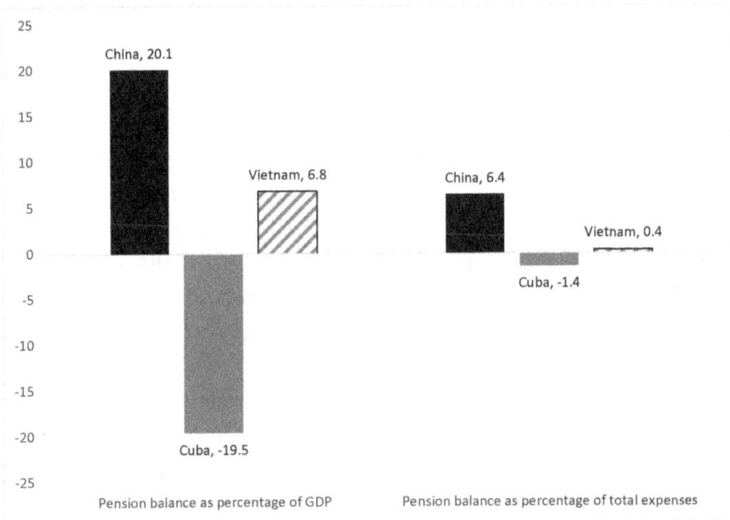

Fig. 5.7. Pension Balance as Percentage of Total Expenses and GDP in the Three Countries, circa 2020. *Source*: My own elaboration based on table 5.13.

contributions were half those of China and Vietnam. Cuba's low relationship of contribution to cost/GDP is at the core of the financial and actuarial unsustainability of its social security system.

Concerning the annual balance of the pension program in the three countries as a percentage of total pension expenses in 2006–2019, China's combined basic pension insurance in both major schemes shows a steady surplus, growing from 12 percent in 2006 to a peak of 57.8 percent in 2013, and thereafter declining to 20 percent in 2019. Conversely, Cuba shows a steady pension deficit relative to expenses: there was a worsening of said deficit from 37.4 percent in 2006 to a peak of 43.8 percent in 2013, followed by a decline to 14.3 percent in 2017 (the result of the parametric reform of 2008), to grow again to 33.4 percent in 2020 (due to accelerated aging and insufficient measures by the reform), showing an increasing trend. Data on Vietnam that combines mandatory and voluntary social insurance pension starts in 2012 and illustrates a surplus, save for a small deficit in 2014; the surplus in the last four years averaged 10.1 percent (see figure 5.6).[90]

In China, the pension balance is a surplus equal to 20.1 percent of expenses and 6.4 percent of GDP. In Vietnam, the surplus is 6.8 percent and 0.4, respectively. Conversely, in Cuba, the balance is a systematic deficit equal to 19.5 percent of expenses and 1.4 percent of GDP. See figure 5.7.

Cost and Sustainability of Healthcare

Broadly, this section is a summary of the cost and sustainability of healthcare in each of the three countries. The focus specifically is on contributions to healthcare by the employee, the employer, and the government (though there is notably none in Cuba); reimbursement of expenses in China; cost of healthcare relative to GDP; public and private sectors in China and Vietnam (only public in Cuba); and annual financial balance (revenue minus expenses) relative to GDP (except for Cuba). Finally, a comparison is made among the three countries on pension and health expenses as percentage of GDP.

Financing of China's basic health program (medical benefits) is different in the two schemes. In the urban-employee scheme, the insured pay 2 percent of their salary to the individual account, whereas employers contribute 6 percent of payroll to basic social insurance (until 2021, part of the employer's contribution was allocated to individual accounts), for a total of 8 percent. The employer also pays 1 percent for sickness-maternity cash benefits, raising the total contribution to 9 percent (see table 5.12).[91] This scheme took 28 percent of the total expenses in 2019.

In the scheme for urban and rural residents, which only has basic social insurance, residents contribute an annual flat rate, which varies across regions. In 2020, the national standard annual per capita contribution was 250 yuan (US$40), and central and local governments subsidized basic social insurance (559 yuan per capita annually, or US$87). The social insurance fund reimburses the cost of medical benefits for both groups up to 600 percent of the local average wage.[92] Any excess must be financed from private insurance or supplemental plans or paid out of pocket (said expenses and insurance premiums can be drawn by urban employees from their individual accounts). Contributions from China's flexible employees (including the self-employed) with voluntary coverage in the resident scheme depend on local conditions.[93]

China's total healthcare cost was 2.1 percent of GDP in 2019, but central and state governments have been increasing transfers to balance the system—the state share is about 30 percent of total expenses and regional subsidies vary (Y. Wang 2022). Private facilities and personnel are allowed to compete with public services and personnel; 58 percent of current health expenditures come from public sources, and 42 percent come from private sources (World Bank 2021b).[94] Between 2006 and 2019, there was a steady annual surplus in the balance of the basic medical social insurance (combining the urban-employee and the resident schemes), but it went from an increase of 37.1 percent in 2006 over 2005 to a decrease of 18.2 percent in 2019 over 2018 (NBSC 2008, 2021b). In

2020, there was a jump in expenses in the national basic medical program that resulted from Covid-19, but there was still an overall surplus of 381,400 million yuan or US$59,968 million (NHSA 2020 and 2021).

Cuba's healthcare system is all public, universal, and free, so workers and employers do not pay any contributions (save 1.5 percent for cash benefits paid by employers). There are no private facilities, unlike in China and Vietnam. All medical care is financed completely by the state out of general revenue, hence there is no balance of revenue and expenses. Cuba's health expenses relative to GDP were 11.9 percent in 2019, five times that of China and Vietnam. However, health expenses as a percentage of the state budget's current expenditures decreased from 20.5 percent in 2015 to 18.2 percent in 2019 (a reversal of a previously increasing trend), hence there are fewer fiscal resources available to finance growing costs (ONEI 2013–2020a).[95] It is remarkable that Cuba still allocates so much of its scarce resources to healthcare despite the economic crisis, but shrinking budget allocations negatively impact the sustainability of the health system, along with its inefficiency, its gratis nature, the aged population, and the scope of coverage. The poor have legal access to the public health system at no cost, but this is also true of owners of microbusiness, the self-employed, members of cooperatives, private farmers, and other employees in the non-state sector, many of whom have high incomes and could afford to pay for healthcare. Legally, citizens cannot be charged copayments, but in practice there are informal payments (bribes) charged to secure faster access and better personal care (Mesa-Lago and Díaz-Briquets 2021).

Vietnam's total contribution to the medical benefits scheme is 4.5 percent of wages (based on minimum and maximum earnings related to the minimum wage of civil servants), wherein 1.5 percent is paid by the insured and the remaining 3 percent is paid by the employer (who also pays 3 percent for sickness-maternity benefits, thus raising the total to 7.5 percent) (see table 5.12); insured persons are also charged copayments. The self-employed must pay the sum of the percentage contributions paid by employees and employers (4.5 percent), hence they may have lower access to care and related services. The healthcare scheme is public and private, 50.3 percent of current expenditures comes from public sources, and 49.7 percent comes from private sources, which is higher than in China (World Bank 2021b). The public sector is partly financed by the state, and if the insured chooses a provider other than the one assigned to them, there are minor copayments at the primary level that increase at higher levels.[96]

Curative care is funded mostly by health social insurance, whereas preventive medicine and public health are financed by the state budget.[97]

All insured persons and their dependents are assigned to a public local clinic, which provides primary care and charges a 5 percent copayment. When special treatment is needed, the doctor refers them to a hospital, and a basic 5 percent fee is also paid, which increases proportionally with more costly treatment. If the insured person goes to a clinic other than the one assigned, they pay 70 percent of all costs. For children aged 6–18, the state pays 30 percent and the parents pay 70 percent (De Miranda and Yamaoka 2014). Primary care is paid from 80 percent to 100 percent depending on the level of medical services, whereas specialized services are paid from 40 percent to 100 percent; the rest is paid out of pocket and most medicines also need to be bought by users. Theoretically, public and private employees have access to private physicians and hospitals, but costs are much higher and usually prohibitive.

Those employed by private foreign companies have better health insurance (paid by the employee and the employer), which allows access to private hospitals and covers more treatments, but a copayment is still charged. Poor households, children younger than age 6, the disabled, and students are entitled to free medical services at public hospitals, but they are subjected to long lines (near-poor households pay a reduced rate). The government pays subsidies for these groups (e.g., 3.2 percent of the minimum wage of civil servants for the near poor and 0.9 percent for students). Dependents of insured persons pay a premium depending on the number of insured persons in the household. Free insurance cards are granted to civil servants, military men, and war veterans, but also to the poor or near poor and children under 6 years of age. About 78 percent of all participants receive government subsidies for their insurance cards, 83 percent among ethnic minorities (Fifth Plenum, 2012; Huong et al. 2013).

In 2020, health expenditure per person was about 5.8 percent of total household expenditure; 10 percent of households had more than 11.7 of total expenditure; only 3 percent had more than 25 percent (GSO 2021a). The healthcare program generated surplus in 2015–2018 but had a small deficit in 2019 (0.6 percent of expenditures), though there was a surplus in 2020 equal to 0.6 percent of expenditures (GSO 2021b). In 2018, 95 percent of the provinces had deficits because revenue from contributions was low, and they demanded state transfers: 43.3 percent of total revenues (ILO 2018a).[98] For a comparison of the costs of pensions and healthcare expenses relative to GDP in the three countries, see figure 5.8.

Cost and Sustainability of Social Assistance

The aim here is to summarize cost and sustainability of social assistance in each of the countries. The focus is on social assistance expenditures as

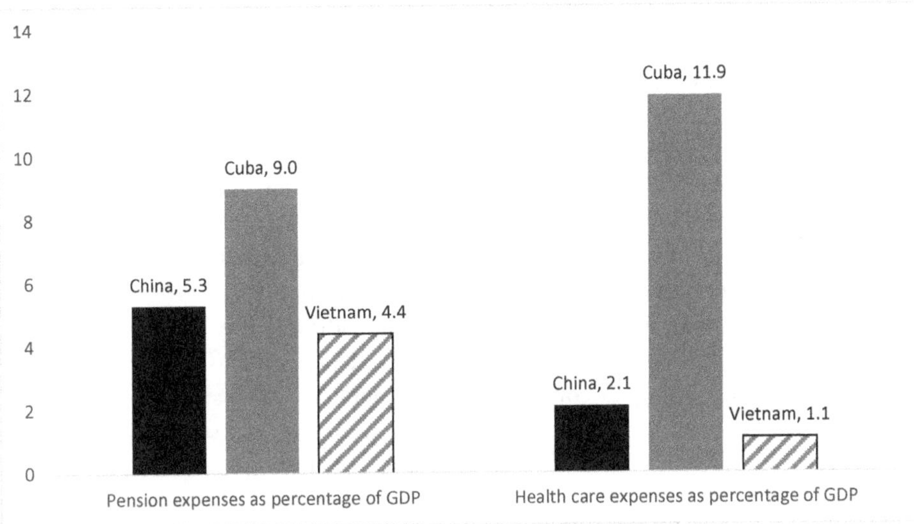

FIG. 5.8. Pension and Health Expenses as a Percentage of GDP in the Three Countries, 2019–2020. *Source*: My own elaboration based on table 5.13.

a percentage of GDP and their trends, the financing of social assistance, and comparisons of social assistance expenditure per capita and impact on the poor. Social assistance costs over GDP are similar in the three countries: 0.37 percent in China, 0.35 percent in Cuba, and 0.5 percent in Vietnam (NBSC 2021b; ONEI 2021; GSO 2021b).

One could argue that being socialist countries, these percentages are very low. Solinger compares dibao (0.25 percent of GDP) with figures in similar programs in other countries, reaching the conclusion that indeed dibao percentage is lower; she cautions that her exercise is not rigorous but "impressionistic," however (2022b, 170). A more satisfactory comparison would be that of the ILO *World Social Protection Report* (2017), which compares 133 nations' data on percentage of general social assistance relative to GDP. One-half of those nations spent from 0.0 percent to 0.5 percent, including socially developed countries ranked much higher than China (as well as Cuba and Vietnam) in the UNDP Social Development Index—for instance, Italy at 0.2 percent, Hungary and Spain at 0.3 percent, Japan at 0.4 percent, and Austria and Czech Republic at 0.5 percent.

In China, social assistance programs are financed mostly by the state (central and local governments) and by social groups and charities (central government financing of dibao has risen to 72 percent of the total and the rest comes from local governments). Urban and rural families whose per capita income is below a minimum receive tax-financed, means-tested medical assistance. It is also common that the most economically advanced areas of the East financially help poor areas in the West and Middle (GOV 2021d).

Cuba's social assistance program is financed entirely by the central government. There are a few charity organizations run by the Catholic Church that receive some state aid (such as a physician and/or a nurse), and the government sells them food at subsidized prices. In 2010–2020, social assistance expenditures decreased by 7.7 percent (ONEI 2016–2021). In 2020, Cuba's annual social assistance expenditures were 372 million CUP (US$15.5 million, equivalent to US$1.38 per capita) (ONEI 2021). All the poor are legally covered by the free public health system.

In Vietnam, several groups (some disadvantaged and some not) receive insurance cards for free medical services at public hospitals, but they are subjected to long lines), and the government also subsidizes these groups. About 78 percent of all participants receive government subsidies for their insurance cards, 83 percent among ethnic minorities (Fifth Plenum, 2012; Huong et al. 2013). In the period between 2012 and 2020, eleven provinces and municipalities had all social assistance expenditures, numbers of beneficiaries, and monthly allowances above the national norm. In the same period, the budget sources (central and local) for social assistance rose by an average of 15.2 percent per annum. Social assistance expenditures climbed 234 percent in the period (compared with a decrease of 7.7 percent in Cuba) from 10,254,000 million dong (US$490 million) to 37,195,000 million dong (US$1,640 million), and economic growth tended to be "pro-poor," or more beneficial to the poor. Social assistance expenditure increased from 0.3 percent to 0.9 percent of GDP in 2012–2020 (ILSSA/ILO 2022).[99] In per capita terms, social assistance expenditure was US$17 in 2020, twelve times the per capita expenditure of Cuba.[100]

The two Asian programs cover a higher percentage of the poor than Cuba does and have been able to substantially reduce the incidence of poverty. In 2020, to confront the pandemic, China increased funding for poverty alleviation, expanded social assistance to an additional 6 million people and 8 million received temporary aid grants (Y. Wang 2022). Conversely, social assistance expenses in Cuba were stagnant in 2020, and although the number of beneficiaries rose slightly, the average assistance per beneficiary decreased by 8.5 percent (ONEI 2021).

Comparison of Actuarial Equilibrium in the Three Countries

Here I summarize the actuarial equilibrium of the three countries based on the latest available actuarial valuation and compare the ratio of active workers to one pensioner. Since 2020, China has separate funds and accounts for the five insurance programs: pensions, healthcare, work injury, unemployment, and maternity (the latter has been integrated into the basic social insurance), which is important because each fund has to be self-sufficient (transfers are not allowed among them). China's latest actuarial study of the urban employees' basic pension insurance in 2019–2050, excluding public agencies and institutions (Zheng 2019), reached the following conclusions assuming a baseline scenario (that is, no change in current conditions). The number of insured will increase until 2047 and then start to decline in 2048; before 2030 such an increasing trend would be due to expansion in coverage of the scheme, and after that year it would depend on population aging. The number of contributions will peak in 2048 and begin to decrease in 2049. The cumulative balance of the scheme in 2019 was 6,287,300 million yuan (based on MOHRSS 2020c), tantamount to 6.3 percent of GDP in that year, and it will peak in 2027 at 6,990,000 million yuan (US$1,012,152 million).[101] Said cumulative balance will become negative starting in 2028 (–118,130 million yuan) and will get significantly worse by 2050 (–11,280,000 million yuan); the latter would be equivalent to 11.3 percent of the GDP in 2019 (99,086,510 million) (NBSC 2021b), though considerably less than the GDP of 2050.[102] The fund will be exhausted by 2035, and it is expected that the central government will provide subsidies to cover part of the gap, whereas provincial governments will be responsible for any remaining shortages.

Actually, the central government has already been subsidizing the fund—otherwise, it would have shown a deficit much earlier (Cousins 2021). The actuarial study considered several different scenarios of reform to the current system—for example, changes in the current enterprise contribution and a five-year raise in the age of retirement from its current ages, 60 (male) and 50–55 (female), to 65 and 60, respectively—but the conclusion was that, "in the end, the system [revenue] will not cover expenditure, and the accumulated balance would be used up [depleted]" (Zheng 2019, 3). There were no actuarial reports available on the urban-employee basic health scheme, the urban-and-rural-resident basic social insurance pension and health schemes, or the military scheme.

Cuba's latest international actuarial study of the main pension scheme was conducted by the ILO (1999) with a *financial* (not actuarial) projection of deficit in 2020 at 1,350 million CUP (1.3 percent of GDP in that year), with a contribution rate of 19.8 percent (which is 0.8 percentage points higher than the current contribution). The ILO study was completed before the parametric pension reform of 2008, which raised retirement ages by five years for both genders and imposed contributions on workers; hence its projections are not adequate. A private study by an actuary conducted in 1994, projected for the old-age pension scheme (excluding the cost of disability and survivors' pensions) an actuarial deficit in the period 1995–2010 as the percentage on the payroll to keep the scheme in equilibrium for each year of the projection. The assumption in the study was that the age of retirement would be increased to 65 (five more years than the current age for women), and the projected contribution rate in 2010 was 63 percent of the payroll, 44 percentage points higher than the 2020 rate of 19 percent (Donate-Armada 1994). Another private projection (not actuarial) for the 1991–2050 period (baseline) estimated that the deficit would grow from 8 percent to 12 percent of GDP in the last twenty-five years of the projection; the combined value of the deficits in 1999–2050 was 36,000 million pesos (in 1991 prices), tantamount to more than twice the 1991 GDP (Cuevas and Pérez 1999).[103]

Two reform alternatives were proposed in Cuba. The first was an increase in the retirement age to 65 for both genders and an increase of the contribution to 25 percent; the second was the same increase in age but an increase only to 20 percent in the contribution, combined with a decrease in the replacement rate by 17 percentage points. Both alternatives reduced but did not eliminate the deficit; in addition, in the second alternative, the pension amount was cut considerably. Finally, although the 2008 reform increased the age of male retirement to 65, the other changes were not introduced, and macroeconomic conditions badly deteriorated, particularly in 2019–2024. The most recent financial projection (not actuarial) for the period 2019–2040 projects that the pension system will systematically generate a financial deficit that reaches 11,127 million CUP (US$463 million) in 2040, tantamount to 10.3 percent of the GDP in 2019 (Mesa-Lago et al. 2022). No further actuarial valuation has been done (or at least published) since 1999—twenty-three years since the ILO study.

In Vietnam, the National Assembly, the Council of Social Insurance, and the government supervise and conduct annual inspections and audits over social insurances. The Council of Social Insurance projects that, without reform, the reserves will be exhausted by 2037, whereas the World Bank estimates 2042.[104] The Bank also projects that the pension system will have a deficit tantamount to 2.5–3.0 percent of GDP in 2043–2050, the cost of the implicit debt without reform would be tantamount to 188 percent of GDP in 2020 and 174 percent of GDP in 2080 (World Bank 2021b; see also A. Minh 2018; Allianz and Hermes 2020; Quy 2020). The ILO (2018b) conducted an actuarial report on the pension program in 2016 with data until the end of December 2015, updated in 2020 with 2019 data, but I did not have access to it. However, the ILO later reported (2019) the financial-actuarial unsustainability of the system. According to Quang (2022), the updated actuarial report concluded that the financial position of the fund is sound in the short term: future increases in contributions are likely to be required over the medium and long term if no changes are made to the benefit structure; reserves will continue to grow in the short term; investment policy should focus on investing the fund prudently; beneficiary coverage, short-term costs, and long-term sustainability are very sensitive to withdrawal patterns and the likelihood of reentry and meeting the vesting period at retirement; long-term sustainability of the scheme will worsen if the rate of withdrawals goes down and more individuals qualify for pensions in the future; even if contributor coverage expands, beneficiary coverage will remain low as long as individuals keep withdrawing early and do not have enough years vested. The World Bank (2021b) has published projections on the impact of aging on pensions, healthcare, and social assistance in the period 2021–2050 based on three scenarios, for a total aggregate oscillating from 1.4 percent to 4.6 percent of GDP in additional expenses. It also projects that the labor force will start to decline in 2035, hence revenue will decrease too, whereas the growing number of pensioners will cause a negative cash flow between 2028 and 2034 in the pension scheme.

The ratio of active insured workers per one pensioner is a useful indicator to assess the long-term actuarial sustainability of pensions. In 2019, in China, it was 3.0 (combining the two major schemes); in Cuba, 2.7; and in Vietnam, 4.9 in the mandatory program—almost twice that of Cuba (partly explained by Vietnam's much younger population and pension program).[105] Due to accelerated aging, China's ratio decreased from 5.5 in 2015 to 3.0 in 2019 (NBSC 2021b, 2021c), whereas the Cuban ratio declined from 2.8 to 2.7 in the same period and is projected to decrease to 1.3 in 2040 (Mesa-Lago et al. 2022). Vietnam's ratio shrank from 5.3 in 2011 to 4.9 in 2019.[106] These ratios exclude Cuba's more generous pension scheme for the armed forces, interior ministry, and communist party personnel; in 1995, the cost of their pensions was equal to the total deficit accumulated by the general pension system that covers two-thirds of the labor force (Donate-Armada 1995). Ages of retirement are too low in China and Vietnam, hence there is ample opportunity to increase them; they are higher in Cuba but still need to be raised in tandem with the high life expectancy at retirement age.

Cuba and Vietnam do not adjust the pension formula based on a demographic factor (life expectancy of the population), and in Cuba, the retirement span exceeds life expectancy of women. In China, the in-

Table 5.13: Indicators of Financial and Actuarial Sustainability in the Three Countries, 2019–2021

Indicators	China	Cuba	Vietnam
Total contribution (%) on salaries (all insurances)	36.75	19.0	32.0
Total social security expenses (% of GDP)[a]	8.0	21.2	6.9
Pensions	5.3	9.0	4.4
Healthcare	2.1	11.9	1.7[b]
Social assistance	0.4	0.3	0.5
Life expectancy at age of retirement (years)			
Men	14.7[c]	16.2[d]	19.7
Women	25.5/30.5[c]	22.7[d]	28.5
Old-age dependency ratio			
2019	17.7	24.9	12.1
2030	27.4	37.0	20.0
Total social insurance balance (% of expenses)[e]	28.7	n.a.	4.7
Total social insurance balance (% of GDP)	9.8	n.a	0.3
Pension balance (% of pension expenses)	20.1	–19.5[f]	6.8
Pension balance (% of GDP)	6.4	–1.4[g]	0.4
Assets individual accounts fund (US$ million)	362,000	0	0
Assets individual accounts fund (% of GDP)	2.5	0	0
Ratio active workers per one pensioner	3.0[h]	2.7[i]	4.9
Projected pension cumulative balance (US$ million)[j]	1,012,152	–11,127	140,000
Projected pension cumulative balance (% of GDP 2019)	6.5	–10.3	0.2
Year that pension reserves will be exhausted	2035	No reserves	2037–2042[i]

Sources: My own elaboration based on NBSC (2021b, 2021c), Zheng (2020), Zhou (2021), B. He (2022) for China; ONEI (2020a, 2021), Mesa-Lago, Moreno, and Kay (2022) for Cuba; GSO (2021b), ILO (2019), Quy (2020), World Bank (2021b), Ramírez and Arza (2021) for Vietnam; other sources ILO (2017), OECD (2018, 2019b), UNDESA (2020).

◀ *Notes:* [a] Includes work injury and unemployment compensation, but expenses are small and they are not disaggregated, except in China.

[b] The figure of 1.7 percent in 2019 is only for contributory health insurance expenditure; the World Bank estimated the cost of healthcare (including capital expenditures) at 5.9 percent of GDP.

[c] Men at age 60, women at age 55 (white-collar) and 50 (blue-collar) in 2020.

[d] Life expectancies peaked in 2012 and then declined; data in the table is an estimate for 2020.

[e] Revenue minus expenses.

[f] In 2020 the deficit increased to −33.4 percent.

[g] In 2020 increased to −2.4 percent.

[h] Contributors to retirees combining the urban-employee and urban-and-rural-resident schemes.

[i] Year depends on scenario and reforms; if all reforms are introduced, reserves are not exhausted until 2071 (ILO) or 2080 (World Bank).

[j] China in 2027, Cuba in 2040, Vietnam in 2030.

dividual account pension formula has been changed, as the pension is based on savings in the account and paid for several months, determined according to the retirement age and the average life expectancy of the population at the time. Before, it was paid for 122 months: now, for those who retire at age 50, it is 195 months; for those who retire at age 55, it is 170 months; and for those who retire at age 60, it is 139 months (GOV 2005). It has been noted that the span of payment for that pension is shorter than life expectancy at age of retirement. In Vietnam, life expectancy at the age of retirement is high when compared with other countries of the region; that of males is above Japan and China, but among females the highest is China's, followed by Vietnam's (World Bank 2021b).[107] The ILO (2018b) projects that life expectancy at retirement age will rise in 2015–2060: from 18.9 to 20.9 years for men and from 21.6 to 25 years for women.

Summary concerning Financial and Actuarial Sustainability

In this section first I summarize all indicators of financial-actuarial sustainability analyzed here. Then, I select the most relevant indicators to rank the three countries on their degree of sustainability. Finally, I summarize in a comparative manner the major findings and rank the three countries. For a summary of the nineteen indicators that could be quantified on financial-actuarial sustainabily in the three countries in 2019–2021, see table 5.13.

For a selection of the nine most important indicators (out of twenty

Table 5.14: Degree of Financial-Actuarial Sustainability in the Three Countries

Indicators	China	Cuba	Vietnam
Total contribution (%) on salaries (all insurances)	36.8 (1)	19.0 (3)	32.0 (2)
Total social security expenses (% of GDP)	8.0 (2)	21.2 (3)	6.9 (1)
Old-age dependency ratio projection 2030	17.7 (2)	24.9 (3)	12.1 (1)
Male life expectancy at retirement (years)	14.7 (1)	16.2 (2)	19.7 (3)
Pension balance (% of GDP)	6.4 (1)	–1.4 (3)	0.4 (2)
Assets individual accounts (% of GDP)	2.5 (1)	0.0 (2)	0.0 (2)
Ratio active workers per one pensioner	3.0 (2)	2.7 (3)	4.9 (1)
Projected pension cumulative balance (% of GDP 2019)[a]	6.5 (1)	–10.3 (3)	0.2 (2)
Year that pension reserves will be exhausted	2035 (2)	No reserves (3)	2037–2042 (1)[b]
Total scores	13	25	15
Total average ranking of nine indicators[c]	1.44 (1)	2.78 (3)	1.67 (2)

Source: My own elaboration based on table 5.13.

Notes: [a] China in 2027, Cuba in 2040, Vietnam in 2030.

[b] Year depends on scenarios and reforms.

[c] The lower the number the better.

total) that are also comparable among the three countries, see table 5.14, where they are ranked accordingly. Some indicators were dropped for a variety of reasons. Cuba lacked data on the total insurance balance as percentages of expenses and GDP (only pension data was used). There was not an aggregate figure for life expectancy (China has two figures for female life expectancy), hence male life expectancy was chosen because it was unified). In the old-age dependency ratio, the projections to 2030 were selected. Some indicators were repetitive as they were given in US dollars and percentage of GDP, and the latter was used (pension balance, assets in individual accounts, and projected pension cumulative balance). In most indicators, the higher the number the better. In pension balance, a surplus follows the same rule but if a deficit (–), then the lower the better. Finally, in years the reserve is projected to be depleted, the later date is the better. Exceptions include total security expenses/GDP, old-age dependency ratio, and life expectancy, where the lower the number the better.

Scores of the nine indicators are China (13), Vietnam (15), and Cuba

(25), the latter twelve points more than China and ten points more than Vietnam, while there are only two points between China and Vietnam. Average rankings of the nine indicators are China first (1.44), Vietnam second (1.67), and Cuba third (2.78). Cuba has a difference of 1.34 points above China and 1.11 points above Vietnam, whereas the difference between the two Asian countries is only 0.23 points.

China probably has the best financial-actuarial equilibrium of the three nations but is increasingly affected by aging. It has the highest salary contributions both to total social security and to the basic pension scheme, and the urban-employee pension scheme is fully financed by such contributions, whereas the urban-and-rural-resident scheme combines contributions with subsidies from the central and local governments. China has the highest assets and reserves in the four pillars, and the individual accounts fund is equal to 2.5 percent of GDP (the other two countries do not have such accounts).

The basic social insurance pension program has steadily generated a surplus equal to 6.4 percent of GDP in 2019, the highest of the three countries. The projected pension cumulative balance is also the biggest of all three countries. The basic social insurance pension of urban employees has reserves but is projected to be exhausted in 2035 (the earliest of the three countries) and the ratio of active workers to one pensioner is 3 (the second-highest). The average return of these reserves is high by international standards, and it peaked in 2020 despite the pandemic.

Until 2015, civil servants had a separate pension scheme fully financed by the state, and probably suffering from financial and actuarial deficit, the scheme was integrated into the urban-employee basic pension insurance. The basic medical program cost is the second-highest among the three countries related to GDP but is still small, and said program has systematically generated a surplus. A negative factor is that the military has a separate military pension scheme and separate health facilities and personnel, and no data is available on financial cost/sustainability of the two programs.

Aging in China is second to Cuba but with a significant gap. In 2021, China's population grew by 0.4 per 1,000, Vietnam's grew by 0.9, whereas Cuba's decreased by 6.1. In the ranking among 235 countries-territories in the world by population growth, Vietnam was 7th, China was 195th, and Cuba was 217th (UNDP 2022). China has just increased ages of retirement by three years for both genders as well as by five years in the period of contributions.

The financial equilibrium of social insurance in Cuba is the worst of the three countries. Total salary contribution is one-half that of China and 60 percent that of Vietnam, whereas Cuban total social security cost related to GDP is about three times that of the two Asian countries. The pension program has endured a steady deficit, which was reduced in the short term by the 2008 parametric reform, but due to still laxer conditions and the most aged population of the three countries, the deficit is climbing again, reaching 33.4 percent of pension expenditures and 2.4 percent of GDP in 2020 (said deficit is financed by the state), and the ratio of workers per one pensioner is 2.7, the lowest of the three countries. Cuba's pension fund lacks a reserve (China and Vietnam have reserves, and in China individual accounts have an accumulated pension fund) and do not have company pension plans and commercial insurance (as in China). Therefore, Cuba's pension revenue is only from contributions, as the absence of investment means there are no capital returns. Cuba's universal and free healthcare system is totally financed by the state, and without data on the balance of revenues and expenses, but cost related to GDP is five times that of China and seven times that of Vietnam. State budget allocation to health is declining and, combined with the export of part of the health personnel, is leading to deteriorating access to and quality of services.

The Cuban armed forces and interior ministry personnel have their own pension scheme totally financed by the state, as well as health facilities that are also state financed, with no available data on their costs and balances. Aging in Cuba is the most advanced of the three countries, and Cuba is among the oldest countries in the world—aging is similar to that of developed countries, but Cuba's economy is lower than in most middle-income countries. Policies to confront the adverse financial effects of aging have so far had no positive effects, and there is no plan to improve the sustainability of social security.

Vietnam is in a middle position, close to China but much better than Cuba. The total social security contribution is smaller than in China but 68 percent bigger than in Cuba, whereas the total cost related to GDP is the smallest of the three countries (less than one-third that of Cuba). The pension program is financed by contributions from employers and employees, and it is the second-highest contribution in the three countries and has generated steady surpluses. To keep the fund in equilibrium, an increase of the contribution is stipulated every other year. The ratio of active workers per one pensioner is 4.9, the highest of the three countries, and projections of the year of the fund's depletion are farther in the future than in the other two countries; but the deficit would equal 2.5 percent to 3 percent of GDP in 2043–2050.

There is a social insurance pension fund, apparently concentrated in government securities, though it was impossible to find out what the real capital returns have been, and there are no individual pension accounts as in China, but voluntary supplementary pension funds have been established in large enterprises, accounting to only 0.8 percent of the labor force. Civil servants and the military are part of the public sector fund and do not have a separate scheme. The health program is financed by employers and insured contributions, government subsidies, and minor copayments at the primary level, but these increase with the complexity of treatment—the health insurance program had a surplus in 2015–2017, endured a small deficit in 2018 (0.24 percent of expenses and virtually zero relative to GDP), but rebounded in 2020. Short-term funds basically guaranteed the solvency of social insurance programs, but the pension fund (though it still had a large surplus) demands careful calculations to ensure a long-term balance. Vietnam has the youngest population of the three countries and aging is not as pressing a problem as in the other two, but it will become more impactful between 2035 and 2042.[108] MOLISA and the ILO have analyzed a number of options that would reduce the cost of the system while also closing gender gaps and reinforcing income distribution (Ramírez and Arza 2021).

Allianz and Hermes (2020) undertook the ranking of seventy countries on the "sustainability of pensions" in 2020.[109] They examine how pension systems react to demographic change (for instance, increasing the age of retirement), surprisingly placing China in fifth place, after Belgium and the Czech Republic and above Sweden, whereas Vietnam is in thirty-second place, after New Zealand and Norway.[110] As already noted, Cuba is not included in the study but would rank below both China and Vietnam, as well as several Latin American countries, based on the previous analysis of the variables used by the Allianz and Homes ranking, the cost of pensions relative to GDP, and the rankings of Peru, Brazil, Argentina, and Chile (thirty-fourth, forty-fifth, fifty-eighth, and sixtieth, respectively) that are in a much better pension financial situation than Cuba (Mesa-Lago 2021b).

PART III

CONCLUSIONS AND RECOMMENDATIONS

CHAPTER 6
CONCLUSIONS

In this chapter I aim to rank the three countries based on the averages previously estimated for each of the six social security principles. Then I discuss some methodological problems in said ranking and confirm the three hypotheses of the book. Finally I explore answers to the question as to why Cuba has not followed the successful Sino-Vietnamese market-socialist model.

FINAL RANKING OF THE THREE COUNTRIES

In chapter 5, 51 key indicators out of a total of 109 were selected according to their relevance to and their comparability among the countries, and average rankings were estimated for each social security principle. For a calculation of the combined average of each of the six principle averages in order to obtain an overall ranking, see table 6.1. In all cases the lower the number is the better. The overall average ranking is China first (1.57), Vietnam a close second (1.74), and Cuba a relatively distant third (2.20). The difference between China and Cuba is 0.63 points, Cuba's difference with Vietnam is 0.46 points, and the difference between China and Vietnam is only 0.17 points; the difference between China and Cuba is almost four times the difference between the two

TABLE 6.1: Average Ranking of the Three Countries by Six Social Security Principles Averages

Average rankings in six principles	China	Cuba	Vietnam
Unity[a]	2.00 (3)	1.25 (1)	1.50 (2)
Coverage	1.25 (1)	2.33 (3)	2.25 (2)
Benefit sufficiency	1.23 (1)	2.54 (3)	2.00 (2)
Social solidarity and gender equity	1.89 (2)	2.11 (3)	1.44 (1)
Efficient administration and tripartite participation	1.58 (1)	2.17 (3)	1.58 (2)
Subtotal average of five social indicators	1.59 (1)	2.08 (3)	1.75 (2)
Financial-actuarial sustainability	1.44 (1)	2.78 (3)	1.67 (2)
Total scores	9.39 (1)	13.18 (3)	10.44 (2)
Total average ranking in six principles	1.57 (1)	2.20 (3)	1.74 (2)

Source: My own elaboration based on tables 5.1–3, 5.9–11, and 5.14.

Note: [a] Equal treatment could not be measured and ranked.

Asian countries.[1] China ranks first in four indicators, second in one (social solidarity and gender equity), and third in one (unity); Cuba ranks third in five indicators and first in one (unity); Vietnam ranks second in five indicators and first in one (social solidarity and gender equity). In the subtotal five social indicators, ranking is the same, but the gap is smaller at a 0.49 point difference between Cuba and China and 0.33 points between Cuba and Vietnam. Conversely, in the principle of financial-actuarial sustainability, the space between Cuba and China expands to 1.34 points (which is almost three times the difference between social indicators) and 1.11 points between Cuba and Vietnam (which is also three times the same difference).

SOME METHODOLOGICAL PROBLEMS IN THE COMPARISONS

There are four methodological problems involved in the comparisons. First, there are different time periods in the operation of the models. Second, in some indicators homogenous data for the three countries was not available. Third, there were three ranking issues. Fourth, the nonquantifiable nature of nonsystemic factors may affect performance.

Different Time Periods

There are no systematic comparisons of China, Cuba, and Vietnam at the time of their revolutions (Vietnam in 1945; China in 1949; Cuba in

1959, and socialism was not officially proclaimed until 1961) nor when each country started its economic reforms. The two Asian countries, Vietnam and China, preceded Cuba by fourteen and ten years, respectively. Economic reforms took a longer time relative to the start of the revolution: twenty-two years in China, forty-one years in Vietnam, and forty-nine years in Cuba. All three countries at first copied the Soviet model of central planning and virtual total state ownership of the means of production.

After the failure of the Soviet model, market-oriented structural economic reforms began. In China, first was Mao's failed Great Leap Forward followed by market-oriented reforms that did not start until 1978; in Vietnam, the reforms began in 1986; and in Cuba, the pure centrally planned model lasted until the first timid reforms occurred in 1994–1995, then were reversed in 2000, resumed modestly in 2007–2015, reversed in 2016, and partly continued without success in 2022. So, which starting year should be used for Cuba—the implementation of the centrally planned model (1961), or the beginning of the modest economic reforms (1994 or 2007)? If 2007 were used, there would be a twenty-nine-year difference with the start of reforms in China (1978) and twenty-one years with the start of the reforms in Vietnam (1986). The base years for the comparison would be distorted because Cuba would have been much more advanced than the two Asian countries. In addition thorough, comparative, reliable data from the early years of the reforms is very hard to find in China and Vietnam.[2]

In conclusion, reforms did not occur in the same time periods and levels of development at the start of the implementation of the two economic models were quite different, with Cuba more advanced than China and Vietnam.[3] The possibility of conducting adequate time comparisons from the start of the economic reforms until the present is practically nil; it is virtually impossible to measure relative improvement during a common time period. Nevertheless, it was possible to give trends during a comparative time period in some indicators: real average pensions, financial balance of pensions, health expenditures/GDP, infant and maternal mortality rates, health facilities and personnel, and ratios of active workers to one pensioner (see chapter 5).

Some Missing Data

Missing data on some indicators has already been noted: coverage of the total population with healthcare in Cuba and of the total labor force with pensions (a surrogate was used); several morbidity rates, particularly in Cuba and Vietnam; data on administrative costs in the three countries; percentage of women's participation in all social security programs in Cuba and Vietnam; average wage of women compared with men in Cuba and Vietnam; better comparative indicators to measure social solidarity and, particularly, gender equity in the three countries; and a recent actuarial study for Cuba, given that the one available is twenty-three years old. The eight missing indicators, however, represent about 7 percent of the total of 109 total social security indicators shown in this book and 15 percent of the fifty-one indicators selected. Although additional research is needed to fill the small vacuum, this is not a significant obstacle for the comparison and ranking.

Potential Ranking Issues

Potential ranking issues have been discussed (see chapter 3), but there are three further potential issues to be considered. The first is that, because there are only three countries, the ranking range is quite narrow: from 1 to 3 (best to worst). The ideal ranking would include more countries, but this was not feasible because, after the collapse of the USSR and the Eastern European countries, there are very few socialist economies left in the world. Laos, a socialist market, and North Korea, which still adheres to the centrally planned model, would have been good candidates, but there is little data available on the former and virtually none on the latter.

The second potential issue is that the ranking does not properly show the relative distance among the three countries; for instance 2 does not mean twice 1. This problem is largely mitigated by the use of scores. In a few cases, two countries have very close scores, but their ranking is different. For instance, in hospital beds per 1,000 inhabitants, Cuba's score is 3.0 and Vietnam is 2.8. Cuba and Vietnam are relatively close, and they are ranked 2 and 3 (see chapter 3). To cope with this problem, in appendix 4, I use the standardized numbers scales approach (as I did in appendix 3), which better measures distances among the three countries (the higher the number the better). The results show the following average rankings in the six social security system principles combined: China first (1.77), Vietnam second (1.04), and Cuba third (–2.81). The ranking orders are similar to those in the simple ranking (see table 6.1), but in appendix 3 the distances are considerably higher: Cuba from China, 4.58 points; Cuba from Vietnam, 3.85 points; and Vietnam from China, 0.73 points; vis-à-vis 0.63, 0.46, and 0.17 in table 6.1 respectively. Furthermore, distances in appendix 4 are also substantially higher than those in appendix 3, which measures economic-social performance: China is ahead of Cuba by 1.08 points, Vietnam ahead of Cuba by 0.96 points, and China ahead of Vietnam by 0.12 points. In terms of the performance in the social security principles, it is obvious that the stan-

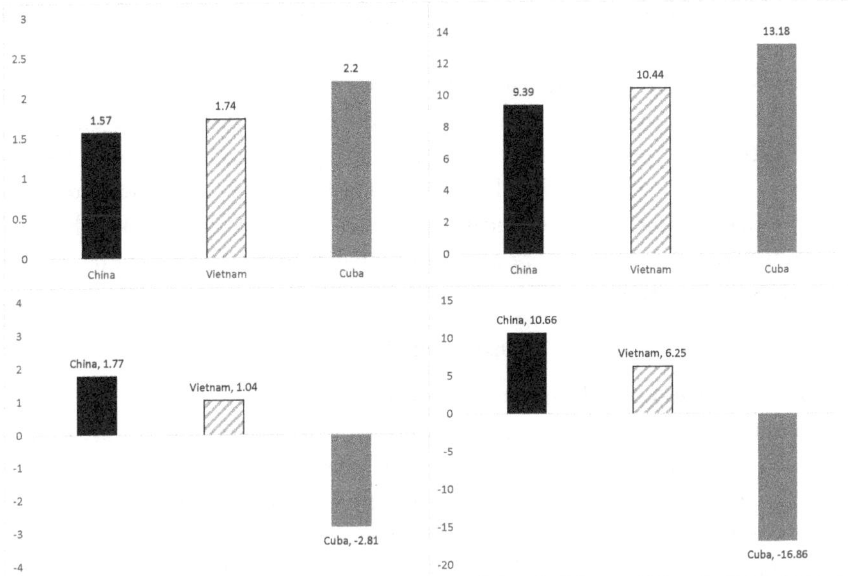

FIG. 6.1. Rankings and Scores on Social Security in the Three Countries, circa 2020. *Source*: My own elaboration based on table 6.1 and appendix 4.

dardized numbers scales approach detects larger distances in the ranking among the countries hence resolving this potential problem.

For a comparison of rankings and scores under the regular (first segment) and standardized number scale (second segment) in the three countries, see figure 6.1. In the regular segment, the lower the number the better; in the standardized number scales, the higher the number the better.

A third snag, however, is that each indicator has the same weight for the calculation of the ranking. Ideally, a weight should be assigned, but this would require a significant level of subjectivity to determine which indicator is more important than another and by how many points. Therefore, in both table 6.1 and appendix 4, the six social security principle indicators were given equal weight. More research is needed on this issue.

The fourth issue is the potential argument that a different combination of indicators could have led to a different ranking; this is addressed by several rationales. The fifty-one indicators selected are essentially those available for the three countries related to the key ILO social security principles. I made an effort to prevent duplication of indicators so as to avoid the overvaluation or the double counting of any one indicator.[4] The number of indicators in each principle is not uniform: there are four in unity and coverage, nine in social solidarity and gender equity (as well as in financial-actuarial sustainability), twelve in administration, and thirteen in financial-actuarial sustainability. Therefore, the unity and coverage indicators appear to be underrepresented in the total. To address this, I acknowledge that there is a lack of comparative indicators in equal treatment (part of the unity principle); and all the key available indicators on coverage were used (on contributory pensions, healthcare, and social assistance).

Nonsystemic Factors

It cannot be assumed that the performance of the three countries is the exclusive result of the model itself or its policies, as nonsystemic factors such as differences in levels of development and endowment might have played a role in the outcome. Concerning development, the most important factor is the sheer size of China (and to a lesser extent Vietnam), both much bigger than Cuba, but small countries, including Cuba, are among the most developed in the world despite their size (see chapter 3). Regarding endowment, it has been noted that Vietnam produces ten times more oil than Cuba, whereas China produces six times more than Cuba. However, in oil per capita, the order is Vietnam, Cuba, and China. Although Vietnam is a net oil exporter, the other two countries are net oil importers. Furthermore, the USSR supplied oil to Cuba in 1960–1990 at preferential prices and in excess of the island's needs. In the early 2000s, Venezuela began to supply oil to Cuba in exchange for professional services (under very generous terms and a substantial hidden price subsidy). Venezuela also built Cuba's oil refinery in Cienfuegos and supplied crude oil to that refinery—part of its output was sent back to Venezuela, but a surplus was kept by Cuba and exported to the world market. Another compensatory factor is that Cuba enjoyed a considerably higher level of economic and social development before its revolution than did China and Vietnam. There are *force majeure* factors, such as hurricanes in Cuba, earthquakes in China, and typhoons in Vietnam, but they have not been decisive in the long run, although they may have caused serious damage for a year or two.

The most important factor is probably exogenous: the effects of external powers (both positive and negative) on the economies of the three countries. China and Vietnam have received significant direct foreign investment (including from the United States), while Cuba has been under a US embargo since 1961; recall, however, that China and Vietnam were also under a US embargo (although for a shorter period). A compensatory factor is that Cuba received generous economic aid provided by the USSR between 1960 and 1990 (the largest granted by that country to any of its CMEA partners), but that aid ended in the early 1990s when the Soviet camp collapsed. Furthermore, the US embargo was intensified under the Trump administration. And yet, Cuba enjoyed even more generous aid from Venezuela until that country entered a grave economic and social crisis, which has been ongoing since 2017 and which has reduced, but not entirely stopped, the aid. Finally, most of the Cuban debt was condoned by the creditors, and external remittances have been the second-largest hard-currency revenue of the country. Combining all these compensatory factors, in 1960–2022 Cuba received US$238,500 million, compared with the cost of the embargo—estimated by the Cuban government (without a clear methodology or sound evidence) as US$165,000 million. Therefore the former exceeds the alleged cost of the latter by 44 percent (Mesa-Lago, 2024c). Furthermore, it can be argued that, if Cuba had followed the Sino-Vietnamese model of a socialist market, it would have increased its domestic production and GDP and generated a surplus to export, hence reducing the adverse impacts of the embargo. In this sense, Vietnam began the socialist-market model and saw beneficial effects for eight years under the US embargo.

In summary, nonsystemic factors cannot be quantified or controlled to measure their potential impact on performance in the three countries, but the most important have been analyzed (see chapter 3). The three countries were very similar in a large majority of factors. Counterarguments have also been presented with the conclusion that the divergent factors did not hinder the comparison, though they may have influenced the outcome.

CONFIRMATION OF THE THREE HYPOTHESES OF THE BOOK

The First Hypothesis

The first hypothesis of this book is that the Sino-Vietnamese socialist-market model has had a better economic and social performance—despite initial lower levels of economic and social development in Vietnam and China—than the Cuban model of predominant central plan and modest-ineffective reforms. In chapter 3, I selected the most relevant and comparable twenty variables (ten economic and ten social) that proved the first hypothesis. Scores of the three countries in the twenty variables were calculated and the countries ranked based on those calculations, showing China ahead in the first place, followed by Vietnam in second, and Cuba lagging behind in third (table 3.2). In addition, in appendix 3, I elaborated a similar exercise but this time based on seventeen variables suitable for Standardized Numbers Scale, which measures better ranking spaces between the three countries and obtained the same conclusion: China was best, followed by Vietnam, with Cuba lagging behind in third place. Finally, I contribute abundant evidence that, at the eve of their revolutions, Cuba was much more economically and socially advanced than either China and Vietnam, hence it took a greater effort from these two Asian countries to match and then exceed Cuba's economic and social levels.

The Second Hypothesis

The second hypothesis is that Cuba developed social security much earlier, faster, and most expansively than it could financially support, which made it unsustainable in the long run, especially with the country's poor economic performance. Conversely, social security in China and Vietnam developed gradually and it is financed by higher contributions and lower costs (as well as reserves that generate investment returns in pensions, which are lacking in Cuba), with much more successful economic performance, hence it is substantially more sustainable for a longer period.

Building upon an already established and relatively advanced social security system in the region, in its first three decades in power, Cuba's revolutionary government developed a universal and virtually free social security system (at the level of some developed countries), which had generous entitlement conditions and benefits, based on government commitment and huge amounts of Soviet aid, but without considering long-term financial sustainability.

The collapse of the USSR and the socialist camp radically changed the situation. The crises of 1990–1995, 2008–2009, and 2019–2024 eroded social security and aggravated the system's lack of sustainability. Raúl Castro's structural reforms subordinated social security to economic growth and available fiscal resources, subsequently cutting social expenses, diminishing access, and reducing benefits. Conversely, China and Vietnam started almost from scratch and prioritized economic development, subordinating social security to growth and fiscal capacity and establishing bare minimum social security that took four and two decades, respectively, for implementation and that still is gradually but steadily expanding.

The combined average of the five social security indicators (unity, coverage, sufficiency, social solidarity–gender equity, and administration) results in rankings of 1.59 for China (first), 1.75 for Vietnam (second), and 2.08 for Cuba (third). Even if this gap between the Asian countries and Cuba is smaller than that of financial sustainability and the overall indicators, it still provides evidence that, around 2020, the two Asian countries had surpassed Cuba despite the wide gap with Cuba at the time of the inception of their socialist economies. Furthermore, out of the nine indicators of financial-actuarial sustainability, Cuba ranks third in seven: total contribution as percentage of wages; total social security expenses as percentage of GDP; old-age dependency ratio; pension balance as percentage of GDP; ratio of active workers to one pensioner; projected pension cumulative balance as percentage of GDP; and year when pension reserves are exhausted (see table 5.14).

In the ranking of financial-actuarial sustainability, the gap between Cuba and China is 1.34 points and between Cuba and Vietnam 1.11 points (out of a total of 3 points), the widest gap in all indicators (table 6.1), which supports the hypothesis that the two Asian countries are more financially and actuarially sustainable than Cuba. Two experts refer to China's stand on the issue discussed above: "Social security . . . requires that benefit levels keep pace with economic capacities, such that social security neither under-demands nor overstretches the economy possibilities to maintain sufficient economic growth. . . . The strategic step-by-step reform approach within a clear policy of growth orientation has proven essential for China. . . . This approach should be maintained in future reforms. It can also be taken as a template for reform policy in other countries" (Gongcheng and Scholz 2019, 76, 78).[5] Concerning Vietnam, a comprehensive study by a team of local experts on social protection who analyzed achievements, challenges, and goals for the future, stressed the importance of sustainability. They stated: "Social policies have to be . . . implemented alongside economic development in line with developmental levels and available resources in each period" (Huong et al. 2013, 39).

The Third Hypothesis

The third hypothesis is that accelerated aging has had a strong adverse effect on the financial sustainability of the Cuban social security system because of the unsustainability of its pension program and relatively higher healthcare costs. See tables 1.1 and 5.13 for confirmation that Cuba has the most accelerated aging process (illustrated by the negative population growth rate, the highest figures on elderly population, the dependency ratio and the old-age dependency ratio, and the lowest fertility rate and the ratio of active workers per one pensioner), followed by China, whereas Vietnam is the youngest of the three countries.

There is an urgent need in Cuba to implement another parametric reform in order to increase retirement ages and raise contributions (see chapter 7), but these measures are politically and socially difficult because of the dire economic conditions endured by the population. China's aging is becoming a serious problem, and the government is taking measures and providing incentives to slow down such effects. The country is relying more on resources than Cuba is, supported by high economic growth (ages of retirement and period of contribution have been increased). Although aging has so far had no significant effect in Vietnam, the government has implemented policies to strengthen sustainability, such as gradually increasing contributions.

Finally, a note on the tradeoff in Cuba between social security financial-actuarial sustainability and social solidarity. Cuba has greater social solidarity than China (but lower than Vietnam) because its pension system lacks individual accounts that impede solidarity transfers, whereas the health system is legally universal and free—there are no private hospitals, health professionals are banned from private practice, and there is one unique public health system for all (save for the armed forces and foreign patients). The government has resisted the expansion of the private sector because of ideological concerns about the concentration of property and wealth, although inequality has substantially risen since the 2000s. And yet, social solidarity is eroding because of rising costs and shrinking state expenditures, as well as the exportation of health personnel, which have all substantially reduced access and quality of health services, prompting bribes to secure faster access and personal care. This contradiction presents justifiable moral problems, but the key issue is that social solidarity cannot be financially sustained if there are not enough economic resources available, something that was recognized by the Cuban leadership in 2007, when they substantially cut social expenditure.

It is also illuminating that the financial deficit in the pension system covered by the state, after a short decline after the 2008 parametric reform, the deficit has been growing again since 2017 (due to accelerated aging and still lax entitlement conditions), and such deficit will continue to grow in the future. In the final instance, the crucial dichotomy is between fictional equality (no longer existent in Cuba) and a certain amount of inequality that allows for better living standards of the population. Furthermore, such inequality could be alleviated by shifting from Cuba's current regressive predominant consumer taxes toward a progressive income tax system that would also generate more revenue for the state.[6]

WHY HAS CUBA NOT FOLLOWED THE SINO-VIETNAMESE PATH?

In view of the demonstration herein of the success of the Sino-Vietnamese model of socialist market in terms of economic and social protection, financial sustainability, and ability to keep the political regime under the communist party control, an intriguing question arises. Why hasn't Cuba followed such an economically rational path making the necessary adaptations to its own features and needs? It is impossible to provide a thorough, fulfilling answer to such an inquiry. Instead, I speculate on the potential reasons.[7]

First, let me summarize the leaders' positions regarding the Sino-Vietnamese approach. On several occasions, Fidel Castro rejected the socialist-market path arguing that China (he did not refer to Vietnam) possessed several key characteristics that were absent in Cuba: a sizable territory and world economic importance, a vast physical distance from the United States, and a domestic market large enough to attract substantial amounts of foreign investment, particularly from the United States (cited by Mesa-Lago and Pérez-López 2013, 174). These arguments have been fully debated (see chapter 1), and without discarding their importance, I reach the conclusion that they were not insurmountable barriers for a Cuban-adapted form of socialist market.[8] There is a fair consensus among Cuban academic economists in favor of a shift to some type of Sino-Vietnamese model, with the proper adjustments or at least acknowledgment of the progress of such model compared to Cuba's.[9]

A matter of concern among some of those scholars has been the inequalities generated by the socialist market, addressed by the Cuban leadership's strong stance against the concentration of property, wealth, and income, a stance that has been enshrined in the 2011 Guidelines of the Party and in the Constitution of 2019 (art. 30). Yet, it has been demonstrated herein that, against the official rhetoric, income distribution in Cuba has become more unequal in the last fifteen years. During a visit to Cuba in 2003, Xu Shicheng, a member of the Chinese Academy of Social Sciences asserted that "Cuba must deepen its reforms . . . establish the mechanisms of the socialist market economy and . . . smash egalitarianism" (quoted by Ratliff 2004, 17). At a lecture at the University of Havana, Nguyen Pho Trong, secretary general of the communist party of Vietnam, strongly defended the role of the market as favorable to, instead of antagonistic to, a socialist economy.

More pragmatic than his brother, Raúl Castro, during his visit to China in 1997, spent long hours with then premier Zhu Rongji and his principal adviser (whom Raúl invited to visit Cuba). When the adviser did visit, he lectured hundreds of Cuban executives and leaders on economic reform, but Fidel refused to meet him (Ratliff 2004). In another trip to China in 2005, Raúl stated: "It is really heartening to see all that you have been able to accomplish. . . . [T]here are people who are concerned about China's evolution, on the contrary I feel confident and happy [by what I see]" (Ministerio de Relaciones Exteriores de Cuba 2020). But once he was the president of Cuba, he was more cautious, saying in 2010: "We are not contemplating copying again what any one else has done [a reference to the failed Soviet pre-Gorbachev traditional economic model of central planning]; doing so brought us enough problems and moreover we copied badly; however, *we do not ignore the experiences of others and learn from them* [emphasis added]" (R. Castro 2010, 1).

In 2012, after Cuba had a massive national discussion on the "updating" of its economic model (Mesa-Lago and Pérez-López 2013), Pope Benedict XVI visited the island and in his main speech noted that the Marxist ideology as it was conceived did not match Cuba's reality. He exhorted Cubans to seek new models. Vice President Marino Murillo responded: "The updating of the Cuban economic model seeks to find sustainable economic development and preserve the achievements of the revolution and of socialism. . . . [W]e will address economic problems within a socialist framework." He added that Cuban officials had studied the economic experiences of other countries such as China and Vietnam, in order to "understand methodologically what these countries had done . . . [but] this does not mean that we are planning to copy automatically what others have done" (cited by Arreola 2012).

After Obama's visit to Cuba in March 2016, where he met with a group of SME owners in Havana, Fidel Castro immediately published an article ("reflexión") criticizing Obama's public speech, where he said that he had visited Cuba to leave behind the last vestiges of the Cold War, asked to forgive the past, and looked to a future when the United States would cooperate with Cuba. Fidel retorted that those "syrupy" words had provoked in him the risk of a heart attack because it was impossible to forget the blockade of sixty years, and that Obama should abstain from elaborating theories on the future of Cuba. Fidel concluded: "Nobody should have the illusion that our people would renounce the glory and the rights that we have won. We are capable of producing the food and material wealth that we need [and] do not need the empire to give us any gifts" (F. Castro 2016). This was the green light to launch a campaign against Obama, promoted by the hard-liners who opposed change. At the seventh party congress, held a few weeks later from April 16 to April 19, 2016, most observers expected announcements of substantial new changes, but nothing happened; some believe that in that congress Fidel (half a year before his death) definitively defeated Raúl's reforms (Bye 2020). In 2016, President Raúl Castro compared the reforms in China and Vietnam with those in Cuba, but he warned that the latter were called "updating," because they would not "change the fundamental objectives of the Revolution" (R. Castro 2016, 9). This was followed by the regression or counterreform of 2016.[10]

In summary, it is plausible that Raúl Castro wanted to implement structural economic reforms that would gradually move the Cuban economy toward some sort of Sino-Vietnamese approach, but unlike Fidel, he did not have full control and had to share leadership with other leaders who were adamantly opposed to that model. This could explain the slow path of Raúl's reforms, their customary zigzags, the reversal of 2016, and the eventual failure of his strategy. Raúl retired to live in relative peace during the last years of his life. His successor, Miguel Díaz-Canel, lacks any individual power and depends on the power of Raúl and other top leaders; therefore, the motto of his presidency has been "continuity," which precludes any movement toward the necessary economic transformation.

A leitmotif in all the above is that Cuba will not copy foreign models but will develop its own model and will preserve the revolutionary achievements. More than a decade has elapsed since the 2011 party congress proposed the "updating" of the Cuban economic model, and after much discussion and tryouts, such a model continues to be elusive, and so far all the reforms implemented have been unsuccessful. Furthermore, in this book I have proved that the previous achievements of the revolution have mostly been eroded by the maintenance of central planning, the lack of a clear economic model, and recurrent economic crises. Therefore, it is essential to search for other, concealed, causes of the Cuban rejection of the Sino-Vietnamese path. Most of them seem to be political rather than economic: to pursue the survival of the regime at any cost.

Political logic has prevailed over economic logic. Cuban leaders in the party, the armed forces, and the executive have painstakingly studied the collapse of the Soviet Union and concluded that any liberalization of the regime (glasnost, perestroika) would weaken their power and prompt its disappearance. In the same vein, they perceive that any significant delegation of economic decision-making—fully legalizing and guaranteeing the SME, authorizing it to expand and absorb the state-sector labor surplus, letting private farmers and cooperatives be truly autonomous, freeing agricultural producers from the mandatory procurement quota or *acopio*, allowing foreign investment by the Cuban diaspora, permitting enterprises to make key decisions on investment and directly import and export—would diminish their political power and might become the proverbial snowball that rolls down the hill and is unstoppable. The armed forces (through the powerful corporation GAESA) are the managers and de facto owners of a major source of the nation hard-currency revenue (tourism), as well as many state enterprises, and army leaders are reluctant to effect any changes that might threaten the status quo. Middle-level bureaucrats face a conflict of interest with non-state entrepreneurs: a small private restaurant that provides good food and service, for example, competes with state restaurants whose service is awful and the food is worse, hence said bureaucrats will do anything to obstruct the success of competitors.[11]

An article published in 2021 by a well-known Cuban think tank acknowledged the case of Vietnam, which has grasped international attention for its fast economic growth and, since the 1990s, has averaged 7 percent annually, second in the world after China. Vietnam's economic policies, including decentralization and enterprise competition, have been very efficient worldwide; its government's openness to international trade and investment (which contribute one-fourth of capital annual expenditure) has generated trust from foreign enterprises (particularly transnationals) to build factories; and its foreign trade represents 150 percent of national production, more than any other nation with a similar GDP per capita. The article also shows that Vietnam's assistance in developing Cuban rice production has not reduced Vietnamese exports of rice to Cuba, and that trade between the two countries steadily led to a deficit against Cuba accounting to 78 percent of total trade in 2021—trade volume peaked in 2018 and declined by 12 percent in 2021 (García 2021; ONEI 2022a). Therefore, the question persists: Why then Cuba does not follow Vietnam's model?

The only possibility of escaping the current freeze comes with the inevitable death of Raúl and the remaining octogenarian intransigent leaders, which could prompt a struggle for succession.[12] The pending question is whether the powerful armed forces and their oligarchs, in alliance with the party, will be successful in keeping power. Recent events show that, made desperate by the severe economic crisis, Cuba is moving in a different direction.

In January and May 2023, the Russian and Cuban leadership announced agreements ("Cuba y Rusia acuerdan," 2023; "Inversiones rusas," 2023) to transform the Cuban economy into the inefficient Russian model of state capitalism based on oligopolistic private enterprises with state support and abundant nepotism and lacking substantial competition.[13] This model is quite attractive to the Cuban leadership and the monopolistic military-complex GAESA, which controls 95 percent of all Cuban enterprises (Morales 2023). Between November 2022 and June 2023, there were visits from top Cuban leaders to Russia and vice versa (Grishin 2023). The agreements were signed by Presidents Putin and Díaz-Canel and approved by the Russian Security Council, and powerful Russian oligarchs have been entrusted to plan implementation. Russia has promised to supply Cuba with 1.64 million tons of oil and oil products annually, plus wheat and fertilizers. In addition, Russia resumed direct flights to Cuba and announced the building of a hotel only for Russians and a new airline terminal for 500,000 tourists. Russia announced investment plans including the assembly of Russian-made cars, modernizing the Cuban steel mill "Antillana de Acero," reconstructing light industry, building four thermoelectric blocs of 200 MG, using new technology in the Boca de Jaruco oil deposit, building a plant to produce construction materials, administering and modernizing sugar mills to increase sugar and rum output, building a hydroelectric plant in Santiago de Cuba, processing agricultural produce, developing a solar plant, building several banks, and digitalizing the economy. Cuba, in turn, has granted Russia thirty-year land leases to Russian investors, the duty-free import of Russian machinery, support to establish a trading house, tax preferences, expediting the repatriation of profits, and the freedom to directly appoint and dismiss employees in Russian enterprises (a right not granted to other foreign investors). Joint educational programs have been announced in agriculture, biomedicine, and biopharmaceuticals. Finally, an interparliamentary commission will collaborate on finance and investment, energy, tourism, agriculture, security, and countering sanctions imposed by foreign nations. Perhaps the most important Cuban contribution is political: Díaz-Canel pledged "unconditional support" and a vote against a WHO resolution condemning the impact of the Russian war in Ukraine on that country's health system (Grishin 2023; "Inversiones rusas en Cuba," 2023; "What Are Cuba & Russia," 2023; Reyes 2023).

Nevertheless, some Russian-Cuban projects do not seem feasible, or they are not as grandiose as they appear on paper, or they are promises to be tested (this paragraph is based on Mesa-Lago 2024b). For instance, increasing sugar production—which declined from 8 million tons in the 1980s to the current 350,000 tons—would require a huge investment to replace, modernize, or expand the mills and enlarge drastically reduced cane plantations. Sergei Baldin, the Russian trade representative in Cuba, stated that the volume of trade with Cuba was US$450 million in 2022, thrice the volume of trade in 2021; but actual figures in 2021 and 2022 were US$633 million and US$846 million respectively, therefore an increase of 33 percent instead of three times. The investment in Antillana de Acero is said to produce 3,000 tons of steel but, in 1989 Cuba's steel output was 314,000 tons. The number of Russian tourists peaked at 177,977 in 2019 but then decreased to 54,383 in 2022, and in the first half of 2023 it was 69 percent below the level of the first half of 2019, making dubious an increase to half a million Russian tourists. Cuban trade with Russia systematically results in a deficit of 99 percent of total exchange, which is unsustainable in the long run.

There is proof that Russia had sent Cuba 1,148,000 oil barrels by February 2023, tantamount to a supply of the promised 32,000 barrels for thirty-five days, but no data is available thereafter. Russia postponed until December 2027 the payment of the debt of US$3,000 million that Cuba defaulted on but then charged interest that led to a US$11 million increase in said debt (the debt could have been forgiven or reduced, which would have been more favorable to Cuba). Another key question is whether Russia will have the economic capacity to fulfill all its promises to Cuba (particularly on investment), as well as to other Latin American and African countries, in the midst of its prolonged war in Ukraine and facing strong Western sanctions, a decline in growth of 2 percent in 2022, dwindling world oil and gas prices, a shrinking trade surplus, the ruble value falling to 100 per one US dollar, its growing fiscal deficit, and the high inflation resulting from printing money for growing military and welfare expenditures. Certainly, Russia cannot spend US$65,000 million in Cuba as it did in 1960–1990 when the island was in a much better economic situation than now.

CHAPTER 7

SUGGESTED POLICIES TO IMPROVE SOCIAL SECURITY AND ITS SUSTAINABILITY

In this chapter, policies to improve social security are suggested for the three countries, disaggregated into pensions, healthcare, and social assistance. The policies in each country are structured based on the previous diagnosis of the problems faced in each of the six social security principles. Suggestions in each country end with a brief comment on the current model's suitability to sustain social security, or whether it is necessary to adjust the model or implement a structural economic reform.[1] Any type of social security reform in the three countries should be preceded by a nationwide social dialogue with participation from all the key sectors—workers, employers, government, and so forth (for concrete recommendations on how to conduct such a dialogue, see Mesa-Lago 2021b).

CHINA

China ranks first in social security indicators. Social security has been significantly expanded to reach very high healthcare coverage of the total population and the elderly population (much lower in the labor force on pensions), social assistance has been significantly extended, and three pillars have been added to supplement basic social insurance pensions. Administrative indicators are fairly good and financial-actuarial sustainability is probably the best of the three countries. Economic performance is one of the best in the world, but some social security problems persist, including system fragmentation, social and regional inequalities, separate groups (the military) with better entitlement conditions and benefits, and the threat to long-term financial and actuarial equilibrium mostly due to population aging. The pros and cons of a parametric reform vis-à-vis a more radical structural reform have been discussed by various scholars.[2] Actually, China has advanced considerably, introducing gradual changes that have tackled many problems, but the country is still in need of more profound reforms rather than a paradigmatic transformation. According to Y. Wang, China's legislation establishes "the fundamental right to social security and thus is not limited to basic security, but demands full insurance protection" (2021, 124). Gongcheng, president of the China Association of Social Security, notes "shortcomings and deficiencies" of the system that "call for a comprehensive improvement of the current social security system" (2022, 8–9), including nationwide unity in the basic old-age insurance, the basic healthcare insurance, and the social assistance system.

Pensions in China

Unity and Equal Treatment

The highly fragmented pension system includes two major schemes—one for urban employees and one for urban-rural residents—with diverse entitlement conditions, benefits, and contributions (the scheme for urban employees is much better than that for urban-rural residents, which is also true of urban-resident insured compared to rural-resident insured). Many migrant and flexible workers (including the self-employed) have voluntary coverage or are not covered, whereas military personnel have a separate scheme with the best conditions and benefits.[3] Furthermore, regions, provinces, and municipalities enact diverse regulations that expand the legal multiplicity.[4] There is a positive ongoing process of unification (for instance, the integration of the civil servant scheme into the urban-employee scheme), but the uneven development of regions and municipalities in China is a significant obstacle for unification and, especially, standardization. As the country advances in its developmental process, those gaps should be reduced. It is advisable to place the existing three branches under one single social insurance pension entity: the contributory branch (urban-employee scheme) financed by employers' and employees' contributions and capital returns from the invested pension fund;[5] the contributory-state subsidized urban-and-rural-resident branch; and the social assistance branch that targets the poor and is fully financed by the state. For the time being, the three branches would continue with their diverse features and separate funds, but the integration would facilitate cross-checks (for instance, that those who receive social assistance are not covered by the other two branches) and would better detect moves from the contributory to the contributory-subsidized and social assistance branches or vice versa. Finally, the integration would ensure that no citizen is left unprotected by the combined three branches.[6]

The state budget should transfer the needed resources to the unified entity that, in turn, would make allocations to the contributory-subsidized and social-assistance branches (although separate funds should continue for the three branches). The existing fund to reduce regional gaps and the proposed fund to reduce inequalities among the two major pension branches (see below) should be under the control of the integrated entity. In the long-term, more standardized entitlement conditions and the calculation of benefits and contributions could be gradually implemented between the contributory and the contributory-subsidized branches. For that purpose, the integrated entity would propose to the executive and legislative branches national rules applicable to the system that would reduce and eventually eliminate the current fragmentation by regional and local norms and strengthen equal treatment and social solidarity.[7] The differentiation between urban and rural hukou is to be abolished, and this has already happened in Beijing and other cities, while a series of steps are slowly underway such as the confirmation and registration of land-related rights, compensation and resettlement measures, and so forth (Y. Wang 2022). This process should be accelerated in order to get rid of such negative divergence.

Coverage

Although there has been a significant expansion of the labor force coverage by contributory pensions, still it is at 42.5 percent, which is less than the minimum of 50 percent established by the ILO. A current plan aims to expand such coverage to achieve universality. Important measures to reach that goal would be the full incorporation, in a mandatory manner, of migrant workers and flexible employees (including the self-employed) into either the urban-employee or the urban-and-rural-resident schemes—these two groups account for almost 43 percent of the labor force and the majority is not effectively covered by basic social insurance in pensions and healthcare. As the gradual process of integration described above advances, eventually there would be only one scheme. Rural residents should also have mandatory coverage in the resident scheme. The payment amounts of migrant workers and flexible employees are lower than the payments of salaried workers, but because of their lower earnings their contributions (and burden) are proportionally higher than the salaried workers, which is an obstacle for their coverage. Therefore, contributions of migrants and flexible employees should be reduced, whereas state, provinces, and local subsidies should be raised to facilitate coverage expansion of these two groups, particularly when they are poor or have very low income. The universalization goal ought to take priority over other objectives, such as the expansion of commercial insurance that is only affordable to higher income groups than the uninsured.

Benefit Sufficiency

The very low retirement ages (60 men and 50/55 women) have been in place since the system inception in the 1950s and are incongruent with the rapidly aging population and the rising life expectancy; between 2025 and 2040, retirement ages are being gradually raised to 63 for men and 55–58 for women. In practice, due to the "deferred retirement plan," men usually retire at 65 and women at 60. Furthermore, retirement is possible five years earlier than the statutory age for those insured who engage in physical work in certain industries, and this is without any discount of the pension for each year of withdrawal earlier than the normal age, a very costly benefit. Ideally, current statutory ages should be increased to 65 for both genders (as an alternative, the women's age could be temporarily set at 60 and later raised to 65).[8]

In addition, the pension formula should be adjusted based on a demographic factor (life expectancy of the population). Incentives should be provided for people to retire later in life, and the government should encourage delayed retirement so as to take full advantage of the "elderly population dividend" (W. Zhang 2022). Norms for earlier retirement should be tightened to avoid misuse, including a discount of at least 2 percent per year of early retirement. The period of contribution is being gradually raised from fifteen to twenty years), but this still is relatively short by international standards and should be expanded to twenty-five years, and this period used to calculate the base salary that is fifteen years prior to retirement. These reforms, however, might be insufficient to balance the system actuarially, and a minor increase in contributions returning to the previous level might well be needed too (this should be balanced vis-à-vis potentially negative effects on the formal sector). In any case, changes in all these parameters should be made dependent on an actuarial evaluation and implemented gradually. These measures would increase the value of pensions and improve the financial-actuarial sustainability of the system.

The current opacity of the total number of pillars should be clarified. According to the Chinese conception, there are three pillars: (1) the basic social insurance plus individual accounts,[9] (2) the occupational plans, and (3) commercial insurance. According to the international literature, there are four pillars, however, and there could be more.

Many experts support a first pillar (also called pillar "zero"). This is a basic noncontributory means-tested old-age pension.[10] It is for all those not covered by either the urban-employee scheme or the urban-and-rural-resident scheme, with full state financing to ensure basic living subsistence. The cost of this pillar has been estimated at about 1 percent of GDP (L. Fang 2014) and between 0.9 percent and 1.6 percent based on a pension at 6.6 percent of GDP per capita (Lu et al. 2019; see also Shen et al. 2020).

The basic social insurance pension (second pillar) could have a guaranteed national pension with a minimum RR of 45 percent (based on the recommendation of the ILO) for all insured).[11] The individual account (third pillar) in the urban-employee scheme is theoretically a nondefined contribution (NDC), but in practice it is set at 139 months for those who retire at age 60 (lower than life expectancy). Its length, level of pension, and indexation should be set by appropriate actuarial criteria (Cousins 2021). The fourth pillar should be the company pension plan. The fifth pillar should be commercial insurance.

In view of the many divergent estimates on the effective RR, it is essential for the NBSC to publish a reliable series. Some experts and organizations suggest further reducing the employer percentage contribution to the basic social insurance pension in the urban-employee scheme in order to give more space for employers to contribute to occupational plans and commercial insurance (Chen and Turner 2021) or to increase competition (World Bank 2021b). This recommendation would expand the gap between the average pension in such scheme and in the resident scheme, increasing inequality and reducing social solidarity. Concerning survivors, the current lump sum and funeral grant should be replaced by a full pension (public discussions on this issue began in 2020), adding the payment of the balance in the insured person's individual account.

Although the average contributory pension in 2020 in the urban-employee scheme was higher than the urban poverty line, the average pension of the urban-and-rural-resident scheme, was one-nineteenth the urban-employee scheme and below the urban and rural poverty lines. Therefore, this pension should be increased above the urban and rural poverty lines. Data is needed on the basic basket of goods and services to properly measure the average pension sufficiency in both schemes.

An effective and harmonious national system for pension adjustment should be designed. The current adjustment of contributory pensions in the urban-employee program to wages and CPI should be gradually unified at the national level, though this measure confronts significant differences in local conditions and across cities. The urban-and-rural-resident pension scheme is adjusted based on the local CPI only because their insured are not employed, and in order to attenuate different urban and rural CPI the state provides social assistance support.

Social Solidarity and Gender Equity

The documented significant inequalities in pensions in the various schemes (e.g., the average pension in the urban-employee scheme is about twenty times the average pension in the urban-and-rural-resident scheme) should be reduced by the creation of a public national adjustment fund that promotes fairness without harming effectiveness of the pension system, similar to the one that exists to reduce the gap on financial balances among regions and provinces. This measure would increase coverage and replacement rates for retired elderly people and improve social solidarity.[12] The announcement of a gradual integration of regional, provincial, and municipal pension pools so far has not materialized into a unified national pension pool, and it should.

Gender equity could be improved with the publication of data on women's average wages relative to men's and the pension degree of coverage for women and men, as well as average pensions for both genders (this data would allow a measure of inequality and permit the adoption of corrective policies). Although there is lack of data on average pensions for women, information on other countries clearly indicates that it is lower than for men, particularly in single-parent families, which are usually led by women. Policies should separately address gender discrimination derived from the labor market. Some regions pay a bonus to mothers for second and third children born alive in order to compensate for the time away from work that women take to raise their children; it should be awarded also for the first child and be made mandatory at the national level. This measure would improve women's pensions and be also an incentive to increase the birth rate.

Administration

The unified system should have one national administration in charge of recordkeeping, accounts, management of the pension fund, and processing pension requests. Local entities such as banks, mail posts, and so forth could oversee payment of the pensions. In 2018, the central committee of the party proposed that all social security fees should be levied by the tax authority in order to increase the efficiency of contribution collection. The People's Congress approved that plan, which should be thoroughly implemented in all regions, provinces, and municipalities based on a realistic strategy (see Cousins 2021). Administrative and tax-collection unification would facilitate the expansion of coverage and the gathering and publication of data on administrative expenses as a percentage of total pension expenditures, which would enhance transparency and provide an indicator of efficiency. In turn, the reduction of said administrative costs could improve pensions and financial sustainability.

An integrated national data management system and ID, which has just recently been approved, should help to strengthen compliance, reduce targeting errors, and control fraud. Enforcement of the law is poor, and many employers evade, underreport, or treat employees (particularly migrant and flexible employees) as service providers, and don't pay due contributions; therefore, compliance has been declining.[13] Enforcement of compliance should be done by the state taxation board in order to cross-check information on taxes and on social insurance contributions. Inspection by the tax authority should be strengthened and more stringent sanctions imposed to get employers to sign contracts and pay their contributions (particularly to the flexible employees and migrant workers who have the minimum time employed). Sanctions imposed for noncompliance in Vietnam and other countries should be studied for potential adoption. The state should be held directly liable if it does not meet its obligation to collect social insurance contributions. Restrictions on household registration for flexible workers to participate in the basic old-age insurance schemes at their place of employment should be relaxed to facilitate the process (Qi 2022). Workers' and employers' direct participation in the management of social security should be institutionalized. An independent and autonomous supervisory agency should be created to oversee the entire pension system.[14]

Financial-Actuarial Sustainability.

The current central adjustment fund among regions and provinces plays a positive role in reducing gaps in financial balances, but it requires an upgrade to a national pooling system (Qi 2022) that transfers surpluses from the most developed wealthiest regions to alleviate deficits in the least developed poorest regions. It requires a raise in the level of transfers and positive incentives to implement the proposed reforms in an efficient manner. This measure would help to improve social solidarity and financial-actuarial sustainability. It is also advisable to incorporate all provinces into the NCSSF for better management of investment and risk.

Data on the total fund amount and annual real capital return of each pillar and of all pillars should be published annually. To increase capital returns, the further diversification of the investment portfolio is recommended—for instance, increasing investment in foreign instruments but carefully avoiding the excessive concentration on that type of investment to reduce the risk of volatility. A more profitable portfolio will increase the pension level, which is the main objective of social security.

The new fourth pillar commercial insurance is managed by both state-owned and private profit-seeking corporations; the former can have shares owned by individuals, whereas the latter includes overseas companies (B. He 2022). Although both types of corporations are under the supervision of the state, the private corporations are exposed to the same problems that are confronted by other countries, such as high administrative costs and profits. In addition, there is a documented history of state pressure on said corporations to invest the funds on government debt—for instance, in Argentina and El Salvador (Mesa-Lago 2021b). Such potential dangers require that the private administrators are strictly regulated against the cited risks and that an autonomous supervisory entity oversees their operation in order to protect the insured savings. This is essential to secure the confidence of the insured in such corporations and to ensure the proper management of their funds.

China has published a recent actuarial report covering the period 2019–2050, which is not the case in the other two countries. However, this report excludes public agencies and institutions and is limited to the urban-employee scheme; the next report should include public entities in the urban-employee scheme and also cover the urban-and-rural-resident and military schemes in order to evaluate their actuarial equilibrium and take the required measures. The 2019 actuarial report projected declining surpluses, a deficit starting in 2028 that will get significantly worse, and the exhaustion of the fund by 2035. This projection leaves a window of only four years to implement the necessary reforms before the scheme suffers a deficit; otherwise, it will be much more difficult to avoid the predicted collapse in twelve years. It is probable that these projections are optimistic because of the exclusion of the public sector (burdened by the integration of the civil servant scheme that likely suffered an actuarial deficit). Furthermore, it is plausible that the resident and military schemes are in worse financial-actuarial shape than the urban-employee scheme. A long-term plan to achieve financial-actuarial sustainability is urgently needed.

Several recent policies have been implemented to address the challenge of aging, and their effects have not been evaluated yet. However, some of these policies in Cuba (admittedly much more modest than in

China) have been followed by decreases in fertility. (The same is true in Japan where much more resources have been invested.) Young Chinese couples are so far not responding to said policies. More radical measures should be implemented, including the possibility of opening to immigration.

Coverage, particularly in remote rural areas as well as in some marginal urban areas, is low partly due to poverty but also because of lack of knowledge; the same is true about affiliates that don't contribute. Cousins (2021) argues that not all policymakers are aware of the disequilibrium of the pension system, even after the actuarial report of 2019, and that they should change the current short-term focus on revenue and expenditure to a long-term actuarial approach. If this is the mindset of leadership, the population's knowledge must be even worse. An educational campaign financed by a public national education fund is needed to improve general financial knowledge on the importance of social security.[15] The central administration should periodically inform the insured of the accumulation from their contributions plus capital returns, as well as their projected pensions, in order to help workers make informed decisions (Barr and Diamond 2010) and to incentivize the affiliation and punctual payment of their contributions. In addition, better financial advice should be provided to the insured in the fully funded pillars and the regulations on those pillars be strengthened to protect the insured.

Last but not least, there should be open national discussion to address the fundamental question of priorities with regards to China's pension policy. On the one hand, there is the need to extend coverage and improve benefits in the urban-and-rural-resident scheme, to consolidate and integrate the social assistance system, to strengthen social solidarity, and to fortify the financial-actuarial equilibrium of social insurance, all of which protect most of the nation's population and labor force. On the other hand, it would benefit a minority of the population and labor force to develop and provide tax incentives for the creation and expansion of another layer of individual accounts (commercial insurance on top of the second pillar already in existence, plus occupational plans). That decision should not be made by technicians but by the people.

Healthcare in China

Unity and Equal Treatment

China has the unified National Healthcare Security Administration (NHSA), but as in pensions, significant differences exist between the urban-employee and the urban-and-rural-resident schemes, as well as the separate military facilities and staff. Therefore, the same recommendations for pensions should be followed in the basic medical social insurance system. This would significantly improve social solidarity and reduce administrative costs.

Coverage

Coverage of the total population on health is virtually universal, but there are significant disparities in degree of access and quality of care among population groups (e.g., migrant workers, or people in remote rural areas) and regions or provinces; such inequalities should be addressed in order to improve effective coverage and access.[16] In addition, dependents of the insured are not protected (except for dependents of unemployed military personnel), and they should be. To this end, an additional modest contribution could be required of workers and employers, or an increase in central and local subsidies in the resident scheme.

Benefit Sufficiency

The urban-employee scheme has individual health accounts, but the urban-and-rural-resident scheme does not. In the future, it should be decided whether to create such accounts in the latter or to eliminate them in the former. This would fortify the basic health social insurance and facilitate transfers among generations, income groups, and genders.

The urban-employee scheme has thresholds, caps, and reimbursement rates that are much better than in the resident scheme, whereas those insured in the resident scheme have higher out-of-pocket expenses than the former. Per capita expenses in the urban-employee scheme are almost five times those in the resident scheme. The urban-employee scheme confronts a gap of 2.5 times the entitlement conditions mentioned before, between the most and the least developed regions. The number of hospital beds per 1,000 inhabitants is twice as high in cities as in rural areas. The two basic medical insurance schemes pay only partial medical expenses below a given amount. The rest of the expenses are partly covered by supplementary catastrophic illness insurance (12.9 percent of the population suffer from catastrophic health expenditure; Hu 2021), but this insurance only covers patients whose out-of-pocket expenses are more than the average disposable income per capita in the local area. There is ample evidence that out-of-pocket expenses have a highly regressive income-distribution effect. A study should be done to measure how many insured are left uncovered by the current rule, and depending on the results, there should be an increase in disposable income so as to expand coverage of catastrophic illnesses. A public national adjustment fund should be established to ameliorate such significant gaps and disparities and improve sufficiency—a pillar of the current government plan to reduce inequality in China.

The heavy reliance on hospitals and the insufficient primary care facilities (save for private services) is costly and inefficient and generates overcrowding and long wait lines. The new plan to expand primary services at the local level would facilitate access, tackle most diseases, and reduce costs and lines; its implementation should be evaluated. Other recommended policies to improve primary care and the family doctor program are to increase the salaries of family physicians up to the level of tertiary level specialists and to recognize the rigor of their training in order to incentivize their enrollment in medical schools (family physicians should be 50–60 percent of all medical practitioners); to transform medical education by shifting from the previous specialized medical service to basic primary medical and healthcare service; to significantly increase investment in basic healthcare services, with the majority of funds to pay the salaries of family doctors working in primary care institutions; and to strengthen teaching in resident training for general practitioners and family doctors (Xu 2014).

Social Solidarity and Gender Equity

Social solidarity could be improved by the recommended unification of the fragmented healthcare system, universalization of coverage, amelioration of current inequalities in access and quality by groups/regions, establishment of a national fund to reduce health gaps and inequalities, and so forth. As the country develops more evenly, the example of prosperous cities (like Dongguan and Shennu) that provide the same package of benefits to diverse groups should be followed. The recently enacted Fourteenth Five-Year Plan has started to deal with some of these issues, especially highlighting the urban-rural gaps in health insurance, but much more needs to be done and outcomes should be evaluated in the future. As far as social solidarity, the urban-employee scheme has individual accounts whereas the urban-and-rural-resident scheme does not. Gongcheng (2022) properly suggests that individual accounts by themselves, together with the diverse treatment between the two schemes, undermine the system function of social solidarity, hence he recommends that such accounts be abolished.

Women's coverage in the urban-employee basic insurance medical scheme is 47 percent (versus 53 percent men), and in the resident scheme it is 44 percent (versus 56 percent men). This is in part a result of the lower participation of women in the labor force, but it is also due to the system itself. The maternity paid leave oscillates between fourteen and twenty-three weeks, depending on the provinces, and it is an outcome of the system. Such gender disparities must be corrected by increasing female participation in the labor force and by forcing provinces to nationally increase maternity paid leave to twenty-three weeks (an alternative is to unify the norm nationally at eighteen weeks). In both cases, the necessary resources could be drawn from the public national adjustment fund already recommended.

Administration

Tax authorities at the regional and local levels are in charge of the collection of contributions; employers and insured people have IDs, and theoretically contributions are registered. An important step was taken in 2019 to unify the collection of taxes and social security contributions at the national level under the State Tax Organization, which should facilitate the detection of evasion, collusion, and payment delays. An evaluation of the results of such unification should be conducted immediately. To effectively prevent medical fraud and abuse, it is essential for the government to recognize the need for tough anti-fraud legislation, backed up by strong criminal and civil penalties. Scientific studies have proposed methods to better detect and reduce fraud and corruption (Li et al. 2022; Zhang et al. 2020). In addition, there should be tight coordination between the nationally unified tax entity and the NHSA in order to improve enforcement and avoid noncompliance. Administrative costs relative to total health expenditures should be published for transparency and efficiency; in the same vein, the government should mandate that private facilities publish such costs to assess their competitiveness with social insurance facilities. Multiple policies to improve administrative efficiency and quality in the health system have been proposed (see World Bank 2013; GOV 2022b). The hospital-centric model should be transformed so as to strengthen primary and preventive healthcare.

Financial-Actuarial Sustainability

The healthcare system has generated a steady annual surplus in the balance of basic medical social insurance (combining the urban-employee and the resident schemes), but such surplus decreased between 2006 and 2019. To the best of our knowledge, no actuarial report has been done of those two schemes and the military scheme. Therefore, there is a need to conduct an actuarial evaluation of all the health schemes to ensure their equilibrium. A modest contribution for healthcare should be charged to retired workers and pensioners.

Social Assistance in China

Unity and Equal Treatment

The current social assistance system is fragmented and multilayered, with intertwined programs geared toward the poor, families with income below local standards, the unemployed, and urgent emergencies. Since 1978, there have been four major social assistance schemes with some overlap, the most important of which is dibao, for families whose members' joint per capita annual income is lower than the locally set minimum living standards. There are not complete nationally unified norms for all social assistance programs; in some of them, conditions are set by regions, provinces, and municipalities, thus generating significant disparities. The minimum in dibao is very low and there are other restrictions. President Xi tightened this program and reduced its beneficiaries by 42 percent, but his measures might cut corruption, improve rural benefits, and shrink the urban-rural gap; an evaluation of these results is needed. The 2022 program that is trying to correct pending problems should be vigorously enforced and expanded.

All social assistance programs should be nationally integrated and unified under a single public national entity that makes them coherent, develops uniform norms to replace regional or local regulations and conditions, and elaborates effective targeting to prevent exclusions and erroneous inclusions particularly in rural areas. Local authorities could oversee means-testing under national standardized norms. Rural and urban social assistance programs should be unified and a mechanism established to determine the share of social expenditure of the central and local government, as well as to stipulate the equal rights of migrant workers and local residents and to create a national social assistance program based on the place of work, through which migrants who live in the area for more than six months acquire the same social benefits as local residents (Yang 2018).

Several specific recommendations have been elaborated to improve dibao. One is to set and adjust the dibao standard to the local living standard, so that more people can meet the assistance conditions. Another is for the central government, every year, to establish the national minimum poverty line and the low-income family poverty line and to mandate that local government poverty lines must be equal or higher. Other recommendations are to broaden population coverage, better integrate it with other social assistance programs, increase collaboration with NGOs, and revise the stigmatizing means-testing procedure through more public education and professionalization of administrators (Gao 2017; Yang 2018).

Coverage and Benefit Sufficiency

Social assistance coverage relative to the total population was difficult to calculate because of the multiple programs and their changes through time, as well as uncertainty as to whether some programs still exist or have been terminated. Coverage was roughly estimated as 10.2 percent excluding long-term care. However, the Social Assistance Explorer estimates the 4.5 percent of the population is covered by social assistance. There is need to integrate all programs and provide consolidated statistics to more accurately determine total coverage and disaggregated by social assistant pension, healthcare, and other schemes. China lacks both a noncontributory pension for the elderly poor and a survivor pension, although these two groups may get social assistance.

A draft law under discussion might introduce a reform of social assistance aimed at broadening that assistance and generalizing its benefits to tackle poverty in a more efficient manner, but still with dual programs and standards set locally. An action plan of 2021 proposes a social safety net and better integration of social assistance with social insurance. The unified social assistance system should have a basic noncontributory old-age pension first pillar, nationally financed by the government, which eliminates remaining poverty pockets. An integrated and comprehensive system of eldercare should be developed by the state, particularly in rural areas that undergo a faster aging process than in urban areas (the departments that oversee medical and nursing care should be well coordinated). The weakening of family help to the elderly, insufficient pensions for farmers, and inadequate service facilities are obstacles that demand urgent government policies to develop the eldercare needed to improve rural governance and stability (B. He 2022). The goals for the expansion of services for the elderly for 2025 should be monitored and their implementation evaluated.[17]

Social Solidarity and Gender Equity

Women are covered by sickness and maternity benefits at 30 percent, and measures should be taken to increase such coverage (Ramírez and Arza 2021). The two pilot programs for long-term care show substantial inequalities among provinces (an 18.0 times difference in the annual per capita contribution and a 3.6 times divergence in the annual average financing between the urban-employee and the urban-and-rural-resident schemes) in addition to a probably sizable gap in the per capita benefit between such schemes, for which data is needed. The guidelines address these challenges by setting a national financial benchmark to balance contribution burdens among regions and groups, and they also set a ratio of 1:1 of insured and government contributions in the resident scheme and stipulate a subsidy for people who face difficulties in joining the insurance (Fan 2022). It is hoped that these policies will mollify the disparities; for instance, financing sources should be adjusted, increasing the shares of social insurance health and public subsidies in the resident scheme to reduce the contribution paid by the insured. No information is available on gender concerning this program, and it should be provided.

Administration

The Fourteenth Five-Year Plan for National Aging and Development for Eldercare Service System for 2021–2025 and Vision for 2035 was enacted in 2022, so it will take time to evaluate the fulfillment of its goals (GOV 2022b). In this sense, the data available on the pilot plans for long-term care for the elderly is very valuable and shows important advances, such as coverage of 10.3 percent of the population, a significant fund already accumulated, a fair average benefit, an average contribution that is only 1.1 percent of the average benefit, and the predominance of the home-care service, which is not only the optimal form of care for the elderly but also the one preferred by 90 percent of elder people and their families.[18]

On the other hand, significant inequalities between the urban-employee and urban-and-rural-resident schemes, as well as among provinces, have been noted. The traditional role of the family as caregivers of the elderly at home ("raising children for old age") is declining, and the demand for elderly services is not satisfied by the family. The state, the private sector, and the community must collaborate with the family to cope with such a demand for eldercare. Implemented policies are not coherent and sustainable, however, and there is a lack of supporting mechanisms and high administrative costs. The government should gradually reduce its role as provider and become a guide, regulator, and coordinator: to develop and improve regulations; to set the boundaries of the state's responsibility (including subsidizing services provided by family, community, and the market); and to establish a standardized service system that is mainly based on home care to develop a national eldercare system involving all social partners. The state also should supervise care providers based on national standards (V. Zhang 2022). The motto of the long-term-care plan is consistent with the general social security approach and should be adjusted to reflect the nation's economic capacity: "Be patient and seek steady rather than speedy development" (cited by Fan 2022).

The guidelines for the long-term-care plan are mostly well-thought-out. Hopefully, the move from urban to rural areas and from urban-employee to urban-and-rural schemes should alleviate the inequalities noted. Priorities also make sense: start with the basic needs of the severely incapacitated elderly and gradually include the moderately incapacitated elderly and then the needs of incapacitated people of other ages.

Suitability of the Current Economic Model

China's socialist-market model has been quite successful in achieving the highest economic growth rates in the world, becoming the largest manufacturer and exporter, and the second-biggest economy (Chinese leaders forecasted growth rates between 6 and 8 percent that would allow their country to surpass the United States by the end of the 2020s), while improving living standards, virtually eradicating poverty, and significantly expanding social security. But after thirty successful years, the export-oriented development strategy has been exhausted. Compounding these problems, President Xi has been critical of the private sector and is restricting it. He launched a movement back to the planned economy model and state enterprises. A long-term economic slowdown appears to be unfolding: growth rates in 2021–2023 have been about half of what they were before. In May 2022, a debate on the future model of China was brewing, concerning the choice between a reversal to a planned economy or continuing with the socialist-market model: "China cannot have both today's statism and yesterday's strong growth rates: it will have to choose" (Rosen 2022). "China's leaders once again [can] demonstrate that they are 'imaginative and flexible' and 'shift policy, decisively, comprehensibly and without regards to procedural or legal 'niceties'" (Brandt and Rawski 2022, 827). "If employment and income growth falter, China's budget would come under pressure, forcing the CCP to choose between providing healthcare, elder care, and pension entitlements on the one hand and pursuing national security goals, industrial policy and the Belt and Road Initiative on the other" (Rudd 2022). The twentieth party congress extended Xi's mandate to a third term, shut out moderates from the standing committee of the politburo, and replaced them with Xi loyalists supportive of the turn back to more state intervention in the economy.[19] Such regression combined with the drastic "Zero Covid" policy and the exhaustion of the development strategy has induced severe economic and social problems and prompted the enactment in 2023 of thirty-five guidelines, which might sign a return to the market and the private sector, but it is too soon to evaluate their success.[20] The government should recognize that without a strong private sector it is not possible to cope with the current economic problems and so it should enact concrete measures including financial-sector liberalization that will help direct more resources to private business rather than stated-owned ones (Prassad 2023).

In order to tackle the social security problems diagnosed and to generate economic resources for the proposed social security reform, China needs to implement a new development strategy in its next phase.[21] A shift to an intensive domestic-oriented strategy would effect several changes. It would expand internal consumption; replace imported technology by national innovation; reform large state enterprises to make them more competitive and reduce government subsidies, shifting them to services such as healthcare and pensions; strengthen the foundations of a market-based economy to improve competition and efficiency; reform its fiscal system; design an effective program to provide adequate jobs for the young, particularly graduates; improve community help and social support; and achieve "a basic but secure social protection system that provides a moderate level of security for all while respecting social constraints" (World Bank 2013, 282).

Recovery policies introduced in August 2023 are not strong enough and should be expanded and deepened (Krugman 2023). In the context of this book, this means no development of social security beyond the country's economic capacity, so as to ensure its financial-actuarial sustainability. The current government has also set a priority in achieving a more balanced growth that would reduce inequalities among regions, among urban and rural areas, and among income groups, whereas the five-year plan (2021–2025) has the target of constructing a unified, equitable, and sustainable pension system with full coverage. The previous recommendations would help to achieve these goals.

CUBA

Cuba ranks third in social security indicators. The social security system reached its peak by the end of the 1980s, when it was ahead of most Latin American and socialist countries, but it has been affected by Cuba's inefficient centrally planned model, the US embargo, the pandemic, and several economic crises, which have wrinkled access to healthcare, decreased the real value of pensions and the quality of health benefits, and worsened financial-actuarial deficits that are already aggravated by accelerated population aging. The 2008 parametric reform did not solve these problems, which have eroded the constitutional right to social security. There is an urgent need to implement wide, deep, and thorough social security reform in order to address the flaws documented in this book concerning pensions, healthcare, and social assistance.[22] A precondition to any social security reform is to implement urgently needed structural economic reforms à la Sino-Vietnamese model or further toward the market to break away from poor economic performance.[23]

Pensions in Cuba

Unity and Equal Treatment

The current system requires the integration of the military and internal security personnel's separate and costly scheme into the general pension system, as well as the standardization of their entitlement conditions and calculation of benefits.[24] There is also a need to standardize the conditions and contributions of special groups such as the self-employed, members of cooperatives, owners of small farms, and so forth. For instance, self-employed persons should not have to pay a sum of the percentage contributions otherwise paid by employers (whom they lack) and salaried workers, because the higher contributions serve as a disincentive for private microenterprises (because of higher operation costs), which must be expanded to stimulate economic growth and productivity. This measure would have positive effects on other social security principles, such as social solidarity and financial sustainability.

Coverage

The only data available on pension coverage is from 2017 and refers to the population aged 60 and over covered by contributory and noncontributory pensions, so this coverage figure is not comparable with those of China and Vietnam (six Latin American countries, two less socially developed than Cuba, have higher coverage on this indicator). The Cuban government neither publishes administrative statistics on labor force coverage, as China and Vietnam do, nor takes annual household surveys, which, in seventeen other countries in Latin America, provide data on coverage of the labor force (disaggregating the coverage of salaried and self-employed workers), as well as coverage of the elderly population. In addition, such surveys show coverage by key variables as income quintiles, educational levels, and locations (rural vis-à-vis urban).

The absence of this data is inexplicable in a planned economy with a predominant state sector and large enterprises that should allow for an easy and fast calculation of coverage. Furthermore, there are many years of regional household survey experience to facilitate this in Cuba. Therefore, a priority for the central statistical agency, the National Office of Statistics and Information (ONEI), should be to publish administrative data and take household surveys on labor force coverage by pensions (disaggregating coverage of salaried and self-employed workers and other groups) and on the elderly population. This data would provide an accurate calculation of coverage to determine who is uncovered and their characteristics (including the degree of informality), to insert Cuba in world statistics, allow comparisons with other countries, and design strategies to reach real universal coverage.

Once the above tasks are completed, a plan to incorporate those uncovered should be designed. Among those not covered would probably be informal workers (particularly the self-employed and employees of microenterprises), owners of small farms, usufruct farmers, and independent peasants. Due to the diverse characteristics of these groups, the plan should be adapted to each of them, setting their contributions and benefits, as well as incentives for incorporation. The state may consider granting a matching contribution to that paid by the worker, as in several countries such as Bolivia, Costa Rica, and Peru (Mesa-Lago 2021b; Colina 2022b). Statistics on the number of pensioners and pension expenditures do not disaggregate among old-age, disability, and survivor pensions, which is needed not only to project future costs but also to estimate old-age-pension coverage.

The Cuban government has not published statistics on poverty incidence in the sixty-four years since its revolution (although there are rough estimates that show an increasing trend), therefore features of the poor are unknown. Moreover, available official statistics illustrate that social assistance has contracted when it should have expanded. Another priority of ONEI, therefore, should be to calculate and publish the poverty incidence and the features of the poor.

Benefit Sufficiency

It is strongly advised to equalize ages of retirement for both genders, raising the woman's age from 60 to 65 years.[25] Furthermore in view of rapid population aging, retirement ages should be adjusted to life expectancy. Such an increase should be done gradually over a short number of years (for instance, one additional year over a five-year period—a previous increase was done over seven years). The current period of contribution of thirty years, if possible, should be maintained; on the other hand, the very short time to estimate the base salary (the best five years) should be expanded at least fifteen years prior to retirement, as in China and Vietnam, and further increased later. Suggested changes in these parameters should be subordinate to an actuarial evaluation. Stronger surveillance is needed to reduce abuses on claims for disability pensions (Hicks and Pérez 2005).

The standard legal replacement rate of 60 percent is significantly above the minimum 45 percent set by the ILO. On the other hand, the contributory pension is not adjusted to the CPI and its real value in 2020 was 36 percent below the 1989 level and is insufficient to meet basic food needs. Compared to the average pension in China and Vietnam, the Cuban pension in 2020 was 4 percent and 10 percent of the respective averages in the two Asian countries. Due to hyperinflation in 2021–2023, that pension must have further deteriorated. It is essential therefore to adjust the pension to the CPI every year.[26] This, however, would require the implementation of economic structural reforms that increase GDP growth (indexing may facilitate the reduction of the too high legal replacement rate). Wages will have to be also indexed to avoid a rising gap with pensions.

Social Solidarity and Gender Equity

Social solidarity is strongest in Cuba, but there are some problems to tackle. The statistical yearbook, for instance, does not publish the mean pension by province, so it is not possible to assess inequalities on this variable. ONEI publishes women's participation in the total and employed labor force but does not publish data on participation in all the social security programs (as China and Vietnam, partially, do). It is quite probable, as in other countries, that said participation is lower than that of men, but we do not know by how much, therefore it is not possible to detect how much of the gender discrimination is generated by the labor market. Those statistics as well as the average pension by gender are needed to enact the proper policies to reduce gender discrimination. In order to increase women's pensions, the granting of one year of contribution for each child born alive should be considered (this measure would be also an incentive to increase the birth rate).

Administration

Because the pension system is totally managed in a centralized manner by the state, it should be easy for the government to estimate and publish its administrative cost as a percentage of total expenditure, which would permit an assessment of the efficiency of the current system and facilitate measures to improve it.[27] A registration system with individual accounts for all workers should be created to compile data on their years of employment, wages, and contributions, which would facilitate the calculation of pensions (Colina 2022b). In addition, such a tool would determine the percentage of salaried workers who contribute to pensions based on their salary (and self-employed contributions based on their declared income), as well as the amount contributed by both groups, which is necessary to assess the financial stability of the pension system and to conduct actuarial studies.

Cuba has the most centralized social security system, which should be decentralized as in China and Vietnam. In the same vein, there is not yet a digital information system and ID card (briefly mentioned in the current long-term plan), which should be implemented, as in China and to less extent, Vietnam. Finally, Cuba lacks a modernization administrative plan (as China and Vietnam have) and should start working on it.

In the context of the current Cuban centrally planned system is the question of whether administration and tax collection should be unified or be mutually independent. I support unification in the pursuit of transparency and accountability. Colina (2022b) believes that independence would save transaction costs and help to achieve financial sustainability.

Workers and employers should supervise and oversee the management and investment of the pension system and propose corrections, as in China and Vietnam as well as in all public pension systems in Latin America (and as is being demanded from privately managed systems). Information and education of the insured and the population on the pension system, rights, and obligations should be amply disseminated (Mesa-Lago 2021b).

Financial-Actuarial Sustainability

The pension system needs to establish a reserve fund that is nourished by contributions from employers and all workers and engrossed by capital returns, as is the case in virtually all PAYG systems in the world. The capital return of this fund would be invested in securities and productive projects, which would generate an interest or annual dividend to increase the fund. The return on the fund's capital, if it is well managed, would contribute much more than contributions to funding pensions, allowing better real pensions with a solid equilibrium. However, Cuba does not have a stock exchange in which national and foreign instruments are traded as in China and Vietnam, so the investment of the fund would be all in state debt. It has been proved that this method results in dependence on the state, which usually pays low interests, involving a subsidy from workers to the government's general expenses. Colina (2022b) proposes a mixed financial system: a public pension and a capitalized supplementary pension based on individual accounts that is publicly managed (as in China). He asks, however, for a separation of the administration of state enterprises from the management of the capitalized pillar, for which transparency and accountability are required. Colina also advises Cuba to invest the capitalization fund in low-risk instruments, which would maximize security but reduce the capital returns needed in a long-term pension system.

ONEI does not publish the financial balance (revenues minus expenditures) of the pension system as China and Vietnam do. This is very easy to do because in Cuba, all pension contributions go to the state, which, in turn, pays all pensions. The annual balance (deficit) in this book was calculated based, on the one hand, on the revenue of "social insurance" (pension) contributions (there are neither reserves nor capital returns) and, on the other hand, pension expenditures. However, the latter does not disaggregate administrative expenditures, hence the expense allocated to benefits must be lower in reality. Said balances should be made public.

For twenty-two years, Cuba has not conducted an actuarial valuation of its pension system, so the magnitude of the actuarial disequilibrium is unknown; it is probably grave in outlook, as the disequilibrium impacts the future fiscal balance. Unlike Vietnam, Cuba does not have a window of opportunity to address the collapse of the pension system, so it is essential to conduct the actuarial valuation immediately, preferably by the ILO (of which Cuba is a member), to determine with certainty the necessary parametric reforms concerning retirement age, period of contribution, base salary, percentage contributions by the worker and the employer,[28] the legal replacement rate, and the formula to calculate the pension.[29] It would be a serious mistake to set such parameters without having a solid foundation and projections based on reliable data. The actuarial evaluation would estimate the current and long-term actuarial deficit of the system: contrasting the present value of all future obligations (current pension expenses and those generated by current actively insured persons) with future revenue (from contributions and, hopefully, from capital returns).

Healthcare in Cuba

Unity and Equal Treatment

Finding solutions to the problems confronting the Cuban healthcare system is difficult, and as has been shown, these problems will get progressively worse—particularly considering the matter of rising health costs due to aging that affects financial sustainability and thus requiring rapid action. The unified and universal health system should be kept, but its efficiency needs to be increased and the operation of private facilities and personnel in competition with the public system allowed. As in the case of pensions, the separate healthcare facilities and staff for the military, internal security, and party officials should be integrated into the general public health system.

Coverage

It is essential that ONEI calculate and publish statistics on coverage of the total population and on effective access, the latter bearing in mind the reduction and closing of facilities (hospitals, polyclinics, posts) and the exportation of doctors and other medical personnel that have reduced the population's access.

Benefit Sufficiency

The deterioration in the quality of health services will require a significant investment, which is quite difficult in view of the current dire economic situation. This demands a significant transformation in the current economic model. To cope with aging and to improve efficiency, scarcely available resources should be assigned more rationally. A significant number of funds are apportioned to facilities and personnel that care for younger-age cohorts (gynecological and pediatric hospitals) to keep reducing the already low infant mortality. Conversely, few funds, facilities, and personnel are allocated to the elderly population—there are virtually no geriatric hospitals and very few homes for the elderly, despite Cuba having the oldest population in the Western Hemisphere (and it is growing in numbers). It would be also advisable to place greater emphasis on inexpensive preventive measures capable of minimizing the need for more expensive curative care. Doing so would require the return of many family doctors from abroad (and, to avoid their potential underutilization, retraining skills attuned to elderly needs), together with sufficient economic growth to import medical inputs that are essential for quality care. Such economic growth would be facilitated if the émigré community were formerly invited to invest in a friendly domestic-policy environment, as is the case in China and Vietnam.

Social Solidarity and Gender Equity

The gap in health indicators (particularly the maternal mortality rate) among the most developed urban provinces and the least developed rural provinces could be reduced by increasing budget allocations or by creating a national fund to invest in the provinces with the biggest gaps. In gender equity, Cuba ranks well below China but slightly higher than Vietnam. Some measures that could be taken are an increase in the percentage of maternity leave from 60 to 100 percent (as in China and Vietnam), an expansion of the period of leave from eighteen to twenty-four weeks, and a calculation of the amount based on the average salary of the previous six months instead of one year.

Financial-Actuarial Sustainability

The potential threat to the long-term financial sustainability of the universal healthcare system could be reduced by policies geared toward increasing revenue and reducing expenditures. Regarding the former, a guaranteed share of hard-currency earnings from the provision of professional medical services abroad could be redirected to improve health infrastructure, purchase medications, and raise the salaries of healthcare personnel. In addition, in view of the increasing income inequality of the population and the regressive nature of taxes in Cuba, it would be appropriate to charge copayments to higher-income patients for more complex and costly procedures; in reality, copayments are made informally and hurt low-income groups (legal copayments are charged in China and Vietnam). The provision of cheap medical services in Cuba could be expanded, particularly by enticing people from developing countries ("medical tourism") and by promoting long-term residential retirement tourism cum medical services among the elderly of middle-income countries whose healthcare expenses are covered by their social security provisions, regardless of where services are received. An additional revenue stream may materialize by sending Cuban mid-level technical personnel to provide long-term-care services in rich countries.

Another long-term option would be to entice elderly US citizens, including those of Cuban descent, to retire in Cuba and to rely on medical services provided by the Cuban healthcare system. This option, however, is not likely in the short-term given the continued bilateral animosity between the two countries and the serious deterioration of Cuba's healthcare services. Even in the long run, this alternative is unlikely to generate much revenue because US federal regulations proscribe the use of Medicare, the US government healthcare program for the elderly, to pay for services accessed beyond the confines of the United States.

Substantial resources could be saved by the suggested policies to improve the allocation of health resources. Another means is to assess the current medical education strategy of continued promotion of medical graduates that results in the export of health professionals to generate hard currency at the expense of reducing domestic access for the population and neglecting graduates in disciplines that are needed for economic development. There are solid reasons to change this strategy, including the decreased demand for buying medical service because of the severe economic crisis in Venezuela, and the return of physicians from Brazil, Bolivia, Ecuador, and some African countries due to changes in governments. A Cuban economist argues that such an export strategy carries high risks not only in terms of the potential vulnerability of political and economic changes in the receiving countries but also because the strategy is circumscribed by modest multiplier effects: health personnel abroad represent only 1 percent of the Cuban labor force but generate 44 percent of total export value (Torres 2018, 2020).

As in China and Vietnam, Cuba should allow the operation of private healthcare facilities such as hospitals, policlinics, and so forth, and should authorize physicians and other health personnel to open private practices. These private services should be regulated by the state and engage in competition with the public system in order to stimulate improvements in efficiency and better quality of services. The social welfare model of Nordic countries and other European nations could provide useful insights on the pros and cons of partial privatization. Bye (2020) compares Sweden and Norway, arguing that the former has gone much further than the latter, with adverse consequences.[30] He argues that many social democrats in Sweden claim today that the Swedish welfare state is being abandoned (even before the current conservative government took power in 2022).

Social Assistance in Cuba

Unity and Equal Treatment

Social assistance in Cuba is the most unified of the three countries, hence there are no recommendations on this principle.

Coverage

ONEI does not provide percentage of coverage of social assistance, although it does publish absolute figures that allowed estimates in this book; these as well as the Social Assistance Explorer rank Cuba last among the three countries. ONEI does not give data on poverty incidence, which impedes an accurate assessment of the impact of social assistance on poverty.

Benefit Sufficiency

The current norm is that people in severe need cannot access social assistance if they have family able to help. This norm should be abolished and replaced by a national social protection system that is well targeted on the poor through an efficient means test. As has been noted already, this will require estimating the population poverty incidence and the features of the vulnerable in order to set the essential base to properly detect the real vulnerable population, calculate the cost of social assistance, and identify financing sources.

A comprehensive system of eldercare should be developed, and the very high ratio of elderly population per bed reduced substantially. In view of the severe scarcity of state resources, it is advisable to expand non-state services, as in China and Vietnam. Churches, charity agencies, and NGOs should be encouraged to build and manage homes for the elderly, which may attract international aid and be supplemented by government subsidies for the needy who receive care at those institutions (Acosta 2022a). A mixed approach is to open existing public welfare homes and residential eldercare facilities to self-paying individuals and provide them with enhanced quality services with government support, as is done already in China and is starting to occur in Vietnam (Glinskaya et al. 2022). Expansion of self-employed eldercare workers should be promoted to facilitate the granting of licenses and reduction of excessive taxes in order to increase competition and reduce prices. The new family code regulation related to the work and training of these workers is a positive step and should be implemented.

Social Solidarity and Gender Equity

Inequality gaps and infringement on the rights of women, the disabled, the elderly, and children—caused by insufficient state services combined with mercantilized provision and unremunerated family caregiving—should be corrected (Acosta 2021; Ación and Colina 2022). ONEI does not provide data on social assistance by gender and province, which impedes an essential evaluation of these two social security principles to elaborate policies for improvement.

Administration

As China and Vietnam have done, Cuba (where central planning predominates) should develop a medium- and long-term plan to address needs and policies related to aging, social assistance, and long-term care for the elderly (Acosta et al. 2018). Currently, the budgeted allocation provided for social assistance is merged with the healthcare allocation; they should be separated to improve transparency and to assess the needs of each unique sector. The government should then assign the necessary resources to social assistance so as to finance the changes suggested above. In addition, the government should regulate, oversee, and monitor eldercare services and regulate their prices. Whenever possible, priority should be given to home care over institutional care. Recently, the training of human resources on eldercare began, and this is an important step; the graduation and proper training of those professionals should be expanded and their salaries increased. Information is badly needed on the quality of social assistance and the satisfaction of users (surveys should be administered for this).

Financial-Actuarial Sustainability

There are no ONEI statistics on the financing of social assistance, the cost of these services, or their financial sustainability. Ación and Colina acknowledge the lack of statistics on expenditures for eldercare, but they state that "the economic sustainability of future programs of social transfers for eldercare—as well as other social assistance policies—is improbable only relying on fiscal support" (2022, 15–16). The two social scientists propose a new financial model for eldercare that is both mixed and decentralized, with diverse types of ownership and management (families, enterprises, cooperatives, NGOs, and the state), and that features multiple financial sources such as social insurance, taxes (central and local), family fees adjusted to income, and donations. Such a model should be guided by the principles of social solidarity, equity, financial sustainability, and social participation in the administration and should be adapted to economic growth and the nation's available resources (Ación and Colina 2022, 1, 17–19).

Options to demographically address the challenge of fast aging are few and unlikely to yield tangible solutions. The former director of the Cuban Center for Demographic Studies at the University of Havana acknowledges that population aging is irreversible (it could be slowed down through immigration, but migrants are unlikely to want to settle in Cuba given its current dismal economic situation), while other long-term demographic trends (e.g., low fertility) are hardly likely to be reversed in the short term (Albizu-Campos 2009, 2016). It has been noted that, despite the implementation of pro-fertility measures, the number of births and the total fertility rates have declined. When results are achieved, they usually entail high price tags, which are not affordable for Cuba, given the country's serious economic difficulties.

Some selected policies could be devised to alleviate the current demographic predicament. The most potentially consequential option—often voiced before, and unlikely to come to fruition unless the national economy undergoes a remarkable turnaround—is ending the long-standing permanent emigration trend by encouraging circular migration. Were this to happen, Cubans would continue emigrating to and working in other countries, but they would routinely return to their homeland to be with family and friends and spend foreign earnings there (Aja and Hernández 2019).

Suitability of the Current Economic Model

The centrally planned model has failed all over the world, including in Cuba. The study recounted in this book has proved that Cuba's minor reforms have not only been unsuccessful in increasing economic growth but have not impeded several crises and significant economic-social deterioration, which adversely affected the early significant gains in social security. Therefore, this model should be replaced by another, such as the successful Sino-Vietnamese socialist-market approach, with the necessary adaptations to Cuban characteristics. Furthermore, the proposed social security reforms would be unviable unless preceded by such transformation to promote rapid and sustained economic growth. In turn, this would generate the needed resources to improve social security. Cuban academic economists agree that the solution lies in accelerating and deepening the necessary structural reforms, along the lines of those successfully implemented in China and Vietnam.[31]

These reforms are intended to shift the central plan to a decentralized one with indicative planning as guidance for development; replace central administrative and physical indicators by market indicators; terminate the state monopoly of foreign trade, permitting all enterprises and the non-state sector to import and export directly without intermediaries; significantly expand the non-state sector (particularly the private sector) to create productive jobs, absorb the labor surplus in the state sector, and increase productivity and GDP. The reforms should also implement agrarian reform that gives freedom to all agricultural producers to decide what to sow, to whom they sell the crops, and at what prices according to supply and demand, which would increase agricultural output, make the country self-sufficient in food (allowing an end to the dependence on imports), and generate a surplus for export. The reforms should also authorize foreign investment in all economic sectors, including from Cubans abroad, and in the non-state sector with proper state regulations. They negotiate the external debt and meet the agreed-upon payments with foreign creditors. The reforms authorize commercial banking (including foreign banks) to expand, so that banking eventually becomes the financier of state enterprises, instead of the state being the financier. They also authorize private enterprises and independent cooperatives. They reform the regressive tax system so as to make it progressive, with an expansion of the personal income tax to eliminate the multiple and heavy taxes that strangle the non-state sector and to allocate funds to develop a social protection net.[32]

These profound reforms would allow the success of monetary and exchange unification. They would control the current hyperinflation and open space for negotiations with the United States to end the embargo (as was done in Vietnam) and for Cuba to enter the World Bank and the IMF, hence receiving loans from both. Unfortunately, in 2023, Cuba appeared to embrace the inefficient Russian model of oligarchic capitalism, which may give some relief from the crisis on the island but will not solve the nation's structural economic and social problems.

VIETNAM

Vietnam ranks second in social security indicators. Healthcare coverage has been rapidly and notably expanded, and the system is shifting its emphasis toward primary care and family medicine. The pension and social assistance system are unified and fairly standardized; gross RR of contributory pensions are high by international standards; social assistance has been extended and poverty incidence reduced significantly. Social solidarity and gender equity are the strongest of the three countries; the non-state sector (especially private) plays an important role in both healthcare and social assistance; the pension system has generated steady surpluses, and the same is true of the health system (save for one year); the country is still young and has a window of opportunity to tackle major problems; and the economy has been growing at strong rates.

On the other hand, there are notable challenges. Coverage of the labor force remains low, because the large incidence of self-employment and its voluntary coverage mean that only a tiny minority is covered (but it is expanding due to state aid). Some fragmentation persists in the health system; retirement ages are quite low, relative to both international standards and life expectancy at retirement age. Despite improvements, particularly in rural areas, inequalities endure among regions, ethnic groups, and genders; and although increasing, social assistance still leaves a sizable segment of the population uncovered. According to an official document: "although the national Constitution states that access to social security is an entitlement, the current social assistance pillar of social security . . . is unable to fulfill the Constitution's mandate" (Kidd et al. 2016, 31). Therefore, there is a need to confirm in legislation that qualifying persons have the right to social insurance and social assistance (as established in the constitution), as well as to ratify the ILO Convention No. 102 on social security minimum standards (Olivier 2022).

Several parametric reforms have been implemented, but there is wide consensus that more are indispensable (World Bank 2019; Ramírez and Arza 2021; ILSSA/ILO 2022; Olivier 2022). These authors provide concrete recommendations on how to execute the reform. Three medium-term plans are geared to solve some of the problems: the communist party orientations for 2018–2025 and a vision to 2030, the ministry of health national action program for 2017–2025, and the prime minister health program for 2018–2030. Because these three programs are now in their fifth year, evaluations and any necessary adjustments are advisable. Scholarly studies on the reliability of Vietnam's statistics are needed, as have been done for China and Cuba. It is in the interest of the nation to know potential statistical problems in order to design proper policies to correct them.

Pensions in Vietnam

Unity and Equal Treatment

Vietnam has the most unified and standardized pension system of the three countries. The armed forces are integrated in the mandatory social insurance pension program (which is not the case in China or Cuba), but they have some entitlement conditions better than the rest of the insured; such conditions should be standardized with those in the general system (save for justified exemptions due to the nature of military work) to strengthen social solidarity. However, the self-employed have voluntary affiliation (this is an important exception to be discussed below). The use of a different salary reference for the public sector (based on the last few years of wages) and for the private sector (the entire working life) should be eliminated. Ideally, the entire working life should be used for both groups, but if this becomes politically unfeasible, the current average of twenty years would be reasonable. The government is considering a reduction of these years to facilitate access to the contributory pension, but such a decision should be evaluated in advance by an actuarial study. In addition, the social security system still needs to be better integrated in order to fulfill its three functions: prevention (social insurance), protection (social assistance), and promotion (a well-defined strategy to operate as an integrated and coherent system) (World Bank 2019). There is need for an integrated legal framework that coordinates all social security laws, preferably in a single consolidated law (Olivier 2022).

Coverage

Vietnam has the lowest coverage of the labor force by pensions (28 percent) of the three countries—for two main reasons. First, self-employment accounts for almost 36 percent of the labor force, and only 1.5 percent of those within this sector had registered in 2017 for voluntary affiliation. A major obstacle is that they pay the total contribution of 22 percent because they lack an employer. However, a new policy implemented in 2018 provides a state subsidy to the contributions paid by the self-employed, farmers, and other informal workers, which has accelerated coverage in the voluntary scheme, but it is still quite low. An official target of 50 percent coverage of the labor force, the ILO minimum standard coverage, has been set for 2025 and to 60 percent for 2030 (ILSSA/ILO 2022). Based on an average annual rate of expansion of

1.3 percentage points in 2018–2020, pension coverage in 2030 would be 45.6 percent.[33]

One alternative to expand coverage is to increase the state aid to expand voluntary affiliation faster. Another would be to mandate the affiliation of professionals and other organized groups with relatively high incomes. This is because those covered by contributory pensions are in the top 40 percent of income (formal sector), while the noncontributory pension for those aged 80 and above is universal. Therefore, the challenge is to extend coverage to the "missing middle" sector that is excluded from both schemes (Kidd et al. 2016; World Bank 2019, 2021b; ILSSA/ILO 2022). Olivier (2022) recommends the gradual incorporation of currently excluded business household heads, business managers, and managers of cooperatives, employees with multiple employers, and certain dependents and survivors. Among the policies intended to expand coverage of SMEs are the aims of simplifying the registration and paying of contributions, gaining more flexibility in negotiating debt payments with employers, spreading the payments of contribution arrears out over time, and allowing partial withdrawals as a lump sum with a strict limit (Castel and Pick 2018). In order to reduce the gap in women's disability pensions, it is essential to provide state incentives to deter those eligible from leaving the labor force early and taking a lump sum. A multilayered child benefit is recommended in order to tackle the lack of coverage on disability, maternity, and sickness cash benefits for the self-employed and domestic workers in the voluntary program; this would provide a lower benefit than in the mandatory system, thereby preserving the incentive to join the latter (ILO 2021c). Coverage of domestic workers should be mandatory so as to force employers to enroll them (Ramírez and Arza 2021). Olivier (2022) goes further, recommending that voluntary affiliation should gradually shift to mandatory insurance, with the government expanding its subsidies.

The Vietnam GSO statistical yearbook (the latest available at the time of ending this book was 2021) has only one page on social security ("insurances"), including the number of insured and beneficiaries by type of program (pensions, health, and unemployment) and total revenue and expenditures (also disaggregated by the three main programs). The household living standards survey taken every other year (latest available is 2020) provides information on healthcare (health treatment) and social assistance (participation in poverty alleviation programs) (GSO 2020). The labor force survey, also taken every other year (latest available is 2020), has plenty of data on employment, unemployment, poverty, and so forth (GSO 2022a). Finally, the VSS publishes occasional indicators but not as a regular statistical series (see as an example, VSS 2019b).

None of these publications offers data on coverage of the labor force (disaggregating coverage of salaried and self-employed workers), coverage of the elderly population, and coverage by key variables such as income quintiles, educational levels, regions, ethnic minorities, and rural versus urban location.[34]

It is therefore recommended that either household or labor surveys include that essential data on coverage or that a new survey is developed with those tasks. It is also suggested that, because the majority of the self-employed lack voluntary pension insurance, surveys on the informal sector add a questionnaire on social protection or that this is included as part of the survey on social security coverage. Finally, there is simultaneous repetition of data among surveys and lacunae, underscoring the importance of coordination among surveys, which is essential in order to design proper policies to expand coverage and meet the 2030 goal (Huong et al. 2013).

Benefit Sufficiency

Statutory ages for retirement in Vietnam (60 for men and 55 for women) are well below ages in countries at the same level of development and even below those in some less developed countries. However, these ages are gradually increasing to 62 for men and 60 for women. The retirement age for women should gradually increase to 62, the same as for men.[35] Ideally, the retirement age for both sexes should be linked to changes in life expectancy.[36] Early retirement is possible in Vietnam five years earlier than the statutory age for insured military personnel, workers with reduced work capacity, and those in dangerous jobs, with a discount of 2 percent for each year of withdrawal earlier than the normal age; this benefit should be tightened to avoid its potential misuse. A better option would be to guarantee access to a disability benefit that is properly certified to all workers suffering from a severe incapacity (Kidd et al. 2016).

The twenty years of contributions required for a minimum old-age pension is a significant barrier for private-sector workers, the self-employed, and women. The Resolution 28 of 2018 envisages a gradual reduction of said period to fifteen years by 2024 and to ten years by 2028, a measure supported by Ramírez and Arza (2021) and ILSSA/ILO (2022). Ramírez and Arza, however, are concerned about the impact on the level of the pension. Another important apprehension is the effect of such a measure on financial-actuarial sustainability. A compensatory alternative could be a state matching contribution already granted to the self-employed in the voluntary program that could also be applied to women; the cost of the two policies should be actuarially assessed. In all cases, incentives should be provided to workers so that they continue working as longevity increases (e.g., a percentage increase in the pension for each year of extra work), whereas stronger penalties should be imposed for early retirement (e.g., 2 percent per year). The full salary, instead of the base salary, of the employee should serve as the basis for the contribution payment and benefit size (Olivier 2022).

In order to evaluate if the current minimum contributory pension of US$193 is indeed sufficient in meeting essential needs, the cost of a basket of food should be estimated and made public. RR in public and private sectors are diverse; a process of equalization is gradually taking place, but its path should be accelerated. The legal maximum RR is 75 percent of the insured's average earnings, whereas the estimated effective gross RR is 63 percent for men and 44 percent for women (a more reliable RR should be estimated by the government); the legal maximum RR is well above the 45 percent ILO minimum and the estimated effective gross RR almost meets it. The OECD projection of a hypothetical RR of 75 percent of men's average earnings in 2056 is well above the OECD member average, almost similar to China and surpassed only by Pakistan, Italy, and India.

The ILO (2018b) considers Vietnam's RR too high to ensure financial sustainability, hence serious consideration should be given to adjusting it. The party is considering a shift from the current actual adjustment to wage growth toward annually adjusting to CPI. The ILO warns that, with merely the latter, pensioners may maintain the purchasing power of pensions but will not share in improving the living standards of active workers. On the other hand, the combination method results in a growing gender gap with age, hence gender equality should be taken into account (Ramírez and Arza 2021).

Terminal lump sums, especially for women at a young age, should be discouraged and alternative mechanisms designed. In general, Resolution 28 of 2018 envisages phasing out lump sums while promoting regular pension payments (Olivier 2022). The lack of protection on disability, maternity, and sickness cash benefits for those in the voluntary program demands that they be made universal. Survival pensions for women require fifteen years of contribution by their husbands, and this requisite should be eliminated or reduced. Some of these measures would improve the financial-actuarial sustainability of the system, whereas others would reduce it; in any case, they should be submitted to an actuarial review in advance and implemented gradually over a predetermined period. Resolution 28 of 2018 outlines a multitiered system: tier 1 as the noncontributory pension, tier 2 as the contributory social insurance pension, and tier 3 as the supplementary voluntary pension insurance. Further direction is needed to ascertain how different tiers relate to each other and how they will be able to cumulatively provide a comprehensive social security system (Olivier 2022).

Social Solidarity and Gender Equity

Although Vietnam has the most unified and standardized pension system of the three countries and has reduced disparities between urban and rural areas, inequalities remain among regions and ethnic groups. A national compensation fund, like the one proposed for China, should be established with adequate central government funding to ameliorate those disparities. Gender policies should be integrated in a package rather than as single measures (Ramírez and Arza 2021). Women have higher pension coverage than men (31.3 percent and 22.1 percent, respectively) and coverage is about the same in health insurance (95 percent). On the other hand, women are overrepresented in self-employment and unpaid family work, thus they are also in the vulnerable population. In addition, women have lower gross RR and pension averages than men (data is needed on female participation in all social security programs). One major reason for low female participation in the labor force is that most women aged 20–43 do not work because of their household responsibilities. Policies should be designed and implemented to improve the state-subsidized training of women, and incentives added to formalize their micro businesses (Huong et al. 2013). This would reduce the burdens of caring for children and the elderly for working-aged women by improving and subsidizing childcare and eldercare services.

In addition, some countries have implemented a bonus or a year of contribution for women for each child born alive ("care credits"); such a benefit in Vietnam would encourage women to keep their contribution in the system rather than withdrawing lump sums because it would increase their chance of meeting qualifying conditions for a pension. A care credit of eighteen months based on the reference salary would increase the value of women's pensions by 8.3 percent and reduce the gender gap at a reasonably low cost (Ramírez and Arza 2021). The planned increase in the age of retirement of women (a higher increase than that of men) raised concerns about adverse effects; however, the ILO has estimated that by equalizing the age of retirement, the gender gap in benefits will decrease by 1–2 percent, which is still not enough (Ramírez and Arza 2021).

Vietnam is ahead of the other two countries on the calculation of the RR. In terms of care, it is advisable to move from the current maternalistic approach toward a model of parenthood leave available to both mothers and fathers (ILO 2021b). Finally, the noncontributory pension and its level should be increased, a measure that will benefit women in particular. Noninsured women should be given the right to a tax-financed maternity benefit, which is estimated to cost only 0.04 percent of GDP (Ramírez and Arza 2021).

Administration

Although Vietnam has the most unified and standardized pension system of the three countries, its social protection policy is still cumbersome and overlapped. There are about 233 policy documents issued and implemented across different periods by the communist party, the National Assembly, the government, various ministries, and different agencies. Therefore, legislation lacks a systematic approach (which creates difficulties in the application of policies and management of the system) and needs full integration (Q. Dao 2017).

The various departments of MOLISA that deal with different benefits should be properly coordinated. MOLISA supervises the whole system, which strengthens enforcement of compliance. And yet, a high debt for evasion and payment delays as well as underdeclaration of earnings is reported (though this is declining). To further reduce it, a new decree enacted in 2022 imposes tougher sanctions for those who infringe the law; it is therefore important to evaluate the impact of this legislation on compliance. In addition, insurable earnings should represent the entire wage so as to guarantee benefit adequacy, and there should be an integration of the contributory and noncontributory pensions (Ramírez and Arza 2021). The plan of integration of MOLISA and the Ministry of Health and the issue of a national ID card for social security by 2020 should have a positive impact on pension compliance. In addition, a national data-sharing platform should be established among all social security agencies and programs (World Bank 2019). These measures would reduce to about one-half those who are entitled to social assistance but who are excluded in the poor list.

Quite positive is that the Vietnam General Confederation of Labor, the Chamber of Commerce and Industry, and cooperatives have representation in the Social Insurance Board, supervise the system, and provide recommendations for social security policy and legislation. In addition, there are mechanisms for employees and employers to complain about social insurance grievances. Still, the autonomy of the Social Insurance Board and the VSS should be strengthened, a better balance of worker and employer representation on the board is required, and the board membership could be expanded to include informal workers and pensioners (Olivier 2022). Ideally, a consolidated structure at the apex level should be entrusted with supervision and policy guidance and with facilitating integrated and coordinated interventions. Alternatively, an independent and autonomous supervisory agency should be created to oversee the entire pension system.

Financial-Actuarial Equilibrium

Contribution rates are already high, hence there is very little space to increase them further to help achieve better equilibrium (an increase in contributions could also discourage participation in the formal sector); reforms suggested in other parameters should be considered. Vietnam has sufficient fiscal space to finance some of the improved benefits out of the general revenue. Savings from the subsidy paid by the government to VSS to cover the pension of civil servants that retired prior to 1995 could be used to improve the most needed benefits, and the same could be said of the Merit program when it ends—these two programs account for 1 percent of GDP (Kidd et al. 2016).

Vietnam is the youngest of the three countries and still has a window of opportunity to adopt policies to cope with aging, but there are signs that the window will not last long. Life expectancy at retirement age is higher than in other countries in the region (for men, it is higher than in Japan); the population aged 65 and above will climb to 18 percent by 2040, and fertility rates are rapidly declining. Some parametric reforms have been introduced to balance finances, such as gradual increases in retirement ages and contributions, an expanded salary base to impose contributions, penalties for early retirement, and so forth, but they could be insufficient. Expanding coverage may be positive in the short run, but in the long run it will not stop a deficit; there is need for a more profound reform.

The social insurance pension program generated steady surpluses in 2015–2020. The ILO (2018b) conducted an actuarial study on the pension program with data at the end of 2015, but the study was not accessible. In any case, it is now seven years old, and in the interim there have been important parametric reforms (positive) and the impact of Covid-19 (negative) that should be evaluated. The Council of Social Security projected exhaustion of the reserves by 2030, but the World Bank (2021b) postponed it to 2042, without reforms; in addition, the Bank projected a growth in the pension system deficit from 2.5 percent to 3 percent of GDP in 2043–2050. Alternatively, the Bank estimated that the exhaustion year of 2042 could be postponed with several parametric reforms: to 2044, with pension indexation to CPI; to 2046, with an increase in retirement age; to 2063, with the convergence of valorization formula by 2048; or to 2080, with all three reforms combined. An actuarial study should be conducted as soon as possible to determine the effects of these reforms as well as the other ones suggested herein, such as the expansion of coverage. The ILO could do such study with simulations that show the effects of each reform or combined reforms; once this is done, there should be a national social dialogue to discuss the needed reforms. Anticipating the end of the window of opportunity, an educational campaign financed by a public national education fund should be created to improve financial knowledge of both the general population and the insured, and to emphasize the importance of social security pensions and health literacy.[37]

The ILO, working with MOLISA, designed the following reform with three tiers. The first tier is a tax-funded and means-tested non-contributory pension, at age 67, that would cover a good part of those now uncovered, including part of the informal sector. The second tier is a mandatory public social insurance pension of defined benefits, financed by contributions from employers and employees, based on PAYG or partial funding, and managed by social insurance (as it is currently under VSS). This tier will require a parametric reform (such as increasing the age of retirement and equalizing it for both genders, adjusting pensions to the CPI, etc.). It will also need incentives for affiliation and a process of formalization of the labor force. The third tier is comprised of voluntary supplementary private pensions of defined contribution, for those who have a capacity to save and increase their basic pensions. The change process should be gradual (in the period 2021–2030), the three tiers should be well coordinated and integrated, paying due consideration to gender equity, and approved by the government through a national dialogue with social partners. The proposal includes a roadmap with two scenarios, each with coverage targets in the years 2025 and 2030 for insured and pensioners and projected costs indexed to inflation for tiers 1 and 2; the noncontributory pension costs range from 0.1 to 0.3 percent of GDP with a declining trend (ILO/Japan 2019).

The World Bank (2021b) has also proposed a three-pillar reform with the following design.[38] First, there is a parametric reform of the current VSS contributory pension for formal workers, including a gradual increase in the retirement age, a reduction in RR, accrual rates, and incentives for early retirement, and a new stimulus mechanism to attract informal workers (a government-financed matching contribution), as well as the incorporation of more workers in the formal sector, such as small firms, and better enforcement and compliance.[39] Second, expansion of the noncontributory pension and lowering the age of 80 and above closer to age 70, this pension could be means-tested or universal. The third is an extension of the voluntary private pension (since RR in the mandatory contributory scheme will have to be reduced) for all workers. Before starting this pillar, the country must have in place a strong regulatory-supervision regime and better government capacity to manage pension-fund investments. It is advisable that the third tier or pillar be mixed, comprised of both public and private agencies competing among themselves with a regulatory frame for all and state supervision.

There are more similarities than differences between the two proposals summarized above, a welcome development in the field: the design is based on three very similar tiers or pillars; implementation is gradual; a noncontributory pension is supported (both proposals evaluate the advantages and disadvantages of universal versus means-tested pensions); the informal sector is to be incorporated with incentives (the ILO reduces qualifying conditions and introduces a set of different minimum pensions, while the Bank supports a matching state contribution); and a gradual formalization of the labor force is considered crucial. The Bank emphasizes the need of proper sequencing—the mandatory contributory pillar coverage cannot be expanded before it is reformed—but does not develop scenarios.[40] Finally, reversing its previous position in favor of "one-model fits all," the Bank acknowledges that "there is no one 'correct' way to build this system" (Mesa-Lago 2021b, 135) and provides alternatives.[41] In 2023, at the time of completing this book, the government had already introduced at least three elements of the proposed reforms: the age of retirement in the contributory pension is being gradually increased to 62 for men and 60 for women; the government has introduced its matching contribution to stimulate affiliation to the contributory tier; and a new voluntary pension scheme has been announced.

Healthcare in Vietnam

Unity and Equal Treatment

There is some fragmentation in the social insurance health system, mainly at the provincial level. There are differences, for instance, among four groups concerning public subsidies, and an attempt should be made to gradually unify subsidies to such groups.

Coverage

Vietnam rapidly expanded coverage of the population with healthcare to 89 percent in 2020, and a goal of 95 percent for 2025 has been set, which seems easy to achieve with current expansion policies. Healthcare coverage of the population is three times the pension coverage of the labor force, and the difference may be reflected by the mandatory enrollment of the self-employed in the health program. Survey data shows that the population treated having healthcare insurance or free healthcare certificates increased from 61 percent to 92 percent in 2008–2018, hence such policies must have helped to expand coverage of the self-employed.

Benefit Sufficiency

The current shift emphasizes primary healthcare and prevention, largely based on the increase in numbers of family doctors (opposite to the loss of those doctors in Cuba due to their exportation), decreased reliance on hospital care (among other reasons, to reduce the costs of and overcrowding at hospitals while making services closer to the people), as well as stronger coordination among health providers. The corresponding section on China provided recommendations on the training, salaries, and incentives for family doctors that are suitable to Vietnam as well.

Hospital beds are expanding in number and that should continue in order to meet needs. On the other hand, the ratio of physicians to hospital beds is the highest among all three countries, which suggests a reallocation of resources among the two demands. Morbidity rates in eight important diseases should be reported.

Social Solidarity and Gender Equity

Existing disparities by regions, areas, quintiles, and ethnic groups in the population that receives health treatment are partly alleviated by government subsidies, but they could be further reduced through the recommended national compensation fund that would give priority and assign more resources to the disadvantaged, thereby strengthening social solidarity. Vietnam leads over China and Cuba as well as most less developed countries, and even some of the most developed ones such as the United States, with regards to the longest paid maternity leave (twenty-four weeks). However, the self-employed are excluded from this benefit, mainly because they lack an employer who often pays for the leave. A state fund to pay for maternity leave that combines an employer contribution and state subsidies would address this and have a progressive effect on distribution, as the self-employed, with a few exceptions, have relatively lower incomes than most salary earners. The absence of individual accounts in Vietnam's health program avoids the accentuation of gender inequity, as is the case in China, but there is no data on female participation compared with male participation in health social insurance and in the other programs, which China provides.

Administration

The holding by MOLISA and MOH of national drug bidding, negotiated with firms and pharmaceutical companies, saves hundreds of billions of dong annually. But there are few mechanisms for effective communication and collaboration between the MOLISA and the MOH, although some progress has been achieved. The MOLISA modernization plan of 2016–2020 was expected to develop a unified information system and database for an integrated social security card ID to be used by MOLISA and the Ministry of Labor, which would facilitate better integration of the social protection system. The plan's implementation has been evaluated with positive results. There is overcrowding at high-level hospitals despite the fact that virtually all districts (communes) have primary healthcare posts—but about half of them do not meet national standards. As a result, it is essential to raise those standards. The concentration of outpatient visits in state hospitals and private health facilities increases costs, such that a shift should occur toward primary healthcare facilities that are less expensive.

Private provision accounts for 42 percent of current health expenditures, geared mainly to those with enough resources to pay the high prices of those services, which make them little accessible to the population with scarce resources. Private hospitals and clinics should be properly regulated by the state and should pay adequate taxes on their profits in order to contribute to healthcare for the population, particularly low-income and poor people. A study comparing administrative costs of public and private providers is necessary in order to evaluate the efficiency of both and to design proper policies to improve efficiency and reduce costs. Consultation with the population (regions and groups) in the design of healthcare plans and legislation should be strengthened in order to meet people's needs properly, as well as accountability and oversight mechanisms, and monitoring of performance and implementation.

Financial-Actuarial Sustainability

The social insurance health program generated a surplus in 2015–2016 but a deficit in 2017–2018; it was covered by government transfers, which took a tiny percentage of GDP. In order to cope with this problem, an increase in contributions has been imposed every other year; this is feasible up to a point because Vietnam's contributions are the smallest of the three countries. The projected expansion of population coverage from 89 percent to 95 percent in 2019–2025 should not help to reduce costs because the added population is expected to have low incomes or to be poor or near poor. To the best of our knowledge, a recent actuarial report—at least by an external international organization—has not been conducted and is needed to implement the necessary parametric reforms that strengthen the equilibrium of the program.

Social Assistance in Vietnam

Unity and Equal Treatment

Social assistance in Vietnam is nationally unified—the central government regulates the standard level for social assistance benefits and the eligibility criteria for selection of beneficiaries. However, the decentralization of social-assistance-policy design allows subnational authorities to decide their own policies based on local economic conditions and the fiscal space. The local authorities at the provincial level (Provincial People's Committee) can decide their own social assistance policy by increasing the standard level of the benefits or loosening the eligibility criteria. For instance, the age for the universal noncontributory pension is 80 and above, but some provinces reduced it to 75 or 70. Better coordination is needed between social insurance and social assistance—for instance, overlapping has been shown to exist on transfers by both institutions (Kidd et al. 2016). The World Bank (2012) argues that an integrative framework for social protection would provide consistency among its different programs, allowing for the use of the same equipment and the same personnel, thus saving costs. According to Olivier (2022), Resolution 28 of 2018 does not provide sufficient policy direction and adequate policies to deal with the shortcomings of social assistance (recommendations will be provided later).

Coverage

The number of all social assistance beneficiaries (including all programs) was 3.2 million in 2021, and as a percentage of the population it was 3.2 percent (vis-à-vis 4.5 percent in China and 1.6 percent in Cuba), whereas coverage of the population aged 60 and above by pensions (both contributory and noncontributory) was 14.7 percent (vis-à-vis 71 percent in China and 3.9 percent in Cuba). General social assistance should accelerate its previous rate of expansion to incorporate some excluded disadvantaged groups. Most of the elderly do not receive either a contributory or a noncontributory pension. As coverage of the labor force by contributory pensions expands slowly (unless more self-employed are insured), priority should be given to the extension of the noncontributory pension.[42]

Benefit Sufficiency

The age for social assistance pensions is 80 and above (universal) and 60–79 (means-tested). A reduction of the age for access to the noncontributory pension at 60–79 could help to expand coverage and further reduce poverty. The ILO (n.d.) advises an expansion of coverage to all ages 67 and above who do not have a contributory pension and that the level of the noncontributory pension is increased. The ILO proposes two options on the pension amount; the higher would reduce poverty from 20.2 percent to 8.3 percent and benefit ethnic minorities and women in particular, and the cost would be only 0.54 percent of GDP. Social assistance should target those groups who lack or have very low coverage, such as poor children and pregnant women, in addition to the poor who need treatment for terminal illness (ILSSA/ILO 2022). The average noncontributory pension is above GDP per capita, whereas the social assistance "norm" is 64.7 percent, which is 35 percentage points below. Furthermore, the norm is also below the poverty line: 60 percent of the urban line and 48.6 percent of the rural line. The norm should be raised annually to the poverty line, differentiating urban and rural ones. Noncontributory pensions are not indexed, and they should be, although keeping a proper difference from contributory pensions.

A good part of eldercare is provided by family caregivers, but these are declining because of migration and lower fertility; it is urgent for the state (combined with the private sector) to expand eldercare facilities. The National Action Plan for the Elderly for the Period 2012–2025 seeks to increase the quality of eldercare, including delivery of health services for those unable to take care by themselves, as well as raising private provision with government stewardship and expanding the network of facilities in geriatric medicine. These are adequate tasks, and the results of the plan by 2022 (ten years since inception) should be evaluated as soon as possible. Other goals should be to continue the diversification of the types of available care (home-based, community-based, and institutional) to clearly incorporate the private sector within the "social" sector in order for the former to be allowed to receive preferential land, loans, etc.; to enact regulations for the non-state sector, as well as a coordination of the provision between it and the state sector; and to train care workers to be able to meet the demand for services.

Social Solidarity and Gender Equity

The identified disadvantaged groups, such as less developed regions, pregnant women, children, ethnic minorities, and the remaining poor (either without coverage or very poor benefits) should be prioritized to receive social assistance and reduce current inequalities.

Administration

The Master Plan for Social Assistance Reform and Development in 2017 assessed performance until 2016 and set goals for 2018–2025 with a vision for 2030. An evaluation of the first five years of said plan should be undertaken in order to ensure the network of social assistance facilities and the provision of social assistance services needed, with an emphasis on the elderly nursing home model (ILSSA/ILO 2022). The existing social assistance policies and programs should be consolidated into a smaller number of better-designed flagship poverty reduction programs, and these should be better coordinated with the ministries that provide social assistance benefits and services, as well as with the wider anti-poverty programs (World Bank 2019). Targeting needs improvement to avoid exclusions, including implementing new technologies to manage information, improve communication with the population, educate the people on their rights, and train more and better qualified social workers (Kidd et al. 2016).

The law encourages the development of the private sector in providing social assistance, which includes foreign companies, particularly in nursing homes that are concentrated in Hanoi and surrounding provinces where affluent people can pay for these high-cost services. The state should regulate private services, and companies should pay adequate taxes to help finance public eldercare for the needy. A professional network of social workers should be trained to improve the quality of care and nurture services for groups in need of social assistance. Priority should be given to enabling vulnerable people to live in a safe home environment, with institutional care as a last resort.

Financial-Actuarial Sustainability

There is a vacuum of data on this important issue (for instance, revenues and expenditures are not provided by the household living standards survey), so it is not possible to estimate the financial balance. In contrast with pension and health social insurances that are mainly financed by contributions from employers and employees (necessitating financial-actuarial equilibrium), social assistance is totally financed by the state, and the government needs to know the long-term sustainability of social assistance programs. Therefore, it is recommended that the necessary data is published. A study of financial sources for the future integrated/expanded social assistance system should include diverse sources, such as progressive income tax, value added tax, property taxes, and so forth, considering their feasibility and progressive-regressive effects (World Bank 2019).

Suitability of the Current Economic Model

Provided that its GDP growth continues at similarly high rates, Vietnam should persist on its economic and institutional reform, restructuring state-owned enterprises and ensuring GDP annual growth of 6.5 percent to generate additional resources for social security expenditures (Q. Dao 2017). It should also continue to take advantage of the benefits of free trade agreements, strengthen trade promotions, and expand and diversify import and export markets to increase domestic production (ILSSA/ILO 2022). Foreign direct investment can be selective to improve labor productivity in the long run and raise the nation's capability to build on its own infrastructure for development in terms of physical assets such as clean water supply, electricity, natural gas, roads, rails, ports, and telecommunication (Viêt Vũ Quang 2020).

Vietnam has made significant progress in the education of its labor force, but technical and professional qualifications remain very limited with slow improvement. The manufacturing industry has developed rapidly, but the quality of its employed labor force remains low and the proportion of workers without a degree or certificate fell slightly in 2011–2019. Therefore, there should be an expansion of technical-vocational education and training (TVET) to build skilled human resources for further development.[43] Additionally, despite a decrease of 13 percentage points in the number of self-employed and unpaid family workers in the last decade, these groups still account for more than half of the labor force, a key reason for their low pension coverage; these groups also require more TVET (ILSSA/ILO 2022).

Despite progress in reducing economic-social differences among regions, substantial inequalities remain, and more investment is required in the least developed regions (the above recommended national compensation fund would be a key mechanism in achieving this goal). National open unemployment rates have decreased impressively but remain high among the youth, and a special program is needed to cope with this problem. Finally, the dependency ratio in Vietnam is projected to increase; the government should immediately start to design and implement policies to confront the aging of the population so as to solidify the financial-actuarial sustainability of social security.

In closing, in the fundamental findings of this book, Cuba serves as a lesson: the performance of the Cuban model of central planning and predominant state ownership of the means of production has badly trailed behind the performance of the Sino-Vietnamese model of socialist market. Furthermore, the impact of the Sino-Vietnamese model on social security has been quite positive, matching and exceeding early Cuban gains, and it is much more sustainable. If China were to significantly reverse its successful movement toward the market in favor of state intervention in the economy, its economic-social performance would probably suffer, as well as the progress of its social security system. An important question is whether Vietnam will continue on the socialist-market path and, if so, gradually close its economic-social and social-security gaps with China and expand its advantage over Cuba.

APPENDIX 1

CHINA POLICY SHIFT IN THE MODEL UNDER PRESIDENT XI AND ITS EFFECTS

Since 2021, President Xi's campaign against corruption has been followed by his increasing control over big business and the "disorderly" expansion of capital, increasing the power of regulators and tax investigators to crack down on tech giants and wealthy celebrities and attempting a more balanced growth and the reduction of inequality. Centralization of state control of fiscal and financial resources was not previously relinquished and is expanding. The socialist-market model prioritized the speed of growth over all else, but Xi has pushed for more equitable and "less-corrupt growth."

Beijing sent a warning that no firm is too big to fall. Officials have turned away from openness and competition, enacting directives that urge local governments to watch for protests related to the troubled property sector; and most companies now have communist party cells that have taken over decision-making. A regulatory crackdown on tech companies and after-school-education enterprises contributed to a wave of dismissals that left one-quarter of youngsters unemployed (Bradsher 2022a). Xi's administration "has moved decisively towards state control. . . . State owned enterprises take the lead in implementing top-down initiates [ignoring] the benefit of shifting from plan to market and redistributing resources from state to private firms" (Brandt and Rawski 2022, 826–27). As early as 2014, Malesky and London showed that growth in China (and Vietnam) was most robust during periods of state withdrawal from the economy and warned about economic difficulties arising from the scale and character of the expanding state role in the economy.

Economists cautioned that "the new policies could hurt competitiveness and private sector dynamism, while favoring the inefficient, monopoly-dominated state sector," which has not been reformed (Mozur 2021, A-1). The big surge of the Covid-19 omicron variant in the spring of 2022 and the government's harsh Zero-Covid policy that shut down the country for almost three years led to the shutdown of dozens of cities, particularly Shanghai, the second-largest in the nation, whose stock market dropped 17 percent in the first three quarters of 2022 (foreign investment stalled during the pandemic). Furthermore, "in the name of pandemic control, the government tightly regulated the economy in ways that the country hasn't seen for decades, wreaking havoc on business" (Mozur 2021, A-1), particularly small ones (shutdowns were worse and more widespread than those in the early 2000s). This not only made it impossible for many private businesses to survive but quickly dampened willingness to invest.

There were conflicting messages from the government. Former premier Li Keqiang and ministers in Beijing urged the government to balance pandemic control measures with the need to encourage growth, but President Xi did not yield, and he was supported by provincial party secretaries, low-level government officials, and the state media (Yuan 2022). The Zero-Covid policy ended in December 2022, influenced by public demonstrations against the lockdowns in many cities (Huang 2022). Real estate prices are sharply decreasing; the property market, which over the last decade contributed about one-quarter of the economy, is suffering a meltdown; and heavily indebted housing developers are defaulting on bond payments to creditors. The government is providing incentives to revive the real estate sector, but the property bubble is no longer a supercharger of growth (Wakabayashi 2022).

There are mounting signs of a considerable fall in growth and productivity. Unemployment among migrant workers and new recent graduates is rising, and migrants lack unemployment insurance if not employed. Exports are shrinking and terms of trade have worsened because of the war in Ukraine and other geopolitical tensions. Many countries are shifting their supply lines away from China. A rapidly aging population is shrinking the workforce resulting in fewer workers and consumers (Bradsher 2022c; Rudd 2022; Y. Wang 2022; Yuan 2023c).

Trying to confront the situation, official guidelines enacted in April 2022 aimed at establishing a unified domestic market to build "a high-standard market system." The guidelines argued that if China's unique super-large domestic market was integrated and unified by the same system and rules, as well as fair and unified supervision, it would allocate resources efficiently, maximize social welfare, help stabilize market expectations, and promote healthy economic development. In the same vein, unified land and labor markets in urban and rural areas would be optimized; barriers to market entry and exit, local protectionism, and negative lists for market access, market intervention, and other impediments restricting economic circulation would be eliminated for domestic entities (enhancing a more transparent business environment), while foreign countries would benefit on a reciprocal basis, better connecting domestic and international markets.

In addition, more work would be done to review anti-monopoly systems and to determine monopolistic behavior. Basic market institutions in property rights protection, market entry, and fair competition would be strengthened. Property rights of enterprises would also be protected, along with the personal and property safety of entrepreneurs, meaning market entities would be treated equally, and the government would promptly review and abolish policies preventing the formation of a unified market and fair competition and comprehensively review preferential policies that discriminate against foreign-invested or non-local enterprises ("Whats and Whys of China's Unified Domestic Market," 2022). However, the guidelines labeled "dual circulation" generated concern among foreign investors and exporters that the government could reserve the domestic market for Chinese companies (Bradsher 2022a).

As expected, the twentieth party congress held on October 16–23, 2022, extended President Xi's mandate for a third term (which has not occurred since Mao Zedong), terminated the mandate of Premier Li Keqiang and took him out of the Politburo Standing Committee along with other pro-market officials, and appointed loyalists to the Politburo to secure strong support for Xi's policy agenda (Buckley and Bradsher 2022; Buckley et al. 2022). At his speech opening the party congress, Xi lauded socialist market economic reform and argued that China's economy should "give full play to the decisive role of the market in resource allocation." But he also pledged "to create a larger role for socialism and the state sector" and emphasized that "state-owned capital and enterprises get stronger, do better and grow bigger" (cited by Wakabayashi et al. 2022).

After the Zero-Covid policy ended, there was a brief economic spurt, but it was followed by stagnation, hence the government seemed to realize that it needed the private sector to help in recovery. Chief economist for Greater China, a real estate management firm in Hong Kong, said: "After years of demonizing private entrepreneurs, the government has lately signaled a pivot to a more . . . pro-business mind set" (cited by Goodman 2023, B-1, B-4). In July 2023, thirty-five guidelines were enacted to reverse the previous regression toward the plan and state enterprises, but some of the measures were not new and one asked entrepreneurs to be "patriotic" and uphold the party leadership over the private sector. Business owners had lost faith in the government and did not expect the new guidelines to be implemented (Yuan 2023b).

Other adverse factors affecting China were the deteriorating relations with the United States and other trading partners, a sharp drop in exports and imports, a decrease in foreign investment of 80 percent in the second quarter of 2023 relative to the same period in 2022, capital flows out of the country, a decline in the manufacturing sector for four consecutive months, stagnating wages after two decades of brisk increases, youth unemployment reaching 21.3 percent, and continuous deterioration in consumer confidence. Falling consumer and producer prices, as well as real estate prices, raised the threat of deflation (denied by the government), which would be particularly serious in China where overall debt is 282 percent of national economic output (Goodman 2023).

In the last decade, a huge construction boom based on indebtedness by central and local governments, developers, and individual borrowers led to soaring real estate prices. Currently there is a housing glut combined with a sharp decrease in demand, a declining birth rate, and increasing youth unemployment, which have left many buildings unfinished, cities with from 65 to 80 million empty apartments, and homeowners with mortgages to pay but no homes. Real estate giant Evergrande defaulted on US$900,000 million in debt in 2021 and filed for US bankruptcy, whereas the country's biggest developer by sales, Country Garden, lost US$7,600 million in the first semester of 2023 and is at risk of default. Fifty other real estate developers have failed to make payments in the past three years. Unpaid bills from private developers alone amounted to US$390,000 million. The exchange rate of yuan to the US dollar dropped to a fourteen-year low, and the Hong Kong stock market plunged to a thirteen-year low (Bradsher 2023a, 2023b, 2023c; Moreno 2023; Stevenson 2023).

In August 2023, an economic stimulus plan was announced to promote consumer spending by providing incentives to buy goods and services, including subsidies, but it relies mostly on local governments that are seriously indebted and that confront other financial difficulties, such as lacking resources to pay their civil servants (Bradsher 2023d).

The central bank reduced the interest rate twice, but the second time by only one-tenth of one percentage point for one-year loans, judged grossly insufficient by most experts. Other measures are tax breaks to small enterprises and increased state investment that may not be able to accelerate growth (Bradsher 2022a, 2022b; Bradsher and Stevenson 2022; Bradsher et al. 2023).

The described events impeded China's ability to reach a growth target of 5.5 percent in 2022; in the second quarter of 2022, growth was only 0.4 percent larger than in the same period in 2021. The scheduled release of the growth rate in the third quarter, to be done at the party congress, was delayed "indefinitely," a very unusual deferral, which prompted speculation that the rate had been lower than expected. The final annual rate for 2022 was 3 percent or 2.5 points lower than the 5.5 percent target, the worst performance in nearly half a century (Cheng 2023; "China's Economic Recovery," 2023). The official GDP target for 2023 was 5 percent, but in August global investment banks forecast growth from 4.6 to 4.8 percent in 2023 and from 4.2 to 3.9 percent in 2024 (Bradsher 2023a). At the end of 2023 the forecast was for a growth of 5.2 percent followed by a slowdown to 4.5 percent in 2024 (World Bank 2023b). A slower economy and less spending power means that leaders will have to worry more about social stability, as choices about public expenditure priorities become more difficult (Rosen 2022).

APPENDIX 2

COMPARISON OF CHINA, CUBA, AND VIETNAM IN KEY INDICATORS OF THE MPI, 2010S

In 2010 the Oxford Poverty and Human Development Initiative (OPHI), in collaboration with the UNDP, developed the global Multidimensional Poverty Index (MPI). Its latest version is 2020, with data from national surveys taken in 2004–2019 from 107 developing countries including China, Cuba, and Vietnam (Alkire, Kanagaratnam, and Suppa 2020). The MPI measures incidence of poverty (H) and intensity of poverty (A) to give an equation (MPI = H x A), applied to ten indicators of deprivation organized into three equally weighted dimensions: two indicators on health (nutrition and child mortality), two on education (years of schooling and school attendance), and four on living standards (cooking fuel, sanitation, drinking water, and assets such as a TV, phone, bike, etc.). Acute poverty is currently measured, and moderate poverty will be added in the future. Data includes headcount on poverty, intensity of deprivation, population in severe and vulnerable multidimensional poverty, the three clusters of multidimensional poverty (health, education, and living standards), and population living below the national income poverty line (percent and PPP $1.90 a day).

Cuba's MPI is ranked the seventh-lowest among the 107 developing countries, after Armenia, Georgia, Kyrgyzstan, Serbia, Turkmenistan, and Ukraine, which all have 0.001; it is also tied with Trinidad and Tobago. The sixty-six countries classified with "very high development" in the HDI are excluded because they are not considered developing countries. This includes five in Latin America: Chile, Argentina, Uruguay, Panama, and Costa Rica in that order. Among the other twelve Latin American countries, the MPI of six of them ranges from 0.015 in Dominican Republic to 0.020 in Colombia, and in the other six from 0.026 in Mexico to 0.200 in Haiti (Bolivia and Venezuela did not participate but probably are in the second group). The worst MPI was found in Niger 0.590, well over Latin America. The table below compares China, Cuba, and Vietnam in the most important indicators of the MPI.

Cuba has the best indicators among the three countries, except for contribution of health to deprivation (better in Vietnam), and the contribution of standards of living to deprivation (better in China). The most important issue, however, is that Cuba does not provide data on the population below the income poverty line, particularly the national line, whereas China and Vietnam do (those indicators are lower than the poverty incidence shown in table 3.2). Data on Cuba comes from a national survey on occupation that is not available on a public platform; furthermore, the Cuban government provided said data on a joint agreement with OPHI requiring the latter to use it solely for computing and publishing the global MPI aggregates (Alkire, Kanagaratnam, and Suppa 2020, 24), meaning that the base data could not be published. Such data has not been available to Cuban researchers either, hence they have not been subjected to academic scrutiny as in most other countries of the world. A key question is how the Cuban government could provide the base data on poverty when it did not publish it in fifty-eight years (1959–2017). Related to this issue and most revealing is the fact that the fundamental two indicators on population below the poverty line, which are usually the most used internationally, were not given by Cuba; only 13 percent of the 107 countries failed to provide such indicators (all Latin American countries including Haiti, the least developed, supplied the data).

In addition, Cuban statistical yearbooks, which publish so much data on health, failed to deliver data on nutrition. The Cuban survey was unclear as to whether the source of water from wells was protected or unprotected whereas water delivered by truck was considered an "unimproved facility" (Alkire, Kanagaratnam, and Suppa 2020, 5). It is internationally known that water in Cuba must be boiled to be drinkable, though this is not noted by the MPI. Finally, the reliability of the infant mortality rate is questionable—in Cuba's national MPI, infant mortality

TABLE APPENDIX 2. Key Indicators of the MPI in the Three Countries, 2010s

Indicators[a]	China	Cuba	Vietnam
MPI (value)	0.016	0.002	0.019
Population in MDP (%)			
Headcount	3.9	0.4	4.9
Intensity of deprivation	41.4	36.8	39.5
Severe MDP	0.3	0.0	0.7
Vulnerable to MDP	17.4	1.6	5.6
Contribution of deprivation to MDP (%)			
Health	35.2	25.8	15.2
Education	39.2	32.2	42.6
Standard of living	25.6	42.0	42.2
Population below income poverty line (%)			
National poverty line	1.7	n.a.	6.7
PPP $1.90 a day	0.5	n.a.	1.9

Source: My own elaboration based on UNDP (2020).

Notes: MDP = multidimensional poverty; PPP = purchasing parity power (international dollars)

[a] Years are 2013–2014 for Vietnam, 2014 for China, 2017 for Cuba.

instead of child mortality was used (Pichs 2021). In summary, out of the ten indicators: of the two on health, one was missing and the other has been academically contested (Vietnam was ahead of Cuba on the contribution of health to deprivation); and out of the four indicators on living standards, one was questionable, and Cuba lagged well behind China on the contribution of living standards to deprivation.

APPENDIX 3

TABLE APPENDIX 3. Ranking of the Economic-Social Performance of the Three Countries Based on the Standardized Numbers Scale

Indicators[a]	China	Cuba	Vietnam
Economic			
GDP per capita (US$)	1.12	–0.79	–0.33
GDP average annual growth rate	0.78	–1.13	0.34
Gross capital formation (% of GDP)	0.99	–1.01	0.02
Inflation (now price stability)[b]	0.62	–1.15	0.54
Fiscal deficit (now fiscal stability)[c]	–0.07	–0.96	1.03
Index of industrial ouput	0.99	–1.01	0.03
Agricultural-cattle-fish output	0.89	–1.08	0.19
Economic (trade) openness	–0.50	–0.65	1.15
Foreign trade balance of goods (% of GDP)	0.54	–1.15	0.62
Annual average growth in HDI 1990–2021	0.80	–1.12	0.32
Social			
Open unemployment (now employment rate)[d]	–1.09	–0.96	1.04
Income inequality (now equality)[e]	–0.08	0.87	0.22
Change in real wage/income growth	0.37	–1.13	0.77
Real average/mean monthly pension (US$)	1.07	–0.91	–0.15
Mean years of schooling	–0.83	1.11	–0.28
Infant mortality (now survival rate)[f]	0.52	0.64	–1.15
Maternal mortality (now survival rate)[g]	0.74	–1.14	0.40
Total score of seventeenindicators[h]	6.96	–11.57	4.76
Average ranking of seventeen indicators[h]	0.40	–0.68	0.28

Source: My elaboration together with Yan Cai.

Notes: Explanation of the standardized numbers scales method: to standardize a batch, the mean is subtracted for every indicator number in the batch and the result is divided by the standard deviation of the batch; the resulting batch has standard scores (z scores), which indicate how many standard deviations are above the mean (for a positive z score) or below the mean (for a negative z score) for each number in the original batch.

[a] From tables 3.1 and 3.2 were selected the ten indicators that have the attribute of the higher score the better: GDP per capita, GDP average growth rate, gross capital formation, index of industrial output, agriculture-cattle-fish output, economic trade openness, foreign trade balance of goods, change in real wage/income growth, real average/mean monthly pension, and mean year of schooling. Six other indicators could be converted to the opposite, they are now the higher the score the better: inflation, fiscal deficit, open unemployment, income inequality, infant mortality, and maternal mortality. Indicators deleted because they are the lower the score the better are: poverty incidence, misery index, and gender inequality index

[b] Inflation was converted to price "stability" with the equation (CPI_x – CPI_{x+1}) divided by $CPI_{x.}$

[c] Fiscal deficit was converted to fiscal "stability" with the equation (total receipts – total expenditure) divided by GDP.

[d] The open unemployment rate was converted to "employment" rate subtracting the open unemployment rate from 100.

[e] Income inequality was converted to income equality, the Gini coefficient formula is A (above the Lorenz curve) divided by (A+B), this was changed to B (below the Lorenz curve) divided by (A+B), hence the result is the higher the score, the more equality.

[f] Infant mortality rate was converted to infant "survival" rate, subtracting infant mortality from 1,000 live births.

[g] Maternal mortality rate was converted to maternal "survival" rate subtracting the maternal mortality rate from 100,000 births.

[h] The higher the score the better; the average ranking resulted from dividing the total score by 16.

APPENDIX 4

TABLE APPENDIX 4. Ranking of Social Security Performance of the Three Countries Based on the Standardized Numbers Scale

Principles/Indicators[a]	China	Cuba	Vietnam
1. Unity			
Diverse groups			
Pensions[b]	−0.58	−0.58	1.16
Healthcare[b]	−0.58	1.16	−0.58
Social assistance	−1.16	0.58	0.58
Private facilities/personnel[c]	−0.58	1.16	−0.58
Total score	−2.90	2.32	0.58
Average ranking of four indicators	−0.73	0.58	0.16
2. Coverage			
Labor force on pensions (%)	−0.29	1.11	−0.83
Total population on health care (%)	0.71	n.a.	−0.71
Needy on social assistance			
All beneficiaries as % of total population	0.96	−1.03	0.07
Pensioners as % of population 60+	1.14	−0.72	−0.42
Total score	2.52	−0.64	−1.89
Average ranking of four indicators	0.63	−0.21	−0.47
3. Benefit Sufficiency			
Contributory pensions			
Effective gross replacement rate (%)	−0.09	−0.96	1.04
Average monthly contributory pension (US$)	1.07	−0.91	−0.17
Indexing of pensions[d]	0.58	−1.16	0.58
Pension amount above poverty line[d]	0.58	−1.16	0.58
Healthcare			
Physicians (per 10,000 inhabitants)	−1.15	0.55	0.60

Principles/Indicators[a]	China	Cuba	Vietnam
Hospital beds (per 10,000 inhabitants)	1.15	–0.51	–0.64
Infant mortality rate (per 1,000 born alive)[e]	0.51	0.64	–1.15
Maternal mortality rate (per 100,000 births)[f]	0.74	–1.14	0.40
Causes of death (NCD % of total)	1.12	–0.32	–0.80
Eldercare (bed per population 65+)	1.12	–0.32	–0.80
Social assistance			
Average/mean monthly assistance pension (US$)	1.10	–0.85	–0.25
Total score	6.73	–6.14	–0.61
Average ranking of eleven indicators	0.61	–0.56	–006
4. Social Solidarity and Gender Equity			
Social solidarity			
Number of separate social security schemes[b]	–1.06	0.13	0.93
Coverage of labor force on pensions	–0.10	1.05	–0.95
Existence of individual accounts[c]	–1.16	0.58	0.58
Central adjustment fund among regions/provinces[d]	1.16	–0.58	–0.58
Gender equity			
Proportion of the labor that is female (%)	0.02	–1.01	0.99
Weeks paid for maternity leave	–0.50	–0.65	1.15
Percentage of previous year average salary paid	0.58	–1.12	0.58
Female advantages over men in calculating RR[d]	–0.58	–0.58	1.16
Total score	–1.64	–2.18	3.86
Average ranking of eight indicators	–0.21	–0.27	0.48
5. Administrative Efficiency and Social Participation			
Decentralization[g]	1.00	–1.00	0.00
Law compliance/enforcement[h]	0.00	0.00	0.00
Centralized collection of contributions/taxes[i]	0.00	0.00	0.00
Digital information system and unified ID card[j]	1.00	–1.00	0.00
Central state mechanism to buy medicines[k]	–1.00	0.00	1.00
Hospital length of stay (days)[l]	–1.11	0.29	0.82
Bed occupancy rate[m]	0.27	0.83	–1.11
Targeting errors (inclusion/exclusion)[n]	0.00	0.00	0.00
Fraud, corruption, informal payments[n]	0.00	0.00	0.00

Principles/Indicators[a]	China	Cuba	Vietnam
Tripartite administration[d]	0.58	–1.16	0.58
Comprehensive modernization plan[o]	0.00	–1.00	1.00
Total score	0.74	–3.04	2.29
Average ranking of eleven indicators	0.07	–0.28	0.21
6. Financial-Actuarial Sustainability			
Total contribution % on wages (all programs)	0.82	–1.12	0.30
Total social security expenses[p]	0.51	–1.15	0.65
Old-age dependency ratio projection (2030)[q]	0.08	–1.04	0.96
Male life expectancy at retirement (years)[r]	0.84	0.26	–1.10
Pension balance (% of GDP)	1.13	–0.78	–0.34
Assets in individual accounts (% of GDP)	1.16	–0.58	–0.58
Ratio active workers per one pensioner	–0.57	–0.58	1.16
Projected pension cumulative balance (% of GDP 2019)	0.91	–1.07	0.17
Year that pension reserves will be exhausted[s]	0.33	–1.12	0.80
Total score	5.21	–7.18	2.02
Average ranking of nine indicators	0.58	–0.80	0.22
Overall total score of indicators in six principles	10.66	–16.86	6.25
Overall average ranking of average rankings in six principles	1.77	–2.81	1.04

Source: My elaboration together with Yan Cai.

Notes: For explanation of the method of standardized numbers scales, see appendix 3. In each of the six social security principles, the corresponding scores of the indicators are summed up and then divided by the number of indicators in order to obtain the ranking of the three countries in each principle. Finally, the overall scores of the six social security principles are added and the result is divided by six to calculate the overall ranking average of the six ranking averages in the six principles.

[a] The higher the score the better; four indicators were deleted because they are the lower the better and could not be converted: Covid-19 excess mortality, changes in six healthcare indicators in 2008–2019, gender inequality, and administrative cost as percentage of total expenses. Several indicators were converted to the opposite in order to change them from the lower the better to the higher the better (see tables 5.1, 5.3, 5.9–11, 5.14, and 6.1).

[b] This batch of numbers was converted to 1/n.

[c] No is 1 and Yes is 0.

[d] Yes is 1 and No is 0.

[e] Converted to infant "survival" rate, subtracting the infant mortality rate from 1,000 live births.

[f] Converted to maternal "survival" rate, subtracting the maternal mortality rate from 100,000 live births.

[g] Most is 1, Middle is 0.5, and Least is 0.

[h] Poor is 0.

[i] Yes is 1.

[j] Yes is 1, Partly is 0.5, and No is 0.

[k] Yes is 1, Not needed is 0.5, and No is 0.

[l] Converted to –X.

[m] Converted to bed vacancy rate (100 – n).

[n] Yes is 0.

[o] Best is 1, Middle is 0.5, and No is 0.

[p] Converted to negative social security expenses (100 – n).

[q] Converted to old-age independency ratio (100 – n).

[r] Converted to –n.

[s] Converted to n – 2021.

NOTES

INTRODUCTION

1. Another successful application of the socialist-market model is Laos People's Democratic Republic, but there is much less information available on this country, and its inclusion would have extended this book and made it more complex (see Monreal 2018b).

2. In 2019, credit to China's government and state-owned enterprises was 32 percent of GDP, and 68 percent went to the non-state sector (NBSC 2019).

3. These three components cover the largest majority of total insured in the three countries and the biggest share of social expenditures; unemployment and employment injury take a small fraction of social expenditures (Cuba lacks unemployment insurance). General note: The ILO considers the terms social "protection" and social "security" to be interchangeable, but "social protection" usually has a wider variety of meanings than "social security," including housing and education. In the 2010s, the ILO Department of Social Security changed its title to Social Protection. Although I do agree with this semantic issue, in this book I prefer to use the more conventional delimited title of social security.

4. I traveled to Cuba six times between 1978 and 2017, established close contacts with many Cuban academic experts on the economy and social security, and have copublished articles with some of them.

5. After explaining that during the first thirty years of the revolution Cuba reached almost incomparable levels in health, education, and social security, helped by Soviet aid, Bye adds: "China and Vietnam . . . , by the time that the USSR collapse came about . . . could start blessing their populations with substantial economic growth. Most notable was the partially dramatic process of upward mobility and social security improvement for increasing segments of the population, lifting millions out of poverty. . . . That it is missing for the majority of Cubans today" (2020, 84–85).

6. According to the UN World Food Programme, in 2022, rationing for the population age group 14 to 60 "only covers 36 per cent of the energy intake, 24 per cent of the protein and 14 per cent of the fat daily recommendations . . . the diet of the average Cuban household is poor in micronutrients [and there is] malnutrition deficiency" (2023, 7).

7. Unless otherwise noted, translations from the Spanish are mine. Translations from Chinese are by Bingzi He, and translations from Vietnamese are by Dat Nguyen Hai.

8. In 2016, P. Vidal (2021) asked Vietnamese economists whether beneficiaries of social services opposed the market-oriented reforms for fear they might curtail their entitlements. The Vietnamese economists answered that the country had just come out of two devastating wars and they did not have anything to lose but only hope to improve.

9. According to OECD (2022b), poverty generally declines more rapidly in countries with strong GDP growth.

10. Gongcheng and Scholz (2019) successfully argue that social security in China has contributed to and stimulated economic development: quasi universal coverage and steady increase in benefits have induced propensity and capacity to consume, a driver of economic growth.

CHAPTER 1: ARE THE THREE COUNTRIES COMPARABLE?

1. The autocratic nature of these regimes is contraposed with their claims that they hold democratic elections. In this book I do not deal with matters of political science, hence the following discussion is for illustrative purposes only. Domínguez (2021) considers the three systems as "one-party authoritarian." For Dussel Peters (2022), China's public sector is not a "vertical monolith," because there is significant competition among and within political institutions (the communist party, the National Popular Assembly, the State Council), as well as between the central government and provinces and municipalities; such competition—he argues—plays an important role in the ascent and decline of officials in their careers. Meng (2019) argues that China has "decentralized authoritarianism" as top local leaders are appointed by "insider-dominated" provinces, not from outside or from the central government; hence promotion-seeking leaders are incentivized to promote economic development and adequate

social security. X. Huang (2020) states that the Chinese state is authoritarian and centralized politically but decentralized economically and fiscally, and that there is considerable power delegation from the center to the provinces and local authorities. Bye, writing in 2018–2019, states that all critical decisions in Cuba are taken at the national level, by a small political elite without any systematic consultation mechanisms with decentralized bodies, let alone with independent or countervailing institutions. Democracy and popular participation are hardly possible without decentralized and bottom-up structures of decision-making; nevertheless, he also contends that there were some indications of declining authoritarianism in the first half of 2010s that gradually evaporated (Bye 2020, 238–39). In China and Vietnam, other than the communist party, there are tiny state-controlled political parties (rooted on ethnic groups), which do not exist in Cuba.

2. Statistics on Cuba's life expectancy stopped in 2013, hence this data is nine years old (ONEI 2021). A demographer has estimated a decline in Cuba's life expectancy for women from 80.6 to 73.9 years (in 2012–2021), that of men from 76.5 to 68.9, and that of both sexes from 78.6 to 71.2; if this data is used, Cuba has the lowest life expectancy of the three countries (Albizu-Campus 2022b).

3. Cuba's fertility rate is rapidly declining: in 2020 it was 1.52, and in 2021 it was 1.45 (ONEI/CEPDE 2022).

4. Country demographic aging is a positive phenomenon, because the population lives longer and contributes to the national well-being. Concerning social security, however, it has negative financial effects such as higher costs of pensions and healthcare.

5. According to the Bank, Vietnam will become an "aged" society (with aged 65 and above comprising 10 percent of the total population) by 2035; Cuba and China are already well above 10 percent.

6. Since 1995, I have publicly opposed the US embargo; for my analysis of its main sanctions and effects, see Mesa-Lago 2015b, 2021a; Mesa-Lago and Vidal 2019; Mesa-Lago and Svejnar 2020.

7. Díaz-Briquets and Albizu-Campos (2024) cite the value of the Marshall Plan at US$135,000 million in 2018 prices.

8. In the second semester of 2019, Cuba did not pay the restructured debt with the Paris Club, and that unpayment continued at least until October 2022; Cuba asked for a postponement of the 2020–2021 payments but only got it for 2020 (deadline unknown), and interest has been charged. Cuba also failed to pay the debt with China and Russia, and both extended the deadline to 2027, also charging interest (Rodríguez 2022).

9. The service sector in China and Vietnam is much more productive than in Cuba because of its different components, as already explained.

10. Rawski (2023) argues that, in China, market forces definitely play a large

role in setting prices of agricultural products, but there is also state intervention (he did not provide specifics).

11. One anonymous referee argued that "China's collectivization in agriculture was mainly done in 1955–1956 and in industry and other urban enterprises in 1953–1956 faster than Cuba's ten years." This is a matter of discussion. I have documented (Mesa-Lago 2000, 342–47) that, by 1963, 70 percent of Cuban agriculture was collectivized (having taken five years) whereas by 1961 industry was 85 percent collectivized, transportation was 92 percent, and wholesale and foreign trade, banking, and education were all 100 percent (having taken three years, not ten as the referee sustains).

12. From 1913 to 1958, Cuba established mandatory pensions for fifty-four labor groups reaching 62.6 percent of the labor force, the second-highest in Latin America and close to the current apparent coverage of 68.5 percent; maternity insurance was created in 1934; the infant mortality rate was the lowest in the region in 1958; there were 4.2 hospital beds per 1,000 inhabitants, the third-highest; but the nation lacked a national healthcare insurance (Mesa-Lago 2003).

13. In 1986, the earliest comparison by the World Bank (2023a) available on GDP per capita in US dollars among the three countries, the figures were Cuba US$2,367, Vietnam US$430, and China US$282.

14. Based on the period 2010–2019, the gap was much wider: China 0.95, Vietnam 0.70, and Cuba 0.03, hence China was thirty-two times higher (better) than Cuba, and Vietnam twenty-three times higher (better) than Cuba.

CHAPTER 2: COMPARISON OF THE TWO ECONOMIC MODELS AND THEIR KEY POLICIES

1. I have compared the ideological economic zigzags between pragmatist and idealist cycles in China and Cuba, largely influenced by the respective revolution leader: Mao in China and Fidel in Cuba (Mesa-Lago 2000). Mao died twenty-seven years after the revolution in 1976, and reform began in 1978; Fidel died after fifty-seven years in power in 2016, but he had passed the authority to his brother Raúl in 2006 and reforms began in 2008. In Vietnam, the leader died before the war victory; Ho Chi Minh passed away in 1969 and reforms started in 1986.

2. Bye (2020) questions the full application of the central plan in Cuba, which is even more limited because of the current economic crisis. He argues that, actually, the Cuban present strategy is "survival without development." And yet, Cuba has had central plans since 1962, as well as central administrative directives. Most scholars concur that Cuba has a "command" economy. North Korea is the only country in the world left with an almost pure Soviet-style central plan and without market reforms, but little hard data is available about this system, and hence it had to be excluded from the comparison.

3. London (2023) characterizes the Vietnamese model as "market Leninist," a combination of party political control, a market economy, and a welfare mixed regime of public and private entities.

4. Dussel Peters (2022) argues, however, that public sector property combined with property of state-owned enterprises generates 40 percent of GDP (with a decreasing trend), and although state ownership in industry has declined sharply, it is predominant in banking and financing. In addition, private companies with state connected investors rose from 16 percent to 35 percent of registered capital in 2000–2019.

5. Among private enterprises, 35.9 percent were urban, 20.4 percent were rural, and 43.7 percent were self-employed.

6. Most Marxist economists argue that a country cannot prosper without one form of a market economy or another. "No matter which transformation model becomes a reality—the economy must be fixed by a much deeper market reform" (Bye 2020, 278).

7. There is not a figure on privately managed agriculture in Cuba (only by farmers that own small land parcels), as it is merged with the figure of service cooperatives; the two jointly accounted for 32.6 percent of the total agricultural land in 2020 (ONEI 2021).

8. Previous estimates for one year were done by Rodríguez (2015) and Bye (2020).

9. Since March 1994, the government of Vietnam has stopped following the central plan with administrative goals as well as physical output targets for state enterprises (Le 1994).

10. An anonymous referee contended that many of the enterprises that sell shares on the stock market are still totally controlled by the state; the public has no control over those enterprises, and management is selected by the organization department of the communist party (which is also true of China).

11. Spadoni (2022) estimates an annual average of US$680 million in 2014–2021. In that period only 285 new foreign businesss were set up, out of which 29 were reinvestments, "considerably lower than the needed foreign investment" (Rodríguez 2022, 2).

12. London (2023) argues that party actors and institutions continue to dominate and guide non-party institutions.

13. Before implementing the agrarian reform at the national level, China conducted several local experiments and, once outcomes were evaluated, extended the reform to the nation (Rozelle 2022).

14. Le (1994) gives several examples on how Vietnam market-oriented reform was initiated by grassroots illegal experiments supported by local party and government officials and later generalized by party and government scholars at the central level.

15. Bye asks a crucial question: "Why is the state not willing to pay bet-

ter prices to domestic producers, and generally incentivize domestic production more, when huge amounts of foreign exchange are spent on food imports?" (2020, 27).

16. China is also self-sufficient in rice and exported 2.5 million tons in 2021–2022.

17. In 2002, Vietnam signed a technical agreement with Cuba to improve its rice production and yield; the increased output was partly consumed by the island and partly shared by Vietnam for export; Vietnamese technicians built dams, cleaned canals, and trained Cuban farmers. The agreement was terminated in 2023 because Cuba kept part of the Vietnamese share, failed to supply the energy promised, and the inefficient state Agroindustrial Enterprise created snags. Vietnam withdrew its equipment and technicians with a negative impact on production (García 2023).

18. These authors provide substantial evidence against the theory that rapid growth in China (and Vietnam) was due to the advantage-of-backwardness (for a discussion, see Malesky and London 2014).

19. The role and contribution of the diaspora in domestic economic development have been very important in both China and Vietnam, while it is still neglected in Cuba; in Vietnam, there was a special Resolution of the Party on the role and mobilization of the Vietnamese diaspora that contributed to domestic economic development (Tran Ngoc 2022).

20. According to Dinh, Mishra, et al. (2013) and Dinh (2021a, 2022), a key factor in China industrialization was that the state seized land from the owners and turned it to the state and co-ops, which in turn sold produce to the government at a price lower than the market, hence generating a profit that was invested in industry, infrastructure, and so forth.

21. For stages of Vietnam's industrialization, see T. T. A. Nguyen et al. (2014).

22. Out of eighteen coastal economic zones, fifteen were regulated in 2008 and three in 2020 (Decree No. 1353 2008 and Decree No. 1453 2020). Before those economic zones, Vietnam had four export zones with favorable conditions (Le 1992).

23. Vietnam is a member of the Program for International Student Assessment and ranked eighth out of seventy-two participating countries in 2015, ahead of Germany and the Netherlands (Eckardt et al. 2018).

24. Le (2015) said that, compared with socialist economies such as Cuba, Vietnam is much more advanced in the implementation of internal reforms and integration with the rest of the world.

25. Viêt Vũ Quang (2020), however, shows that China, Thailand, and Malaysia have bigger shares of industry/GDP than Vietnam.

26. Statistics on open unemployment in the three countries are questionable: in China, statistics exclude rural residents and rural migrants living or

working in cities whereas in Cuba they are underestimated due to substantial underemployment.

27. The average rate rose to 4.9 percent in 2022 and 5.2 percent in mid-2023. In April 2023, the government reported that 20.4 percent of people aged 16–24 looking for a job were unemployed, the highest level since China started announcing that statistic in 2018. The causes are the strict pandemic restrictions, declining small businesses, and slowed-down economic growth (Fu 2023a).

28. Bye (2020) obtained information from Cuban officials that showed as many as 2.5 million state employees were redundant, 1.4 times higher than the previous estimate.

29. Private enterprises create productive employment at a higher rate than the rest of the economy, absorb unneeded labor in unprofitable state enterprises (hence saving budget subsidies allocated to them), and also pay taxes.

30. Cuban economist Juan Triana estimated that, without compensatory measures, 60 percent of state enterprises would be shut down and 40 percent of total jobs would disappear (cited by Bye 2020).

31. Because of the pandemic, tourism was halted in April 2020, falling 77 percent that year and another 67 percent in 2021, for a two-year combined decrease of 91.7 percent. In 2022, with the decline in Covid-19, the number of tourists rose four times relative to 2021, but still it was 62 percent below that of 2019 (ONEI 2022b, 2023).

32. The UN World Food Programme previously warned that the government had "reduced food subsidies, pushing inflation higher than forecasted and household vulnerability to food insecurity. As a result, the country experienced food shortages, including main cereals (wheat flour, rice and corn), beans, vegetables, daily products and meat (beef and pork)" (2023, 7–8).

33. The drastic and sudden devaluation of the dong more than ten times is the reason some economists argue that a "big bang" approach was applied.

CHAPTER 3: ECONOMIC AND SOCIAL PERFORMANCE OF THE THREE COUNTRIES

1. GDP per capita in US$ in 2020 were 10,361 in China, 3,552 in Vietnam, and 400 in Cuba (China from NBSC 2022a; Cuba from ONEI 2021; Vietnam from GSO 2022b).

2. The World Bank publishes series of GNI per capita, in PPP, for China and Vietnam but not for Cuba.

3. Because of the severity of the Cuban economic crisis, on July 11, 2021, massive national protests took place all over the nation, but the government suppressed them harshly; in September–October 2022 new protests occurred. In January–August 2022, 178,000 emigrants left the island, The total exceeded 200,000 by the end of the year, equal to the sum of the two biggest emigration waves in 1980 and 1994 and equal to 1.8 percent of the total population (Pérez

Villanueva 2022a; Pumar 2022; Stephen 2022). Such an exodus has not happened in China and Vietnam in modern times.

4. In 2020 gross capital formation/GDP in Cuba decreased to 9.9 percent whereas it was stagnant in Vietnam at 27 percent and in China at 43.1 percent (ONEI 2021; GSO 2021b; NBSC 2021b).

5. China's output in major manufactured products increased tremendously in 1978–2019; for instance, 3,593 percent in cement, 3,032 percent in steel, and 1,183 percent in natural gas (NBSC 2008–2021b). Vietnam's manufacturing output in 2005–2019 rose by 977 percent in iron and steel, 545 percent in rolled steel, 336 percent in electricity, 242 percent in cement, and 80 percent in chemical fertilizers (GSO 2009, 2020b). Conversely, Cuba's manufacturing output in 1989–2019 decreased 93 percent in textiles, 76.4 percent in cement, 60 percent in steel, and 24 percent in natural gas in 2015–2019. The decline in natural gas did not occur in the entire 1989–2019 period but between 2015 and 2019, it has continued thereafter together with a decline in oil output (CBSC 2020a; GSO 2021b; ONEI 2020a.). In 2022 Cuba's electricity output was operating at 38 percent of installed capacity (Rodríguez 2022), and the electric network collapsed across the entire island when Hurricane Ian hit in September 2022.

6. In 2020, out of Cuba's twenty-four most important agricultural-cattle-fishing-mining-manufacturing products, output decreased in all but one—and in half of them, it was below the 1989 level (CEE 1991; ONEI 2021).

7. In 2019, China's balance of payments under the current account had a surplus of US$141,300 million, tantamount to 1 percent of GDP (State Administration of Foreign Exchange 2020).

8. Cuba's combined five major sources of hard-currency revenue (exports of medical services, remittances, tourism, exports of goods, and telecommunications) decreased by one-half in 2018–2021, from US$15,899 million to US$7,959 million (Spadoni 2022).

9. In 2019 the surplus was US$10,570 million, and in 2020 it was US$19,938 million (GSO 2021b).

10. Cuba's reported external debt in 2019 (latest year available) was US$19,618 million (ONEI 2022a), but limited to the negotiated debt (that is, circumscribed to the negotiated debt excluding the standing non-negotiated debt), the total debt might be three times higher. In 2020, Vietnam's total external debt was US$38,500 million and international reserves were US$94,800 million (IMF 2021); China's external debt in the same year was US$2,400,800 million and international reserves were 3,216,500 million (GOV 2021f, 2021g). Respective figures per capita were Vietnam US$399 and US$982 and China US$1,731 and US$2,320.

11. Vietnam's 2006–2018 series shows a decrease from 15.5 to 6.8 percent (GSO 2020). In 2021, poverty decreased to 4.4 percent, 1 percent in urban areas and 6.5 percent in rural areas (GSO 2022b). There are reports of higher poverty

incidence in practice, in China, as well as government censorship of criticism of the official series (Yuan 2023a).

12. International/regional organizations such as the ILO, ECLAC, and the World Bank have not published Cuba's poverty incidence. However, a Multidimensional Poverty Index (MPI) published by the Oxford Poverty and Human Development Initiative and UNDP includes Cuba, as well as China and Vietnam. For an analysis of the MPI, the ranking of the three countries, and an evaluation of the reliability of Cuban data, see appendix 2.

13. Monreal estimated the Cuban poverty rate at 25 percent in 2014.

14. In 2016, buying essential goods in CUC exclusively available at state shops was possible only for those with access to hard currency. External remittances of about US$3,000 million annually go mainly to urban families and whites (for other racial inequalities, see Hansing and Hoffmann 2020).

15. In 2018, the gap between the first (poorest) income quintile and the fifth (wealthiest) quintile in Vietnam was only ten times and the Gini coefficient was 0.375 in 2020 (GSO 2020, 2021a). Cuba's Gini coefficient is not published by UNDP 2020. According to OECD (2022b), Vietnam has a lower Gini coefficient than China; among twenty-eight countries in OECD and Asia/Pacific, Vietnam is ranked twelfth (about midpoint) and China is ranked eighth.

16. This index is based on five women indicators: participation in the labor force, maternal mortality ratio, population with at least some secondary education, adolescent birth rate, and share of seats in parliament.

17. Unemployment in China increased in 2022 largely because of the wide lockdowns imposed by the Zero Covid policy, as well as strict regulations that caused hundreds of thousands of layoffs; particularly affected were migrant workers and new graduates. Government policies to reduce youth unemployment have been affected by the economic slowdown (V. Yang 2022; Fu 2023a). Unemployment in Vietnam was lower in rural areas (1.5 percent) than in urban areas (2.9 percent) (ILSSA/ILO 2022).

18. The UN World Food Programme states that "the minimum monthly salary was insufficient [in 2022] to cover the . . . nutritional requirement recommended for the Cuban population (2,300 kcal); furthermore, since 55–65 percent of household expenditures goes to food, inflation poses a major challenge for many Cuban families" (2023, 7). According to official data, Cuba's median wage in the state sector rose 125 percent in 2022, but inflation increased 1,212 percent (based on GDP deflator), hence the real salary contracted substantially (ONEI 2023).

19. Cuba's 2021 maternal mortality rate was reported by the party newspaper ("Cuba registra," 2022); that rate was the highest on record; in comparison, in 1955 it was 145.0 (Albizu-Campos and Jiménez 1995).

20. One anonymous reader suggested an alternative method to cope with the problem: "data reduction techniques like principal component analysis."

21. This is a problem of this method: three indicators could not be used because all indicators must show the higher score the better. In six indicators, it was possible to estimate the "opposite" (for instance, the infant mortality rate is converted to infant survival rate), but in other indicators that was not possible. In addition, the indicator GDP average growth was deleted to avoid potential overlapping with GDP per capita and gross capital formation. So, this method has the advantage of measuring the distances among indicators, but it has the disadvantage of impeding the use of key indicators. And yet the two methods show the same ranking and similar scores among the three countries.

CHAPTER 4: GENERAL OVERVIEW OF SOCIAL SECURITY INSTITUTIONS AND PROGRAMS

1. These programs have the largest shares of total social security expenses and percentages of GDP.

2. Dependent survivors of an insured person do not get a pension but, rather, a lump sum as well as a funeral grant and the balance that is in the individual account of the diseased insured worker.

3. An anonymous referee contended that social policy in the early USSR, China, and Vietnam was structurally different from that in capitalist economies because the state provided jobs and social security protection to all workers through state enterprises, farms, and so forth. The referee then asked if socialist-market economies continue to show substantially different social policies. In this book the answer is in the negative: social policies in socialist-market economies have more similarities with fully market economies than with pure centrally planned economies.

4. The 2015 social insurance reform integrated the private sector and civil servant schemes of pensions, medical-maternity, employment injury, and unemployment (the latter was granted to civil servants who lacked it before).

5. "Market sector" includes private employees as well as employees in the state sector with market-type contracts; the term "market" is commonly used to differentiate the two groups: private employees from civil servants.

6. Since 2008, the central government has tried to align the civil servants' costly and unequal scheme with the urban-employee program, but there was strong resistance from the former affiliates. This resistance was finally overcome by the 2015 reform, which integrated 40 million civil servants and public sector employees. However, the 2015 reform adjusted salaries and pensions of public employees to offset any financial losses resulting from the merge.

7. According to the Social Insurance Law, persons in flexible employment are the self-employed registered as "individual industrial and commercial households" without employees, part-time employees not participating in the scheme through their employers, and other persons in this category. Workers in the informal sector, home workers, household hourly workers, street vendors, and so

forth are also considered flexible employees. Part-time workers are those with an average of four hours daily and twenty-four hours weekly for the same employer, hence they participate in basic social insurance pensions and sickness-maternity; if they work for several employers, they may not accumulate the minimum time required to be insured (MOHRSS 2012).

8. This new scheme is officially called a "third pillar," but occupational pension plans should be such a third pillar, and the new commercial insurance would then be a fourth pillar.

9. At the end of 2020, 30 million impoverished people who reached age 60 began to receive pensions from this scheme ("China's Social Security," 2021).

10. In 2016, 95 percent of the insured in this scheme chose the lowest level (Chen and Turner 2021).

11. All Chinese citizens, urban and rural, must register at the time of birth in a hukou based on their parents' residence, although a rural person that migrates to urban areas is able to change said registration (B. He 2022).

12. According to B. He (2022), the communist party does not have paid employees but, rather, volunteers who enroll in the pension scheme corresponding to the sector in which they work. This is different from the situation in Cuba and Vietnam, where party officials are paid salaries and have separate coverage and benefits. X. Huang (2020) states that China party officials are covered by the urban-employee scheme.

13. Vietnam has a social assistance "Merit" program to compensate those who served in the wars of independence, as well as their families (Kidd et al. 2016).

14. For legislation on social security in Vietnam, see https://thuvienphapluat.vn/.

15. X. Huang (2020) divides the history of healthcare under socialism into three phases: health provided by work units (*danwei*) in cities and by communes in rural areas (1949–1978); danwei become inadequate due to the collapse of state enterprises and communes (1978–1987); the social insurance health system is introduced to replace danwei and expands outside of the formal urban workforce to peasants and urban poor (1988–2011).

16. Flexible employees (including the self-employed) have different treatment according to their income and whether they have a labor relationship with employers. Those who are poor and low-income might receive social assistance concerning maternity and sickness leave; those who have adequate income or who have labor relations with an employer could be affiliated in the urban-employee or urban-and-rural-resident schemes and partly pay for their maternity and sickness leave cash benefits; those who are not affiliated with either of those programs and are not poor or low income don't have said benefits. The government encourages them to join one of the two schemes (B. He 2022).

17. The NRPS covered almost 99 percent of the rural population (Dongxiao

et al. 2007); it improved health status among rural adults aged 60 and above, particularly women (Nikolov and Adelman 2019).

18. Although out-of-pocket spending has decreased significantly, it remains high: 35 percent of total spending in 2019 vis-à-vis 20 percent in OECD members (WHO 2022c).

19. Prior to the revolution, there was no health social insurance either. Instead, there was a fragmented health system comprised of a national public health sector (free), the maternity hospitals (also free), medical cooperatives and associations (sort of HMOs) financed by members' fees, and private for-profit hospitals and clinics. In addition, there was maternity and sickness paid leave for those employed, financed by the employer (CERP 1964).

20. Shi and Yangyang (2021) categorize four stages in the evolution of social assistance in China: poverty reduction (1978–1985); development-oriented poverty alleviation on a regional basis (1986–2000); poverty alleviation for villages (2001–2012); and targeted poverty reduction to eliminate extreme poverty (2013–2020). Solinger (2022b) identifies three stages that correspond with China's economic model transition: economic conversion at the end of 1978; political conversion in 1997; and social transmutation in 2000.

21. Still, in 2020 when the program had declined, dibao took 75.6 percent of total social assistance allowances (Y. Wang 2022, based on 2021c). In turn, Solinger (2022b) estimates that only 0.25 percent of GDP was spent on dibao and declining.

22. Solinger (2022b) estimates that dibao allowance relative to the average wage in eighteen large cities in 2004 ranged from 11.7 percent in Beijing to 20.5 percent in Qingdao. It was 22 percent of the average urban disposable income in 2002 and fell to 17 percent in 2008. She describes the hardships of dibao recipients based on one hundred interviews.

23. The antecedents of this targeted poverty reduction program go back to the Seven-Year Poverty Alleviation Program of 1994–2000; see Ringen and Ngok 2013. The first assistance program for the disabled began in 2015; a rehabilitation program was added in 2018.

24. Local governments had to establish medical social assistance such as reduction and exemption of medical expenses in rural areas since 2003 and in urban areas since 2005. The targeted recipients were mainly dibao and low-income families (L. Yang 2018). At the start, medical social assistance only provided inpatient care, but it is expanding to outpatient care; the government reimburses most expenses but the beneficiary has a copayment.

25. A debate has recently evolved on whether the Chinese government has used dibao largely to detect and, in a sense, reward potential negative behavior (e.g., by bestowing the dibao on previous protesters, former prisoners, and drug dealers) and thereby win their cooperation, a practice that has enraged those who did not receive the assistance but who thought they should get it.

This deprivation ironically caused small protests by nonrecipients, even though the program is aimed at preventing misbehavior (Pan 2020). Other views on this issue are that dibao has functioned as both a social safety net and a way of maintaining social control and political stability (Gao 2017), and that it was instituted to pacify protesting workers who had lost their jobs and has since been modified to attend to the disabled, the elderly, and those who lack a person legally responsible for their care (Solinger 2022b).

26. The law of the new Family Code does not regulate the role of the state in supporting poor elderly persons (Ley 156, 2022; Acosta 2022b).

27. In 2011–2020, the number of beneficiaries of social assistance had an average growth of 4.65 percent annually. However, groups of the population lacked access: disadvantaged children and pregnant women, those aged 75 and above in ethnic minorities and mountainous areas, and disadvantaged patients undergoing long-term treatment for terminal illnesses (ILSSA/ILO 2022).

28. For access to social assistance for the disabled, see Banks et al. 2019.

CHAPTER 5: COMPARISON OF FEATURES AND PERFORMANCE BASED ON SOCIAL SECURITY PRINCIPLES

1. Civil servants' pensions once averaged two to three times those of employees in the private sector (L. Fang 2014).

2. X. Huang (2020) reports that local government officials do not have to pay health insurance contributions when they retire, and this is true also of certain civil servants (after they were integrated into the urban-employee scheme, the state subsidizes their contribution). Most civil servants, however, must pay for the urban-employee scheme, though local authorities provide medical subsidies and assistance according to local conditions (B. He 2022).

3. Many employers evade payment, underreport numbers of employees, or treat migrants and flexible employees as service providers and refuse to pay their due contributions.

4. For instance, a man who enters the army at age 17 can retire after twenty-five years of service at age 42 and receive a pension equal to 90 percent of his last year's salary during an average retirement period of thirty-seven years (the regime is totally financed by the state). The general system, on the other hand, requires 60/65 years of age and thirty years of contribution, and the pension is based on 60 percent of the average of the best five years of wages (the system is financed by contributions of employers, workers, and the state covers the deficit).

5. B. He (2022) calculated basic insurance coverage for urban employees as 56.1 percent in 2019 (based on China Statistical Yearbook and contrasting 434.88 million participants and 774.71 million employed workers), but that figure excluded those participating in the urban-and-rural-resident scheme so the total must be higher. OECD (2018) estimated labor force coverage in 2017 as 51.2 percent (higher than in table 5.1 in 2020) and, within twenty-one coun-

tries in OECD and Asia, ranks China in ninth place (from lowest to highest), thus about midpoint. Allianz and Hermes (2020) roughly appraised coverage on pensions as 60 percent of the population aged from 15 to 64 in China and 20 percent in Vietnam, whereas pension coverage of the population aged 65 and over has similar estimates.

6. According to Zhao and He (2021), in 2014 only 16.4 percent of those covered by the urban-employee pension scheme were migrant workers, who were covered by the health scheme at 18.2 percent. Migrants are not a major problem in Vietnam as they are in China, and they account for only 1.2 percent of the labor force (GSO 2022a); however, they may be classified as temporary residents and face difficulties in getting proper jobs (Kidd et al. 2016). The same is true of Cuba where internal migrants account to only 0.9 percent of the labor force (ONEI 2022b).

7. OECD (2018), based on its 2015 estimate, ranks Vietnam coverage as the fourth-lowest among twenty-one OECD and Asian countries. The World Bank (2021b) estimates that 25 percent of the elderly received a contributory pension in 2018. The ILO calculates coverage of those aged 65 and above at 33.5 percent in 2016 (Kidd et al. 2019).

8. Ramírez and Arza cite female coverage as being lower than male coverage, opposite to the text figures.

9. The ILO (2018b) estimated the informal sector as 76.2 percent of employment in 2015 and 97.6 percent of them not covered by any type of pension.

10. It is argued that the amount of the matching is small and only 2.3 percent of the labor force is currently covered. See https://baotintuc.vn/chinh-sach-bhxh-bhyt/so-nguoi-tham-gia-bhxh-tu-nguyen-tang-vuot-bac-trong-gan-4-nam-gua-20211030110645011.htm/.

11. Underreporting of salaries and a low portion of the worker's salary subjected to contribution (due to the exclusion of fringe benefits) leads to low pensions.

12. In 2009, a special national scheme was announced for rural-to-urban migrant workers with a combination of PAYG and individual accounts, enterprises were to contribute 12 percent and workers from 4 percent to 8 percent (Leung and Xu 2015), but this measure was postponed and apparently does not exist yet (B. He 2022; Y. Wang 2022).

13. X. Huang (2020) tests his hypotheses of a dichotomy between coverage and generosity of benefits concluding that local leaders in provinces with high social risks and not enough resources are most likely to expand coverage (to enlarge the pooling of resources), whereas provinces with high fiscal revenues are more likely to enhance the generosity of social insurance health benefits.

14. Coverage in 2018 was 87.7 percent and the target for 2020 was 90.7 percent (ILO 2018a, 2021b). According to the World Bank (2021b), coverage reached 95 percent among age groups from 0 to 14 and 80 and above; coverage

expanded faster in rural areas. Coverage of women on sickness and maternity benefits is estimated at 30 percent (Ramírez and Arza 2021).

15. Ación and Colina (2022) show also the decline of other social assistance beneficiaries, such as persons with disability and mothers with children with severe disability.

16. Another dataset, ASPIRE, that provides data on social assistance expenditures includes China and Vietnam but excludes Cuba.

17. In September 2024, retirement ages were set to raise gradually, starting in January 2025, from 60 to 63 years for men (by 2040), from 55 to 58 for white-collar women workers, and from 50 to 55 for blue-collar women. The period of contribution will also be increased gradually from fiteen to twenty years. Insured will have the option to retire three years earlier, if they have met the twenty-year contribution period (V. Wang 2024).

18. Life expectancy in China varies greatly: it is over 80 years in most developed Beijing, Shanghai, and Tianjin, but 69 years in least developed Yunnan. There are also differences between urban and rural areas (B. He 2022).

19. The legal calculation of the basic social insurance pension is based on the average monthly wage of the local employee in the previous year and the indexed average monthly wage of the insured person; 1 percent of this amount is assigned for each year of the employee's contribution payment. The individual account pension is a monthly lifelong annuity based on dividing the capital accumulated from contributions and investment yields by the number of months of payments, determined by factors such as the average life expectancy at the time of retirement, the age of retirement, and the interest (Y. Wang 2020a, 2020b).

20. OECD (2019b) gives RR of 69 percent and 44 percent. According to the China Household Finance Survey, the RR was 70 percent in 2016 but declined to 54 percent in 2018 and could not maintain the living standard of the beneficiary (L. He 2022). Based on a survey of 2018, Giles et al. (2021) estimate RR in the urban-employee scheme from 45.5 percent to 48.9 percent, and in the urban-and-rural-resident scheme from 10.7 percent to 15.3 percent (rural residents are at the low end of the range).

21. OECD (2018) assumes the worker enters the labor force at age 20 in 2016, earns an average wage throughout his entire career without any interruption (a total of forty years), and retires at age 60.

22. According to Chen and Turner (2021), RR in the various China pension schemes/pillars were from 45.5 percent to 48.9 percent in the basic insurance urban-employee scheme, from 10.7 percent to 15.3 percent in the basic insurance resident scheme, from 3 percent to 5 percent in the occupational plans, and from 4 percent to 5 percent in the commercial insurance plans.

23. The individual pension in both schemes is calculated based on the balance in the account at the time of retirement and divided into 139 monthly

installments paid over a ten-year period (the estimated life span average after retirement at 60), whereas the basic social insurance pension is paid until the death of the insured.

24. Calculations were done dividing total pension expenses by number of retirees; conversion of yuan to the US dollar was based on international exchange rates.

25. According to ILSSA/ILO (2022), monthly per capita income in 2020 was 4,249,000 dong (US$184), below the first two estimates and 22 percent below the third one (ILSSA/ILO 2022).

26. Rehabilitation services are centralized, but the implementation policy is localized. There are many differences in the services provided, but twenty are provided nationally. Since 2021, there is a trend to integrate the three-level rehabilitation system.

27. Reimbursement of medical expenses and medicine varies greatly; there are central guidelines, but applications are left to local medical insurances. Additionally, there are differences between the urban-employee scheme and the urban-and-rural-resident scheme, as well as between active and retired workers, first- and second-level designated hospitals, first hospitalization and subsequent ones, and so on, all very complex to even synthesize herein (B. He 2022). One of the most important problems is that many expensive and foreign drugs are not included in the payable list of the basic medical insurance (Y. Wang 2020a, 2020b).

28. According to WHO (2022d), out-of-pocket health expenditure as a percentage of total health expenditures in 2019 was 42.9 percent in Vietnam, 35.2 percent in China, and only 10.6 percent in Cuba. Legally, healthcare is free in Cuba, but informal payments (bribes) are typical to get faster and better care. Since these payments are secret, however, there are no records of them. WHO neither provides a source nor explains how Cuba's out-of-pocket expenses were estimated.

29. Community health service institutions set up a family doctor team comprised of family doctors, nurses, pharmacists, and medical practitioners. The team members classify the residents according to their health status and needs, sign different service packages, and provide targeted family-doctor-signed services for the various categories.

30. Salaries of family doctors were very low, with the result that few students were willing to become family doctors (Xu 2014).

31. In 2016–2020, out of a total of eleven vaccines administered to the population, seven decreased from 39 percent to 99 percent, three from 5 percent to 16 percent, and only one rose by 17 percent (ONEI 2021).

32. However, the latest household survey taken in 2018 showed that 59.4 percent of communes had a private physician and 49 percent had a private nurse, all increasing since 2016 (GSO 2020).

33. Cuba had 138 local health posts located in urban and rural areas in 2007 that were shut down in 2011; 21 rural hospitals were also closed in 2011 (ONEI 2008a, 2012, 2020a); patients were transported to regional hospitals, but in urgent cases, patients have had to travel longer, thus increasing health risks.

34. Cuba's maternal mortality rate escalated from 31.1 per 100,000 child births in 2007 to 40.0 in 2020, whereas the Chinese rate decreased from 34.2 to 18.3 from 2008–2019 (ONEI 2008a, 2021; NBSC 2008, 2021b).

35. Among the twenty Latin American countries, eleven have lower means than Cuba.

36. National Office of Statistics and Information, Cuba (ONEI) deaths 167,645; WHO mean 117,985; excess means 167,645 – 117,985 = 49,660; population (Nx) 11,147,405. Calculation: excess mean = (deaths ONEI-expected mean / NX.) x 100,000; [(167,645 – 117,985) / 11,147,405] x 100,000 = [(49,660 / 11,147,405)] x 100,000 = 0.0044548 x 100,000 = 445.5.

37. For a comprehensive analysis of long-term-care coverage, adequacy, eligibility, package of benefits, administration, and financing in the world, see ISSA (2022).

38. Ratios for fifteen OECD countries in 2019 have been calculated on beds in *residential* long-term-care facilities per 1,000 population aged 65 and over—the higher the ratio the better (Szweda-Lewandowska 2022). China's ratio of 25.8 (calculated from table 5.8) is above the ratios of Italy (18.8) and Poland (11.3), but below the ratios of the other thirteen countries.

39. China's public-private partnership is a commonly used mechanism for provision of long-term care (Glinskaya et al. 2022).

40. In 2020, two self-employed caregivers of an incapacitated elderly person in her home were paid daily (day and night shifts) 240 CUC each (US$20 both), the monthly equivalent of 14,400 CUC or twelve times the average mean monthly salary in the state sector. Only families with relatives abroad who send the needed US dollars could afford that service.

41. Cuba has not ratified the Interamerican Convention that protects the rights of elderly persons, approved in 2015 and in force since 2017 (Acosta 2022b).

42. The deficit in care for the elderly induced an increase in the number of licenses granted to the self-employed devoted to this task in the private sector—from 300 in 2010 to 3,000 in 2013, and the number keeps rising (Acosta et al. 2018).

43. According to a survey conducted by Jackson and Peter (2015), 20 percent of the population expected that the family would be mostly responsible for providing income to retired people, but 90 percent expected to live with their grown children.

44. Several experts consider this a noncontributory "social pension" (Zhao and He 2021).

45. In 2021 the average social assistance benefit was 1.9 percent of GDP per capita (ONEI 2022a).

46. The value of external remittances sank 70.8 percent in 2019–2021, from US$3,716 million to US$1,084 million (Morales 2021; Spadoni 2022).

47. In 1995, a team of Cuban academic economists recommended a change from state subsidies to consumer goods, on one hand, to subsidies to people in need, on the other. This benefits all the population including those who have high incomes (Carranza et al. 1995). The Cuban government at the time (Fidel Castro had implemented the policy of state subsidies to food and other essential goods) ignored such a recommendation. Raúl Castro, however, took steps to eliminate rationing (although it still exists), but he did not implement adequate subsidies to the vulnerable population. In fact, social assistance has been significantly cut. At the end of 2023, the government announced the replacement of state subsidies to consumer goods by subsidies to the needy, starting in 2024 (Gámez 2024b).

48. The "Merit" program for those who served in the wars of independence and their families (a total of 800,000 around 2014) paid an average monthly assistance benefit for those aged 60 and above of 870,000 dong (US$41), one-quarter of the average contributory pension for the minimum-skilled insured in the mandatory program but three times the average social assistance transfer of 270,000 dong (Kidd et al. 2016).

49. According to the World Bank (2021b), in 2018 more than one-half of all elderly received neither a contributory pension nor a noncontributory pension.

50. Another ILO (2018b) study found that, despite universal coverage among those aged 80 and above who are poor, 60 percent of them do not receive a pension.

51. Shen et al. (2020) measure pension inequalities among seven groups based on China's health pension surveys. Data indicates that the military (and civil servants before their unification to the urban-employee scheme) had RR between 90 and 100 percent.

52. Since 2018 the adjustment fund draws at least 3 percent from capital pools of regions that then is redistributed based on the number of pensioners in each region; this is a first step in the right direction but not yet a national pooling based on a unified pension scheme (Gongcheng and Scholz 2019).

53. Starting in January 2022, the vice minister of finance ordered an interregional pooling of pension resources; gaps in economic development and in population age structures have resulted in some regions having fund surpluses, whereas others face payment difficulties, and therefore transfers will be made among them ("China Starts Nationwide Pooling," 2022).

54. According to Gao (2017), the dibao's reduction of the inequality gap in income is minimal. Solinger (2022b) makes a strong case that dibao has failed to meet expectations—that is, it does not protect the unemployed resulting from

the shutting down of state enterprises with the reform, and that there are significant gaps among provinces and cities.

55. Ho khau is an important document used to prove residential information, it is necessary for anyone to go through many administrative procedures and to provide key documents such as birth registration, death declaration, marriage registration, transferring land use rights, buying a house, confirmation of marital status, etc.

56. Inequalities among regions have also been documented (ILSSA/ILO 2022); for instance, on multidimensional poverty (lowest 1.3 percent in Red River Delta versus 14.4 percent in Northern Midlands) and on Gini Coefficient (lowest 0.291 in southeast versus 0.420 in Northern Midlands and Mountains). The poverty rate among ethnic minorities is 59 percent, wherein the majority Kinh and Hoa are only 9.9 percent (Kidd et al. 2016).

57. In 2020, there were 1.5 million women "inactive," a good part of them housewives doing home labor and caring for relatives—activities not considered employment (Ación and Colina 2022). Among women aged 60 and above, 27 percent have never had remunerated work, compared to 2 percent of men, whereas only 7 percent of women found another job after retirement vis-à-vis 16 percent of men (ONEI 2019b). In addition, because women are more likely to be employed in the informal economy, they are less able to achieve access to social insurance contributory pensions than men (ILO, n.d.).

58. UNDP (2020) provides the labor force participation rate by gender in 2019 of the three countries: Vietnam 82.4 percent male and 72.7 percent female, China 75.3 percent and 60.5 percent, and Cuba 66.8 percent and 40.7 percent. The gender gaps in percentage points were 10.0 in Vietnam, 14.8 in China, and 26.1 in Cuba, a similar ranking as in the gender shares of the labor force.

59. In 2016, in the voluntary program, coverage of women was 47.7 percent and 52.3 percent of men; by 2019, however, due to government gender policies, the proportions reversed to 58.8 percent of women and 41 percent of men (ILSSA/ILO 2022).

60. At the subnational level, there are thirty-one jurisdictions: twenty-two provinces, four cities, and five autonomous regions; at lower levels of administrations, there are more than three hundred cities and about three thousand counties, towns, and villages (Lu et al. 2019).

61. In Latin America, individual accounts in private pension schemes are normally managed by private profit-seeking corporations. In a couple of countries, there is a public administrator that competes with the private corporations under equal norms. In 2022, Bolivia shut down the two private corporations and transferred all their functions to a unified state agency (Mesa-Lago 2021c).

62. Meng (2019) shows that "insider-dominated" provinces tend to have a decentralized pension scheme more than centrally dominated provinces, because municipal leaders have incentives to keep pensions localized.

63. Olivier (2022) notes that, although MOLISA unifies the administration of social security saved for healthcare, the various benefits are managed by different MOLISA departments, which are lacking in adequate coordination.

64. Conversely, Zheng (2019) estimates that, in 2019, 80 percent of the insured punctually contributed to the urban-employee scheme. In the resident scheme, there is no data on how many of the affiliates actively contribute.

65. Smaller enterprises face relatively higher and rising costs (564 percent in 2003–2016) than large enterprises, hence their profit margins decrease (ILO 2021a).

66. Another source reports a slight increase in compliance from 58 percent to 62 percent in 2005–2016 (ILO 2021a).

67. The proportion above 100 percent in Vietnam is explained by patients receiving alternative treatments in a single day who occupy the same bed, particularly during high demand. See https://www.moh.gov.vn.web/guest/thong-ke-y-te?p_p_id/.

68. For instance, some hospitals tend to oversupply expensive services, and there are few incentives for cost control or efficiency improvements at facility levels.

69. This is high compared to other countries in the region: 40 percent in the Philippines, 53 percent in Malaysia, and 60 percent in Indonesia.

70. One referee argued that in one-party states, as in the three countries analyzed herein, there are no business actors, and worker organizations operate within the party structure; hence it is likely that social policies are more resilient and have few avenues for challenges from below. Although it is not possible to deal with this question here, there are examples in this book suggesting that provincial and local governments have substantial input in policy implementation and changes in China. This is not the case in Cuba.

71. The overall source for legislation on social security in Vietnam is https://thuvienphapluat.vn/.

72. The Social Insurance Law (2010) of China established (art. 3) that the system had to be sustainable according to the economic and social development of the nation.

73. In Vietnam, the health contribution is obligatory for those in both mandatory and voluntary programs (Castel and Pick 2018).

74. Before its incorporation with the urban-employee scheme, the mandatory pension for civil servants and public service employees was on PAYG and was entirely financed by public funds; it had laxer conditions than in the urban-employee scheme.

75. In line with the flexibility of the resident scheme, participants between the ages of 45 and 60 and with less than fifteen years of contributions are encouraged to increase monthly payments to cover the absence of contributions during their earlier working years (Nikolov and Anderson 2019).

76. China's individual account fund of US$362,000 million is relatively low compared with considerably smaller economies in some Latin American countries—for example, US$215,400 million in Chile. Related to GDP, China's individual account fund is only 2.5 percent, but in Chile it is 80 percent (Mesa-Lago 2021c).

77. Zheng (2020) also gives a total of 11,600,000 million yuan (US$1,680,000 million), equal to 11.7 percent of GDP in 2019. KPMG (2020) gives a total for all pillars of 15,000,000 million yuan in 2019, equal to US$2,365,930 million.

78. Chinese households held US$15,300,000 million in 2020 (an amount similar to China's GDP) in local bank deposits, when they could be invested to provide a third (or fourth) pension pillar. The CBIRC began a pilot program in mid-2021 to foster endowment plans offering stable returns over ten years of retirement ("China Turns to Private Insurers," 2021).

79. KPMG (2020) gives annual average real growth rates by pillar in 2009–2019 as 4.94 percent in pillar 1 (probably basic insurance plus individual accounts), 1.07 percent in pillar 2 (occupational plans), and 2.07 percent in pillar 3 (the new commercial insurance). The average of the three was 2.7 percent. Although returns of the national fund are in double digits, those of provincial schemes have dropped to low single digits, and some provinces such as Heilongjiang, Liaoning, Inner Mongolia, Jilin, and Qinghai already face funding shortfalls (A. Lee 2021).

80. China's population is expected to decline from 1,410 million in 2020 to 730 million in 2100, when the country will have as many 85 year olds as 18 year olds (Cave et al. 2021).

81. The projection for China's elderly population for 2050 is 28 percent of its total population, which is 487 million, more than the total population of the European Union (M. Vidal 2021). The aging degree in the rural population is significantly higher than in the urban population: those aged 60 and above account for 23.8 percent of the total rural population, nearly 8 percentage points higher than the urban ratio, and this will rise to 37.7 percent by 2035 (National Aging Development Bulletin 2021). There are significant differences also among provinces concerning their degree of aging: the age group of 65 and above is the largest group in Liaoning (17.4 percent), Shanghai (16.2 percent), and Jilin (15.6 percent), all "deeply aging"; conversely it is the smallest group in Xizhang (5.6 percent), Xinjiang (7.7 percent), and Guangdong (8.5 percent) (2021 Census, GOV 2021e). Due to the decrease in the productive age population and the increase in the elderly population, the latter's dependency on the former rose from 8.9 percent in 2011 to 13.5 percent in 2020. However, that proportion is still below those of Japan, Germany, the United Kingdom, and France (A. Lee 2021).

82. Beijing Dabeinong Technology Group is offering its employees up to 90,000 yuan (US$14,100) for having a third child ("China Rolling Out Perks," 2022).

83. A fund has been developed to redistribute the surplus from younger provinces to the older provinces (MOHRSS 2021; "China's Social Security System," 2021).

84. Cuba's 19 percent total contribution to the pension scheme is smaller than those in Latin American countries with both an aged population and a mature pension system (for instance, 21.2 percent in Argentina, as high as 40 percent in Brazil, and 22.5 percent in Uruguay) but also lower than in countries with a younger population and less mature pension system, such as 23 percent in Paraguay (Mesa-Lago 2021c).

85. The number of female children born per fertile women was 0.76 in 2019. Contributing to this phenomenon has been a high rate of contraceptive use, a high reliance on induced abortion, and harsh living conditions.

86. For projections to 2050 and 2100, see ECLAC 2020.

87. Previously, the World Bank (2012) argued that there were conflicting interests between the social insurance fund and the government: the former interest was to get the highest capital returns and the latter interest was to obtain funds at the lowest costs, hence the pressure to invest in government securities.

88. Regions have significantly diverse fertility rates, which are highest in the least developed areas and lowest in the most developed; they are higher among H'Mong ethnic groups and lower among Kinh groups (World Bank 2021b).

89. The population aged 60 and above is projected to increase to 18 percent in 2030 and 30 percent in 2050 (Kidd et al. 2016).

90. Another series for 2016–2020 based on contribution-revenue and benefit-expenditure gives much higher positive balances: 46.5 percent in 2016, 51.6 percent in 2017, 55.4 percent in 2018, 59.2 percent in 2019, and 57.4 percent in 2020 (ILSSA/ILO 2022).

91. None of the three countries charges healthcare contributions to retired workers.

92. Also, only the expenses that exceed around 10 percent of average annual wage for local workers could be reimbursed, and only a specific proportion of the costs could be reimbursed. The applying percentages for urban employees are higher than those for the urban-and-rural-resident scheme.

93. For instance, in 2021 in Beijing, they paid a total of 11.8 percent plus 3 yuan, out of which 2.8 percent and 3 yuan went to the individual account.

94. Utilization of public hospitals was 50 percent vis-à-vis 30.5 percent private hospitals. The public outpatient treatment increased from 30.7 percent to 50.9 percent between 2008–2018, whereas that of private health facilities decreased from 38.4 percent to 27.9 percent; concerning inpatient treatment, 88 percent went to public hospitals in 2020 (GSO 2020, 2021a).

95. In 2014–2021, Cuban investment in health decreased from 2.2 percent

to 0.3 percent of total investment, whereas investment in enterprise and real estate services grew from 21.8 percent to 50.3 percent (Monreal 2021).

96. In 2016, according to the World Bank (2021b), 45 percent of insured members got premiums paid by the state budget.

97. Employers in Vietnam must pay and provide a free annual checkup (blood tests, X-rays, etc.) to their employees.

98. In the next three decades, annual expenditures in health for the elderly are projected to increase from four to five times (World Bank 2021b).

99. The "Merit" program cost was 1.1 percent of GDP in 2014—that is, 3.7 times the cost of the rest of social assistance at the time (0.3 percent), but it is closed now (no new beneficiaries are accepted) and eventually will disappear (Kidd et al. 2016).

100. Vietnam's social protection eight-year plan aimed to achieve a universal system by 2020, but the focus was on those in especially difficult circumstances: children in need, low-income elderly, severely disabled persons, and the poor (Fifth Plenum, 2012).

101. The World Bank (2021b) projected the start of the deficit for 2029. Zhou (2021) estimates a deficit from US$1,130,000 million to US$1,400,000 million in 2025–2030 (from 8 percent to 10 percent of the GDP of 2019) and widening further over time due to the aging process and annual raises in pensions indexed to wages and the CPI. The Insurance Association of China projected in November 2020 that a shortfall of 10,000,000 million yuan would occur in 2030 instead of 2050 (cited by A. Lee 2021).

102. The statistical series of the basic pension balance (revenue minus expenditures) in 2006–2019 shows a steady surplus, but the rate of annual increase in the surplus decreased from 35.8 percent to 8.1 percent in the period (NBSC 2008, 2021b).

103. The deficit should be worse, because the assumptions used (GDP, wages, inflation, and demographic aging) deteriorated considerably in 1992–2023.

104. With reforms, the year could be postponed to 2044 (based on inflation indexation to pension), to 2046 (based in increase in retirement age), to 2063 (based on convergence of valorization formula by 2048), or to 2080 (all three reforms combined).

105. The accuracy of this comparison cannot be assessed: in China there are active worker contributors to old-age pensioners whereas in Cuba there are workers (who may or may not be contributors) to all types of pensioners—including old-age, disabled, and survivors (NBSC 2021a, 2021c; ONEI 2021). In Vietnam, the ratio of workers paying premiums per one pensioner decreased from 9.4 to 7.8 in 2011–2020. These are much higher ratios than in the text (ILSSA/ILO 2022).

106. ILO (2018b) estimates that in Vietnam the ratio of workers aged 15–

59 for each elder person aged 60 and above will increase from 6.6 to 2.1 in 2015–2055. The World Bank (2021b) projects an ascending ratio of *pensioners to contributors* in 2019–2080 but does not provide numbers to estimate *contributors to pensioners* in order to do a comparison with China and Cuba.

107. The estimate of OECD (2018) of an average life expectancy of 18.7 years at retirement age 65 is close to the OECD average of 19.7 years. Eleven out of twenty-one countries have higher life expectancies at the age of retirement than Vietnam does, they are the most developed; China has lower life expectancy.

108. The population aged 60 and above was 12 percent in 2020 and will increase to 18 percent by 2030 and 23 percent by 2040 (Olivier 2022). Cuba's population aged 60 and above was 21.6 percent in 2020 and by 2030 will be 29.3 percent (ONEI 2022a)—that is, 1.8 and 1.6 times Vietnam's proportion, respectively.

109. A general index that combines three sub-indices (adequacy or sufficiency and financial sustainability already explained, plus the demographic situation, places China in eleventh place, after Canada, and Vietnam in fifty-seventh place followed by Greece; Cuba should be at the bottom, well below Argentina in the fifty-ninth place (Allianz and Hermes 2020).

110. I could not check the study methodology but have questions about the ranking.

CHAPTER 6: CONCLUSIONS

1. Concerning scores, Cuba is 3.8 points behind China and 2.7 points behind Vietnam, whereas the difference between the two Asian countries is 1 point.

2. I was able to compare the diverse socioeconomic models of Chile (market), Cuba (planned), and Costa Rica (mixed) throughout forty years, because the models' starts were much closer in date and plenty of data was available for the starting years (Mesa-Lago 2000).

3. For the sake of comparison, let us use a common social indicator: infant mortality. In 1990, Cuban infant mortality rates were, respectively, one-fifth and one-third those of China and Vietnam. Furthermore, thirty-seven years before (1958) at the eve of the revolution, the Cuban rate of 33.4 was similar to Vietnam's (32.6 in 1990) and substantially smaller than China's (50.2 in 1991). Comparisons based on NBSC 2021b; GSO 2020; ONEI 2020a; Mesa-Lago 2009.

4. Due to the lack of concrete indicators in social solidarity, we used segmentation among schemes and pension coverage (these are also used in unity and coverage) but these are only 4 percent of the total indicators.

5. I have already cited the social security expert X. Huang (2020), who argues that the expansion of China's healthcare system was carried out in a

gradual and incremental manner, tied to economic development and available resources, thus avoiding a commitment to an excessively generous system. A pertinent element of government advice: "Be patient and seek steady rather than speedy development" (Fan 2022).

6. Cuba's tax system is regressive. In 2020, out of all taxes, 66 percent were indirect (mostly from sales taxes) and 34 percent were direct (Mesa-Lago 2015a; ONEI 2021).

7. I gratefully acknowledge Vegard Bye's suggestion to add this section to the book, following his own book's analysis (chapter 10, "Conclusions").

8. It has been argued that Vietnam is more agricultural and less urban than Cuba (I discussed this issue in chapter 1).

9. See Davies 2007; García 2007; Pérez Villanueva 2008; De Miranda and Pérez Villanueva 2012; Nova 2013, 2022; P. Vidal 2014; Torres 2016; Monreal 2018a, 2018c.

10. In 2017, when he was vice president, Díaz-Canel (2017) said in relation to market reforms like those of China and Vietnam: "the intention is to impose a platform for the capitalist and neo-liberal restoration . . . a return to the Cuba we had in 1959 . . . every thing would be privatized."

11. Bye (2020) argues that the incompetence of the pro–status quo actors made them afraid of becoming the "losers" vis-à-vis the "winners": SME, private farmers, and the new emerging middle class.

12. Bye (2020) elaborates a scheme to explore different outcomes or "routes."

13. The large majority of former nations that were under Soviet rule currently have a market economy with much better performance than Russia. The Czech Republic and Estonia almost double Russian GDP per capita, and Latvia, Lithuania, Poland, Hungary, and Rumania have a higher GDP (IMF 2023).

CHAPTER 7: SUGGESTED POLICIES TO IMPROVE SOCIAL SECURITY AND ITS SUSTAINABILITY

1. A deep analysis of this issue is beyond the scope of this book.

2. See Zheng (2008), Barr and Diamond (2010), Dorfman et al. (2013), World Bank (2013), L. Fang (2014), Lu et al. (2019), and Cousins (2021), among others. For various types of social security reforms, see Mesa-Lago 2007, 2021c; Olivier 2022.

3. This is not exclusive to China but is common in most countries of the world—for instance, in nineteen out of twenty Latin American countries.

4. Gongcheng (2022) advises an integration of social security multiple norms into one sound unified legal system.

5. The military separate scheme should be incorporated into this branch, and the former entitlement conditions should be standardized as much as feasible.

6. Meng makes a case for keeping positive aspects of decentralization and localism because they foment competition and pension development: "In ad-

dition to establishing [a] nationally integrated pension program, China should allow its municipal governments to run their own pension schemes and retain the authority to set the parameters of their pension programs, like contribution rate and benefit level, according to their local condition" (2019, 211). He does not elaborate, however, on how to harmonize this goal with social security principles such as equal treatment and social solidarity.

7. Zheng (2008) and L. Fang (2014) recommend a target that both reduces benefits of the very well protected workers and improves the conditions of the poorest protected, whereas Dorfman et al. (2013) propose maintaining diverse pension rules for salaried workers and nonsalaried workers but gradually merging them.

8. The argument of young Chinese workers that increasing the retirement age will reduce job opportunities for them is refuted by Giles et al. (2021).

9. Gongcheng and Scholz (2019) recommended the elimination of individual accounts in the two major pension schemes so as to facilitate transfers among generations, income groups, and genders, thus improving social solidarity. Gongcheng (2022) also called for abolishing the individual accounts of urban employees' healthcare insurance.

10. The World Bank (2013) and Lu et al. (2019) proposed a means-tested pension. Another alternative is a universal pension, except for those who receive a basic contributory pension, to be detected by an affluence test (Barr and Diamond 2010). Although this pension is easier to administer (important in China's rural areas) and avoids the stigma, the affluence test may be complex to implement (see Shen et al. 2020; Mesa-Lago 2021c).

11. Barr and Diamond (2010), Zheng (2012), Dorfman et al. (2013), L. Fang (2014), and Lu et al. (2019) recommended that either the individual accounts or all contributory pillars are based on nondefined contribution (NDC); the latter claim that the NDC "is already effectively embodied" in the urban-employee scheme, "although it is not so labeled" (Lu et al. 2019, 6). Chen and Turner (2021) affirm that individual accounts are in practice NDC.

12. President Xi has stated the goal of integrating urban and rural areas in social security (cited by Tang 2022).

13. Y. Wang (2021) argues that the state legal responsibility for collecting contributions and protecting the insured and the social insurance system can be effectively met on the basis of the existing legal institutions: the state should be held directly liable if it does not meet its obligations to collect social insurance contributions.

14. This independent agency exists in Chile and Costa Rica and has proved successful.

15. Chile, Costa Rica, Mexico, and Uruguay have created public educational funds, introduced social security courses in the school curricula, and increased advising on financial issues to the insured and the population.

16. A significant cause of lower healthcare in rural areas is that doctors and other health personnel are paid much lower salaries there than in urban areas, and they work with poorer facilities and equipment (Y. Wang 2022). To address this problem, the government should provide wage incentives and better facilities and equipment in rural areas. An option that is not feasible in China because of the freedom of medical personnel to choose their jobs and locations is for graduates to have a one-year social service in the countryside, as is offered in Cuba and other Latin American countries.

17. For other recommendations, see the special issue on long-term care for the elderly in *International Social Security Review* 75, no. 2–3 (2022).

18. The guidelines encourage home-care services to reduce dependency on hospitals and institutions for the elderly.

19. Xi's stand against corruption and his reduction of inequalities are positive features of his policies, but his strengthening of the state intervention in the economy and his turn away from a socialist-market economy are adverse features.

20. Johnson (2023) argues that Xi will not return to the previous socialist-market model.

21. "The critical question for China in the 2020s is whether Xi can engineer a course correction to recover from the significant slowing of economic growth" (Rudd 2022).

22. For previous recommendations (some of them applied in the 2008 reform), see Hicks and Pérez (2005) and Mesa-Lago (2003, 2018b).

23. Hicks and Pérez (2005) propose a change to a market economy; for multiple proposals on the latter, see the collection in ASCE (1991–2021).

24. The main source of this section, unless specified, is Mesa-Lago et al. (2022).

25. There is a solid consensus on this recommendation among the experts on Cuban pensions (Donate-Armada 1994; Cuevas and Pérez 1999; Mesa-Lago 2003; Hicks and Pérez 2005; Mesa-Lago et al. 2022).

26. It is reasoned that adjustment to the CPI is better than adjustment to wages because increases in the latter would tend to reflect increases in productivity in better functioning labor markets (Hicks and Pérez 2005).

27. Administrative cost is a key indicator that should be tabulated and published by international organizations, which should also provide standards for reasonable costs.

28. It has been shown before that Cuba's total current contribution on wages to the pension scheme is lower than those of China and Vietnam, despite these two countries having less mature pension systems; the same is true of several Latin American countries with systems as mature as Cuba's and similarly aged populations. In addition, Cuba's pension expenditures relative to GDP are higher than those of China and Vietnam. The conclusion is that Cuba's contribution

must be increased, as real pensions are already too low to endure any reduction, but in order to effect said increase, steady economic growth must be achieved by shifting to the socialist-market model.

29. The ILO has a proven simulation tool, tried in many countries, that can change the variables of the system (e.g., retirement age, contribution, base salary, replacement rate) based on key economic variables (such as GDP growth, wages, inflation, interest rate, etc.) in order to project equilibrium over a long period.

30. In Latin America, Chile under Pinochet rule was the pioneer in trying to privatize healthcare, with the dictatorial regime weakening the public health system and providing incentives for the expansion of private providers that endured many flaws. When democracy was restored, the "Concertación" coalition reinstated resources for public health, and the private sector sharply decreased (Mesa-Lago 2007).

31. Bye analyzes the differences in the structural reforms between the two models. In Cuba "the process has been mostly about *survival without development*, dictated by the fear of giving the private sector a strategic economic role as a platform for challenging the monolithic political power structure. In China and Vietnam, on the other hand, there has been extremely successful economic development and social improvement as a result of far-reaching market reforms that may explain why the political regimes have survived" (2020, 246). See also Bye's analysis of diverse scenarios for the future.

32. For an analysis of the failed state reforms, Cuban economist opinions and more details on the proposed policies, see Mesa-Lago and Svejnar (2020), 42–51. In August 2022, the best-known social science journal asked seven prominent economists, all residing in Cuba, to identify the major challenges and reforms required with the following score: control/reduce current hyperinflation, three points; increase domestic production, particularly food, three points; renegotiate the foreign debt, three points; terminate central planning, two points; and eliminate state monopoly of foreign trade, increase foreign investment, terminate restrictions to the private sector, abolish state monopolies and oligopolies and increase competition, recover the purchasing power of salary, restore electricity output and reduce emigration, one point each ("¿Cuáles son los principales nudos," 2022).

33. This period may be too short to project the coverage growth annual rate, a longer period could result in a higher rate.

34. The annual statistical yearbook offers absolute data that permits calculations on coverage and also plenty of financial data, health statistics, and so forth, but not the detailed data on coverage as described in the text. A quarterly publication on the social economic situation does not provide statistics on social security.

35. Vietnam has an advantage over China in that women's retirement age

is already unified at 55 and will be 60 by 2030. The increase in China's age of retirement to 55/58 for women is an improvement, but retirement age will still be below 60 by 2040.

36. According to OECD (2018), average life expectancy at age 65 in Vietnam is 18.7 years, close to the OECD average of 19.7 years and higher than China's 16.1 years.

37. According to the World Bank, a survey showed that 62 percent of respondents thought that the government should bear primary responsibility for "providing income to retired people," whereas only 27 percent were in favor of raising taxes to "provide a basic benefit to the elderly in financial need" (2021b, 135), an outcome that stresses the need for policymakers to explain the challenges as well as the urgency of the reform.

38. A previous study by the World Bank (2012) on Vietnam has been superseded by later reforms, many of which are incorporated in the longer and more updated 2021c version—this one was preceded by a policy-oriented more succinct document (World Bank 2019).

39. A 1995 law stipulated mandatory coverage of enterprises with at least ten employees; it was not possible to find data on the enforcement and results of that norm.

40. The World Bank (2019) offers a table that contrasts the current situation in social protection key components and its proposed reforms in various phases by 2030.

41. A previous World Bank publication stated: "There is no ideal pension system for every country situation, as different pension systems developed under different historical, cultural, political, institutional and developmental circumstances" (2019, 34). This is the stand I have supported during the last forty years.

42. The 2018 resolution of the central committee of the party recognized that universal pension coverage could only be achieved by expanding the noncontributory pension within the social security system (Socialist Republic of Vietnam 2018).

43. The World Bank (2021b) concurs that Vietnam should invest more in human capital to build its own intellectual infrastructure for the future.

REFERENCES

Ación, Ahmed, and Henry Colina. 2022. *Reflexiones sobre el Marco de Financiamiento de las Políticas de Cuidados en Cuba.* Santo Domingo: Friedrich Ebert Stiftung and Universidad de la Habana.

Acosta, Elaine. 2019. "Economía y sociedad en Cuba. El presente como malestar subjetivo y el futuro como promesa estancada." In *Cuba Pos-Castro. ¿Espejismo o realidad? Miradas diversas sobre una sociedad en transición*, edited by Sergio Angel Baquero and Armando Chaguaceda, 113–32 Bogotá: Universidad Sergio Arboleda.

Acosta, Elaine. 2021. "Migration and Elderly Care When Women Leave, Who Cares for Older Adults? A Case Study of Cuba." In *The Palgrave Handbook on Gender and Migration*, edited by Claudia Mora and Nicola Piper, 167–83. Camden, London: Palgrave Macmillan.

Acosta, Elaine, ed. 2022a. "Agencia y propuestas de la sociedad civil y la comunidad en la asistencia y cuidados a las personas mayores en Cuba." *Foro Cubano. Revista de Divulgación* 5, no. 46 (July). https://www.programacuba.com/agencia-y-propuestas-de-la-sociedad-civil/.

Acosta, Elaine. 2022b. "Los derechos de las personas mayores en el nuevo Código de las Familias en Cuba." *Demo Anlat*, April 4, 5–9. https://demoamlat

.com/los-derechos-de-las-personas-mayores-en-el-nuevo-codigo-de-las-familias-en-cuba/.

Acosta, Elaine, and Sergio Ángel Baquero. 2020. "Radiografía del envejecimiento poblacional en Cuba. Desigualdades acumuladas y nuevas vulnerabilidades." In *Crisis de cuidados, envejecimiento y políticas de bienestar en Cuba*, 101–38. Bogotá: Editorial Sergio Arboleda.

Acosta, Elaine, Florencia Picasso, and Valentina Perrotta. 2018. *Cuidados en la vejez en América Latina. Los casos de Chile, Cuba y Uruguay*. Santiago: Konrad Adenauer Foundation.

Aja, Antonio, and William Hernández. 2019. "Dinámica de la población y sus interrelaciones en Cuba y sus territorios. Recomendaciones para la acción." *Novedades en Población* 15, no. 29: 69, 72–73.

Albizu-Campos, Juan Carlos. 2009. "La fecundidad en Cuba. Viejas interrogantes y algunas respuestas." *Novedades en Población* 5, no. 10: 42–123.

Albizu-Campos, Juan Carlos. 2016. "Fertility, GDP and Average Real Wage in Cuba." *MEDICC Review* 18, no. 1–2 (January–April): 71–76.

Albizu-Campos, Juan Carlos. 2020. "Una mirada a la población económicamente activa." *Novedades en Población* 16, no. 32. http://www.novpob.uh.cu/index.php/NovPob/article/view/457/.

Albizu-Campos, Juan Carlos. 2021. "Projections of Cuban Life Expectancies, 2020–2030." Havana, August 31. *Novedades en Población* 1 no. 21 Recovered October 26, 2024. http://scielo.sld.cu/scielo.php?script=sci_arttext&pid=S1817-40782015000100001&lng=es&tlng=es/.

Albizu-Campos, Juan Carlos. 2022a. Comparison of diverse inflation rates in 2021–2022 according to ten sources. Communication by e-mail to the author, Havana, April 13.

Albizu-Campos, Juan Carlos. 2022b. "Investigación en curso sobre la esperanza de vida en Cuba." Based on data from Dirección Nacional de Estadísticas y Registros Médicos-MINSAP, *Datos de certificados de defunción*, and ONEI, *Anuario demográfico de Cuba*, 2012 to 2022. Havana, July. https://www.onei.gob.cu/anuario-demografico-de-cuba-enero-diciembre-2022/.

Albizu-Campos, Juan Carlos. 2022c. "El uso de epítetos apocalípticos es ante todo contraproducente." Interview by Elaine Acosta, *Cuido 60*, February 25. https://www.cuido60.com/juan-carlos-albizu-campos/.

Albizu-Campos, Juan Carlos. 2024a. "Cuba. Una rápida mirada a la emigración y la población," Horizonte Cubano, Columbia University Law School, July 15. https://horizontecubano.law.columbia.edu/news/cuba-una-rapida-mirada-la-emigracion-y-la-poblacion

Albizu-Campos, Juan Carlos. 2024b. La población cubana y la emigración que el viento se llevó," La Joven Cuba. Havana, July 24. https://jovencuba.com/poblacion-cubana-emigracion/.

Albizu-Campos, Juan Carlos, and Sergio Díaz-Briquets. 2023. "Cuba y la emigración. La salida como voz." *Horizonte Cubano*, Cuba Capacity Building Project, Columbia Law School, January 26. https://horizontecubano.law.columbia.edu/news/cuba-y-la-emigracion-la-salida-como-voz/.

Albizu-Campos, Juan Carlos, and Tomás Jiménez. 1995. *Cuba transición de la fecundidad. Cambio social y conducta reproductiva.* Havana: MINSAP, CEDEM, UNICEF. July. https://www.researchgate.net/publication/283524053_Cuba_Transicion_de_la_fecundidad_Cambio_social_y_conducta_reproductiva/.

Alkire, Sabina, Usha Kanagaratnam, and Nicolai Suppa. 2020. "The Global Multidimensional Poverty Index (MPI) 2020." *OPHI MPI Methodological Poverty Index*, note 49: 1–58.

Allianz, and Euler Hermes. 2020. *Allianz Pension Report 2020: The Silver Swan.* Munich, May 28.

Álvarez, José. 2004. *Cuba's Agricultural Sector.* Gainesville: University Press of Florida.

Añé, Lía. 2007. "Contribución a los estudios de pobreza en Cuba." Paper at Congress of the Latin American Studies Association, Montreal, September 6–8.

Arreola, Gerardo. 2012. "En Cuba no habrá una reforma política, advierte el Vicepresidente Marino Murillo." *La Jornada*, March 28, 5.

ASCE (Association for the Study of the Cuban Economy). 1991–2021. *Cuba in Transition*, Vols 1 to 30.

Aspalter, Christian, ed. 2023. *The Routledge International Handbook to Welfare State Systems.* Abingdon: Routledge.

Banks, Lena M., Matthew Walsham, Hoang Van Minh, Doan Thi Thuy Duong, Tran Thu Ngan, Vu Quynh Mai, Karl Blanchet, Hannah Kuper. 2019. "Access to Social Protection among People with Disabilities: Evidence from Vietnam." *International Social Security Review* 72, no,1: 59–82.

Barr, Nicholas, and Peter Diamond. 2010. "Pension Reform in China: Issues, Options and Recommendations." London School of Economics and MIT. February. https://www.lse.ac.uk/european-institute/Assets/Documents/nick-barr-research/Barr-Diamond-China-Pensions-2010.pdf.

Barrientos, Armando. 2018. Social Assistance in Low and Middle-Income Countries Dataset—SALMIC. Manchester: Global Development Institute, University of Manchester. https://research.manchester.ac.uk/en/publications/social-assistance-in-low-and-middle-income-countries/.

BCC (Banco Central de Cuba). 2014. Resolución No. 35. *Gaceta Oficial de Cuba.* Havana, May 21.

Bradsher, Keith. 2022a. "As China's Party Congress Begins, the Economic Impact Is Considered." *New York Times*, October 10: B-2.

Bradsher, Keith. 2022b. "Beijing Pauses GDP Release as Communist Party Gathers." *New York Times*, October 18: B-5.

Bradsher, Keith. 2022c. "China's Covid Policies Spook European Companies." *New York Times*, May 6. https://www.nytimes.com/2023/05/04/business/china-foreign-business-security.html/.

Bradsher, Keith. 2023a. "Beijing's Central Bank Cuts Key Interest Rate." *New York Times*, August 22: B-3

Bradsher, Keith. 2023b. "China Faces New Threat to Economy: Falling Prices." *New York Times*, August 10: B-1, B-4.

Bradsher, Keith. 2023c. "China's Plan for Stimulus Loses Steam." *New York Times*, August 23: B-1, B-4.

Bradsher, Keith. 2023d. "China's Plan to Stimulate an Increase in Spending." *New York Times*, August 1: C-1, C-3.

Bradsher, Keith, and Alexandra Stevenson. 2022. "Xi Secures an Iron Grip on Power." *New York Times*, October 25. https://www.nytimes.com/2022/10/23/business/china-gdp-economy.html/.

Bradsher, Keith, Daisuke Wakabayashi, and Claire Fu. 2023. "For China, No Easy Fix as Recovery Hits a Wall." *New York Times*, June 20: B-1, B-2.

Brandt, Loren. 2022. Information provided by e-mail to the author, Toronto, June 26.

Brandt, Loren, Debin Ma, and Thomas G. Rawski. 2017. "Industrialization in China." In *The Spread of Modern History to the Periphery since 1971*, edited by Kevin H. O'Rourke and Jeffrey G. Williamson, 197–228. Oxford: Oxford University Press.

Brandt, Loren, and Thomas G. Rawski. 2008. *China's Great Economic Transformation*. Cambridge: Cambridge University Press.

Brandt, Loren, and Thomas G. Rawski. 2022. "China's Great Boom as a Historical Process." In *The Cambridge Economic History of China*, edited by Debin Ma and Richard Von Glahn, 2:775–828. 2 vols. Cambridge: Cambridge University Press.

Bray, David. 2005. *Social Space and Governance in Urban China: The Danwei from Origins to Reform*. Stanford, CA: Stanford University Press.

Brundenius, Claes, and Le Dang Doanh. 2014. "Innovation, Entrepreneurship and SMEs: What Can Cuba Learn from the Vietnam Reform Process?" In *No More Free Lunch: Reflections on the Cuban Economic Reform Process and Challenges for Transformation*, edited by Claes Brundenius and Ricardo Torres, 129–51. Cham: Springer.

Bruni, Michele. 2018. *Ageing, the Socioeconomic Burden, Labour Market and Migration: The Chinese Case in an International Perspective*. Maastricht: Global Labor Organization Discussion Paper Series No. 222.

Buckley, Chris. 2013. "China's Leaders Urge More Market Control of the Economy." *New York Times*, November 12.

Buckley, Chris, and Keith Bradsher. 2022. "Xi Expands His Power, Elevating Loyalists and Forcing Out Moderates." *New York Times*, October 23.

https://www.nytimes.com/2022/10/22/world/asia/china-xi-jinping-congress.html/.

Buckley, Chris, and Keith Bradsher. 2023. "Li Keqiang, 68, Premier Sidelined in China as Xi Tightened Grip, Is Dead." *New York Times*, October 28.

Buckley, Chris, Keith Bradsher, and Chang Che. 2022. "In Third Term, Xi Strengthens Grip on Power." *New York Times*, October 24.

Buckley, Chris, Alexandra Stevenson, and Cao Li. 2021. "Xi Eyes Richest in Bid to Build a Middle Class." *New York Times*, September 7: A-1.

Bye, Vegard. 2020. *Cuba, from Fidel to Raúl and Beyond*. Cham: Palgrave Macmillan/Springer.

Cai, Meng, and Ximing Yue. 2020. "The Redistributive Role of Government Social Security Transfers on Inequality in China" *China Economic Review* 62 (August): 101512.

"Can China's Creaky Health Insurance Scheme Withstand Its Ageing Population and Corona Virus?" 2022. *Pension Policy International*, January 3.

Carmona, Edilberto, Lissett Izquierdo, and Ismael Francisco. 2021. "Hogar de ancianos. Sin tiempo para el olvido." *Cubadebate*, Havana, February 1. http://www.cubadebate.cu/especiales/2021/02/01/hogar-de-ancianos-sin-tiempo-para-el-olvido/.

Carranza, Julio, Luis Gutiérrez, and Pedro Monreal. 1995. *Cuba la restructuración de la economía. Una propuesta para el cambio*. Havana: Editorial de Ciencias Sociales.

Castel, Paulette, and Alexander Pick. 2018. *Increasing Social Insurance Coverage in Viet Nam's SMEs*. Paris: OECD Development Policy Papers, October, No. 13.

Castro Ruz, Fidel. 2016. "El hermano Obama." *Granma*, March 28. Internet@granma.cu>reflexiones-fidel>2016-03-28/.

Castro Ruz, Raúl. 2010. "Discurso en la clausura de la Asamblea Nacional del Poder Popular." *Granma*, December 18. Internet@granma.cu/.

Castro Ruz, Raúl. 2011. "Texto íntegro del discurso de Raúl en las conclusiones del congreso del PCC." *Cubadebate*, Havana, April 19. http://www.cubadebate.cu/noticias/2011/04/19/texto-integro-del-discurso-de-raul-en-las-conclusiones-del-congreso-del-pcc/.

Castro Ruz, Raúl. 2016. "Informe Central al 7mo. Congreso del Partido Comunista de Cuba." *Granma*, April 27.

Cave, Damien, Emma Bubola, and Choe Sanh-Hun. 2021. "World Is Facing First Long Slide in Its Population." *New York Times*, May 23. https://www.nytimes.com/2021/05/22/world/global-population-shrinking.html/.

CBIRC (China Bank and Insurance Regulatory Commission). 2020a. "Opinions on Promoting the Development of Commercial Insurance in the Field of Social Services." http://www.cbirc.gov.cn/.

CBIRC (China Bank and Insurance Regulatory Commission). 2020b. "Shandong Banking and Insurance Regulatory Bureau Actively Promotes the Construction of the Third Pillar of Pension Insurance." https://www.sohu.com/a/372206635_123753/.

CEE (Comité Estatal de Estadísticas). 1991. *Anuario estadístico de Cuba 1989*. Havana.

CERP (Cuban Economic Research Project). 1964. *Social Security in Cuba*. Coral Gables: University of Miami.

Chen, Tianhong, and John A. Turner. 2021. "China's Development of a Multi-tier Pension System." *International Social Security Review* 74, no. 1: 35–58.

Cheng, Evelyn. 2023. "China Reports 3% Growth Rate for 2022." Beijing, *CNBC*, January 16.

"China: Raising Pension Levels to Ensure Senior Citizens Have No Pension." 2021. *Pension Policy International*, June 23.

China Government Network. 2022. Beijing. http://www.gov.cn/shuju/2022-01/29/content_5671104.htm/.

"China Is Going to Have to Figure Out How to Care for 400 Million Elderly People by 2040." 2023. *Business Insider Newsletter*, January 19.

"China Issues Guidance for Basic Elderly Care System by 2025." *Reuters*, May 22. https://www.linkedin.com/posts/farah-master-48a02145_china-issues-guidance-for-basic-elderly-care-activity-7066267292615004160-lmcl/.

"China Rolling Out Perks to Encourage Couples to Have 3rd Child amid Demographic Crisis." 2022. *Pension Policy International*, January 31. https://www.pensionpolicyinternational.com/tag/china (no longer active, accessed February 1).

"China's Birth Rate Drops to Record Low in 2021." 2022. *Pension Policy International*, January 17. https://www.pensionpolicy international.com/tag/china (no longer active, accessed January 18).

"China's Economic Recovery Is Spluttering: The Prognosis Is Not Good." 2023. *The Economist*, June 23. https://www.economist.com/leaders/2023/06/22/chinas-economic-recovery-is-spluttering-the-prognosis-is-not-good/.

"China's Social Security System." 2021. CLB, *China Labour Bulletin*. Hong Kong, August 18.

"China Starts Nationwide Pooling of Basic Pension Funds." 2022. Xinhua, February 22. https://english.news.cn/20220223/7c13e77ba40b44a9b600ddf824f1bb96/c.html/.

China State Council. 2014. "Opinions of the State Council on Further Promoting the Reform of the Household Registration System," July 24.

China State Council. 2016. "Opinions on Integrating the Basic Medical Insurance System for Urban and Rural Residents," January 3.

"China to Accelerate Development of Multi-tiered Social Security System: Action Plan." 2021. *Pension Policy International*, September 9. https://www

.pensionpolicyinternational.com/tag/social-protection (no longer active, accessed September 10).

"China Turns to Private Insurers to Help Unlock US$15.3 Trillion of Savings and Avert a Crisis in the Pension System." 2021. *Pension Policy International* (no longer active, accessed May 19).

CiberCuba. 2021. "Padre de joven con discapacidad se queja de maltrato de trabajadores sociales." Havana, January 18. https://www.cibercuba.com/noticias/2021-01-18-u1-e199482-s27061-trabajadores-sociales-sancti-spiritus-niegan-ayuda-joven/.

Circular No. 86 TT-BTC. 2017. "On Supplementary Pension Plans." Ministry of Finance, Hanoi, August 15.

Circular No. 115 TT-BTC. 2013. "On Guidelines for Supplementary Pension Funds." Ministry of Finance, Hanoi, October 15.

Colina, Henry. 2016. "Sistemas de pensiones de la seguridad social. La experiencia internacional y Cuba." Tesis de Maestría, Facultad de Economía, Universidad de La Habana.

Colina, Henry. 2020. "Sistema de pensiones de seguridad social en Cuba. Un debate presente para el futuro." Havana: Friedrich Ebert Stiftung and Universidad de La Habana, April.

Colina, Henry. 2021a. Calculations on Cuba's pension gross replacement rate, 2000–2020. Havana: e-mail to the author, August 11.

Colina, Henry. 2021b. Clarifications on coverage of domestic workers and contributions to social security in Cuba. Havana: e-mail to the author, July 19.

Colina, Henry. 2022a. Information on pensions, maternity leave, digitalization, and ID card. Havana: e-mails to the author, April 5, 27, and October 18–19.

Colina, Henry. 2022b. "Sistema de pensiones de seguridad social en Cuba. Un debate presente para el futuro." Doctoral dissertation, University of Havana, March 23.

"Con dengue y alta infección del mosquito transmisor en Cuba." 2022. *Diario de Cuba*, Havana, July 6.

Conglong, Liu, Yang Yongheng, and Wang Jianfeng. 2022. "Promoting the Equalization of Basic Social Services to Solidly Move Forward Common Prosperity." http://www.cntheory.com/zkjy/202201/t20220110_48611.html/.

Consejo de Ministros. 2021. Acuerdo 9151, Asistencia social, *Gaceta Oficial Ordinaria*, Havana, No. 98 GOC-2021-820-O98. https://www.gacetaoficial.gob.cu/es/gaceta-oficial-no-98-ordinaria-de-2021/.

Constitution of the Republic of Cuba. 2019. Approved by National Referendum on February 24.

Cousins, Mel. 2021. "The Sustainability of China's Urban Employees' Pension Programme: A Case of Getting Old before Getting Rich?" *International Social Security Review* 74, no. 1: 59–77.

"¿Cuáles son los principales nudos que Cuba tiene que enfrentar en 2022?" 2022.

Catalejo en Letra de Temas, Havana, January 7. https://temas.cult.cu/la-letra-de-temas-2022-cuales-son-los-principales-nudos-que-cuba-tiene-que-enfrentar-en-2022 (no longer active, accessed January 7, 2022).

"Cuba jubila la chequera. Las pensiones se pagarán por nóminas electrónicas." 2020. *On Cuba News*, Havana, July 27. https://oncubanews.com/cuba-jubila-la-chequera-las-pensiones-se-pagaran-por-nominas-electronicas/?fbclid=IwAR3YFEFOILaj-n7QF4bNwfZdwTLtRBPwG!Ngmmiv-raJn5tMFKPnx4qqsoQ/.

"Cuba registra una tasa de mortalidad infantil de 7,6 por mil nacidos vivos." 2022. *Cubadebate*, Havana, January 2. http://www.cubadebate.cu/noticias/2022/01/02/cuba-registra-una-tasa-de-mortalidad-infantil-de-76-por-mil-nacidos-vivos-en-un-ano-complejo-debido-a-la-pandemia/.

Cuba Standard. 2014. *Economic Trend Report*, no. 1, 2, and 3 quarter.

"Cuba y Rusia acuerdan transformar la economía de la Isla desde la empresa privada." 2023. *14ymedio*, Havana, January 20. https://www.14ymedio.com/cuba/cuba-rusia-transformar-economia-isla_1_1097058.html/.

Cuevas, Alfredo, and Lorenzo Pérez. 1999. "The Pension System of Cuba: Implications of International Pension Reform Expenses for Addressing Cuba's Problems and Preliminary Proposal for Reform." Paper presented at the 1999 annual convention of the Allied Social Science Association, New York City.

Dao, Ngoc Dung. 2018. Minister of Labor, Invalids and Social Affairs, Report on implementation of social insurance regimes and policies at the end of December 31, 2017. Hanoi.

Dao, Quang Vinh. 2017. "Social Protection in Vietnam: Achievements, Challenges and Development Orientation." Hanoi: ILSSA, December 7. http://www.ilssa.org.vn/en/news/social-protection-in-vietnam-achievements-challenges-and-development-orientation-171 (no longer active, accessed January 20, 2018).

Darimont, Barbara. 2022. Information provided to the author on healthcare in China. Munich January 28, and May 16.

Darimont, Barbara, and Louis W. Margraf. 2018. "Analysis of Quality Assurance in the Hospital Sector of the People's Republic of China." *Journal of Global Health Reports* 2 (October). https://www.joghr.org/article/11945-analysis-of-quality-assurance-in-the-hospital-sector-of-the-people-s-republic-of-china/.

Davies, Bob. 2007. "Cuban Economists Envision Role for Markets in Post-Castro Era." *Wall Street Journal*, December 10. https://www.wsj.com/articles/SB116840262503872329/.

De Miranda, Mauricio, and Omar Everleny Pérez Villanueva. 2012. "Los problemas actuales de la economía cubana y las reformas necesarias." In *Cuba. Hacia una nueva estrategia del desarrollo para los inicios del siglo XXI*, 190–224. Cali: Pontificia Universidad Javeriana and SSRC.

De Miranda, Mauricio, and Kanako Yamaoka. 2014. Interview answering author's questions with a Vietnam top official who asked for anonymity (notes in author's possession). Hanoi: Social Security Policy Studies, Institute of Labor Science and Social Affairs, Vietnam's Ministry of Labor, October 30.

Decision No. 488/DQ-TTg. 2017. Renovation and development of social assistance for the period 2017–2025 and vision to 2030. Hanoi, April 14.

Decision No. 708/QD-TTg. 2017. Prime Minister Office, Building a national data base on social security, applying information technology to society, solving social security policies until 2020 and development orientations to 2030. Hanoi, May 25.

Decree No. 12ND-CP. 2022. Penalties for administrative violations on social insurance law. Hanoi.

Decree No. 20N/D. 2021. Stipulating social assistance policies for beneficiaries of social assistance, including allowances for the elderly without pension from July 1, 2021. Hanoi.

Decree No. 88 ND-CP. 2016. On supplementary pension schemes. Hanoi, July 1.

Decree No. 146 ND-CP. 2018. On healthcare subsidies. Hanoi, October 17.

Decree No. 1353/QD-TTg. 2008. On development of coastal economic zones. Hanoi, September 23.

Decree No. 1453/QD-TTg. 2020. On development of coastal economic zones. Hanoi, September 24.

Decreto-Ley 56. 2021. Regulations of maternity and sickness leave. Havana.

Decreto-Ley 88. On SME (mipymes). Havana, August 19.

Decreto Presidencial 261. 2021. Sobre la implementación del plan nacional de desarrollo económico social hasta el 2030. Havana, May 29.

Devereux, John. 2021. "The Absolution of History: Cuban Living Standards after 60 Years of Revolutionary Role." *Journal of Iberian and Latin American Economic History* 39, no. 1: 5–36.

Díaz-Briquets, Sergio, and Juan Carlos Albizu-Campos. 2024. "System Failure and Demographic Outcomes: Cuba's Perfect Storm." Occasional Paper, Cuban Research Institute, Florida International University, Miami.

Díaz-Briquets, Sergio, and Jorge Pérez-López. 2006. *Corruption in Cuba: Castro and Beyond*. Austin: University of Texas Press.

Díaz-Canel, Miguel. 2017. Talk to communist party leaders in February 2017, later leaked to the public. https://www.youtube.com/watch?v=zNaw_Hj9f88. Also https://www.cibercuba.com/videos/noticias/2017-08-22-u177600-e177600-diaz-canel-digan-censuramos-aqui-todo-mundo-censura/.

Diep, Pham-Thi-Hong, and Nguyen-Thu Hang. 2023. "The Vietnamese Welfare State System: A Special Focus on the Old-Age Income Maintenance System." In *The Routledge International Handbook to Welfare State System*, edited by Christian Aspalter, 657–81. Abingdon: Routledge.

Dinh, Hinh T. 2021a. Comments by e-mail on Vietnam in a preliminary version of this book, Washington DC, September 5.

Dinh, Hinh T. 2021b. "Vietnam." In *Covid-19 & Developing Countries—The Road to Recovery*, edited by Hihn T. Dinh, 143–47. Rabat: Policy Center for the New South.

Dinh, Hinh T. 2022. Comments by e-mail on Vietnam in a preliminary version of this book, Washington DC, January 6.

Dinh, Hinh T., Deepak Mishra, Le Duy Binh, Duc Minh Pham, and Pham Thi Thu Hang. 2013. *Light Manufacturing in Vietnam: Creating Jobs and Prosperity in a Middle-Income Economy*. Washington, DC: World Bank.

Dinh, Hinh T., Ali Zafar, Lihong Wang and Eleonora Mavroeidi. 2013. *Tales from the Development Frontier: How China and Other Countries Harness Light Manufacturing to Create Jobs and Prosperity*. Washington, DC: World Bank.

Domínguez, Jorge. 2021. "The Democratic Claims of Communist Regime Leaders." *Communist and Post-Communist Studies* 54, no. 1–2: 45–65.

Donate-Armada, Ricardo A. 1994. "Cuban Social Security: A Preliminary Actuarial Analysis of Law # 24 of Social Security." In *Cuba in Transition*, vol. 4, 155–73. Miami: Association for the Study of the Cuban Economy.

Donate-Armada, Ricardo A. 1995. "Preliminary Analysis of Retirement Programs for Personnel in the Ministry of the Armed Forces and Ministry of Interior." In *Cuba in Transition*, vol. 5, 448–57. Miami: Association for the Study of the Cuban Economy.

Dongxiao, Gu, Xuejie Yang, Xingguo Li, Changyong Liang, Jinhong Zhong, and Nanping Feng. 2007. "Innovating New Rural Cooperative Medical Scheme (NSMS) for Better Patient Satisfaction in Rural China." *International Journal of Environmental Research and Public Health* 15, no. 9 (September). https://pmc.ncbi.nlm.nih.gov/articles/PMC6164713/.

Dorfman, Mark, Robert Holzmann, Philip O'Keefe, Dewen Wang, Yvonne Sin, and Richard Hinz. 2013. *China's Pension System: A Vision*. Washington, DC: World Bank Group.

Dussel Peters, Enrique. 2022. "Capitalismo con características chinas. Conceptos y desarrollo en la tercera década del siglo XXI." *El Trimestre Económico* 69, no. 354 (April–June): 647–89.

Eckardt, Sebastian, Deepak Mishra, and Viet Tuan Dinh. 2018. "Vietnam's Manufacturing Miracle: Lessons for Developing Countries." Washington, DC: Brookings Institution, April 17. https://www.brookings.edu/articles/vietnams-manufacturing-miracle-lessons-for-developing-countries/.

ECLAC (Economic Commission for Latin America and the Caribbean). 2020. *Population Estimates and Projections*. Santiago de Chile: Demographic Observatory Latin America and the Caribbean.

ECLAC (Economic Commission for Latin America and the Caribbean). 2021.

Preliminary Overview of the Economies of Latin America and the Caribbean, 2021. Santiago de Chile, December.

"Editorial." 2008. *Granma*, Havana, March 9 and 21. Internet@granma.cu/.

EIR (Economist Intelligence Report). 2022. *Cuba.* London.

EIU (The Economist Intelligence Unit). 2022. *EIU Cuba Country Report*, March.

Espina, Mayra. 2008. *Políticas de atención a la pobreza y la desigualdad. Examinando el rol del estado en la experiencia cubana.* Buenos Aires: CLACSO.

Espina, Mayra. 2020. "Reforma y emergencia de capas medias en Cuba." *Nueva Sociedad* 285: 108–21.

Espina, Mayra. 2022a. "Cuba. Crisis, desigualdades y prácticas de vida cotidiana." Paper at the 32nd Congress of the Association for the Study of the Cuban Economy. Florida International University, Miami, September 16.

Espina, Mayra. 2022b. E-mail to the author on social assistance in Cuba. Havana, March 10.

Fan, Weidong. 2022. "Long-Term Care Insurance Policy in China." Paper at International Conference on "The Future of Social Security for New Forms of Work," sponsored by China State Council and ILO. Beijing, July.

Fang, Hai, Karen Egglenton, Kara Hanson, and Ming Wu. 2019. "Enhancing Financial Protection under China's Social Health Insurance to Achieve Universal Health Coverage." *China's Health System Reforms: Review of 10 Years of Progress*, March 2. https://pmc.ncbi.nlm.nih.gov/articles/PMC6598720/.

Fang, Lianquan. 2014. "Towards Universal Coverage: A Macro Analysis of China's Public Pension Program." In *Reforming Pensions in Developing and Transition Countries*, edited by Katja Hujo, 187–219. Basingstoke: UNRISD, Palgrave Macmillan.

FIAP (International Federation of [Private] Pension Funds). 2021. *Marcha de los sistemas de pensiones*, no. 4 (June–July). Santiago de Chile.

FIAP (International Federation of [Private] Pension Funds). 2023. "China: The Nation Advances in the Implementation of a Voluntary Capitalization Pension Program." Santiago de Chile, February 22.

Fifth Plenum 11th Central Committee. 2012. *Resolution No. 15-NQ/TW Vietnam Social Policies for 2012–2020.* Hanoi.

Frank, Marc. 2013. "Russian-Cuba Deal Creates Waves among Creditors." *Reuters*, March 14. Frank, Marc. 2015. "Cuba, Paris Club Members Agree on Debt Total: $15 B." Paris, *Reuters*, June 8.

Frank, Marc. 2021. "Cuba, Paris Club Reach Deal to Skip 2021 Debt Payment." Paris, *Reuters*, October 24.

Frank, Marc. 2022. "Cuba to Exchange Some Foreign Currency for Pesos." *Reuters*, August 23.

Frota, Luis. 2021. ILO specialist on social security, information provided by e-mail to the author, Bangkok, November.

Fu, Claire. 2023a. "China Says 1 in 5 Young People Is Unemployed." *New York Times*, May 20. https://www.nytimes.com/2023/05/19/business/china-youth-unemployment.html/.

Fu, Claire. 2023b. "China Scraps Jobs Report on the Young." *New York Times*, August 1: B-1, B-3.

Gámez, Nora. 2024a. "As the Economy Craters, the Cuba Government Hits Private-Sector Workers with Income Tax Hike." *Miami Herald*, January 18. https://www.thedailynewsonline.com/news/as-the-economy-craters-the-cuban-government-hits-private-sector-workers-with-tax-hike/article_38ed78fa-b651-11ee-8934-738eba247d0a.html/.

Gámez, Nora. 2024b. "Resisting Reforms, Cuba Announces Price Hikes and New Restrictions on the Private Sector." *Miami Herald*, January 11. https://twitter.com/ngameztorres/status/1745483622268740023/.

Gao, Qin. 2017. *Welfare, Work and Poverty: Social Assistance in China*. Oxford: Oxford University Press.

García, Edmundo. 2007. "Entrevista a Pedro Monreal." *La Noche se Mueve*. Montreal, September.

García, Indira. 2021. "Las relaciones económicas entre Cuba y Vietnam." In *Resumen preliminar del proyecto 'Evolución de la Economía Internacional y su Impacto en Cuba,'* edited by José Luis Rodríguez and Ramón Pich, 70–85. Havana: Centro de Investigaciones de la Economía Mundial, October.

García, Mercedes. 2023. "Cansados de la ineficiencia cubana, los vietnamitas abandonan su exitoso proyecto de arroz." *14ymedio*, Sancti Spiritus, May 8. https://www.14ymedio.com/Cansados-ineficiencia-vietnamitas-abandonan-proyecto_0_3524647508.html/.

García Quiñones, Rolando. 2019. "Cuba. Envejecimiento, dinámica familiar y cuidados." *Novedades de Población* 29, no 1: 129–40.

Giles, John, Xiaoyan Lei, Gewei Wang, Yafeng Wang, and Yaohui Zhao. 2021. *One Country, Two Systems: Evidence of Retirement Patterns in China*. Bonn: IZA Institute of Labor Economics, Discussion Papers No. 14725.

Glinskaya, Elena, Zhanlian Feng, and Guadalupe Suarez. 2022. "Understanding the 'State of Play' of Long-Term Care Provision in Low- and Middle-Income Countries." *International Social Security Review* 75, no. 3–4: 71–101.

Gongcheng, Zheng. 2022. "China Social Security: Overview, Challenge and Future Prospects." Paper at the International Conference "The Future of Social Security for New Forms of Work sponsored by China State Council and ILO," Beijing, July 27.

Gongcheng, Zheng, and Wolfgang Scholz. 2019. *Global Social Security and Economic Development: Retrospect and Prospect*. Friedrich Ebert Stiftung, China's Association on Social Security and ILO, Asia-Pacific Working Paper Series.

González, Víctor. 2014. "Un éxito empresarial, las carnicerías sin moscas." *14ymedio*, Havana, November 6.

González-Corzo, Mario. 2022. "Economic Reforms and Beef Cattle Production in Cuba." Paper at 32nd Congress of the Association for the Study of the Cuban Economy, Florida International University, Miami, September 16.

Goodman, Peter. 2023. "Slowdown in China Puts World On Notice." *New York Times*, August 12: B-1, B-4.

GOV (Government of the People's Republic of China). 2005. Decision of the State Council on Improving the Basic Endowment Insurance System for Enterprise Employees. https://www.gov.cn/gongbao/content/2006/content_169950.htm/.

GOV (Government of the People's Republic of China). 2007. Labor Contract Law of the People's Republic of China. http://www.gov.cn/flfg/2007-06/29/content_669394.html/.

GOV (Government of the People's Republic of China). 2014. Opinions of the State Council on Establishing a Unified Basic Pension Insurance System for Urban and Rural Residents. http://www.gov.cn/zhengce/content/2014-02/26/content_8656.htm/.

GOV (Government of the People's Republic of China). 2015. Decision of the State Council on the Reform of the Pension Insurance System for Staff of Government and Public Institutions. http://www.gov.cn/zhengce/content/2015-01/14/content_9394.htm/.

GOV (Government of the People's Republic of China). 2016. Opinions of the State Council on Integrating the Basic Medical Insurance System for Urban and Rural Residents. http://www.gov.cn/zhengce/content/2016-01/12/content_10582.htm/.

GOV (Government of the People's Republic of China). 2017. Notice of the General Office of the State Council on the Implementation of Maternity Insurance and Basic Medical Insurance for Employees. http://www.gov.cn/zhengce/content/2017-02/04/content_5164990.htm/.

GOV (Government of the People's Republic of China). 2018. Reform Plan for the Collection and Administration of National Taxes and Local Taxes. http://www.gov.cn/zhengce/2018-7/20/content_5308075.htm/.

GOV (Government of the People's Republic of China). 2019. Notice on Doing a Good Job in Basic Medical Security for Urban and Rural Residents in 2019. https://www.gov.cn/zhengce/zhengceku/2019-10/12/content_5438753.htm/.

GOV (Government of the People's Republic of China). 2020. Law of the People's Republic of China on the Protection of Veterans. http://www.gov.cn/xinwem/2020.

GOV (Government of the People's Republic of China). 2021a. Employee Medical Insurance for Urban Employees Will Have These Big Changes. http://www.gov.cn/zhengce/2021-04/23/content_5601542.htm/.

GOV (Government of the People's Republic of China). 2021b. Final Statistical Monitoring Report of the Outline for the Development of Chinese Women (2011–2020). http://www.gov.cn/xinwen/2021-12/21/content_5663667.htm/.

GOV (Government of the People's Republic of China). 2021c. Ministry of Civil Affairs, *Statistical Bulletin on the Development of Civil Affairs*. https://www.mca.gov.cn/images3/www2017/file/202208/2021mzsyfztjgb.pdf.

GOV (Government of the People's Republic of China). 2021d. Opinions of the General Office of the State Council on Improving Medical Insurance and Relief System for Major and Serious Diseases. http://www.gov.cn/zhengce/contet/2021-11-19/content_5651446.htm/.

GOV (Government of the People's Republic of China). 2021e. Seventh National Census Communiqué. http://gov.cn/guoqing/2021-05/13/content_5606149.htm/.

GOV (Government of the People's Republic of China). 2021f. State Administration of Foreign Exchange Announces China's Full-Scale External Debt Data at the End of 2020. http://www.gov.cn/xinmen/2021-03/26/content_5596085.htm/.

GOV (Government of the People's Republic of China). 2021g. Statistical Communiqué of the PRC on National Economic Development in 2020. http://www.gov.cn/xinwen/2021-02/28/content5589283.htm/.

GOV (Government of the People's Republic of China). 2022a. "Guiding Opinions of the State Council on Strengthening the Construction of Digital Government," June 23. http://www.gov.cn/zhengce/content/2022-06/23/content_5697299.htm/.

GOV (Government of the People's Republic of China). 2022b. State Council 14th Five-Year Plan for National Ageing Development and Elderly Care Service System for 2021–2025, with a Vision for 2035, February 21. https://www.gov.cn/zhengce/content/2022-02/21/content_5674844.htm/.

GOV (Government of the People's Republic of China). 2022c. State Council Opinions on Promoting the Development of Individual Pensions, April 21. http://www.gov.cn/zhengce/content/2022-04/21/content_5686402.htm/.

GOV (Government of the People's Republic of China). 2023. *Statistical Bulletin on National Economic and Social Development 2022*, Beijing. http://www.gov.cn/xinwen/2023-02/28/content_5743623.htm/.

Grishin, Vadim. 2023. "Are Russian Flavored Reforms Possible in Cuba?" Paper presented at the 33rd Annual Conference of Association for the Study of the Cuban Economy, Florida International University, Miami, August 5.

GSO (General Statistical Office). 2009. *Statistical Yearbook of Vietnam, 2008*. Hanoi: Statistical Publishing House.

GSO (General Statistical Office). 2017. *Statistical Yearbook of Vietnam, 2016*. Hanoi: Statistical Publishing House.

GSO (General Statistical Office). 2018. *Statistical Yearbook of Vietnam, 2017.* Hanoi: Statistical Publishing House.

GSO (General Statistical Office). 2019. *Statistical Yearbook of Vietnam, 2018.* Hanoi: Statistical Publishing House.

GSO (General Statistical Office). 2020. *Result of the Viet Nam Household Living Standards Survey, 2018.* Hanoi: Statistical Publishing House. https://www.gso.gov.vn/en/data-and-statistics/2020/05/result-of-the-vietnam-household-living-standards-survey-2018/.

GSO (General Statistical Office). 2021a. *Result of the Viet Nam Household Living Standards Survey, 2020.* Hanoi: Statistical Publishing House. https://www.gso.gov.vn/en/data-and-statistics/2022/06/results-of-the-viet-nam-household-living-standards-survey-2020/.

GSO (General Statistical Office. 2021b. *Statistical Yearbook of Vietnam, 2020.* Hanoi: Statistical Publishing House.

GSO (General Statistical Office). 2022a. *Report on Labor Force Survey, 2020.* Hanoi: Statistical Publishing House. https://www.gso.gov.vn/en/data-and-statistics/2022/02/report-on-labor-force-survey-2020-2/.

GSO (General Statistical Office). 2022b. *Statistical Yearbook of Vietnam, 2021.* Hanoi: Statistical Publishing House.

Hanke, Steve H. 2022. *Misery Index, 2021.* Baltimore, MD: Johns Hopkins University, March 16.

"Hanoi Former Chairman Earns 3-Year Commutation after Fulfilling $1mm Compensation." 2022. *tuổi trẻ news*, Hanoi, June 24. https://tuoitrenews.vn/news/society/20220624/hanois-former-chairman-earns-3year-commutation-after-fulfilling-1mn-compensation/67775.html/.

Hansing, Katrin, and Bert Hoffmann. 2020. "When Racial Inequalities Return: Assessing the Restratification of Cuban Society 60 Years after the Revolution." *Latin American Politics and Society* 62, no. 2 (May): 29–52.

Hawkins, Amy. 2024. "Cost of raising children in China second-highest in the world, thinktank reveals." The *Guardian*, February 21. https://www.theguardian.com/world/2024/feb/21/cost-of-raising-children-in-china-is-the-second-highest-in-the-wold-think-tank-reveals.

He, Bingzi. 2022. Comments by e-mail on the manuscript and materials supplied, Beijing, December 2021 to December 2022.

He, Linxin. 2022. Interviews with the author on social security in China (notes in author's possession). Munich: Max Planck Institut für Sozialrecht und Sozialpolitik, June 2 and 4.

Hernández, Yosvani. 2019. "La sanidad en Cuba no discrimina." *14ymedio*, Pinar del Río, January 21.

Hicks, Norman L., and Lorenzo L. Pérez. 2005. *Reforming the Cuban Safety Net System.* Miami: University of Miami, Institute for Cuban and Cuban-American Studies.

Hirschfeld, Katherine. 2007a. *Health, Politics and Revolution in Cuba since 1989.* New Brunswick, N.J.: Transaction.

Hirschfeld, Katherine. 2007b. "Re-examining the Cuban Healthcare System: Towards a Qualitative Critique." *Cuban Affairs* 2, no. 3: 1–27.

Hoàng, Quynh. 2022. Answers by e-mail to questionnaire elaborated by the author, Hanoi, June 21.

Holz, Carsten A. 2003. "Fast, Clear and Accurate: How Reliable Are Chinese Output and Economic Growth Statistics?" *China Quarterly* 173 (March): 122–63.

Hongqiao, Fu, Ling Li, Mingqiang Li, Chunyu Yang, and William Hsiao. 2017. "An Evaluation of Systemic Reforms of Public Hospitals: The Sanming Model in China." *Health Policy and Planning* 32 (May): 1135–45.

Hu, Kaixuan. 2021. "Challenges Facing the Chinese Healthcare System." *Asia Pacific Journal of Public Health* 33, no. 1: 160–61.

Huang, Xian. 2020. *Social Protection under Authoritarianism: Health Politics and Policy in China.* New York: Oxford University Press.

Huang, Yanzhong. 2022. "The Reckoning ahead for China Zero-Covid Policy." *Wall Street Journal*, December 24–25: C-3.

Huang, Yasheng. 2008. *Capitalism with Chinese Characteristics: Entrepreneurship and the State.* Cambridge: Cambridge University Press.

Huong, Nguyen Thi Lan, Luu Quan Tuan, Matthias Meissner, Bui Sy Tuan, Dang Do Quyen, and Nguyen Hai Yen. 2013. "Social Protection for the Informal Sector and the Informally Employed in Vietnam: Literature and Data Review." Bochum: Ruhr-Universität Bochum, IIE Working Paper No. 199.

Huy, Duong Quang. 2022. Answers to author's questionnaire on economics and statistics in Vietnam. Hanoi, October 23.

IADB-SIMS (Inter-American Development Bank). 2019. Data Base SIMS. https:/www.iadb.org/en/sector/socialinvestments/sims/home (no longer active, accessed September 22).

ILO (International Labor Organization). 1999. *Cuba Technical Note: Application of the ILO Pension Model to the Social Security System in Cuba.* Geneva: Social Security Department.

ILO (International Labor Organization). 2017. *World Social Protection Report, 2017–2019.* Geneva.

ILO (International Labor Organization). 2018a. *Expanding Social Health Protection: Towards Equitable Coverage in Vietnam.* Geneva: Social Protection Department.

ILO (International Labor Organization). 2018b. "Viet Nam—Report to the Government Actuarial Valuation as December 2015 of Long-Term Benefits Administered by the Viet Nam Social Security Organization." Geneva.

ILO (International Labor Organization). 2019. "Actuarial Valuation of as December 2019 of Long-Term Benefits Administered by the Vietnam Social Security Administration." Geneva.

ILO (International Labor Organization). 2021a. *Extending Social Insurance for Informal Workers.* Hanoi. https://www.ilo.rg/hanoi/Whatwedo/Publications/WCMS_779251/lang—en?index.htm (no longer active, accessed March 9).

ILO (International Labor Organization). 2021b. *Gender Gaps in the Social Insurance System.* Hanoi, August 5. https://www.ilo.org/publications/gender-gaps-social-insurance-system/.

ILO (International Labor Organization). 2021c. *Multi-tiered Social Security for Universal Coverage: A Focus on Families in Viet Nam.* Hanoi. https://www.ilo.org/publications/multi-tiered-social-security-universal-coverage-focus-families-viet-nam/.

ILO (International Labor Organization). 2021d. *Social Protection Data Dashboard.* Geneva. https://www.social-protection.org/.

ILO (International Labor Organization). N.d. *A Comprehensive Old Age Pension System for Vietnam: Delivering on Resolution 28/NQ-TW.* Hanoi.

ILO/Japan (International Labor Organization and Japan Multi Bilateral Program). 2019. "Summary Note on Options for the Design of a Multi-Tier Pension System in Viet Nam." Geneva.

ILO/WIEGO (International Labor Organization/Woman in Informal Employment). 2018. *Women and Men in the Informal Economy: A Statistical Picture.* 3rd ed. Geneva.

ILSSA/ILO (Institute of Labor, Science and Social Affairs/International Labor Organization). 2022. *Labour and Social Trends in Vietnam 2021, Outlook to 2030.* Hanoi: Ministry of Labor, Invalids and Social Affairs. https://www.ilo.org/sites/default/files/wcmsp5/groups/public/@asia/@ro-bangkok/@ilo-hanoi/documents/publication/wcms_837244.pdf.

IMF (International Monetary Fund). 2021. *Vietnam: 2020 Article IV Consultation-Press Release; Staff Report; and Statement by the Executive Director for Vietnam.* Washington, DC: IMF Country Report No. 21/42, March.

IMF (International Monetary Fund). 2023. GDP per capita current prices, World Economic Outlook, October 2022. https://www.imf.org/external/datamapper/NGDPDPC@WEO/OEMDC/ADEVEC/WEO/WORLD/.

Insurance Industry Association of China. 2021. Cited in "China Plans $1.7bn Pension Company." *Pension Policy International.* https://www.pensionpolicyintenational.com/china-plans-1-72bn-pension-company (no longer active, accessed August 20).

Interim Provisions on the Medical Benefits for Soldiers and Related Military Personnel in China. 2021. Beijing, October 17, came into force January 1, 2022.

"Inversiones rusas en Cuba. Negocios y acuerdos desde 2020." 2023. *El Toque*, Havana, May 29. https://eltoque.com/es/inversiones-rusas-en-cuba-negocios-y-acuerdos-desde-2020/.

ISSA (International Social Security Association). 2022. Special Issue "The Human Right to Long-Term Care for the Elderly: Extending the Role of Social Security Programmes." *International Social Security Review* 75, no. 3–4 (July–December): 3–191.

Jackson, Richard, and Tobias Peter. 2015. *From Challenge to Opportunity: The Future of Retirement in Vietnam.* Global Ageing Institute. http://pensionreform.ru/files/111920/2015.09.%20Global%20Aging%20Institute.%20Vietnam.pdf.

Jales, Hugo, Thomas H. Kang, Guilherme Stein, and Felipe Garcia Ribeiro. 2018. "Measuring the Role of the 1959 Revolution on Cuba's Economic Performance." *World Economy* 41, no. 3: 2243–74.

Jiandong, Chen, and Armando Barrientos. 2006. "Extending Social Assistance in China: Lessons from the Minimum Living Standard Scheme." University of Sussex CPRC Working Paper 67. https://assets.publishing.service.gov.uk/media/57a08c2a40f0b6497400103c/67Chen_Barrientos.pdf.

Johnson, Ian. 2023. "Xi's Age of Stagnation." *Foreign Affairs* (September–October): 1–18.

Kidd, Stephen, Tareq Abu-el-Haj, Bazlul Khondker, Carol Watson and Sharlene Ramkissoon. 2016. *Social Assistance in Viet Nam: Review and Proposals for Reform.* Hanoi: MOLISA and UNDP, July 22. https://www.developmentpathways.co.uk/wp-content/uploads/2018/06/3.Social-Assistance-in-VN-A-review-and-proposal-for-reform-EN-1.pdf.

Kidd, Stephen, Bjorn Gelders, and Anh Tran. 2019. *Potential Impacts of Social Pensions in Vietnam.* Geneva: ILO, April. https://www.developmentpathways.co.uk/wp-content/uploads/2019/11/Potential-impacts-of-social-pensions-in-Viet-Nam.pdf.

KPMG. 2020. *China Pensions Outlook: Looking Ahead after a Year of Change.* Hong Kong. https://assets.kpmg.com/content/dam/kpmg/cn/pdf/en/2020/03/china-pensions-outlook-looking-ahead-after-a-year-of-change.pdf.

KPMG and ASIFMA. 2023. *China Pension Reforms: Winning Strategies for Global Asset Managers amid Evolution in Retirement Market.* Hong Kong, June 26. https://kpmg.com/cn/en/home/media/press-releases/2023/06/china-pensions-reform-report.html/.

Krugman, Paul. 2023. "How Scary Is China's Crisis?" *New York Times*, August 22: A-23.

La Forgia, Jerry. 2022. Information by e-mail provided to the author. Washington, DC, October 15–17.

"La ineficiencia de las empresas estatales y otras malas noticias para la economía." 2022. *El Toque*, Havana, December 12.

Lardy, Nicholas. 2019. *The State Strikes Back: The End of Economic Reform in China?* Washington, DC: Peterson Institute for International Economics.

Law No. 58. 2014. QH13 On Social Insurance. Hanoi.

Law of the People's Republic of China on Basic Medical Hygiene and Health Promotion. 2019. Adopted at the 15th Meeting of the Standing Committee of the National People's Congress. Beijing, December 28.

Le, Dang Doanh. 1992. *Economic Reform and Development in Vietnam.* Australian National University, Research School of Pacific Studies, Economic Division Working Papers, 92/1.

Le, Dang Doanh. 1994. *Vietnam Country Report.* Hanoi: Asian Transitional Economies Project.

Le, Dang Doanh. 2015. "The Past and Hopeful Future of Vietnam Economy." *Asian Management Insights* 2, no. 1: 28–35.

Le, Dang Doanh. 2018. "Reform and Industrialization in Vietnam." In *Industrialization for Inclusive Development in Tanzania,* Economic Society of Tanzania Annual Congress, Dar es Salaam, December 7. http://baijiaho.baidu.com/s?id=1725421105118931369&wfr=spider&for=pc/.

Lee, Amanda. 2021. "China Population: State Pension Fund under Pressure from 'Unprecedented Challenge' as Nation Gets Old." *South China Morning Post,* May 13. https://www.scmp.com/economy/china-economy/article/3133372/china-population-state-pension-fund-under-pressure/.

Lee, Carmel K. M. 2023. "The Chinese Welfare System: A Special Focus on Aging of Society and Social Policy." In *The Routledge International Handbook to Welfare State System,* edited by Christian Aspalter. Abingdon: Routledge.

Leng, Chang, Zhang Yan, and Ryan Woo. 2021. "Ageing China Boosts Private Sector Role as Pensions Time Bomb Ticks." *Reuters,* May 20.

Leung, Joe C. B., and Yuebin Xu. 2015. *China's Social Welfare: The Third Turning Point.* Cambridge: Polity Press.

Ley 156. 2022. "Código de Familia." *Gaceta Oficial,* no. 87, Ordinaria, Havana, August 17. https://www.gacetaoficial.gob.cu/sites/default/files/goc-2022-ex4.pdf.

Li, Jie, Qiaoling Lan, Enya Zhu, Yong Xu, and Dan Zhu. 2022. "A Study of Health Insurance Fraud in China and Recommendations for Fraud Detection and Prevention." *Journal of Organizational and End User Computing* 34, no. 4: 1–19.

Li, Xiaoyun. 2020. "Why Are Chinese Hospitals Always Overcrowded?" https://nanduguancha.blog.caixin.com/archives/223449/.

Li Keqiang. 2021. "Full-Text Report to the Fourth Session of the 13th National People's Congress on March 5." *Xinhua,* March 12.

London, Jonathan D. 2023. "The Communist Party of Vietnam: Consolidating Market Leninism." In *The Routledge Handbook of Contemporary Vietnam,* 21–47. Abingdon: Routledge.

Lu, Bei, John Piggott, and Bingwen Zheng. 2019. *The Notional and the Real in China's Pension Reforms*. World Bank Social Protection & Jobs Discussion Paper No. 1921, Washington, DC.

Luis, Luis. 2023. "Inflation and Macro Policies in Cuba." Association for the Study of the Cuban Economy, Miami, January 7. https://www.ascecuba.org/17426-2/.

Malesky, Edmund, and Jonathan London. 2014. "The Political Economy of Development in China and Vietnam." *American Review of Political Science* 17: 395–419.

Mao, Xianglin. 2013. Answers by e-mail to author's questions on China reforms. Beijing, November 8.

"Marino Murillo: No habrá cambio del modelo político en Cuba." 2012. *Cubadebate*, March 27. http://cubadebate.cu/noticias/2012/03/27/marino-murillo-no-habra-cambio-del-modelo-politico-en-cuba-fotos/

Meng, Ke. 2019. *China's Pension Reforms: Political Institutions, Skill Formation and Pension Policy in China*. New York: Routledge.

Mesa-Lago, Carmelo. 1968. "Unemployment in Socialist Countries: USSR, East Europe, China and Cuba." Ph.D. dissertation, Cornell University, Ithaca, New York, mimeographed.

Mesa-Lago, Carmelo. 1969. "Availability and Reliability of Statistics in Socialist Cuba." *Latin American Research Review* 4, no. 1 (Spring 1969): 53–91; no. 2 (Summer 1969): 47–81.

Mesa-Lago, Carmelo. 2000. *Market, Socialist and Mixed Economies: Comparative Policies and Performance—Chile, Cuba and Costa Rica*. Baltimore, MD: Johns Hopkins University Press.

Mesa-Lago, Carmelo. 2001. "The Resurrection of Cuban Statistics." *Cuban Studies* 31:139–50.

Mesa-Lago, Carmelo. 2003. "La seguridad social en Cuba en el período especial. Diagnóstico y sugerencias de políticas en pensiones, salud y desempleo." In *La seguridad social en Cuba. Diagnóstico, retos, perspectivas*, edited by Lothar Witte, 33–115. Caracas: Nueva Sociedad.

Mesa-Lago, Carmelo. 2007. *Reassembling Social Security: A Survey of Pension and Healthcare Reforms in Latin America*. Oxford: Oxford University Press.

Mesa-Lago, Carmelo. 2009. "Balance económico-social de 50 años de revolución en Cuba." *América Latina Hoy* 52 (August): 41–61.

Mesa-Lago, Carmelo. 2014. "Institutional Changes of Economic-Social Reforms: State and Market Roles, Progress, Hurdles, Comparisons, Monitoring and Effects." In *Cuba Economic Change in Comparative Perspective*, edited by Richard Feinberg and Ted Piccone, 49–69. Washington, DC: Brookings Institution and Universidad de La Habana.

Mesa-Lago, Carmelo. 2015a. "La desigualdad del ingreso y la experiencia en

América Latina." *Revista Temas* (Havana), no. 84 (October–December): 35–43.

Mesa-Lago, Carmelo. 2015b. *Normalización de relaciones entre EEUU y Cuba. Causas, prioridades, progresos, obstáculos, efectos y peligros.* Madrid: Real Instituto Elcano de Estudios Internacionales, Documento de Trabajo No. 6, May 8.

Mesa-Lago, Carmelo. 2018a. "Cuban Social Security Reforms Compared with Latin America, China and Vietnam." In *Reforming Communism: Cuba in Comparative Perspective*, edited by Scott Morgensten, Jorge Pérez-López, and Jerome Branche, 211–43. Pittsburgh, PA: University of Pittsburgh Press.

Mesa-Lago, Carmelo. 2018b. "Social Welfare and Structural Reforms in Cuba, 2006–2017." In *Cuba in Transition*, vol. 27. Washington, DC: Association for the Study of the Cuban Economy. https://ideas.repec.org/a/qba/annpro/v27y2017id1171.html/.

Mesa-Lago, Carmelo. 2020b. "Vidal's Results and Cuba's Ranking in the Human Development Index." *Cuban Studies* 49: 119–28.

Mesa-Lago, Carmelo. 2020a. "Impacto del envejecimiento en la protección social en Cuba." In *Crisis de cuidados, envejecimiento y políticas de bienestar en Cuba*, edited by Elaine Acosta, 139–72. Bogota: Editorial Sergio Arboleda.

Mesa-Lago, Carmelo. 2021d. *La unificación monetaria y cambiaria en Cuba. Normas, efectos, obstáculos y perspectivas.* Madrid: Instituto Elcano de Estudios Internacionales, Documento de Trabajo 2/2021, February.

Mesa-Lago, Carmelo. 2021a. "Causes of the Protests and Magnitude of the Economic Crisis in Cuba: 2021." Paper at 30th Congress of the Association for the Study of the Cuban Economy, August 12.

Mesa-Lago, Carmelo. 2021c. *Evaluation of Four Decades of Pension Privatization in Latin America (1980–2020): Promises and Reality.* Mexico City: Friedrich Ebert Stiftung, August.

Mesa-Lago, Carmelo. 2022. "Disponibilidad y credibilidad de las estadísticas oficiales cubanas." *Revista Foro Cubano* (Bogota) 3, no. 5: 4–13.

Mesa-Lago, Carmelo. 2024a. "A Comparative Analysis of Structural Reforms in Cuba and China." In *China and Cuba: Trajectories of Post-Revolutionary Governance*, edited by Martin Dimitrov, in preparation.

Mesa-Lago, Carmelo. 2024b. "Cuba's Economic Crisis of 2019–2023: Back to the 1990s." In *Proceedings of the 2023 Conference of the Association for the Study of the Cuban Economy (ASCE).*

Mesa-Lago, Carmelo. 2024c. "El Embargo de los EE,UU. Contra Cuba y sus Efectos: Un Balance de 62 Años." In *El Impacto Real de las Sanciones sobre Cuba y Venezuela: Una Mirada Plural Alejada de la Propaganda Oficial*, edited by Sergio Angel Baquero. Bogota: Editorial Universidad Sergio Arboleda.

Mesa-Lago, Carmelo, and Christian Aspalter. 2023. "The Cuban Welfare State System: A Special Focus on Universalism." In *The Routledge International Handbook to Welfare State System*, edited by Christian Aspalter, 163–83. Abingdon: Routledge.

Mesa-Lago, Carmelo, and Carl Beck, eds. 1975. *Comparative Socialist Systems: Essays on Politics and Economics*. Pittsburgh, PA: University of Pittsburgh Center for International Studies.

Mesa-Lago, Carmelo, and Sergio Díaz-Briquets. 2021. "Healthcare in Cuba: Sustainability Challenges in an Ageing System." *Journal of Latin American Studies* 53, no.1 (February): 133–59.

Mesa-Lago, Carmelo, Carla Moreno, and Steven Kay. 2022. "Sustainability of Public Pensions in Cuba." *International Social Security Review* 75, no. 2 (April): 2500–546.

Mesa-Lago, Carmelo, and Jorge Pérez-López. 2009. "Cuban GDP Statistics under the Special Period: Discontinuities, Obfuscation and Puzzles." In *Cuba in Transition*, vol. 19, 153–67. Washington, DC: Association for the Study of the Cuban Economy and Institute of Cuban and Cuban American Studies, University of Miami.

Mesa-Lago, Carmelo, and Jorge Pérez-López. 2013. *Cuba under Raúl Castro: Assessing the Reforms*. Boulder, CO: Lynne Rienner Publishers.

Mesa-Lago, Carmelo, Omar Everleny Pérez Villanueva, and Pavel Vidal. 2020. "Nuevos desarrollos en el sector no estatal cubano." *Cuban Studies* 50: 3–29.

Mesa-Lago, Carmelo, and Jan Svejnar. 2020. *The Cuban Economic Crisis, Its Causes and Possible Policies for the Transition*. Miami: FIU Vaclac Havel Program for Human Rights & Diplomacy, October.

Mesa-Lago, Carmelo, and Pavel Vidal. 2019. *El impacto en la economía cubana de la crisis en Venezuela y las políticas de Trump*. Madrid: Instituto Elcano de Asuntos Internacionales, Documento de Trabajo, May.

Mesa-Lago, Carmelo, Roberto Veiga, Lenier González, Sofía Vera, and Aníbal Pérez-Liñán. 2018. *Voices of Change in Cuba*. Pittsburgh, PA: University of Pittsburgh Press.

Military Status and Rights Protection Law in China. 2021. Beijing, June 10, came into force on August 1.

Minh, Anh. 2018. *Vietnam Needs to Save Pension Fund or Economy Will Be at Risk*. Hanoi: World Bank.

Minh, Duong Xuan. 2022. Comments by e-mail on economic sections on Vietnam. Hanoi, March 28.

Ministerio de Relaciones Exteriores de Cuba. 2020. "A 15 años de una visita histórica." *Representatciones Diplomáticas de Cuba en el Exterior*. April 27. https://misiones.cubaminrex.cu/es/articulo/15-anos-de-una-visita-historica.

Ministries of Civil Affairs and Finance. 2020. Notice on Public Comments on the Draft of the Social Assistance Law of the People's Republic of China. Beijing, September 7.

MINSAP (Ministerio de Salud Pública). 2021. *Anuario estadístico de salud 2020.* Havana.

MOH (Ministry of Health) of Vietnam. 2007. "Evaluation of Inappropriate Hospital Stays." Hanoi: Health Policy Unit, Department of Planning and Finance.

MOH (Ministry of Health) of Vietnam. 2018. *Health Statistics Yearbook, 2018.* Hanoi.

MOHRSS (Ministry of Human Resources and Social Security of the People's Republic of China). 2012. Interpretation of the Social Insurance Law of the People's Republic of China. http://www.mohrss.gov.cn/fgs/syshehuibaoxianfa/201208/t20120806_28571.html/.

MOHRSS (Ministry of Human Resources and Social Security of the People's Republic of China). 2018. "Establishing a Mechanism for the Determination of Basic Pension Insurance Benefits for Urban and Rural Residents and the Normal Adjustment of Basic Pensions." Beijing.

MOHRSS (Ministry of Human Resources and Social Security of the People's Republic of China). 2019. *China's Social Security.* Beijing: China Labor & Social Security Publishing House.

MOHRSS (Ministry of Human Resources and Social Security of the People's Republic of China). 2020a. *China's Social Security.* Beijing: China Labor & Social Security Publishing House.

MOHRSS (Ministry of Human Resources and Social Security of the People's Republic of China). 2020b. Data on number of beds for the elderly. Beijing.

MOHRSS (Ministry of Human Resources and Social Security of the People's Republic of China). 2020c. Statistical Bulletin of the Development of Human Resources and Social Security 2019. https://www.mohrss.gov.cn/SYrlzyhshbzb/zwgk/szrs/tjgb/202006/W020200608534647988832.pdf.

MOHRSS (Ministry of Human Resources and Social Security of the People's Republic of China). 2020d. Statistical Communiqué on the Development of Human Resources and Social Security 2019. https://www.mohrss.gov.cn/SYrlzyhshbzb/zwgk/szrs/tjgb/202006/W020200608534647988832.pdf.

MOHRSS (Ministry of Human Resources and Social Security of the People's Republic of China). 2021. *Fourteenth Five-Year Plan for the Development of Human Resources and Social Security.* https://www.mohrss.gov.cn/xxgk2020/fdzdgknr/ghtj/fzgh/202107/W020210728368284387709.pdf.

MOHRSS (Ministry of Human Resources and Social Security of the People's

Republic of China) and Ministry of Finance. 2005. "Decision on Improving the Basic Insurance System for Enterprise Employees." Beijing.

Molina, Hilda. 2005. *Algunas consideraciones sobre el sistema de salud en Cuba*. Buenos Aires: Documentos del Centro para la Apertura y el Desarrollo en América Latina, 3, no. 46, December 20. https://www.cadal.org/documentos/documento_46.pdf.

Mondorf, Alessa. 2020. "Datenvaliditát." In *Wirtschaftspolitik der Volksrepublic China*, edited by Barbara Darimont, 13–24. Gabler, Wiesbaden: Springer.

Monreal, Pedro. 2018c. "Las reformas del socialismo con características chinas, vietnamitas y cubanas en diez gráficos." *ElEstadocomotal*, Havana, April 3.

Monreal, Pedro. 2018b. "El peliagudo camino de la pragmática reforma económica laosiana." *ElEstadocomotal*, Havana, November 10.

Monreal, Pedro. 2018a. "Esperando la reforma empresarial en Cuba. Notas sobre la experiencia vietnamita." *ElEstadocomotal*, Havana, April 9.

Monreal, Pedro. 2021. "Sobre el empoderamiento político de los pobres." Facebook, Havana, July 21.

Monreal, Pedro. 2023. "Notas sobre consumo, inflación, salarios, pobreza y desigualdad." Havana, March 2. https://twitter.com/pmmonreal/status/1631355907077554182?s=46&t=JjUpoMN_olTaRu-m8z5ndQ/.

Morales, Emilio. 2021. "Remesas a Cuba en el peor declive de su historia." *THCG Business Report*, no. 6, December.

Morales, Emilio. 2023. "Cuba. Crisis de gobernanza y futuro incierto." Real Instituto Elcano de Estudios Internacionales, Madrid, July 28.

"More Party Cells Needed in VN's Private Business." 2019. *Vietnam News*, Hanoi. March 29. https://vietnamnews.vn/politics-laws/507929/more-party-cells-needed-in-vn-s-private-businesses.html/.

Moreno, Edward. 2023. "China's Economy Shaken by Crisis in Real Estate." *New York Times*, August 22, B-3.

Mozur, Paul. 2021. "An Emboldened Xi Remakes China's Business World in His Image." *New York Times*, October 6, A-1.

National Aging Development Bulletin. 2021. Beijing. https://baijiao.baidu.com/s?id=1713757047387132959&wfr=spider&for=pc (no longer active, accessed November 17).

National Assembly of Vietnam. 2006. Social Insurance Law No. 71. Hanoi.

National People's Congress of the PRC. 2019. Constitution of the People's Republic of China. http://www.npc.gov.cn/englishnpc/constitution2019/201911/1f65146fb6104dd3a2793875d19b5b29.shtml/.

NBSC (National Bureau of Statistics of China). 2008. *China Statistical Yearbook, 2007*. Beijing: China Statistic Press. https://ghdx.healthdata.org/record/china-statistical-yearbook-2007/.

NBSC (National Bureau of Statistics of China). 2009. *China Statistical Yearbook,*

2008. Beijing: China Statistic Press. https://www.stats.gov.cn/sj/ndsj/2008/indexeh.htm/.

NBSC (National Bureau of Statistics of China). 2010. *China Statistical Yearbook, 2009*. Beijing: China Statistic Press. https://www.stats.gov.cn/sj/ndsj/2009/indexeh.htm/.

NBSC (National Bureau of Statistics of China). 2011. *China Statistical Yearbook, 2010*. Beijing: China Statistic Press. https://www.stats.gov.cn/sj/ndsj/2010/indexeh.htm/.

NBSC (National Bureau of Statistics of China). 2012. *China Statistical Yearbook, 2011*. Beijing: China Statistic Press. https://www.stats.gov.cn/sj/ndsj/2011/indexeh.htm/.

NBSC (National Bureau of Statistics of China). 2013. *China Statistical Yearbook, 2012*. Beijing: China Statistic Press. https://www.stats.gov.cn/sj/ndsj/2012/indexeh.htm/.

NBSC (National Bureau of Statistics of China). 2014. *China Statistical Yearbook, 2013*. Beijing: China Statistic Press. https://www.stats.gov.cn/sj/ndsj/2013/indexeh.htm/.

NBSC (National Bureau of Statistics of China). 2015. *China Statistical Yearbook, 2014*. Beijing: China Statistic Press. https://ghdx.healthdata.org/record/china-statistical-yearbook-2014/.

NBSC (National Bureau of Statistics of China). 2016. *China Statistical Yearbook, 2015*. Beijing: China Statistic Press. http://www.stats.gov.cn/sj/ndsj/2015/indexeh.htm/.

NBSC (National Bureau of Statistics of China). 2017. *China Statistical Yearbook, 2016*. Beijing: China Statistic Press. http://www.stats.gov.cn/sj/ndsj/2016/indexeh.htm/.

NBSC (National Bureau of Statistics of China). 2018. *China Statistical Yearbook, 2017*. Beijing: China Statistic Press. http://www.stats.gov.cn/sj/ndsj/2017/indexeh.htm/.

NBSC (National Bureau of Statistics of China). 2019. *China Statistical Yearbook, 2018*. Beijing: China Statistic Press. http://www.stats.gov.cn/sj/ndsj/2018/indexeh.htm/.

NBSC (National Bureau of Statistics of China). 2020a. *China Statistical Yearbook, 2019*. Beijing: China Statistic Press. http://www.stats.gov.cn/sj/ndsj/2019/indexeh.htm/.

NBSC (National Bureau of Statistics of China). 2020b. *Women and Men in China: Facts and Figures*. Beijing: Department of Social Science, Technology and Cultural Statistics.

NBSC (National Bureau of Statistics of China). 2021a. *China Labour Statistical Yearbook, 2020*. Beijing: Department of Population and Employment Statistics. https://icst.cnki.net/KNavi/YearbookDetail?pcode=CYFD&pykm=YZLDT (no longer active, last accessed December 20).

NBSC (National Bureau of Statistics of China). 2021b. *China Statistical Yearbook, 2020.* Beijing: China Statistic Press. http://www.stats.gov.cn/sj/ndsj/2020/indexeh.htm/.

NBSC (National Bureau of Statistics of China). 2021c. Main Data of the Seventh National Population Census. Beijing, May 11. https://www.stats.gov.cn/english/PressRelease/202105/t20210510_1817185.html/.

NBSC (National Bureau of Statistics of China). 2022a. *China Statistical Yearbook, 2021.* Beijing: China Statistic Press. https://www.stats.gov.cn/sj/ndsj/2021/indexeh.htm/.

NBSC (National Bureau of Statistics of China). 2022b. Real Sector Time Series Data. Beijing. https://www.stats.gov.cn/english/Statisticaldata/nsdp/201508/t20150831_1238096.html/.

NCSSF (National Council for Social Security Fund of the People's Republic of China). 2017–2019a, 2020, 2021. *Annual Report of the National Council for Social Security Fund of the People's Republic of China, 2016 to 2020.* https://www.top1000funds.com/asset_owner/national-council-for-social-security-fund-china/.

NCSSF (National Council for Social Security Fund of the People's Republic of China). 2019b. Notice of Full Implementation of the Transfer of Part of the State-Owned Capital to Supplement the Social Security Fund. Beijing, September 10. https://www.sec.gov/Archives/edgar/data/1268896/000119312520036596/d882926dex991.htm/.

Nguyen, Julia. 2020. "Vietnam Sets Ambitious Goals in New National Industrial Policy but Can It Stay Competitive?" *Vietnam Briefing*, October 5. https://www.vietnam-briefing.com/news/author/vietnam-briefing/.

Nguyen, Khac Tuan. 2017. *Some Solutions to Ensure Pension Fund Finance in the Context of Population Ageing.* Hanoi. http://www.ilssa.org.vn/en/news/some-solutions-to-ensure-pension-fund-finance-in-the-context-of-population-aging-172/.

Nguyen, Nguyen Nga, Paulette Castel, and Minna Hahn Tong. 2012. *Vietnam: Developing a Modern Pension System: Current Challenges and Options for Future Reform.* Washington, DC: World Bank.

Nguyen, Phu Trong. 2018. Lecture at the University of Havana, *Cubadebate*, March 29. http://www.cubadebate.cu/noticias/2018/03/29/nguyen-phu-trong-recibe-doctor-honoris-causa-de-la-universidad-de-la-habana/#WsEMYZe-kl0/.

Nguyen, Thi Tue Anh, Luc Minh Due, and Trinh Duc Chieu. 2014. *The Evolution of Vietnamese Industry.* Learning to Compete Working Paper 19. Washington, DC: Brookings Institution.

NHC of the PRC (National Health Commission of the PRC). 2020. Notice of the General Office of the National Health Commission on Printing and Distributing the 2020 Special Action Plan for the Style Construction Work of the Medical Industry. http://www.nhc.gov.cn/yzygj/hfgw/202007/978e4ab30586460ba56986fe09e5f6f7.shtml (no longer active, last accessed February 20, 2021).

NHSA (National Healthcare Security Administration). 2021. National Medical Security Development *Statistical Bulletin*, 2020. https://www.cdc.gov/nchs/products/nhsr.htm/.

NICE (National Institute for Health and Care Excellence). 2018. Bed Occupancy. https://www.nice.org.uk/guidance/ng94/evidence/39.bed-occupancy-pdf-172397464704/.

Nikolov, Plamen, and Alan Adelman. 2019. "Short-Run Health Consequences of Retirement and Pension Benefits: Evidence from China." *Forum for Health Economics and Policy*, April.

Nova, Armando. 2013. *El modelo agrícola y los lineamientos de la política económica y social en Cuba*. Havana: Editorial Ciencias Sociales.

Nova, Armando. 2022. "Intercooperación, alimentación y desarrollo local." Paper at 32nd Congress of the Association for the Study of the Cuban Economy, Florida International University, Miami, September 16.

OECD (Organization of Economic Cooperation and Development). 2017. *Health at a Glance*. Paris. https://www.oecd-ilibrary.org/docserver/health_glance-2017-en.pdf?expires=1665759370&id=id&accname=guest&checksum=F051C8250E2E9C9FF8A6101CFDA98640/.

OECD (Organization of Economic Cooperation and Development). 2018. *Pension at a Glance, Asia/Pacific, 2018*. Paris.

OECD (Organization of Economic Cooperation and Development). 2019a. *Pensions at a Glance, 2019*. Paris.

OECD (Organization of Economic Cooperation and Development). 2019b. *Pensions at a Glance, 2019: Country Profiles, China*. Paris.

OECD (Organization of Economic Cooperation and Development). 2022a. *Health Statistics*. Paris.

OECD (Organization of Economic Cooperation and Development). 2022b. *Society at a Glance, Asia/Pacific, 2019, 2022*. Paris.

Olivier, Marius. 2022. *Viet Nam Social Security Legal Reform: An Integrated Framework*. Hanoi: ILO.

ONEI (Oficina Nacional de Estadísticas e Información). 2007. *Anuario estadístico de Cuba, 2006*. Havana.

ONEI (Oficina Nacional de Estadísticas e Información). 2008a. *Anuario estadístico de Cuba, 2007*. Havana.

ONEI (Oficina Nacional de Estadísticas e Información). 2008b. *El estado actual y perspectivo de la población cubana. Un reto para el desarrollo territorial sostenible*. Havana.

ONEI (Oficina Nacional de Estadísticas e Información). 2009. *Anuario estadístico de Cuba, 2008*. Havana.

ONEI (Oficina Nacional de Estadísticas e Información). 2010a. *Anuario estadístico de Cuba, 2009.* Havana.

ONEI (Oficina Nacional de Estadísticas e Información). 2010b. *Encuesta nacional de fecundidad informe de resultados, 2009.* Havana.

ONEI (Oficina Nacional de Estadísticas e Información). 2011. *Anuario estadístico de Cuba, 2010.* Havana.

ONEI (Oficina Nacional de Estadísticas e Información). 2012. *Anuario estadístico de Cuba, 2011.* Havana.

ONEI (Oficina Nacional de Estadísticas e Información). 2013. *Anuario estadístico de Cuba, 2012.* Havana.

ONEI (Oficina Nacional de Estadísticas e Información). 2014. *Anuario estadístico de Cuba, 2013.* Havana.

ONEI (Oficina Nacional de Estadísticas e Información). 2015. *Anuario estadístico de Cuba, 2014.* Havana.

ONEI (Oficina Nacional de Estadísticas e Información). 2016. *Anuario estadístico de Cuba, 2015.* Havana.

ONEI (Oficina Nacional de Estadísticas e Información). 2017. *Anuario estadístico de Cuba, 2016.* Havana.

ONEI (Oficina Nacional de Estadísticas e Información). 2018. *Anuario estadístico de Cuba, 2017.* Havana.

ONEI (Oficina Nacional de Estadísticas e Información). 2019a. *Anuario estadístico de Cuba, 2018.* Havana.

ONEI (Oficina Nacional de Estadísticas e Información). 2019b. *Encuesta nacional de envejecimiento de la población ENEP-2017.* Havana.

ONEI (Oficina Nacional de Estadísticas e Información). 2020a. *Anuario estadístico de Cuba, 2019.* Havana.

ONEI (Oficina Nacional de Estadísticas e Información). 2020b. *El envejecimiento de la población cubana, 2019.* Havana.

ONEI (Oficina Nacional de Estadísticas e Información). 2021. *Anuario estadístico de Cuba, 2020.* Havana.

ONEI (Oficina Nacional de Estadísticas e Información). 2022a. *Anuario estadístico de Cuba, 2021.* Havana.

ONEI (Oficina Nacional de Estadísticas e Información). 2022b. *Indicadores demográficos para Cuba y sus territorios, enero–diciembre 2021.* Havana.

ONEI (Oficina Nacional de Estadísticas e Información). 2023. *Anuario estadístico de Cuba, 2022.* Havana.

ONEI (Oficina Nacional de Estadísticas e Información). 2024. *Anuario estadístico de Cuba, 2023.* Havana.

ONEI/CEPDE (ONEI and Centro de Estudios de Población y Desarrollo). 2019, 2020, 2021, 2022, *Anuario demográfico de Cuba, 2018, 2019, 2020, 2021.* Havana.

Orlik, Tom. 2011. *Understanding China's Economic Indicators.* FT Press.

Pan, Jennifer. 2020. *Welfare for Autocrats: How Social Assistance Cares for the Rulers*. Oxford: Oxford University Press.

Pérez-López, Jorge. 1974. "An Index of Cuban Industrial Output, 1930–1958." PhD dissertation, SUNY Albany.

Pérez Villanueva, Omar Everleny. 2008. "Entrevista a Omar Everleny." *La Jornada*, March 15.

Pérez Villanueva, Omar Everleny. 2021. "La economía cubana. La Tarea Ordenamiento y su repercusión social." Paper at 30th Congress of the Association for the Study of the Cuban Economy, Florida International University, Miami, August 13.

Pérez Villanueva, Omar Everleny. 2022a. "La economía cubana. Riesgos y desafíos." Paper at 32nd Congress of the Association for the Study of the Cuban Economy, Florida International University, Miami, September 17.

Pérez Villanueva, Omar Everleny. 2022b. Information by e-mail provided to the author, Havana, June 24.

Pichs, Ramón. 2021. "Índice de desarrollo humano e índice de pobreza multidimensional para Cuba. De lo global a lo local." *Resumen Preliminar del Proyecto 'Evolución de la Economía Internacional y su Impacto sobre Cuba,'* edited by José Luis Rodríguez and Ramón Pichs, 129–43. Havana: Centro de Investigaciones de la Economía Mundial.

Plekhanov, Dmitry. 2017. "Quality of China's Official Statistics: A Brief Review of Academic Perspectives." *Copenhagen Journal of Asian Studies* 35, no. 1: 76–101.

Politburo. 2018. Resolution No. 23-NQ/TW, Orientations for building national industrial development policies to 2030 with a vision to 2045. Hanoi, March 22.

Prassad, Eswar. 2023. "What Ails China's Economy?" *New York Times*, August 27: SR-4.

Presidential Decree of the People's Republic of China No. 35. 2010. Social Insurance Law of the People's Republic of China, Beijing, October 28. Updated by National People's Congress in 2018. http://www.gov.cn/npc/c30834/201901/4a6c13e9f73541ffb2c1b5ee615174f5.shtml/.

"Prevención y asistencia social. ¿Cuánto queda por hacer?" 2022. Mesa Redonda (video), Havana, February 15. http://mesaredonda.cubadebate.cu/mesa-redonda/2022/02/15/prevencion-y-asistencia-social/.

Pumar, Enrique. 2022. "The Persistent Social Dilemmas of the Revolution." Paper at 32nd Congress of the Association for the Study of the Cuban Economy, Florida International University, Miami, September 15.

Qi, Tao. 2022. "Adapting to Population Ageing, Promoting Quality and Sustainable Development of Pension System in China." Paper at International Conference on "The Future of Social Security for New Forms of Work," sponsored by China State Council and ILO. Beijing, July 27.

Quang, Huy Duong. 2022. Consultant in Vietnam, answers by e-mail to author's questionnaires. Hanoi, September and October.

Quy, Nguyen. 2020. "Vietnam's Pension System World's 57th Best: Report." *Express International*, June 3. https://e.vnexpress.net/news/news/vietnam-pension-system-world-s-57th-best-report-4109754.html/.

Ramírez, Betina, and Camila Arza. 2021. *Adapting Social Insurance to Women's Life Courses: A Gender Impact Assessment of Vietnam*. Hanoi: ILO, May. https://www.ilo.org/sites/default/files/wcmsp5/groups/public/@asia/@ro-bangkok/@ilo-hanoi/documents/publication/wcms_819801.pdf.

Rapoza, Kenneth. 2019. "China Has Forgiven Nearly $10 Billion in Debt. Cuba Accounts for Over Half." *Forbes*, May 29. https://www.forbes.com/sites/kenrapoza/2019/05/29/china-has-forgiven-nearly-10-billion-in-debt-cuba-accounts-for-over-half/?sh=576432c615b/.

Ratliff, William. 2004. *China's "Lessons" for Cuba's Transition?* Cuba Transition Project, University of Miami, Miami.

Rawski, Thomas. 2001. "What's Happening to China's GDP Statistics?" *China Economic Review* 12, no. 4: 347–54.

Rawski, Thomas. 2022a. Information provided to the author, Pittsburgh, June 25.

Rawski, Thomas. 2002b. "Measuring China's Recent GDP Growth" (in Chinese). *Jingjxue* (China Economic Quarterly) 2, no. 1 (October): 53–62.

Rawski, Thomas. 2023. Comments to an article by the author, June 23.

Resolución No. 351. 2020. Tarifas para Casas de Abuelos y Hogares de Ancianos. *Gaceta Oficial Extraordinaria* 71, Havana (December 10): 934–35.

Reuters Staff. 2021."U.S. Trade Embargo Has Cost Cuba $130 billion, U.N. Says." Havana, May 8.

Reyes, José Luis. 2023. "¿Qué quiere Rusia de Cuba a cambio de sus inversiones en la isla?" *Diario de Cuba*, Madrid, May 19.

Rich, Motoko. 2024. "Policies to Raise Fertility Rates Haven't Produced Baby Booms." *New York Times*, October 14, A-1, 5.

Ringen, Stein, and Kinglun Ngok. 2013. "What Kind of Welfare State Is Emerging in China?" UNRISD Working Paper No. 2013-2.

"Rising Pension Levels to Ensure Senior Citizens Have No Tension." 2021. *China Daily Global*, June 23.

Ritter, Archibald R. M., and Ted A. Henken. 2015. *Entrepreneurial Cuba: The Changing Policy Landscape*. Boulder, CO: First Forum Press.

Rodríguez, José Luis. 2015. "Cuba y los primeros pasos de las reformas estructurales." *Inter-Press Service*, Havana, June 25.

Rodríguez, José Luis. 2022. "Cuba. Factores de la compleja coyuntura económica en el primer semestre del 2022." *Debate Económico*, Havana, August 26.

Romanò, Sara, and Davide Barrera. 2021. "The Impact of Market-Oriented Reforms on Inequality in Transitional Societies: New Evidence from Cuba." *Socio-Economic Review* 19, no 2: 765–87.

Rosen, Daniel H. 2022. "The Age of Slow Growth in China." *Foreign Affairs*, April 15. https://www.foreignaffairs.com/articles/china/2022-04-15/age-slow-growth-china/. Rozelle, Scott. 2022. "Agricultural Reform in Former Socialist Countries." Paper at 32nd Congress of the Association for the Study of the Cuban Economy, Florida International University, Miami, September 16.

Rudd, Kevin. 2022. "The World according to Xi Jinping." *Foreign Affairs*, November/December. https://www.foreignaffairs.com/china/world-according-xi-jinping-china-ideologue-kevin-rudd/.

Sachs, Jeffrey D. 1996. "Reforms in Eastern Europe and the Former Soviet Union in Light of the East Asian experience." Working Paper No. 5404, National Bureau of Economic Research, Cambridge., Massachusetts.

"Seventy Per Cent of Chinese Population to Be Registered with Family Doctors by 2035." 2022. *ChinaDaily*, March 16.

Shen, Ce, Jessica Johnson, Zhenhe Chi, and John Williamson. 2020. "Does a Universal Non-contributory Social Pension Make Sense for Rural China?" *International Social Security Review* 73, no 2: 3–26.

Shi, Li, and Shen Yangyang. 2021. "Experience and Prospects for Poverty Reduction in China." *Issues on Agricultural Economy* 5: 12–19.

Silva, Yenia. 2019. "Retos de un país que peina canas." *Granma*, Havana, July 9. https://www.granma.cu/cuba/2019-07-09/retos-de-un-pais-que-peina-canas-09-07-2019-00-07-29/.

Socialist Republic of Vietnam. 2012. "Resolution 15-NQ/TW of the Central Committee of the Communist Party: Some Issues on Social Policies during the Period 2012–2020." Hanoi, June 1.

Socialist Republic of Vietnam. 2013. Constitution of the Socialist Republic of Vietnam, Approved by the National Assembly, 6th Session. Hanoi, November 28.

Socialist Republic of Vietnam. 2018. Resolution 28-NQ/TW of the Seventh Plenum of the XII Central Committee of the Communist Party on Social Insurance Policy Reforms. Hanoi, May 23.

Solinger, Dorothy J. 2022a. Information provided to the author by e-mail, Irvine, July 3–5, 15–16.

Solinger, Dorothy J. 2022b. *Poverty and Pacification: The Chinese State Abandons the Old Working Class.* Lanham, MD: Rowan and Littlefield.

Spadoni, Paolo. 2022. "The External Sector of Cuba's Economy: Performance and Challenges." Paper at 32nd Congress of the Association for the Study of the Cuban Economy, Florida International University, Miami, September 16.

State Administration of Foreign Exchange. 2020. https://www.safe.gov.cn/en/file/file/202030/fcdd31c2ab414449b42d53a0275f5cb5.pdf?n=/.

State Council Information Office of the PRC. 2021. *Poverty Alleviation: China's Experience and Contribution.* Beijing.

State Council Information Office of the PRC. 2022. "Report on the 2021 Status of the Social Insurance Fund." Beijing.

Stephen, Wicari. 2022. "More People Are Fleeing Cuba now than during 1980 and 1994 Crises." *Bloomberg*, August 17.

Stevenson, Alexandra. 2023. "Another Chinese Developer Teeters, Threatening Broader Implications." *New York Times*, August 10, B-4.

Szweda-Lewandowska, Zofia. 2022. "The Role of Health and Social Care Workers in Long-Term Care for Elders." *International Social Security Review* 75, no. 3–4: 159.

Tang, Xiaoli. 2022. Director General Social Insurance Fund Supervision Board MOHRSS. "Multi-channel Financing for Basic Pensions in China." Paper at International Conference on "The Future of Social Security for New Forms of Work," sponsored by China State Council and ILO. Beijing, July 26.

"Tasa representativa del mercado informal en Cuba." 2022, 2024. *El Toque*, Havana, September 25, October 9, 2022, and October 2024. https://eltoque.com/en/tasas-de-cambio-de-moneda-en-cuba-hoy/. This blog daily reports the informal exchange rate in Cuba.

Torres, Ricardo. 2016. "Vicinity Matters: Cuba's Reforms in Comparative Perspective." *International Journal of Cuban Studies* 8, no. 2: 169–84.

Torres, Ricardo. 2018. "Mirando a través de las ventas de servicios médicos." *Progreso Semanal*, December 12.

Torres, Ricardo. 2020. Information provided to the author by e-mail, Havana, April 23.

Torres, Ricardo. 2023. Book review of Carmelo Mesa-Lago and Jan Svejnar, "The Cuban Economic Crisis: Its Causes and Possible Policies for the Transition." *Cuban Studies* 51: 458–60. Also expanded comments at the author's request, March 20.

Tran Ngoc, Ca. 2022. Information provided by e-mail to the author. Hanoi, September 24.

Trinh, Minh. 2019. *Statistical Misreporting from Below, as Seen from (Very High) Above.* MIT Political Science Department Research Paper 2019–2022, Boston.

UNDESA (United Nations Department of Economic and Social Affairs). 2020. *World Population Ageing, 2019.* New York.

UNDP (United Nations Development Program). 2009, 2020, 2022. *Human Development Report, 2009, 2020, 2022.* New York.

UNDP (United Nations Population Division). 2020. *World Population Prospects. 2019.* New York.

UNDP (United Nations Population Division). 2022. *Countries in the World by Population*. New York. https://www.worldometer.info/world/population-by-country/.

UN World Food Programme. 2023. *Cuba Annual Country Report, 2022: Country Strategic Plan, 2021–2024*. Rome, March 31.

US.SSA-ISSA (U.S. Social Security Administration/International Social Security Association). 2019. *Social Security Programs throughout the World: Asia and the Pacific, 2018*. Washington, DC.

US.SSA-ISSA (US Social Security Administration/International Social Security Association). 2020. *Social Security Programs throughout the World: The Americas, 2019*. Washington, DC.

Vicent, Mauricio. 2022. "Cuba y su éxodo al que no se le ve fin." *El País*, Madrid, November 13.

Vidal, Macarena. 2021. "La bomba de relojería demográfica que amenaza a China." *El País*, May 1.

Vidal, Pavel. 2014. "Monetary and Exchange Rate Reform in Cuba: Lessons from Vietnam." In *No More Free Lunch: Reflections on the Cuban Economic Reform Process and Challenges for Transformation*, edited by Claes Brundenius and Ricardo Torres, 63–81. Cham: Springer.

Vidal, Pavel. 2016. "Cuba's Reform and Economic Growth: A Comparative Perspective with Vietnam." *Journal of Economic Policy Reform* 19, no. 2: 148–65.

Vidal, Pavel. 2021. "De oportunidades y otros demonios en la reforma monetaria cubana." Madrid: Instituto Elcano de Estudios Internacionales, July 7.

Vidal, Pavel. 2022. "La inflación sigue fuera de control en Cuba." *Inter Press Service in Cuba*, Havana, April 19. https://www.ipscuba.net/economia/la-inflacion-sigue-fuera-de-control-en-Cuba/.

Vidal, Pavel, and José A. Alonso. 2022. "Why Is Cuba's Economic Reform Progressing So Slowly?" *Third World Quarterly* 44: 115–33.

"Vietnam Minister, Hanoi Mayor Expelled from Party over Corruption." 2022. *CAN*, June 6. https://x.com/ChannelNewsAsia/status/1533834989443264512/. The news was reproduced by international press agencies such as AP, AFP, Reuters, Barron's, etc.

"Vietnam Strives to Maintain Replacement Fertility Rate." 2023. *Pension Policy International*, June 7. https://www.Pensionpolicyinternational.com/tag/Vietnam (no longer active, last accessed June 9).

Viêt Vũ Quang. 2020. "A Comparative Statistical View of the Vietnamese Economy under Reform since 1985." *Symposium on Vietnamese Party 13th Congress: Dilemmas of Development and Global Integration*. Singapore: The Institute of Southeast Asian Studies, no. 16.

VSS (Vietnam Social Security). 2018. Decision No. 2489A/QD-BHXH, July 12.

VSS (Vietnam Social Security). 2019a. Official Dispatch to MOF, No.-108A/BHXH-KHDT, January 15.

VSS (Vietnam Social Security). 2019b. "VSS's Achievements by March 2019," March 29.

VSS (Vietnam Social Security). 2021. Decision No. 135/QD-BHKH. January 21.

VSS (Vietnam Social Security). 2022. Decision No. 457/QD-BHXH, March 9.

Vu Hoàng. 2014. "In Depth Vietnamese Statistics" (translated from Vietnamese), *RFA*, March 2. https://www.rfa.org/vietnamese/in_depth/vietnamese-statistic-data-03022014131718.html/.

Wakabayashi, Daisuke. 2022. "China's Once-Hot Housing Market Rapidly Cools." *New York Times*, June 20: B-1, B-4.

Wakabayashi, Daisuke, Chang Che, and Claire Fu. 2022. "In Xi's China, the Business of Business Is State-Controlled." *New York Times*, October 17. https://www.nytimes.com/2022/10/17/business/china-xi-jinping-business-economy.html/.

Wallace, Jeremy. 2022. *Seeking Truth and Hiding Facts*. Oxford: Oxford University Press.

Wang, Jiao, Junhui Xiao, Xiali Li, Lin Zhang, and Na Wang. 2021. "Status Quo and Influencing Factors of Family Doctors' Performance in Dongguan City." medRxiv, September 23. https://www.medrxiv.org/content/10.1101/2021.09.23.21263974v1/.

Wang, Vivian. 2024. "China Rises Retirement Age for the First Time since the 1950s," *New York Times*, September 13. https://www.nytimes.com/2024/09/13/world/asia/china-retirement-age.html/.

Wang, Vivian, and Joy Dong. 2023. "Fatal Hospital Fire Puts Spotlight on China's Shortage of Elder Care." *New York Times*, May 8, A-4.

Wang, Yifei. 2020a. *Fact Sheet on Age Security in China*. Munich: Max Planck Institute for Social Law and Policy.

Wang, Yifei. 2020b. *Pension Map of China*. Munich: Max Planck Institute for Social Law and Policy.

Wang, Yifei. 2021. "Legal Protection in Case of Employer's Non-compliance to Pay Social Security Contributions in China." In *Report 2018–2020 Max Planck Institute for Social Law and Social Policy*, Munich, 123–24.

Wang, Yifei. 2022. Comments on this book and answers to questionnaire, Munich, February 21, March 11, May 18–25, August 14.

Wang, Zhikai. 2011. "Social Security for China's Migrant Workers." *International Social Security Review* 150, no. 1–2: 177–87.

Wee, Sui-Lee. 2021. "China Wants to Boost Births. But It's Wary of Losing Control." *New York Times*, May 12 (updated May 31). https://www.nytimes.com/2021/05/12/business/china-births-limits.html/.

Wei Chen, Xilu Chen, Chang-Tai Hsieh, and Zheng Song. 2019a. "A Forensic

Examination of China's National Accounts." Brookings Papers on Economic Activity, BPEA Conference, March 7–8.

Wei Chen, Xilu Chen, Chang-Tai Hsieh, and Zheng Song. 2019b. "A Forensic Examination of China's National Accounts." National Bureau of Economic Research (NBER) Working Paper No. 25754.

Werner, Johannes. 2014. "Industrial Co-op Growing Fast." *Cuba News*, November.

"What Are Cuba & Russia Getting from Each Other?" 2023. *Latin American Advisor*, Washington, DC, Inter-American Dialogue, June 6.

"Whats and Whys of China's Unified Domestic Market." 2022. Guidelines to accelerate the establishment of a unified domestic market amid efforts to build a high-standard market system and promote high-quality development. Beijing, *Xinhua*, April 13 (updated May 13). http://ningbo.chinadaily.com.cn/2022-05/13/c_751359.htm/.

WHO (World Health Organization). 2020. *How Will Population Ageing Affect Health Expenditures Trends in Vietnam and What Are the Implications of People's Age in Good Health*? https://iris.who.int/handle/10665/337713/.

WHO (World Health Organization). 2021. *World Health Statistics 2021: Monitoring Health for the SDGs, Sustainable Development Goals*. Geneva, May 20. https://www.who.int/publications/i/item/9789240027053/.

WHO (World Health Organization). 2022a. "Estimates of Excess Mortality Associated with Covid-19 Pandemic (as of 25 March 2022)." Geneva. WHO_COVID_Excess_Deaths-EstimatesByCountry.xlsx/.

WHO (World Health Organization). 2022b. "Global Excess Deaths Associated with Covid-19, January 2020–December 2021: A Comprehensive View of Global Deaths Directly and Indirectly Associated with the Covid-19 Pandemic." Geneva. https://www.int/data/stories/global-excess-deaths-associatedwith-covid-19-January-2020-december-2021/.

WHO (World Health Organization). 2022c. Global Health Expenditure Database. Geneva. January 30. https://apps.who.int/nha/database/.

WHO (World Health Organization). 2022d. "Out-of-Pocket Expenditures as a Percentage of Total Health Expenditures." Geneva. apps.who.int/nha/database/.

WIPO (World Intellectual Property Organization). 2022. Global Innovation Index. Geneva. https://www.wipo.int/web/global-innovation-index/2022/index/.

World Bank. 1994. *Averting the Old-Age Crisis: Policies to Protect the Old and Promote Growth*. Washington, DC.

World Bank. 2011. *Vietnam and the World Bank: A Strong and Enduring Partnership, A Brief Annotated History*. Washington, DC.

World Bank. 2012. *Vietnam: Developing a Modern Pension System: Current Challenges and Options for Future Reform*. Washington, DC.

World Bank. 2013. *China 2030: Building a Modern Harmonious and Creative Society*. Washington, DC: Development Research Center of the State Council of the People's Republic of China.

World Bank. 2019. *A Vision for the 2030 Social Protection System in Vietnam*. Washington, DC.

World Bank. 2020. "Total Population, Direct Investment, Life Expectancy at Birth." https://data.worldbank.org/indicator/BX.KLT.DINV.CD.WD/.

World Bank. 2021a. "Total Population, Direct Investment, Life Expectancy at Birth." https://data.worldbank.org/indicator/SP.DYN.LE00.FE.IN?locations=CN/.

World Bank. 2021b. *Vietnam: Adapting to an Ageing Society*. Washington, DC.

World Bank. 2021c. *The World Bank in Vietnam*, April 7. http://worldbank.org/en/country,vietnam/.

World Bank. 2022a. "GDP Growth Annual, China and Vietnam." Washington, DC. https://www.data.worldbank.org/indicator/NY.GDP.MKTP.KD.ZG/.

World Bank. 2022b. "Overall Level of Statistical Capacity (Scale 0–100) Country Ranking." Washington, DC. https://databank.worldbank.org/reports.aspx?source=Statistical-capacity-indicators/.

World Bank. 2023a. "GDP per Capita in U.S. Dollars." Washington, DC. https://data.worldbank.org/indicator/NY.GDP.PCAP.CD?locations=CU/.

World Bank. 2023b. "Sustained Policy Support and Deeper Structural Reforms to Revive China's Growth Momentum." *China's Economic Update*, December 14.

World Bank. N.d. "Causes of Death by Non-communicable Diseases, and Causes of Death by Communicable Diseases and Maternal, Prenatal and Nutrition Conditions." Washington, DC, November 25, 2022. https://data.worldbank.org/indicator/SH.DTH.COMM.ZS?locations=CN/.

World Bank/State Council of the PRC. 2022. *Four Decades of Poverty Reduction in China: Drivers, Insights for the World and the Way Ahead*. Washington, DC. https://openknowledge.worldbank.org/handle/10986/37727/.

World Bank/WHO. 2019. *Healthy China: Deepening Health Reform in China. Building High-Quality and Value-Service Delivery*. Washington, DC: World Bank Group.

"The World's Largest Pension Fund May Be Running Dry." 2024 *Pension International*, May 29.

Wu, Jingliau. 2005. *China's Long March toward a Market Economy*. Shanghai: Shanghai Press Publishing Development Company.

Xu, Guoping. 2014. "A Perspective on the Development of Family Medicine in China." *Family Medicine and Community Health* 2, no. 1: 28–34.

Xu, Jin, Martin Gorsky, and Anne Mills. 2019. "Historical Roots of Hospital Centrism in China (1835–1949): A Path Dependence." *Social Science and Medicine* 226 (April): 56–62.

Yake, Wang, and Xi Huizhen. 2021. "The Pension Gender Gap and Its Changes in My Country." *Academic Research* 1: 57–65. Survey taken by Beijing Normal University.

Yang, Lixiong. 2018. "The Social Assistance Reform in China: Towards a Fair and Inclusive Social Safety Net." Paper at Conference "Addressing Inequalities and Challenges to Social Inclusion through Fiscal, Wage and Social Protection Policies," New York, United Nations, June 25–27.

Yang, Vivian. 2022. "Millions Lose Jobs as China Locks Down." *New York Times*, May 6. https://www.nytimes.com/2022/05/05/business/china-shanghai-covid-lockdown-economy.html/.

Yingyao, Hu, and Jiaxiong Yao. 2021. "Illuminating Economic Growth." *Journal of Econometrics*: 1–20. https://www.econ2.jhu.edu/people/hu/Hu-Yao-JoE.pdf.

Yuan, Li. 2022. "China's Covid Lockdowns Revive the Ghosts of a Planned Economy." *New York Times*, April 26. https://www.realclearmarkets.com/2022/04/26/chinas_covid_lockdowns_revive_the_ghosts_of_a_planned_economy_828990.html/.

Yuan, Li. 2023a. "China Is Deleting Poverty, One Video at a Time." *New York Times*, May 8: A-1, A-6.

Yuan, Li. 2023b. "Entrepreneurs Aren't Buying China Government's Pep Talk." *New York Times*, July 24: B-1, B-3.

Yuan, Li. 2023c. "They Bolstered China's Backbone, Now They Have Nothing to Fall Back On." *New York Times*, November 1: B-1, B-6.

Zhang, Conghai, Xinyao Xian, and Chao Wu. 2020. "Medical Fraud and Abuse Detection System Based on Machine Learning." *International Journal of Environmental Research and Public Health*, 19), 7265. https://pmc.ncbi.nlm.nih.gov/articles/PMC7579458/pdf/ijerph-17-07265.pdf.

Zhang, Mo. 2008. *From Public to Private:* "The Newly Enacted Chinese Property Law and the Protection of Property Rights in China." *Berkeley Business Law Journal*, 5 (2). https://lawcat.berkeley.edu/record/1121584?v=pdf.

Zhang, Wentao. 2022. "Improving Ageing Society Governance in China." Paper at International Conference on "The Future of Social Security for New Forms of Work," sponsored by China State Council and ILO, Beijing, July 27.

Zhao, Litao, and Xiaobin He. 2021. "Lessons from China on Different Approaches to Pension Coverage Extension." *International Social Security Review* 74, no. 1: 5–34.

Zheng, Bingwen W. 2008. "30 Years of Reforms and Openness in China: Development and Challenges of Social Security System for Floating Population." *Chinese Journal of Population Science* 128, no. 5: 2–17.

Zheng, Bingwen W. 2012. "China: An Innovative Hybrid Pension Design Proposal." In *Notional Defined Contribution Pension Schemes in a Changing*

Pension World, edited by Robert Holzmann, Edward Palmer, and David Robalino, 189–209. Washington, DC: World Bank.

Zheng, Bingwen W., ed. 2019. *China Pension Actuarial Report, 2019–2050*. Beijing: China Labor and Social Security Press.

Zheng, Bingwen W. 2020. *China Pension Development Report, 2020*. Beijing: Economic and Management Press.

Zhou, Twinkle. 2021. "China Pensions Starved of Alternatives to Stabilize Returns." *Pension Policy International*, July 27. https://www.pensionpolicyinternational.com/china-pensions-starved-of-alternatives-to-stabilise-returns/471332/.

INDEX

Note: Page numbers in *italics* indicate figures and tables.